Edward Jewitt Wheeler

Pulpit and grave

A volume of funeral sermons and addresses from leading pulpits of America,

England, Germany and France

Edward Jewitt Wheeler

Pulpit and grave
A volume of funeral sermons and addresses from leading pulpits of America, England, Germany and France

ISBN/EAN: 9783337104757

Printed in Europe, USA, Canada, Australia, Japan

Cover: Foto ©Lupo / pixelio.de

More available books at **www.hansebooks.com**

PULPIT AND GRAVE:

A VOLUME OF

FUNERAL SERMONS AND ADDRESSES,

FROM

LEADING PULPITS OF AMERICA, ENGLAND, GERMANY, AND FRANCE.

CONTAINING 90 SERMONS, SKETCHES OF SERMONS, AND OBITUARY ADDRESSES ; ALSO, 450 CLASSIFIED TEXTS, SCRIPTURE READINGS, DEATH-BED TESTIMONIES, POINTS ON FUNERAL ETIQUETTE, ETC., ETC.

EDITED BY

E. J. WHEELER, A.M.

FUNK & WAGNALLS COMPANY
NEW YORK AND LONDON

Entered, according to Act of Congress, in the year 1890,
By FUNK & WAGNALLS,
in the Office of the Librarian of Congress at Washington, D. C.

PREFACE.

In no department of his work is the minister of the Gospel called upon to perform duties more onerous, to meet claims more exacting, than in the conducting of funeral services. The demands upon the time of a popular pastor in a large community are enormous, while the preacher in rural districts, who is called upon to traverse miles of muddy road in the most inclement weather, rarely fares better and often fares worse. Yet still more taxing is the drain upon the vital energies of a sympathetic pastor, who, both as man and as minister, weeps with those that weep, and is filled with solicitude that they mourn not as those who have no hope. In addition to this, if his heart has bled over its own personal losses, how are the wounds opened afresh as he is summoned again and again to the house of mourning and to the side of the open grave!

Moreover, the responsibilities of his position are at such a time so awful that no minister who appreciates them can feel other than a sense of insufficiency, and an instinctive shrinking which no length of experience can entirely remove. Life is full of crises, but what one is fraught with more consequence than that which overtakes the parent at the grave of a loved child, the child at the grave of a parent? None pass through it without change; no change carries with it vaster issues for weal or woe. Upon the preacher, often to an extent terrible to contemplate, depends the outcome. One earnest word from him at such a time may mean a useful life saved to God and to the world; one opportunity slighted may cost a life lost to all eternity.

Upon young ministers these duties and responsibilities rest at times with an almost crushing weight. Upon none should they rest lightly. If by this volume they may be guided in the performance of the one, and better prepared for the bearing of the other, its purpose is accomplished, and an apology for its existence is needless. In the effort to compass this, resort has been had to a wide variety of the richest sermonic literature, from which the compiler has gleaned with a view to satisfying the practical needs of the preacher rather than to furnishing mere specimens of eloquence. Many of the sermons given have never before been published, having been supplied, upon request, by their authors, to whom hearty thanks are hereby tendered. It is fitting also to express my obligations to Dr. J. M. Sherwood for the rare judgment with which he has aided both in the selection and arrangement of material.

Upon the list of classified texts much care and labor have been expended to render it a valuable aid to the preacher in the saving of time. Many clergymen have adopted the custom of omitting the text altogether and delivering what are known as obituary addresses. The custom has its advantages, but it has not yet obtained such favor either among clergymen or people as greatly to impair the usefulness of a list of texts arranged for ready reference.

In conclusion, while the object sought has been chiefly the assistance of pastors in their ministrations among the dying and the bereaved, it is believed that no volume but the Book of books will be found fuller of consolation for the mourning. There are here gathered thoughts from many minds, lessons from many experiences, promptings from many hearts; but they all teach the one lesson of hope, trust, submission to an all-loving Father. The reader will be led by many paths, but he will find them all converging to the same point—the Cross of Christ.

E. J. W.

CONTENTS.

INDEX OF AUTHORS AND CONTRIBUTORS............... xi

SERMONS.

SUBJECT.	NAME.	PAGE
The Fall of Hamilton..............	Eliphalet Nott, D.D., LL.D....	13
Consolation in Christ.............	Christian E. Luthardt, D.D.....	31
Christ the Destroyer of Death......	Rev. C. H. Spurgeon..........	37
Confessions of Dying Men.........	Joel Hawes, D.D..............	52
A Mother's Death	Rev. Albert Barnes............	66
An Overcoming Faith.............	Richard Fuller, D.D...........	79
The National Bereavement	Rev. Henry Ward Beecher.....	94
Sorrow for Death of Friends.......	I. S. Spencer, D.D............	102
The Purpose of Divine Chastisements........................	Arthur T. Pierson, D.D.......	113
God's Voice to the Nation.........	Tryon Edwards, D.D..........	123
The Funeral of the Soul...........	H. B. Hooker, D.D............	133

OBITUARY ADDRESSES.

Responsibilities of the Living......	C. F. Deems, D.D.............	141
Life's Review	Theodor Christlieb, D.D........	147
Death of an Only Daughter........	William M. Taylor, D.D.......	153
A Mother's Removal..............	John Hall, D.D................	158
Living After Death................	J. M. Sherwood, D.D..........	161
A Time to Die...................	Anonymous...................	164
The Master's Shepherd Dog........	Justin D. Fulton, D.D.........	167
Infidelity and the Grave..........	Robert G. Ingersoll............	170
Funeral Oration for the Prince of Condé (peroration)..............	James Benigné Bossuet........	172
Funeral Oration on Louis the Great (peroration)	Jean Baptiste Massillon........	174

SERMONS ABRIDGED.

SUBJECT.	NAME.	PAGE
Sorrow for the Death of Friends....	Rev. James Saurin............	176
Victory over Death...............	Rev. Frederick W. Robertson..	181
The Christian's Final Triumph.....	George W. Bethune, D.D......	186
Character and Death of Washington Irving.........................	John A. Todd, D.D............	190
The Speed of Life Impressing Probation........................	Tryon Edwards, D.D..........	194
The Darkness of Providence.......	B. M. Palmer, D.D...........	198
Thoughts on Immortality..........	Rt. Rev. Samuel Fallows, D.D..	202
Lessons from Life's Brevity........	W. W. Ramsay, D.D..........	207
Transition to the Life Beyond......	Lyman Abbott, D.D...........	211
The Christian's Gain by Death.....	Rev. Zephaniah Meek.........	215
Preparing for Death...............	William Ives Budington, D.D.	218
Abiding and Departing............	Alexander McKenzie, D.D. ...	221
Afflictions not Accidental..........	Rev. John Burton.............	223
Death of Believers................	B. M. Palmer, D.D...........	226
The Christian's Victory over Death.	Rev. John Logan..............	228
The Master's Call in Affliction.....	Rev. William Cochrane........	230
Ripe for the Harvest..............	Rev. W. P. Tiddy............	232
The Approach of Death	Erskine Mason, D.D...........	234
Words of Comfort for Afflicted Parents	Rev. Lewis O. Thompson......	235
The Tent Home and the Eternal Home.....................	T. L. Cuyler, D.D............	237
No Night in Heaven	J. M. Sherwood, D.D..........	239
Glad Home-going	Rev. John Lobb..............	244
The Death of a Mother...........	Rev. J. M. Johnson...........	245
Preparations for Meeting God......	R. S. Storrs, D.D............	247
Human Life Transitory	Edward N. Kirk, D.D.........	248
Emotion of a Saint in Heaven......	Rev. A. S. Gardner	251
The Blessed Dead.................	Rev. William Lloyd	252
The Hidings of God's Providence...	M. W. Hamma, D.D..........	254
How Christ Takes away Fear of Death.....................	Rev. R. S. S. Dickinson	255
Christ's Resurrection the Promise and Prophecy of our Own.......	T. DeWitt Talmage, D.D......	256
Christ and the Immortal Life	W. J. Tucker, D.D............	257
The Death of Lazarus..............	Rev. Henry Blunt.............	259
The Years Fleeting and Heaven Nearing.....................	C. L. Goodell, D.D...........	260
The Life and Death of a Child.....	Rev. Wm. Veenschoten........	262

SUBJECT.	NAME.	PAGE
Preparation for Eternity	Justin Edwards, D.D.	263
Death in the Midst of Life	Jabez Burns, D.D.	264
Death-bed Repentance	Most Rev. John MacHale, D.D.,	265
The Changing and the Changeless	Jabez Burns, D.D.	265
Not Here, but Risen	Rev. John Lobb	266
Sudden Death	Rev. E. C. Cure	267
The Web of Life	Rev. Edward Blencowe	268
The Secret of a Successful Ministry	Thomas Armitage, D.D.	268
The Death of the Righteous	David Thomas, D.D.	269

SERMONS IN OUTLINE.................... 270

EXTRACTS AND ILLUSTRATIONS.

Thoughts on Life 281
Thoughts on Death.......................... 283
Thoughts on Heaven 289
Thoughts on Affliction..................... 290

PRAYERS.

At the Funeral of Cornelius Vanderbilt. By C. F. Deems, D.D.... 292
Before a Sermon on "The Rest of God." By Rev. H. W. Beecher. 294
At the Funeral of President Lincoln. By Rev. Dr. Grey 296

TEXTS FOR FUNERAL DISCOURSES.

1. Death in the Prime of Life.................................. 298
2. Death of an Obscure Worker................................. 298
3. Death of a Parent... 299
4. Death of the Unrepentant................................... 299
5. End of an Unhappy Life 300
6. Consolation for the Bereaved 301
7. Sudden or Accidental Death 303
8. Death of a Young Man or Woman............................. 304
9. Death of an Aged Christian................................. 305
10. Death of Children.. 306
11. Death of a Prominent Person.............................. 308
12. Admonition and Exhortation............................... 310
13. Transiency of Life 312
14. Death of the Righteous................................... 317
15. Heaven and Immortality 323
16. Miscellaneous 329

MISCELLANY.

	PAGE
About Funeral Addresses. By Pastor Rudolph Müller	332
Points of Etiquette in Funerals	337
Words from the Dying	347
Curious Facts concerning Funeral Rites	349
Appropriate Hymns for Funeral Services	352
Scripture Readings	354
Practical Hints	354
List of Appropriate Poems for Quotation and Reading	355
The Carnage of War	356
Textual Index	359
Index of Subjects	363

INDEX OF AUTHORS AND CONTRIBUTORS.

Abbott, Lyman, D.D., 211.
Armitage, Thos., D.D., 268.
Aurelius, Marcus, 281.
Barnes, Rev. Albert, 66.
Beecher, Rev. H. W., 94, 294.
Behringer, Rev. G. F., 332, 338.
Bethune, G. W., D.D., 186.
Blunt, Rev. Henry, 259.
Blencowe, Rev. Edward, 268.
Bossuet, J. B., 172.
Brooks, Thomas, D.D., 284.
Budington, W. I., D.D., 218.
Burns, Jabez, D.D., 264, 265.
Burton, Rev. John, 223.
Chapman, J. A. M., D.D., 290.
Christlieb, Theodor, D.D., 147.
Cochrane, Rev. Wm., 230.
Cook, Joseph, 283.
Cure, Rev. E. C., 267.
Cuyler, T. L., D.D., 237, 338.
Davis, Rev. W. R., 250.
Deems, C. F., D.D., 141, 292, 339.
Dickinson, Rev. R. S. S., 255.
Drelincourt, 288.
Edwards, Justin, D.D., 263.
Edwards, Tryon, D.D., 123, 194.
Fallows, Rt. Rev. Samuel, 202.
Fuller, Richard, D.D., 79.
Fulton, J. D., D.D., 167.
Gardner, Rev. A. S., 251.
Goethe, 281.
Goodell, C. L., D.D., 260.
Grey, Rev. Dr., 296.
Hall, John, D.D., 158.
Hamma, M. W., D.D., 254.
Hawes, Joel, D.D., 52.
Haynes, E. J., D.D., 340.
Hooker, H. B., D.D., 133.
Ingersoll, R. G., 170.

Johnson, Rev. J. M., 245.
Kirke, E. N., D.D., 248.
Lobb, Rev. John, 244, 266.
Logan, Rev. John, 228.
Lloyd, Rev. William, 252.
Luthardt, Chr. E., D.D., 31.
MacHale, Most Rev. John, D.D., 265.
Mason, Erskine, D.D., 234.
Massillon, J. B., 174, 284.
McKenzie, Alexander, D.D., 221.
Meek, Rev. Zephaniah, 215.
Montaigne, 284.
Müller, Pastor Rudolph, 332.
Nott, Eliphalet, D.D., LL.D., 13.
Palmer, B. M., D.D., 198, 226.
Park, Prof., 282.
Peck, J. O., D.D., 341.
Pierson, A. T., D.D., 113.
Ramsay, W. W., D.D., 207.
Richter, 287.
Robertson, Rev. F. W., 181.
Saurin, Rev. James, 175.
Sherwood, J. M., D.D., 161, 239, 342.
Spencer, I. S., D.D., 102.
Spurgeon, Rev. C. H., 37.
Sterne, 283.
Storrs, R. S., D.D., 247, 283, 286.
Stowe, Mrs. H. B., 291.
Talmage, T. D., D.D., 256, 286 seq., 289.
Taylor, W. M., D.D., 153, 284, 290.
Thomas, David, D.D., 269.
Thompson, Rev. L. O., 235.
Tiddy, Rev. W. P., 232,
Tiffany, O. H., D.D., 342.
Todd, John A., D.D., 190.
Tucker, W. J., D.D., 257.
Veenschoten, Rev. Wm., 262.
Wedekind, A. C., D.D., 344.

SERMONS.

THE FALL OF HAMILTON.

BY ELIPHALET NOTT, D.D., LL.D., UNION COLLEGE.

How are the mighty fallen !—2 SAMUEL i. 19.

THE occasion explains the choice of my subject—a subject on which I enter in obedience to your request. You have assembled to express your elegiac sorrows, and sad and solemn weeds cover you. Before such an audience, and on such an occasion, I enter on the duty assigned me with trembling. Do not mistake my meaning. I tremble, indeed — not, however, through fear of failing to merit your applause; for what have I to do with that, when addressing the dying and treading on the ashes of the dead? —not through fear of failing justly to portray the character of that great man who is at once the theme of my encomium and regret. He needs not eulogy. His work is finished, and death has removed him beyond my censure, and, I would fondly hope, through grace, above my praise.

You will ask, then, why I tremble? I tremble to think that I am called to attack from this place a crime, the very idea of which almost freezes one with horror—a crime, too, which exists among the polite and polished orders of society, and which is accompanied with every aggravation—committed with cool deliberation, and openly in the face of day ! But I have a duty to perform; and difficult and awful as that duty is, I will not shrink from it. Would to God my talents were adequate to the occasion · but such as they are, I devoutly proffer them to unfold the nature and counteract the influence of that barbarous custom, which, like a resistless torrent, is undermining the foundations of civil government, breaking down the barriers of social happiness, and sweeping away virtue, talents, and domestic felicity, in its desolating course. Another and an illustrious character—a father, a general, a statesman—the very man who stood on an eminence, and without a rival among sages and heroes, the future hope of his country in danger—this man, yielding to the influence of a custom which deserves our eternal reprobation, has been brought to an untimely end !

That the deaths of great and useful men should be particularly noticed, is equally the dictate of reason and revelation. The tears of Israel flowed at the decease of good Josiah, and to his memory the funeral women chanted the solemn dirge. But neither examples nor arguments are necessary to wake the sympathies of a grateful people on such occasions. The death of public benefactors surcharges the heart, and it spontaneously disburdens itself by a flow of sorrows. Such was the death of Washington, to embalm whose memory, and perpetuate whose deathless fame, we lent our feeble but unnecessary services. Such, also, and more peculiarly so, has been the death of Hamilton. The tidings of the former moved us—mournfully moved us—and we wept. The account of the latter chilled our hopes and curdled our blood. The former died in a good old age ; the latter was cut off in the midst of his usefulness. The former was a customary providence : we saw in it, if I may speak so, the finger of God, and rested in His sovereignty. The latter is not attended with this soothing circumstance.

The fall of Hamilton owes its existence to mad deliberation, and is marked by violence. The time, the place, the circumstances, are arranged with barbarous coolness. The instrument of death is levelled in daylight, and with well-directed skill pointed at his heart. Alas ! the event has proven that it was but too well directed. Wounded, mortally wounded, on the very spot which still smoked with the blood of a favorite son, into the arms of his indiscreet and cruel friend, the father fell. Ah ! had he fallen in the course of nature, or jeopardizing his life in defence of his country ; had he fallen—but he did not. He fell in single combat. Pardon my mistake—he did not fall in single combat : his noble nature refused to endanger the life of his antagonist. But he exposed his own life. This was his crime ; and the sacredness of my office forbids that I should hesitate explicitly to declare it so. He did not hesitate to declare it so himself : " My religious and moral principles are strongly opposed to duelling." These are his words before he ventured to the field of death. "I view the late transaction with sorrow and contrition." These are his words after his return. Humiliating end of illustrious greatness! *How are the mighty fallen!* And shall the mighty thus fall? Thus shall the noblest lives be sacrificed and the richest blood be spilt! *Tell it not in Gath ; publish it not in the streets of Askalon.*

Think not that the fatal issue of the late inhuman interview was fortuitous. No : the hand that guides unseen the arrow of the archer, steadied and directed the arm of the duellist. And why did it thus direct it? As a solemn *memento*—as a loud and awful warning to a community where justice has slumbered, and slumbered, and slumbered—while the wife has been robbed of her partner, the mother of her hopes, and life after life rashly, and with an air of triumph, sported away. And was there, O my God! no other sacrifice valuable enough? Would the cry of no other blood reach the place of retribution, and wake justice, dozing over her awful seat? But though justice should still slumber and retribution be delayed, we, who are the ministers of that God who will judge the judges of the world, and whose malediction rests on him who does his work unfaithfully—we will not keep silence.

I feel, my brethren, how incongruous my subject is with the place I occupy. It is humiliating, it is distressing, in a Christian country, and in churches consecrated to the religion of Jesus, to be obliged to attack a crime which outstrips barbarism, and would even sink the character of a generous savage. But humiliating as it is, it is necessary. And must we, then, even for a moment, forget the elevation on which grace hath placed us, and the light which the gospel sheds around us? Must we place ourselves back in the midst of barbarism? And instead of hearers softened to forgiveness by the love of Jesus, filled with noble sentiments toward enemies, and waiting for occasions, after the example of divinity, to do them good—instead of such hearers, must we suppose ourselves addressing hearts petrified to goodness, incapable of mercy, and boiling with revenge? Must we, O my God! instead of exhorting those who hear us to go on unto perfection, adding to *virtue charity, and to charity brotherly kindness ;* must we, as if surrounded by an auditory just emerging out of darkness, and still cruel and ferocious, reason to convince them that revenge is improper, and that to commit deliberate murder is sin? Yes, we must do this. Repeated violations of the law, and the sanctuary which the guilty find in public sentiment, prove that it is necessary.

Withdraw, therefore, for a moment, ye celestial spirits, ye holy angels, accustomed to hover around these altars, and listen to those strains of grace which heretofore have filled this house of God. Other subjects occupy us. Withdraw, therefore, and leave us; leave us to exhort Christian parents to restrain their vengeance, and at least to keep back their hands from blood—to exhort youth nurtured in Christian families, not rashly to sport with life, nor lightly to wring the widow's heart with sorrows, and fill the orphan's eye with tears.

In accomplishing the object which is before me, it will not be expected, as it is not necessary, that I should give a history of duelling. You need not be informed that it originated in a dark and barbarous age. The polished Greek knew nothing of it; the noble Roman was above it. Rome held in equal detestation the man who exposed his life unnecessarily, and him who refused to expose it when the public good required it.* Her heroes were superior to private contests. They indulged no vengeance, except against the enemies of their country. Their swords were not drawn, unless her honor was in danger; which honor they defended with their swords not only, but shielded with their bosoms also, and were then prodigal of their blood. But though Greece and Rome knew nothing of duelling, it exists. It exists among us; and it exists at once the most RASH, the most ABSURD, and GUILTY practice that ever disgraced a Christian nation.

GUILTY—because it is a violation of the law. What law? The law of God: THOU SHALT NOT KILL. This prohibition was delivered by God Himself, at Sinai to the Jews. And that it is of universal and perpetual obligation is manifest, not only from the nature of the crime prohibited, but also from the express declaration of the Christian lawgiver, who hath recognized its justice and added to it the sanction of his own authority.

"Thou shalt not kill." Who? Thou, creature. I, the Creator, have given life, and thou shalt not take it away! When,

---

* Sallust, de Bell. Catil., ix.

and under what circumstances, may I not take away life? Never, and under no circumstances, without my permission. It is obvious that no discretion whatever is here given. The prohibition is addressed to every individual where the law of GOD is promulgated, and the terms made use of are express and unequivocal. So that life cannot be taken under any pretext, without incurring guilt, unless by a permission sanctioned by the same authority which sanctions the general law prohibiting it. From this law, it is granted, there are exceptions. These exceptions, however, do not result from any sovereignty which one creature has over the existence of another, but from the positive appointment of that Eternal Being, whose " is the world and the fulness thereof. In whose hand is the soul of every living creature, and the breath of all mankind." Even the authority which we claim over the lives of animals is not founded on a natural right, but on a positive grant made by the Deity Himself, to Noah and his sons. This grant contains our warrant for taking the life of animals. But if we may not take the life of animals without permission from God, much less may we the life of man made in His image.

In what cases, then, has the sovereign of life given this permission? IN RIGHTFUL WAR; BY THE CIVIL MAGISTRATE, and IN NECESSARY SELF-DEFENCE. Besides, these, I do not hesitate to declare, that in the oracles of God there are no other.

He, therefore, who takes life in any other case, under whatever pretext, takes it unwarrantably—is guilty of what the Scriptures call murder, and exposes himself to the malediction of that God who is an avenger of blood, and who hath said, "At the hand of every man's brother will I require the life of man. Whoso sheddeth man's blood, by man shall his blood be shed." The duellist contravenes the law of God not only, but the law of man also. To the prohibition of the former have been added the sanctions of the latter. Life taken in a duel by the common law is murder. And where this is not the case, the giving and receiving of a challenge only is by statute considered a high misdemeanor, for which the principal and his second are declared infamous and disfranchised for twenty years.

Under what accumulated circumstances of aggravation does the duellist jeopardize his own life, or take the life of his antagonist! I am sensible that in a licentious age, and when laws are made to yield to the vices of those who move in the *higher circles*, this crime is called by I know not what mild and accommodating name. But, before these altars—in this house of God—what is it? It is MURDER—*deliberate, aggravated murder!* If the duellist deny this, let him produce his warrant from the author of life for taking away from his creature the life which had been sovereignly given. If he cannot do this, beyond all controversy he is a murderer; for murder consists in taking away life without the permission, and contrary to the prohibition, of Him who gave it.

Who is it, then, that calls the duellist to the dangerous and deadly combat? Is it God? No: on the contrary, He forbids it. Is it, then, his country? No: she also utters her prohibitory voice. Who is it, then? A man of honor! And who is the man of honor? A man, perhaps, whose honor is a name; who prates with polluted lips about the sacredness of character, when his own is stained with crimes, and needs but the single shade of murder to complete the dismal and sickly picture. Every transgression of the divine law implies great guilt, because it is the transgression of infinite authority. But the crime of deliberately and lightly taking life has peculiar aggravations. It is a crime committed against written law not only, but also against the dictates of reason, the remonstrances of conscience, and every tender and amiable feeling of the heart. To the unfortunate sufferer it is the wanton violation of his most sacred rights. It snatches him from his friends and his comforts; terminates his state of trial, and precipitates him, uncalled for, and perhaps unprepared, into the presence of his Judge.

You say the duellist feels no malice. Be it so. Malice, indeed, is murder in principle. But there may be murder in reason, and in fact, where there is no malice. Some other unwarrantable passion or principle may lead to the unlawful taking of human life. The highwayman, who cuts the throat and rifles the pocket of the passing traveller, feels no malice. And could he, with equal ease and no greater danger of detection, have secured his booty without taking life, he would have stayed his arm over the palpitating bosom of his victim, and let the plundered suppliant pass. Would the imputation of cowardice have been inevitable to the duellist, if a challenge had not been given or accepted? The imputation of want had been no less inevitable to the robber, if the money of the passing traveller had not been secured. Would the duellist have been willing to have spared the life of his antagonist, if the point of honor could otherwise have been gained ? So would the robber, if the point of property could have been. Who can say that the motives of the one are not as urgent as the motives of the other, and the means by which both obtain the object of their wishes are the same ? Thus, according to the dictates of reason, as well as the law of God, the highwayman and the duellist stand on ground equally untenable, and support their guilty havoc of the human race by arguments equally fallacious.

Is duelling guilty? So it is ABSURD. It is absurd as a punishment, for it admits of no proportion to crimes : and besides, virtue and vice, guilt and innocence, are equally exposed by it to death or suffering. As a reparation it is still more absurd, for it makes the injured liable to still greater injury. And as the vindication of personal character, it is absurd even beyond madness. One man of honor, by some inadvertence, or perhaps with design, injures the sensibility of another man of honor. In perfect character, the injured gentleman resents it. He challenges the offender. The offender accepts the challenge. The time is fixed. The place is agreed upon. The circumstances, with an air of solemn mania, are arranged ; and the principals, with their seconds and surgeons, retire under the covert of some solitary hill, or upon the margin of some unfrequented beach, to settle this important question of honor by stabbing or shooting at each other. One or the other or both the parties fall in this polite and gentlemanlike contest. And what does this prove ? It proves that one or the other, or both of them, as the case may be, are marksmen. But it affords no evidence that either of them possesses honor, probity, or talents. It is true, that he who falls in single combat has the honor of being murdered : and he who takes his life the honor of a murderer. Besides this, I know not of any glory which can redound to the infatuated combatants, except it be what results from having extended the circle of wretched widows, and added to the number of hapless orphans.

And yet, terminate as it will, this frantic meeting, by a kind of magic influence, entirely varnishes over a defective and smutty character ; transforms vice to virtue, cowardice to courage ; makes falsehood truth, guilt innocence. In one word, it gives a new complexion to the whole state of things. The Ethiopian changes his skin, the leopard his spot; and the debauched and treacherous, having shot away the infamy of a sorry life, comes back from the field of PERFECTIBILITY quite regenerated, and in the fullest sense an honorable man. He is now fit for the company of gentlemen. He is admitted to that company, and should he again by acts of violence stain this purity of character so nobly acquired, and should any one have the effrontery to say that he has done so, again he stands ready to vindicate his honor, and by another act of homicide to wipe away the stain which has been attached to it.

I might illustrate this article by example. I might produce instances of this mysterious transformation of character, in the sublime circles of moral refinement, furnished by the higher orders of the fashionable world, which the mere firing of pistols has produced. But the occasion is too awful for irony.

Absurd as duelling is, were it absurd only, though we might smile at the weakness and pity the folly of its abettors, there would be no occasion for seriously attacking them. But, to what has been said, I add, that duelling is RASH and PRESUMPTUOUS. Life is the gift of God, and it was never bestowed to be sported with. To each, the sovereign of the universe has marked out a sphere to move in, and assigned a part to act. This part respects ourselves not only, but others also. Each lives for the benefit of all. As in the system of nature the sun shines, not to display its own brightness, and answer its own convenience, but to warm, enlighten, and bless the world; so in the system of animated beings, there is a dependence, a correspondence and a relation through an infinitely extended, dying, and reviving universe, *in which no man liveth to himself, and no man dieth to himself.* Friend is related to friend; the father to his family; the individual to community. To every member of which, having fixed his station and assigned his duty, the God of nature says, "Keep this trust—defend this post." For whom? For thy friends—thy family—thy country. And having received such a charge, and for such a purpose, to desert it is rashness and temerity.

Since the opinions of men are as they are, do you ask how you shall avoid the imputation of cowardice, if you do not fight when you are injured? Ask your family how you will avoid the imputation of cruelty—ask your conscience how you will avoid the imputation of guilt—ask God how you will avoid His malediction if you do. These are previous questions. Let these first be answered, and it will be easy to reply to any which may follow them. If you only accept a challenge, when you believe in your conscience that duelling is wrong, you act the coward. The dastardly fear of the world governs you. Awed by its menaces, you conceal your sentiments, appear in disguise, and act in guilty conformity to principles not your own, and that, too, in the most solemn moment, and when engaged in an act which exposes you to death.

But if it be rashness to accept, how passing rashness is it, in a sinner, to *give* a challenge? Does it become him, whose life is measured out by crimes, to be extreme to mark, and punctilious to resent, whatever is amiss in others? Must the duellist, who now, disdaining to forgive, so imperiously demands satisfaction to the uttermost—must this man, himself trembling at the recollection of his offences, presently appear a suppliant before the mercy-seat of God? Imagine this, and the case is not imaginary, and you cannot conceive an instance of greater inconsistency or of more presumptuous arrogance. Wherefore, *avenge not yourselves,* **but rather give place unto wrath ;** *for vengeance is mine, I will repay it, saith the Lord.*

Do you ask, then, how you shall conduct toward your enemy who hath lightly done you wrong? If he be hungry, feed him ; if naked, clothe him ; if thirsty, give him drink. Such, had you preferred your question to Jesus Christ, is the answer He had given you ; by observing which, you will usually subdue, and always act more honorably than your enemy. I feel, my brethren, as a minister of Jesus, and a teacher of His gospel, a noble elevation on this article. Compare the conduct of the Christian, acting in conformity to the principles of religion, and of the duellist acting in conformity to the principles of honor, and let reason say which bears the marks of the more exalted greatness. Compare them, and let reason say which enjoys the more calm serenity of mind in time, and which is likely to receive the plaudits of his Judge in immortality. God, from His throne, beholds not a nobler object on His footstool, than the man who loves his enemies, pities their errors, and forgives the injuries they do him.

This is, indeed, the very spirit of the heavens; it is the image of His benignity whose glory fills them.

To return to the subject before us: GUILTY, ABSURD, and RASH as duelling is, it has its advocates. And, had it not had its advocates—had not a strange preponderance of opinion been in favor of it, never, O lamented HAMILTON! hadst thou thus fallen, in the midst of thy days, and before thou hadst reached the zenith of thy glory! O that I possessed the talent of eulogy, and that I might be permitted to indulge the tenderness of friendship, in paying the last tribute to his memory. O that I were capable of placing this great man before you. Could I do this, I should furnish you with an argument, the most practical, the most plain, the most convincing, except that drawn from the mandate of God, that was ever furnished against duelling—that horrid practice, which has, in an awful moment, robbed the world of such exalted worth. But I cannot do this; I can only hint at the variety and exuberance of his excellence.

The MAN, on whom nature seems originally to have impressed the stamp of greatness; whose genius beamed from the retirement of collegiate life, with a radiance which dazzled, and a loveliness which charmed the eyes of sages. The HERO, called from his sequestered retreat, whose first appearance in the field, though a stripling, conciliated the esteem of WASHINGTON, our good old father; moving by whose side, during all the perils of the Revolution, our young chieftain was a contributor to the veteran's glory, the guardian of his person, and the compartner of his toils. The CONQUEROR, who, sparing of human blood, when victory favored, stayed the uplifted arm, and nobly said to the vanquished enemy, "LIVE!" The STATESMAN, the correctness of whose principles, and the strength of whose mind, are inscribed on the records of Congress, and on the annals of the council-chamber; whose genius impressed itself upon the CONSTITUTION of his country, and whose memory, the government—ILLUSTRIOUS FABRIC—resting on this basis, will perpetuate while it lasts; and, shaken by the violence of party, should it fall (which may heaven avert!) his prophetic declarations will be found inscribed on its ruins. The COUNSELLOR, who was at once the pride of the bar, and the admiration of the court; whose apprehensions were quick as lightning, and whose development of truth was luminous as its path; whose argument no change of circumstances could embarrass ; whose knowledge appeared intuitive, and who, by a single glance, and with as much facility as the eye of the eagle passes over the landscape, surveyed the whole field of controversy—saw in what way truth might be most successfully defended, and how error must be approached. And who, without ever stopping, ever hesitating, by a rapid and manly march, led the listening judge and the fascinated juror, step by step, through a delightsome region, brightening as he advanced, till his argument rose to demonstration, and eloquence was rendered useless by conviction ; whose talents were employed on the side of righteousness ; whose voice, whether in the council-chamber or at the bar of justice, was virtue's consolation, at whose approach oppressed humanity felt a secret rapture, and the heart of injured innocence leapt for joy.

Where HAMILTON was—in whatever sphere he moved—the friendless had a friend, the fatherless a father, and the poor man, though unable to reward his kindness, found an advocate. It was when the rich oppressed the poor—when the powerful menaced the defenceless—when truth was disregarded, or the eternal principles of justice violated—it was on these occasions that he exerted all his strength. It was on these occasions that he sometimes soared so high, and shone with a radiance so transcendent, I had almost said, so '' heavenly as filled those around him with awe, and gave to him the force and authority of a prophet.''

The PATRIOT, whose integrity baffled the scrutiny of inquisition ; whose manly virtue never shaped itself to circumstances ; who, always great, always himself, stood amid the varying tides of party, *firm*, like the rock, which, far from land, lifts its majestic top above the waves, and remains unshaken by the storms which agitate the ocean. The FRIEND, who knew no guile ; whose bosom was transparent, and deep in the bottom of whose heart was rooted every tender and sympathetic virtue ; whose various worth opposing parties acknowledged while alive, and on whose tomb they unite with equal sympathy and grief to heap their honors.

I know he had his failings. I see on the picture of his life, a picture rendered awful by greatness, and luminous by virtue, some dark shades. On these let the tear that pities human weakness fall ; on these let the veil which covers human frailty rest.

As a Hero, as a Statesman, as a Patriot, he lived nobly ; and would to God, I could add, he nobly fell.

Unwilling to admit his error in this respect, I go back to the period of discussion. I see him resisting the threatened interview. I imagine myself present in his chamber. Various reasons, for a time, seem to hold his determination in arrest. Various and moving objects pass before him, and speak a dissuasive language. His country, which may need his counsels to guide and his arm to defend, utters her *veto*. The partner of his youth, already covered with weeds, and whose tears flow down into her bosom, intercedes ! His babes, stretching out their little hands and pointing to a weeping mother, with lisping eloquence, but eloquence which reaches a parent's heart, cry out, "Stay, stay, dear father, and live for us !" In the meantime, the spectre of a fallen son, pale and ghastly, approaches, opens his bleeding bosom, and as the harbinger of death, points to the yawning tomb, and forewarns a hesitating father of the issue. He pauses, reviews these sad objects, and reasons on the subject. I admire his magnanimity ; I approve his reasoning, and I wait to hear him reject with indignation the murderous proposition, and to see him spurn from his presence the presumptuous bearer of it.

But I wait in vain. It was a moment in which his great wisdom forsook him, a moment in which HAMILTON was not himself. He yielded to the force of an imperious custom, and yielding, he sacrificed a life in which all had an interest ; and he is lost—lost to his country—lost to his family—lost to us ! For this act, because he disclaimed it, and was penitent, I forgive him. But there are those whom I cannot forgive, I mean not his antagonist, over whose erring steps, if there be tears in heaven, a pious mother looks down and weeps. If he be capable of feeling, he suffers already all that humanity can suffer. Suffers, and wherever he may fly will suffer with the poignant recollection of having taken the life of one who was too magnanimous in return to attempt his own. Had he have known this, it must have paralyzed his arm while it pointed, at so incorruptible a bosom, the instrument of death. Does he know this now, his heart, if it be not adamant, must soften—if it be not ice, it must melt.

But on this article I forbear. Stained with blood as he is, if he be penitent, I forgive him ; and if he be not, before these altars, where all of us appear as suppliants, I wish not to excite your vengeance, but rather, in behalf of an object rendered wretched and pitiable by crime, to wake your prayers.

But I have said, and I repeat it, there are those whom I cannot forgive. I cannot forgive that minister at the altar, who has hitherto forborne to remonstrate on this subject. I cannot forgive that public prosecutor, who, intrusted with the duty of avenging his country's wrongs, has seen those wrongs, and taken no measures to avenge them. I cannot forgive that judge upon the bench, or that governor in the chair of State, who has lightly passed over such offences. I cannot forgive the public, in whose opinion the duellist finds a sanctuary. I cannot forgive you, my brethren, who, till this late hour, have been silent, while successive murders were committed. No, I cannot forgive you, that you have not, in common with the freemen of this State, raised your voice to the *powers that be*, and loudly and explicitly demanded an execution of your laws. Demanded this in a manner which, if it did not reach the ear of government, would at least have reached the heavens, and plead your excuse before the God that filled them. In whose presence, as I stand, I should not feel myself innocent of the blood which crieth against us, had I been silent. But I have not been silent. Many of you who hear me are my witnesses—the walls of yonder temple, where I have heretofore addressed you, are my witnesses, how freely I have animadverted on this subject, in the presence both of those who have violated the laws, and of those whose indispensable duty it is to see the laws executed on those who violate them.

I enjoy another opportunity; and would to God I might be permitted to approach for once the late scene of death! Would to God I could there assemble, on the one side, the disconsolate mother with her seven fatherless children, and on the other those who administer the justice of my country! Could I do this, I would point them to these sad objects. I would entreat them, by the agonies of bereaved fondness, to listen to the widow's heartfelt groans; to mark the orphans' sighs and tears. And having done this, I would uncover the breathless corpse of HAMILTON—I would lift from his gaping wound his bloody MANTLE—I would hold it up to heaven before them, and I would ask, in the name of God, I would ask, whether at the sight of IT they felt no compunction.

You will ask, perhaps, what can be done to arrest the progress of a practice which has yet so many advocates? I answer, *nothing*—if it be the deliberate intention to do NOTHING. But if otherwise, much is within our power. Let, then, the governor see that the laws are executed—let the council displace the man who offends against their majesty. Let courts of justice frown from their bar, as unworthy to appear before them, the murderer and his accomplices. Let the people declare him unworthy of their confidence who engages in such sanguinary contests. Let this be done; and should life still be taken in single combat, then the governor, the council, the court, the people, looking up to the Avenger of sin, may say, "We are innocent—we are innocent." Do you ask how proof can be obtained? How can it be avoided? The parties return, hold up before our eyes the instruments of death, publish to the world the circumstances of their interview, and even, with an air of insulting triumph, boast how coolly and how deliberately they proceeded in violating one of the most sacred laws of earth and heaven.

Ah, ye tragic shores of Hoboken! crimsoned with the richest blood, I tremble at the crimes you record against us—the annual register of murders which you keep and send up to God! Place of inhuman cruelty, beyond the limits of reason, of duty, and of religion, where man assumes a more barbarous nature, and ceases to be man, what poignant, lingering sorrows do thy lawless combats occasion to surviving relatives! Ye who have hearts of pity—ye who have experienced the anguish of dissolving friendship—who have wept, and still weep, over the mouldering ruins of departed kindred, ye can enter into this reflection.

O thou disconsolate widow! robbed, so cruelly robbed, and in so short a time, both of a husband and a son, what must be the plenitude of thy sufferings! Could we approach thee, gladly would we drop the tear of sympathy, and pour into thy bleeding bosom the balm of consolation. But how could we comfort her whom God hath not comforted! To His throne let us lift up our voice and weep. O God! if thou art still the widow's husband, and the father of the fatherless—if in the fulness of thy goodness, there be yet mercies in store for miserable mortals, pity, O pity this afflicted mother, and grant that her hapless orphans may find a friend, a benefactor, a father, in THEE!

On this article I have done: and may God add His blessing. But I have still a claim upon your patience. I cannot here repress my feelings, and thus let pass the present opportunity.

How are the mighty fallen! And regardless as we are of vulgar deaths, shall not the fall of the mighty affect us? A short time since, and he who is the occasion of our sorrows was the ornament of his country. He stood on an eminence, and glory covered him. From that eminence he has fallen—suddenly, forever fallen. His intercourse with the living world is now ended; and those who would hereafter find him must seek him in the grave. There, cold and lifeless, is the heart which just now was the seat of friendship. There, dim and sightless, is the eye whose radiant and enlivening orb beamed with intelligence; and there, closed forever, are those lips on whose persuasive accents we have so often and so lately hung with transport.

From the darkness which rests upon his tomb there proceeds, methinks, a light in which it is clearly seen that those gaudy objects which men pursue are only phantoms. In this light how dimly shines the splendor of victory—how humble appears the majesty of grandeur! The bubble which seemed to have so much solidity has burst, and we again see that all below the sun is vanity. True, the funeral eulogy has been pronounced. The sad and solemn procession has moved. The badge of mourning has already been decreed, and presently the sculptured marble will lift up its front, proud to perpetuate the name of HAMILTON, and rehearse to the passing traveller his virtues. Just attributes of respect! And to the living useful. But to him, mouldering in his narrow and humble habitation, what are they? How vain! how unavailing!

Approach and behold, while I lift from his sepulchre its covering. Ye admirers of his greatness, ye emulous of his talents and his fame, approach, and behold him now. How pale! How silent! No martial bands admire the adroitness of his movements. No fascinated throng weep, and melt, and tremble at his eloquence. Amazing change! A shroud! a coffin! a narrow subterraneous cabin! This is all that now remains of HAMILTON! And is this all that remains of him? During a life so transitory, what lasting monument, then, can our fondest hopes erect?

My brethren, we stand on the borders of an AWFUL GULF, which is swallowing up all things human. And is there, amid this universal wreck, nothing stable, nothing abiding, nothing immortal, on which poor, frail, dying man can fasten? Ask the hero, ask the statesman, whose wisdom you have been accustomed to revere, and he will tell you. He will tell you, did I say? He has already told you, from his death-bed, and his illumined spirit still whispers from the heavens with well-known eloquence, the solemn admonition, "Mortals, hastening to the tomb, and once the companions of my pilgrimage, take warning, and avoid my errors. Cultivate the virtues I have recommended. Choose the Saviour I have chosen. Live disinterestedly. Live for immortality; and would you rescue anything from final dissolution, lay it up in God."

Thus speaks, methinks, our deceased benefactor; and thus he acted during his last sad hours. To the exclusion of every other concern, religion now claims all his thoughts. Jesus! Jesus is now his only hope. The friends of Jesus are his friends. The ministers of the altar his companions. While these intercede he listens in awful silence, or in profound submission whispers his assent. Sensible, deeply sensible of his sins, he pleads no merit of his own. He repairs to the mercy-seat, and there pours out his penitential sorrows—there he solicits pardon. Heaven, it should seem, heard and pitied the suppliant's cries. Disburdened of his sorrows, and looking up to God, he exclaims, "Grace, rich grace!" "I have," said he, clasping his dying hands, and with a faltering tongue, "I HAVE A TENDER RELIANCE ON THE MERCY OF GOD IN CHRIST." In token of this reliance, and as an expression of his faith, he receives the holy sacrament. And having done this, his mind becomes tranquil and serene. Thus he remains, thoughtful indeed, but unruffled to the last, and meets death with an air of dignified composure, and with an eye directed to the heavens.

This last act, more than any other, sheds glory on his character. Everything else death effaces. Religion alone abides with him on his death-bed. He dies a Christian. This is all which can be enrolled of him among the archives of eternity. This is all that can make his name great in heaven. Let not the sneering infidel persuade you that this last act of homage to the Saviour resulted from an enfeebled state of mental faculties, or from perturbation occasioned by the near approach of death. No; his opinions concerning the divine mission of Jesus Christ, and the validity of the holy Scriptures, had long been settled, and settled after laborious investigation and extensive and deep research. These opinions were not concealed. I knew them myself. Some of you who hear me knew them. And had his life been spared, it was his determination to have published them to the world, together with the facts and reasons on which they were founded.

At a time when scepticism, shallow and superficial indeed, but depraved and malignant, is breathing forth its pestilential vapor, and polluting, by its unhallowed touch, everything divine and sacred, it is consoling to a devout mind to reflect that the great, and the wise, and the good of all ages—those superior geniuses, whose splendid talents have elevated them almost above mortality, and placed them next in order to angelic natures; yes, it is consoling to a devout mind to reflect, that while *dwarfish infidelity* lifts up its deformed head and mocks, these ILLUSTRIOUS PERSONAGES, though living in different ages, inhabiting different countries, nurtured in different schools, destined to different pursuits, and differing on various subjects, should all, as if touched with an impulse from heaven, agree to vindicate the sacredness of revelation, and present, with one accord, their learning, their talents, and their virtue, on the gospel altar, as an offering to Emanuel.

This is not exaggeration. Who was it, that, overleaping the narrow bounds which had hitherto been set to the human mind, ranged abroad through the immensity of space, discovered and illustrated those laws by which the Deity unites, binds, and governs all things? Who was it, soaring into the sublime of astronomic science, numbered the stars of heaven, measured their spheres, and called them by their names? It was NEWTON. But Newton was a Christian. Newton, great as he was, received instruction from the lips, and laid his honors at the feet of Jesus. Who was it that developed the hidden combination, the component parts of bodies? Who was it that dissected the animal, examined the flower, penetrated the earth, and ranged the extent of organic nature? It was BOYLE. But Boyle was a Christian. Who was it that lifted the veil which had for ages covered the intellectual world, analyzed the human mind, defined its powers, and reduced its operations to certain fixed laws? It was LOCKE. But Locke, too, was a Christian.

What more shall I say? For time would fail me to speak of HALE, learned in the law; of ADDISON, admired in the schools; of MILTON, celebrated among the poets; and of WASHINGTON, immortal in the field and in the cabinet. To this catalogue of professing Christians, from among, if I may speak so, a higher order of beings, may now be added the name of ALEXANDER HAMILTON —a name which raises in the mind the idea of whatever is great, whatever is splendid, whatever is illustrious in human nature, and which is now added to a catalogue which might be lengthened— and lengthened—and lengthened with the names of illustrious characters, whose lives have blessed society, and whose works form a COLUMN big as heaven—a column of learning, of wisdom, and of greatness, which will stand to future ages, an ETERNAL MONUMENT of the transcendent talents of the advocates of Christianity, when every fugitive leaf from the pen of the canting infidel witlings of the day shall be swept by the tide of time from the annals of the world, and buried with the names of their authors in oblivion.

To conclude. *How are the mighty fallen!* Fallen before the desolating hand of death. Alas! the ruins of the tomb! . . . The ruins of the tomb are an emblem of the ruins of the world! When not an individual, but a universe, already marred by sin, and hastening to dissolution, shall agonize and die! Directing your thoughts from the one, fix them for a moment on the other. Anticipate the concluding scene—the final catastrophe of nature. When the sign of the Son of man shall be seen in heaven. When the Son of man himself shall appear in the glory of his Father, and send forth judgment unto victory. The fiery desolation envelops towns, palaces, and fortresses. The heavens pass away! The earth melts! And all those magnificent productions of art, which ages, heaped on ages, have reared up, are in one awful day reduced to ashes!

Against the ruins of that day, as well as the ruins of the tomb which precede it, the gospel in the CROSS of its great HIGH PRIEST offers you all a sanctuary. A sanctuary secure and abiding. A sanctuary which no lapse of time nor change of circumstances can destroy. No; neither life nor death; no, neither principalities nor powers. Everything else is fugitive; everything else is mutable; everything else will fail you. But this, the CITADEL of the Christian's hopes, will never fail you. Its base is adamant. It is cemented with the richest blood. The ransomed of the Lord crowd its portals. Embosomed in the dust which it incloses, the bodies of the redeemed "rest in hope." On its top dwells the church of the first-born, who, in delightful response with the angels of light, chant redeeming love. Against this citadel the tempest beats, and around it the storm rages and spends its force in vain. Immortal in its nature, and incapable of change, it stands, and stands firm amid the ruins of a mouldering world, and endures forever. Thither fly, ye prisoners of hope! that when earth, air, elements, shall have passed away, secure of existence and felicity, you may join with saints in glory to perpetuate the song which lingered on the faltering tongue of HAMILTON, "GRACE, RICH GRACE."

God grant us this honor. Then shall the measure of our joy be full, and to His name shall be the glory in Christ. AMEN.

CONSOLATION IN CHRIST.

BY CHRISTIAN E. LUTHARDT, D.D., LEIPSIC.

[From the German.]

And as it is appointed unto men once to die, but after this the judgment: so Christ was once offered to bear the sins of many; and unto them that look for Him shall He appear the second time without sin unto salvation.— HEBREWS ix. 27, 28.

"IT is appointed unto men once to die, and after this cometh judgment." These are words of solemn import, and they fall heavily upon our heart. Death is the law of our life; we cannot by any means evade or resist it. "It is appointed unto men," unto all men as sons of Adam. For by one man sin entered into the world, and death by sin. This *once dying* closes our earthly life, and after it comes judgment. Every word falls like the blow of a hammer on our souls.

The lamentation over death, and the transitoriness of earthly things, is the oldest and the commonest of all. "All flesh is grass, and all the glory of man as the flower of grass. The grass withereth, the flower fadeth." This is the moan of every age. All that is good and bright—greatness, power, riches, honor, beauty, life, wisdom, knowledge—all passes away. The wail over the first death has not come down to us, but our hearts can picture the stony anguish in which our first parents gazed on the white face of their dead son, and realized that the life was fled. And ever since the air has been "full of farewells to the dying and mournings for the dead;" the old pain is ever new, and we ourselves see the "shadow feared of men" drawing daily nearer.

Our whole life is thus under the law of evanescence. Merry youth passes into the stern struggle of manhood and the weakness of old age. And what remains? One after another we bury the hopes of youth, the thoughts of later years, our wishes, joys, and, last of all, our loves. How full are those graves of all that made life dear!

Our thoughts wander away now to days of bygone happiness, and our hearts cry,

"O for the touch of a vanished hand,
And the sound of a voice that is still."

We think of quiet graves where, it may be, we have sadly laid gray and honored heads, old men full of life and full of labors, but careworn and weary, to whom death was a welcome messenger. There is much to soothe our sorrow when men die after a long day of life well spent. And yet how little, at the largest, is the work we any of us do, compared to that which we had hoped and planned and purposed! And what is all the love we have enjoyed or given, to the blank which it leaves behind?

Then we have buried not the old alone, but the young in the blossom of their years, the morning of their life, bright with hope and promise. What a wealth of parental love, love of brothers and sisters and sweet friends, what hopes for the fatherland may be covered by one little mound of earth!

"There is a reaper whose name is Death;" he reaps for the Lord of the harvest, and he reaps all over the field. "All flesh is grass, and all the glory of man as the flower of the grass. The grass withereth, the flower fadeth." "It is appointed unto men once to die." *It is appointed.* "What means our trembling soul to be thus shy of death?" Sorrowfully, indeed, but without pain, we see the flowers fade and the rose-leaves flutter to the ground. But man is more than a flower. We see the beasts die, not without pity for them, and a natural sorrow for their suffering. We know this is their destiny. But man is more than a beast. That *he* should die strikes us with a sense of sympathetic awe. Life is ever pointing man on to the future; each step leads to another— youth to manhood, manhood to old age, and at length death comes in and breaks the chain. No life fulfils itself to its utmost; it seems broken off even at the longest. This is what makes us shudder. Death is so merciless. We feel it is a judgment. "All our days are passed away in Thy wrath; we spend our years as a tale that is told." This song, a thousand years old, is as true to-day as ever. "It is *appointed* unto man,"—this is the doom hanging over him. Death is a judgment of God. We feel it to be so, and oh! how hard man often wrestles against it; how life contends with death! And even when it is not so, when the fair and beautiful "life is rounded with a sleep," yet how one moment effaces all! It is gone! What was it, after all? And what will it be? "It is appointed unto men once to die, and after this cometh judgment." Death does not end all; this we know. We leave this world and enter on another. What is that then? A world of stillness, where the voices of life are silent; all the ten thousand voices of the busy mart and the loud, striving tide of men, which were wont to be so loud in our ears that we could not hear the still, small voice within—all these will be silenced, and the inward voice alone will speak audibly. And what will it say? What will be the verdict of those thoughts of ours which accuse or excuse one another? There will be no more self-deception then. We enter on a world of realities, where all shams and shows are done away, where we appear before God Himself, not as we appear to our fellow-men here, not perhaps even as we appeared to ourselves. All the cloaks in which we were wont to wrap ourselves fall away; for there is no creature that is not naked and open before Him with whom we have to do. Who shall abide that searching gaze? God will make manifest the secrets of all hearts, and pronounce His sentence upon us; He will render to every man according to his works. There will be no time then to form resolves of improvement. It will be too late; now is the time for that. This life is the time appointed for us to turn to God. For this end is His Word given us, and all the means of grace by which He would educate us in this life.

What is put off here, cannot be done there. "It is appointed unto men once to die, and after this cometh judgment." Who shall stand? There are even among our fellow-men eyes that seem to search out the very secrets of our soul. But what are human eyes to those eyes which shall be fixed upon us by and by?

> "That I the chief of sinners am,
> Thou art the witness, Lord;
> When questioned on the judgment-day
> I will not speak one word."

If we meditate much on these things, if we let them take possession of our minds, they must overwhelm us, unless we believe in the mercy of God unto eternal life. I confess I cannot understand the self-deception of those who live here on earth a life which they know ends in death and the judgment, and yet think they can do without the mercy of God. Where will they sink to, if, when death comes, they do not fall into the arms of God's mercy outstretched to them in Jesus Christ, where alone help and safety are found in the hour of death and in the day of judgment?

We rejoice in the SURE CONSOLATION we have in Christ, which should banish the fear of death. We need a strong consolation in view of death, one which can bear the strain of that dark hour when the accuser of souls is so busy. Without this whither shall we turn for comfort? We may put away the thought of death, we may try to forget that which we cannot alter, but he will come upon us as an armed man, and where then is our defence? We may cover the grave with flowers, but the worm is there and the flowers fade. Death is the abyss which divides this life from another, and we cannot bridge an abyss with flowers. He who does not know the arm that can guide him safely across must linger shivering on the brink, till the inevitable moment comes, and he is swallowed up of the deep waters, without help and without hope. Without hope! this is the latest wisdom which the gospel of despair proclaims; and holding fast to this as its ultimatum, it declares it had been better for a man had he never been born. And, indeed, if this is its final utterance, life is not worth the living, and the sooner we find a way of escape from it the better.

But we turn instinctively from this gospel of death. Where then shall we seek comfort? Has human wisdom any balm for us? Alas! its well-meant utterances never reach the mark; they flutter to the ground like autumn leaves in the evening wind. Shall we take comfort in our own uprightness, duty doing, faithfulness to our calling? Alas! our good works flare away like so much tinder in the fire when we stand before God. "All our righteousnesses are as filthy rags, and our iniquities, like the wind, have carried us away." To whom then shall we turn for help? To God alone! Oh, Almighty Lord, and everlasting God, preserve us, body and soul, unto everlasting life, through our Lord and Saviour Jesus Christ!

"As it is appointed unto men once to die, and after this cometh judgment, so Christ also, having been once offered to bear the sins of many, shall appear a second time, apart from sin, to them that wait for Him unto salvation."

This is our comfort. It is a wonderful message which the Christian faith brings to us, when it teaches us that God, the Lord Himself, stooped from His throne in heaven to clothe Himself in our flesh and blood, to become one of us, and trod the pathway of death, and in His inmost soul tasted death for every man. Truly a wonderful message! That God should manifest Himself in His glory, were easy to understand. But that He should take upon Him such a body of humiliation, and humble Himself even to the death of the Cross, this is above our thoughts and ways as high as the heaven is above the earth. It is so wonderful a message that we might well hesitate to believe it, but to those who do believe it brings joy unspeakable and full of glory. And we know that it is true. Is not love the highest attribute of God—higher than power or wisdom? So the deed of the highest love is the most divine. "Greater love hath no man than this," said the Lord Himself, "that a man should lay down his life for his friends. But God commendeth His love toward us, in that while we were yet sinners, Christ died for us." This is our consolation. If our thoughts should turn to the grave, let us repair first of all, in spirit, to the grave of Jesus, and there meditate what it means for us. The sermon preached to us by that grave is this: "He died for our sins and rose again for our justification." "He was once offered to bear the sins of many."

There is one thing which can help us alike in times of joy and sorrow, in life and death and at the judgment: this is the forgiveness of sins. That Christ died for our sins will be our all-sufficient plea when God reckons with us, and when the enemy of souls accuses us. "The sting of death is sin." If we had no sin we should not be afraid to appear before God. Therefore forgiveness casts out the fear, and takes away the sting of death.

A dying bed is a solemn place. There all earthly comforts fail. We must have something stronger to hold by. What can we say to the weeping parents who see their child's last hour at hand? What shall we say to the husband, when the last look of love falls on him from the fast dimming eyes of the dying wife? Every earthly prop breaks with a crash in such an hour, and pierces through the hand that leans on it. One only pillar bears—the everlasting love and faithfulness of our God and Saviour. "I have redeemed thee, I have called thee by my name; thou art mine." When we can commit our dying ones into the hands of God and say, "For them Christ died; for their sin He atoned on the Cross; He has found eternal redemption for them;" then we can be still and know that He is God. Just as there is nothing so dark as a death-bed without hope; so there is nothing more blessed than to watch a soul departing in peace, because it has seen the Lord's salvation.

We all know how memory is wont to be quickened as the end draws near; how the conscience wakes to new sensitiveness, and the old sins start up before the soul in awful vividness. How shall we dare to pass into the presence of God, if we have not heard the words, "Go in peace, thy sins be forgiven thee;" if we do not know that our debt is cancelled? There, on the Cross, the handwriting that is against us is blotted out.

Our hope! He who was once offered to take away sin by the sacrifice of Himself, will appear again, apart from sin, unto salvation for those who wait for Him. He will come again, not to atone—that is forever done—but to bless with salvation. This is our hope. By one man sin came into the world, and death by sin; and by the new Man Christ Jesus have come righteousness and life. As in Adam all die, so in Christ shall all be made alive who are His. There is a resurrection of the dead, and eternal life. That which is sown in corruption is raised in incorruption; sown in dishonor, it is raised in glory; sown in weakness, it is raised in power; sown a natural body, it is raised a spiritual body. "He will come again unto salvation to them that look for Him."

In the Book of the Revelation we read, "I heard a great voice out of the throne saying, Behold the tabernacle of God is with men, and He shall dwell with them, and they shall be His people, and God Himself shall be with them and be their God. And He shall wipe away every tear from their eyes; and death shall be no more; neither shall there be mourning, nor crying, nor pain any more; the first things are passed away. And He that sitteth on the throne said, Behold, I make all things new. And He saith, Write, for these words are faithful and true." This is our hope. We go out weeping, bearing precious seed, and we come again with joy, bringing our sheaves with us. Then shall we once more embrace our dear ones, with whom we were one in faith and hope, and shall be united with them all in one great family of God. Then shall we delight in the fellowship of prophets, patriarchs, apostles, most of all of Christ Himself. Then shall we hail Him whom our souls love, and whose we are. We shall see Him who hung on the Cross for us, and now appears in heaven as our Forerunner, our royal High Priest. And we shall live with Him in His Kingdom, and serve Him in everlasting righteousness and blessedness. This is our hope.

CHRIST THE DESTROYER OF DEATH.

BY REV. C. H. SPURGEON, LONDON.

The last enemy that shall be destroyed is death.—1 COR. xv. 26.

I. DEATH AN ENEMY. *It was so born*, even as Haman, the Agagite, was the enemy of Israel by his descent. Death is the child of our direst foe, for "sin when it is finished bringeth forth death." "Sin entered into the world, and death by sin." Now, that which is distinctly the fruit of transgression, cannot be other than an enemy of man. Death was introduced into the world on that gloomy day which saw our fall, and he that had the power of it is our arch enemy and betrayer, the devil ; from both of which facts we must regard it as the manifest enemy of man. Death is an alien in this world ; it did not enter into the original design of the unfallen creation ; but its intrusion mars and spoils the whole. It is no part of the Great Shepherd's flock, but it is a wolf which cometh to kill and to destroy. Geology tells us that there was death among the various forms of life from the first ages of the globe's history, even when as yet the world was not fitted up as the dwelling of man. This I can believe, and still regard death as the result of sin. If it can be proved that there is such an organic unity between man and the lower animals, that they would not have died if Adam had not sinned, then I see in those deaths before Adam the antecedent consequences of a sin which was then uncommitted. If by the merits of Jesus there was salvation before He had offered His atoning sacrifice, I do not find it hard to conceive that the foreseen demerits of sin may have cast the shadow of death over the long ages which came before man's transgression. Of that we know little, nor is it important that we should know much ; but certain is it, that as far as this present creation is concerned, death is not God's invited guest, but an intruder, whose presence mars the feast. Man, in his folly, welcomed Satan and sin when they forced their way into the high festival of Paradise ; but he never welcomed death : even his blind eyes could see in that skeleton form a cruel foe. As the lion to the herds of the plain, as the scythe to the flowers of the field, as the wind to the sere leaves of the forest, such is death to the sons of men. They fear it by an inward instinct, because their conscience tells them that it is the child of their sin.

Death is well called an enemy, for *it does an enemy's work* toward us. For what purpose doth an enemy come, but to root up, and to pull down, and to destroy ? Death tears in pieces that comely handiwork of God, the fabric of the human body, so marvellously wrought by the fingers of divine skill. Casting this rich embroidery into the grave among the armies of the worm, to its fierce soldiery death divideth " to every one a prey of divers colors, of divers colors of needlework," and they ruthlessly rend in pieces the spoil. This building of our manhood is a house fair to look upon, but death, the destroyer, darkens its windows, shakes its pillars, closes its doors, and causes the sound of the grinding to cease. Then the daughters of music are brought low, and the strong men bow themselves. This vandal spares no work of life, however full of wisdom or beauty, for it looseth the silver cord and breaketh the golden bowl. Lo! at the fountain the costly pitcher is utterly broken, and at the cistern the well-wrought wheel is dashed in pieces! Death is a fierce invader of the realms of life, and where it comes it fells every good tree, stops all wells of water, and mars every good piece of land with stones. See you a man when death has wrought his will upon him, what a ruin he is! How is his beauty turned to ashes, and his comeliness to corruption! Surely an enemy hath done this.

Look, my brethren, at the course of death throughout all ages and in all lands. What field is there without its grave? What city without its cemetery? Whither can we go to find no sepulchres? As the sandy shore is covered with the upcastings of the worm, so art thou, O earth! covered with those grass-grown hillocks, beneath which sleep the departed generations of men. And thou, O sea, even thou art not without thy dead! As if the earth were too full of corpses, and they jostled each other in their crowded sepulchres, even into thy caverns, O mighty main, the bodies of the dead are cast! Thy waves must become defiled with the carcasses of men, and on thy floor must lie the bones of the slain. Our enemy, death, has marched, as it were, with sword and fire, ravaging the human race. Neither Goth nor Hun nor Tartar could have slain so universally all that breathed, for death has suffered none to escape. Everywhere it has withered household joys and created sorrow and sighing; in all lands where the sun is seen it hath blinded men's eyes with weeping. The tear of the bereaved, the wail of the widow, and the moan of the orphan—these have been death's war music, and he has found therein a song of victory.

The greatest conquerors have only been death's slaughtermen, journeymen butchers working in his shambles. War is nothing better than death holding carnival, and devouring his prey a little more in haste than is his common wont.

Death has done the work of an enemy *to those of us who have as yet escaped his arrows.* Those who have lately stood around a new-made grave and buried half their hearts, can tell you what an enemy death is. It takes the friend from our side, and the child from our bosom; neither does it care for our crying. He has fallen who was the pillar of the household; she has been snatched away who was the brightness of the hearth. The little one is torn out of its mother's bosom, though it almost breaks her heart-strings; and the blooming youth is taken from his father's side, though the parent's fondest hopes are thereby crushed. Death has no pity for the young and no mercy for the old; he pays no regard to the good or to the beautiful. His scythe cuts down sweet flowers and noxious weeds with equal readiness. He cometh into our garden, trampleth down our lilies, and scattereth our roses on the ground; yea, and even the modest flowers planted in the corner, and hiding their beauty beneath the leaves that they may blush unseen, death spieth out even these, and cares nothing for their fragrance, but withers them with his burning breath. He is thine enemy, indeed, thou fatherless child, left for the pitiless storm of a cruel world to beat upon, with none to shelter thee. He is thine enemy, O widow! for the light of thy life is gone, and the desire of thine eyes has been removed with a stroke. He is thine enemy, husband, for thy house is desolate, and thy little children cry for their mother, of whom death has robbed thee!

He is the enemy of us all, for what head of a family among us has not had to say to him, "Me thou hast bereaved again and again!" Especially is death an enemy to the living when he invades God's house and causes the prophet and the priest to be numbered with the dead. The church mourns when her most useful ministers are smitten down, when the watchful eye is closed in darkness, and the instructive tongue is mute. Yet how often does death thus war against us! The earnest, the active, the indefatigable, are taken away. Those mightiest in prayer, those most affectionate in heart, those most exemplary in life, those are cut down in the midst of their labors, leaving behind them a church which needs them more than tongue can tell. If the Lord does but threaten to permit death to seize a beloved pastor, the souls of his people are full of grief, and they view death as their worst foe, while they plead with the Lord and entreat Him to bid their minister live.

Even *those who die* may well count death to be their enemy; I mean not now that they have risen to their seats, and, as disembodied spirits, behold the King in His beauty; but aforetime while death was approaching them. He seemed to their trembling flesh to be a foe, for it is not in nature, except in moments of extreme pain or aberration of mind, or of excessive expectation of glory, for us to be in love with death. It was wise of our Creator so to constitute us that the soul loves the body and the body loves the soul, and they desire to dwell together as long as they may, else had there been no care for self-preservation, and suicide would have destroyed the race.

> "For who would bear the whips and scorns of time,
> The oppressor's wrong, the proud man's contumely,
> When he himself might his quietus make
> With a bare bodkin?"

It is a first law of our nature that skin for skin, yea, all that a man hath, will he give for his life, and thus we are nerved to struggle for existence, and to avoid that which would destroy us. This useful instinct renders death an enemy, but it also aids in keeping us from that crime of all crimes the most sure of damnation, if a man commit it wilfully and in his sound mind—I mean the crime of self-murder.

When death cometh, even to the good man, he cometh as an enemy, for he is attended by such terrible heralds and grim outriders as do greatly scare us.

> "Fever with brow of fire;
> Consumption wan; palsy, half-warmed with life,
> And half a clay-cold lump; joint-torturing gout,
> And ever-gnawing rheum; convulsion wild;
> Swoln dropsy; panting asthma; apoplex
> Full gorged."

None of these add to the aspect of death a particle of beauty. He comes with pains and griefs; he comes with sighs and tears. Clouds and darkness are round about him, an atmosphere laden with dust oppresses those whom he approaches, and a cold wind chills them even to the marrow. He rides on the pale horse, and where his steed sets its foot the land becomes a desert. By the footfall of that terrible steed, the worm is awakened to gnaw the slain. When we forget other grand truths, and only remember these dreadful things, death is the king of terrors to us. Hearts are sickened and reins are loosened, because of him.

But, indeed, he is an enemy, for what comes he to do to our body? I know he doeth that which ultimately leadeth to its betterness, but still it is that which, in itself and for the present, is not joyous, but grievous. He comes to take the light from the eyes, the hearing from the ears, the speech from the tongue, the activity from the hand, and the thought from the brain. He comes to transform a living man into a mass of putrefaction, to degrade the beloved form of a brother and friend to such a condition of corruption that affection itself cries out, "Bury my dead out of my sight." Death, thou child of sin, Christ hath transformed thee marvellously, but in thyself thou art an enemy before whom flesh and blood tremble, for they know that thou art the murderer of all of woman born, whose thirst for human prey the blood of nations cannot slake.

If you think for a few moments of this enemy, you will observe some of his points of character. He is the *common* foe of all God's people, and the enemy of all men; for however some have been persuaded that they should not die, yet is there no discharge in this war; and if in this conscription a man escapes the ballot many and many a year, till his gray beard seems to defy the winter's hardest frost, yet must the man of iron yield at last. It is appointed unto all men once to die. The strongest man has no elixir of eternal life wherewith to renew his youth amid the decays of age; nor has the wealthiest prince a price wherewith to bribe destruction. To the grave must thou descend, O crowned monarch! for sceptres and shovels are akin. To the sepulchre must thou go down, O mighty man of valor! for sword and spade are of like metal. The prince is brother to the worm, and must dwell in the same house. Of our whole race it is true, "Dust thou art, and unto dust shalt thou return."

Death is also a *subtle* foe, lurking everywhere, even in the most harmless things. Who can tell where Death has not prepared his ambuscades? He meets us both at home and abroad; at the table he assails men in their food, and at the fountain he poisons their drink. He waylayeth us in the streets, and he seizeth us in our beds; he rideth on the storm at sea, and he walks with us when we are on our way upon the solid land. Whither can we fly to escape from thee, O Death, for from the summit of the Alps men have fallen to their graves, and in the deep places of the earth, where the miner goeth down to find the precious ore, there hast thou sacrificed many a hecatomb of precious lives. Death is a subtle foe, and with noiseless footfalls follows close at our heels when least we think of him.

He is an enemy whom *none of us will be able to avoid*, take what by-paths we may; nor can we escape from him when our hour is come. Into this fowler's nets, like the birds, we shall all fly; in his great *seine* must all the fishes of the great sea of life be taken when their day is come. As surely as sets the sun, or as the midnight stars at length descend beneath the horizon, or as the waves sink back into the sea, or as the bubble bursts, so must we all, early or late, come to our end, and disappear from earth, to be known no more among the living.

Sudden, too, full often, are the assaults of this enemy.

> "Leaves have their time to fall,
> And flowers to wither at the north wind's breath,
> And stars to set—but all,
> Thou hast all seasons for thine own, O Death!"

Such things have happened as for men to die without an instant's notice; with a psalm upon their lips, they have passed away; or engaged in their daily business, they have been summoned to give in their account. We have heard of one who, when the morning paper brought him news that a friend in business had died, was drawing on his boots to go to his counting-house, and observed with a laugh, that as far as he was concerned, he was so busy he had no time to die. Yet, ere the words were finished, he fell forward and was a corpse. Sudden deaths are not so uncommon as to be marvels, if we dwell in the centre of a large circle of mankind. Thus is death a foe not to be despised or trifled with. Let us remember all his characteristics, and we shall not be inclined to think lightly of the grim enemy whom our glorious Redeemer has destroyed.

II. Let us remember that death is AN ENEMY TO BE DESTROYED. Remember that our Lord Jesus Christ has already wrought a great victory upon death, so that he has delivered us from lifelong bondage through its fear. He has not yet *destroyed death*, but he has gone very near to it, for we are told that he has "abolished death, and hath brought life and immortality to light through the gospel." This surely must come very near to having destroyed death altogether.

In the first place, our Lord has subdued death in the very worst sense, by having delivered His people from spiritual death. "And you hath he quickened who were dead in trespasses and sins." Once you had no divine life whatever, but the death of original depravity remained upon you, and so you were dead to all divine and spiritual things ; but now, beloved, the Spirit of God, even He that raised up Jesus Christ from the dead, has raised you up into newness of life, and you have become new creatures in Christ Jesus. In this sense, death has been subdued.

Our Lord in His lifetime also conquered death by restoring certain individuals to life. There were three memorable cases in which at His bidding the last enemy resigned his prey. Our Lord went into the ruler's house, and saw the little girl who had lately fallen asleep in death, around whom they wept and lamented ; he heard their scornful laughter, when he said, "She is not dead, but sleepeth," and He put them all out, and said to her, "Maid, arise !" Then was the spoiler spoiled, and the dungeon door set open. He stopped the funeral procession at the gates of Nain, whence they were carrying forth a young man, "the only son of his mother, and she was a widow," and He said, "Young man, I say unto thee, arise." When that young man sat up, and our Lord delivered him to his mother, then again was the prey taken from the mighty. Chief of all, when Lazarus had lain in the grave so long that his sister said, "Lord, by this time he stinketh ;" when, in obedience to the word, "Lazarus, come forth !" forth came the raised one with his grave-clothes still about him, but yet really quickened, then was death seen to be subservient to the Son of Man. "Loose him and let him go," said the conquering Christ, and death's bonds were removed, for the lawful captive was delivered. When, at the Redeemer's resurrection, many of the saints arose and came out of their graves into the holy city, then was the crucified Lord proclaimed to be victorious over death and the grave.

Still, brethren, these were but preliminary skirmishes, and mere foreshadowings of the grand victory by which death was overthrown. The real triumph was achieved upon the cross.

> He hell in hell laid low ;
> Made sin, He sin o'erthrew :
> Bowed to the grave, destroyed it so,
> And death, by dying, slew."

When Christ died, He suffered the penalty of death on the behalf of all His people, and therefore no believer now dies by way of punishment for sin, since we cannot dream that a righteous God would twice exact the penalty for one offence. Death, since Jesus died, is not a penal infliction upon the children of God ; as such He has abolished it, and it can never be enforced. Why die the saints, then ? Why, because their bodies must be changed ere they can enter heaven. "Flesh and blood," as they are, "cannot inherit the kingdom of God." A divine change must take place upon the body before it will be fit for incorruption and glory ; and death and the grave are, as it were, the refining pot and the furnace, by means of which the body is made ready for its future bliss. Death, it is true, thou art not yet destroyed, but our living Redeemer has so changed thee that thou art no longer death, but something other than thy name ! Saints die not now, but they are dissolved and depart. Death is the loosing of the cable, that the bark may freely sail to the fair havens. Death is the fiery chariot in which we ascend to God ; it is the gentle voice of the great King, who cometh into his banqueting hall, and saith, "Friend, come up higher." Behold, on eagle's wings we mount, we fly, far from this land of mist and cloud, into the eternal serenity and brilliance of God's own house above. Yes, our Lord has abolished death. The sting of death is sin, and our great Substitute has taken that sting away by His great sacrifice. Stingless, death abides among the people of God, but it so little harms them that to them "it is not death to die."

Further, Christ vanquished Death and thoroughly overcame him when He rose. What a temptation one has to paint a picture of the resurrection, but I will not be led aside to attempt more than a few touches. When our great Champion awoke from his brief sleep of death, and found Himself in the withdrawing-room of the grave, He quietly proceeded to put off the garments of the tomb. How leisurely He proceeded ! He folded up the napkin and placed it by itself, that those who lose their friends might wipe their eyes therewith ; and then He took off the winding-sheet, and laid the grave-clothes by themselves, that they might be there when His saints came thither, so that the chamber might be well furnished, and the bed ready sheeted and prepared for their rest. The sepulchre is no longer an empty vault, a dreary charnel, but a chamber of rest, a dormitory furnished and prepared, hung with the arras which Christ Himself has bequeathed. It is now no more a damp, dark, dreary prison; Jesus has changed all that.

" 'Tis now a cell where angels use
To come and go with heavenly news."

The angel from heaven rolled away the stone from our Lord's sepulchre, and let in the fresh air and light again upon our Lord, and He stepped out more than a conqueror. Death had fled. The grave had capitulated.

" Lives again our glorious King!
' Where, O death, is now thy sting?'
Once He died our souls to save;
' Where's thy victory, boasting grave?' "

Well, brethren, so surely as Christ rose, so did He guarantee as an absolute certainty the resurrection of all His saints into a glorious life for their bodies, the life of their souls never having paused even for a moment. In this He conquered death; and since that memorable victory, every day Christ is overcoming death, for He gives His Spirit to His saints, and having that Spirit within them, they meet the last enemy without alarm; often they confront him with songs, perhaps more frequently they face him with calm countenance, and fall asleep with peace. I will not fear thee, Death; why should I? Thou lookest like a dragon, but thy sting is gone. Thy teeth are broken, oh, old lion! wherefore should I fear thee? I know thou art no more able to destroy me, but thou art sent as a messenger to conduct me to the golden gate, wherein I shall enter and see my Saviour's unveiled face forever. Expiring saints have often said that their last beds have been the best they have ever slept upon. Many of them have inquired,

" Tell me, my soul, can this be death?"

To die has been so different a thing from what they expected it to be, so lightsome and so joyous; they have been so unloaded of all care, have felt so relieved instead of burdened, that they have wondered whether this could be the monster they had been so afraid of all their days. They find it a pin's prick, whereas they feared it would prove a sword-thrust ; it is the shutting of the eye on earth, and the opening of it in heaven, whereas they thought it would have been a stretching upon the rack, or a dreary passage through a dismal region of gloom and dread. Beloved, our exalted Lord has overcome death in all these ways.

But now, observe, that this is not the text—the text speaks of something yet to be done. The last enemy that *shall be* destroyed is death, so that death, in the sense meant by the text, is not destroyed yet. He is to be destroyed, and how will that be ?

Well, I take it death will be destroyed in the sense, first, that, at the coming of Christ, *those who are alive and remain shall not see death*. They shall be changed ; there must be a change, even to the living, before they can inherit eternal life ; but they shall not actually die. Do not envy them, for they will have no preference beyond those that sleep ; rather do I think theirs to be the inferior lot of the two in some respects. But they will not know death ; the multitude of the Lord's own who will be alive at His coming will pass into glory without needing to die. Thus death, as far as they are concerned, will be destroyed.

But the sleeping ones, the myriads who have left their flesh and bones to moulder back to earth, death shall be destroyed even as to them, for when the trumpet sounds they shall rise from the tomb. *The resurrection is the destruction of death*. We never taught, nor believed, nor thought that every particle of every body that was put into the grave would come to its fellow, and that the absolutely identical material would rise ; but we do say that the identical body will be raised, and that as surely as there cometh out of the ground the seed that was put into it, though in a very different guise—for it cometh not forth as a seed, but as a flower —so surely shall the same body rise again. The same material is not necessary ; but there shall come out of the grave, ay, come out of the earth, if it never saw a grave, or come out of the sea, if devoured by monsters, that self-same body for true identity, which was inhabited by the soul while here below. Was it not so with our Lord ? Even so shall it be with His own people, and then shall be brought to pass the saying that is written, "Death is swallowed up in victory. O, Death ! where is thy sting ? O, grave ! where is thy victory ?"

There will be this feature in our Lord's victory, that death will be fully destroyed, because *those who rise will not be one whit the worse for having died.* I believe, concerning those new bodies, that there will be no trace upon them of the feebleness of old age, none of the marks of long and wearying sickness, none of the scars of martyrdom. Death shall not have left his mark upon them at all, except it be some glory mark which shall be to their honor, like the scars in the flesh of the Well-beloved, which are His chief beauty, even now, in the eyes of those for whom His hands and feet were pierced. In this sense death shall be destroyed, because He shall have done no damage to the saints at all ; the very trace of decay shall have been swept away from the redeemed.

And then, finally, there shall, after this trumpet of the Lord, be no *more death,* neither sorrow, nor crying, for the former things have passed away. "Christ being raised from the dead, dieth no more, death hath no more dominion over Him ;" and so also the quickened ones, His own redeemed, they too shall die no more. Oh, dreadful, dreadful supposition, that they should ever have to undergo temptation or pain or death a second time. It cannot be. "Because I live," says Christ, "they shall live also." Yet the doctrine of the natural immortality of the soul having been given up by some, certain of them have felt obliged to give up with the eternity of future punishment the eternity of future bliss, and assuredly, as far as some great proof texts are concerned, they stand or fall together. "These shall go away into everlasting punishment, and the righteous into life eternal ;" if the one state be short, so must the other be : whatever the adjective means in the one case, it means in the other. To us the word means endless duration in both cases, and we look forward to a bliss which shall never know end or duration. Then in the tearless, sorrowless, graveless country death shall be utterly destroyed.

III. And now, last of all—and the word "last" sounds fitly in this case—DEATH IS TO BE DESTROYED LAST. Because he came in last he must go out last. Death was not the first of our foes ; first came the devil, then sin, then death. Death is not the worst of enemies ; death is an enemy, but he is much to be preferred to our other adversaries. It were better to die a thousand times than to sin. To be tried by death is nothing, compared with being tempted by the devil. The mere physical pains connected with dissolution are comparative trifles, compared with the hideous grief which is caused by sin, and the burden which a sense of guilt causes to the soul. No, death is but a secondary mischief, compared with the defilement of sin. Let the great enemies go down first ; smite the shepherd, and the sheep will be scattered ; let sin and Satan, the lord of all these evils, be smitten first, and death may well be left to the last.

Notice that death is the last enemy to each individual Christian, and the last to be destroyed. Well, now, if the Word of God says it is the last, I want to remind you of a little piece of practical wisdom—leave him to be the last. Brother, do not dispute the appointed order, but let the last be last. I have known a brother wanting to vanquish death long before he died. But, brother, you do not want dying grace till dying moments. What would be the good of dying grace while you are yet alive ? A boat will only be needful when you reach a river. Ask for living grace, and glorify Christ thereby, and then you shall have dying grace when dying time comes. Your enemy is going to be destroyed, but not to-day. There is a great host of enemies to be fought to-day, and you may be content to let this one alone for a while. This enemy will be destroyed, but of the times and the seasons we are in ignorance ; our wisdom is to be good soldiers of Jesus Christ as the duty of every day requires. Take your trials as they come, brother ! As the enemies march up, slay them, rank upon rank ; but if you fail in the name of God to smite the front ranks, and say, " No, I am only afraid of the rear rank," then you are playing the fool. Leave the final shock of arms till the last adversary advances, and meanwhile, hold you your place in the conflict. God will, in due time, help you to overcome your last enemy, but meanwhile see to it that you overcome the world, the flesh, and the devil. If you live well you will die well. That same covenant in which the Lord Jesus gave you life contains also the grant of death, for " All things are yours, whether things present or things to come, or life or death, all are yours, and ye are Christ's, and Christ is God's."

Why is death left to the last ? Well, I think it is because Christ can make much use of him. The last enemy that shall be destroyed is death, because death is of great service before he is destroyed. Oh, what lessons some of us have learned from death! "Our dying friends come o'er us like a cloud to damp our brainless ardors;" make us feel that these poor fleeting toys are not worth living for; that as others pass away so must we also be gone, and thus they help to make us set loose by this world, and urge us to take wing and mount toward the world to come. There are, perhaps, no sermons like the deaths which have happened in our households; the departures of our beloved friends have been to us solemn discourses of divine wisdom, which our heart could not help hearing. So Christ has spared death to make him a preacher to His saints.

And you know, brethren, that if there had been no death the saints of God would not have had the opportunity to exhibit the highest ardor of their love. Where has love to Christ triumphed most? Why, in the death of the martyrs at the stake and on the rack. O Christ! Thou never hadst such garlands woven for Thee by human hands as they have brought Thee who have come up to heaven from the forests of persecution, having waded through streams of blood. By death for Christ the saints have glorified Him most.

So is it, in their measure, with saints who die from ordinary deaths. They would have had no such test for faith and work for patience as they now have, if there had been no death. Part of the reason of the continuance of this dispensation is that the Christ of God may be glorified; but if believers never died, the supreme consummation of faith's victory must have been unknown. Brethren, if I may die as I have seen some of our church members die, I court the grand occasion. I would not wish to escape death by some by-road, if I may sing as they sang. If I may have such hosannas and hallelujahs beaming in my very eyes, as I have seen as well as heard from them, it were a blessed thing to die. Yes, as a supreme test of love and faith, death is well respited awhile to let the saints glorify their Master.

Besides, brethren, without death we should not be so conformed to Christ as we shall be if we fall asleep in Him. If there could be any jealousies in heaven among the saints, I think that any saint who does not die, but is changed when Christ comes, could almost meet me and you, who probably will die, and say, "My brother, there is one thing I have missed; I never lay in the grave, I never had the chill hand of death laid on me, and so in that I was not conformed to my Lord. But *you* know what it is to have fellowship with Him, even in His death." Did I not well say that they that were alive and remain should have no preference over them that are asleep? I think the preference, if anything, shall belong to us who sleep in Jesus, and wake up in His likeness.

Death, dear friends, is not yet destroyed, because he brings the saints home. He does but come to them and whisper his message, and in a moment they are supremely blessed;

> " Have done with sin and care and woe,
> And with the Saviour rest."

And so death is not destroyed yet, for he answers useful purposes.

But, beloved, he is going to be destroyed. He is the last enemy of the Church collectively. The Church, as a body, has had a mass of foes to contend with; but after the resurrection we shall say, "This is the last enemy. Not another foe is left." Eternity shall roll on in ceaseless bliss. There may be changes, bringing new delights; perhaps in the eternity to come there may be eras and ages of yet more amazing bliss, and still more superlative ecstasy; but there shall be

> " No rude alarm of raging foes,
> No cares to break the last repose."

The last enemy that shall be destroyed is death, and if the last be slain there can be no future foe. The battle is fought and the victory is won forever. And who hath won it? who but the Lamb that sitteth on the throne, to whom let us all ascribe honor and glory and majesty and power and dominion and might forever and ever. The Lord help us in our solemn adoration.

> "The piteous image of Death stands
> Not to the wise as a terror, and not as the end to the pious.
> Wisely the wise man is driven from thought of death into action;
> Wisely the pious from death draws hope of bliss for the future.
> Each is wise in his way, and death to life is transmuted
> Wisely by both."
> GOETHE.

CONFESSIONS OF DYING MEN.

BY JOEL HAWES, D.D., HARTFORD, CONN.

It is appointed unto men once to die.—HEBREWS ix. 27.

THE fact asserted in this text is admitted by all; but how few appear to feel its practical influence. Who would infer from the conduct and conversation of most men, that they believed themselves to be mortal, or that they expected anything less than that their residence on earth is to be perpetual? They live as carelessly, plan as confidently, and pursue the world with as much eagerness, as if they were exempted from change, and could set at defiance the attacks of disease and death. Yet they must die—must die soon, and may die suddenly; and after death cometh the judgment. This is the appointment of God, and in this war there is no discharge. It is wise, then, to consider our latter end, to be familiar with the thought of dying, often and seriously to consider what will be our feelings and views when we shall come to lie upon our death-bed, and feel that we are going into eternity. This is a duty which especially demands our attention now, as we have just taken leave of the old year, and are entering upon the unknown, untried scenes of a new one, which, to some of us, no doubt, will be the last year of life.

Let us, then, endeavor to bring the closing scene near, to think of ourselves as having reached the end of our earthly course, and about to take our final leave of the world and all its busy cares. The question arises, What, in such a case, would be our feelings, what the reflections that would press upon our minds with the greatest weight and solemnity? We may, indeed, die so suddenly that we shall have no time to think till we think in eternity. We may drop in a moment into the unseen world, as many do, without any warning of our end, till the blow is struck, and the spirit finds itself in the immediate presence of God. Or the last sickness may come in such a form as to rack the body with agonizing pain, put out the light of reason, and cloud the mind in wild delirium. But on the supposition that we shall be notified of our approaching end by the usual precursors of death, and that the dying scene shall find us in the exercise of our reason, capable of reflecting upon the past, and anticipating the future, let us inquire how we shall feel, what will be our judgment as to our present course of life, and what our thoughts, as we draw near the invisible world, and know that we are standing on the verge of a boundless eternity. We cannot, indeed, know all that we shall feel and think in that solemn hour. It will be to each of us a new and untried scene, till we are actually called to pass through it, and learn from dying what it is to die. But it is certain we shall feel and think very differently from what we now do. On many subjects our views will be wholly changed; they will appear to us in an entirely new light, and awaken new feelings within, of which we can now form but a very faint conception. We know this from the nature of the case, and also from the feelings and views which are wont to be expressed by men when they come to die. We have seen many persons die, and we have authentic accounts of the manner in which many others died whom we did not see. Let us, then, study the experience of the dying. It is the last school of wisdom to which the children of men can be advanced; and as we shall all ere long be placed in that school, let us recall a few particulars respecting which the feelings and sentiments of men are wont to undergo a great change as they view themselves near to the close of life. shall illustrate the subject by a frequent recurrence to what persons have felt and said in that situation, I may entitle my discourse—CONFESSIONS OF DYING MEN.

I. In the first place, when men come to die, they are wont to feel, with a vividness of impression wholly unknown before, the shortness of life, and the unspeakable value of time. Viewed in prospect, or in the season of health and happiness, life usually seems long, and time is but little valued. To the young, a year is wont to appear longer than a whole life does to him who is about to depart out of it; and time hangs so heavily on their hands that they know not what to do with it. And even when they have attained to the meridian of their days, and their sun is on the decline, they usually have but a very faint impression of the shortness of life, or of the immense value of the hours that are flitting by them. Especially is this the case with the irreligious and worldly-minded. Immersed in the cares and pursuits of earth and sense, they perceive not how rapidly the little span of life is wasting away, nor how soon all the time allotted them in this state of probation will have passed with the years beyond the flood. They still live under the delusive impression that they have time enough before them to accomplish all their plans, and to do what they please.

But when they come to die the whole scene is changed. Life is then seen to be indeed but a vapor, that appeareth for a little moment, and then vanisheth away. All the months and years they have passed on earth are then compressed, as it were, into a point, and seem more like a dream than a reality. Hear how the worthies, whose names are recorded in the Bible, spoke on this subject, as they approached the close of life. "My days," says Job, "are swifter than a post, they are passed away as a shadow." "Remember how short thy time is," cries the Psalmist. "Behold thou hast made my days as a handbreadth, and mine age is as nothing before thee; as for man, his days are as grass; in the morning it is green; in the evening it is cut down and withered." And the patriarch Jacob, though he had lived an hundred and thirty years, felt constrained to say, "Few and evil have the days of the years of my life been."

Such are the feelings of all men at the close of life. It seems but a transient moment, and the events of it as a dream when one awaketh. Lord Chesterfield, though a sceptic, and devoted to a life of pleasure, was compelled to say, near the close of his days, "When I reflect upon what I have seen, what I have heard, and what I have done myself, I can hardly persuade myself that all the frivolous hurry and bustle and pleasure of the world are a reality; but they seem to have been the dreams of restless nights." Voltaire, after having spent a long life in blaspheming the Saviour and opposing His Gospel, said to his physician on his dying-bed, "I will give you half of what I am worth, if you will give me six months of life." "O, time! time!" exclaimed the dying Altamont, "how art thou fled forever. A month! oh, for a single week! I ask not for years, though an age were too little for the much I have to do." Said Gibbon, "The present is a fleeting moment, the past is no more, and my prospect of futurity is dark and doubtful." Hobbes said, as the last hour approached, "If I had the whole world to dispose of, I would give it to live one day." "Oh!" cried the Duke of Buckingham, as he was closing a life devoted to folly and sin, "what a prodigal have I been of the most valuable of all possessions, time! I have squandered it away with the persuasion that it was lasting; and now, when a few days would be worth a hecatomb of worlds, I cannot flatter myself with the prospect of half a dozen hours."

You see from these examples what are the impressions of dying men, whether good or bad, respecting the brevity of life and the worth of time. One sentiment is then felt by all—life is very short, and time is of infinite value.

II. Another confession which is wont to be made by dying men is, that there is nothing in this world that can satisfy the wants of the immortal soul. This is a lesson which men in general are extremely slow to learn. Though they are continually taught by the Word and the Providence of God, that all things earthly are but for a moment, and perish in the using, they still pursue them as their supreme good, and vainly flatter themselves that when this plan is accomplished, and that object attained, they shall be satisfied; they shall be happy. This is the delusion of the young, the middle-aged, and the aged; and it is the mainspring of that restless activity and ambition, and aspiring after the world, which we witness around us. All wish to be happy, and all expect to be happy in the possession of worldly good.

But in the dying hour this is discovered to be a most fatal mistake, and men look back with amazement upon the folly and madness with which they pursued the world, and looked to its possessions for a satisfying portion. As they stand upon the verge of time, and extend their view to the boundless eternity that stretches before them, the world sinks into utter insignificance, and they wonder how they ever could have been so enamored of its glittering toys, and how the living can be so deluded as to chase its fleeting vanities in the expectation of deriving from them a satisfying good. When Salmasius, one of the greatest scholars of his time, drew near to death, he exclaimed bitterly against himself: "Oh, I have lost a world of time; time, the most precious thing on the earth, whereof if I had but one year more, it should be spent in David's Psalms and Paul's Epistles. Oh, mind the world less and God more!" Grotius possessed the finest genius ever recorded of a youth in the learned world, and rose to an eminence in literature and science which drew upon him the admiration of all Europe; yet, after all his attainments and high reputation, he was constrained at last to cry out, "Ah, I have consumed my life in a laborious doing of nothing! I would give all my learning and honor for the plain integrity of John Urick"—a poor man of eminent piety. John Mason, on his death-bed, said, "I have lived to see five princes, and have been privy counsellor to four of them; I have seen the most important things in foreign parts, and have been present at most state transactions for thirty years together; and I have learned, after so many years' experience, that seriousness is the greatest wisdom, temperance the best physic, and a good conscience the best estate. And were I to live again, I would change the whole life I have lived in the palace for an hour's enjoyment of God in the chapel." Philip the Third, King of Spain, when he drew near the end of his days, expressed his deep regret for a worldly and careless life in these emphatic words: "Ah, how happy it would have been for me, had I spent these twenty-three years I have held my kingdom, in retirement!" "Good God!" exclaimed a dying nobleman, "how have I employed myself! In what delirium has my life been passed! What have I been dong while the sun in its race and the stars in their courses have lent their beams, perhaps only to light me to perdition! I have pursued shadows, and entertained myself with dreams. I have been treasuring up dust, and sporting myself with the wind. I might have grazed with the beasts of the field, or sung with the winged inhabitants of the woods, to much better purpose than any for which I have lived."

Examples of this kind might be multiplied to almost any extent, but enough have been cited to show how men regard the riches and honors of the world when they find themselves drawing near to a dying hour, and are called to look into eternity.

III. When men are laid upon a dying bed, they are wont to feel and to acknowledge the utter insufficiency of a mere moral life to prepare them to appear in the presence of God. Many there are who trust to such a life as their only ground of hope for eternity. They do not, perhaps, believe in the reality of a change of heart wrought by the Holy Spirit, or at least they do not feel the need of such a change in themselves. They mean to lead a correct moral life, to be honest in their dealings, and kind in their treatment of their fellow-men, and this, they imagine, will avail to secure the approbation of their final Judge. They have no just sense of sin, nor of their need of pardon through the blood of Christ, but trust all to a moral life. There is no more common delusion than this, and it is a delusion which vanishes at the approach of death, and leaves the soul trembling in prospect of going to appear before God. The actions of life then appear in a far different light from what they do in the days of health and thoughtlessness. Many things which are indulged, without the slightest apprehension of their being wrong, are then seen to be sins deeply offensive to God, and dangerous to the soul. The law is seen to be unspeakably more strict and holy, sin to be a much greater evil, and the trial before the judgment seat of Christ far more dreadful. What the sinner needs in the dying hour is something to take away the sting of death; something to sustain his spirit as he passes into the dark valley, and to assure him of the forgiveness and favor of that Almighty Being before whom he is about to appear. But this the fairest morality is utterly insufficient to do. It meets not the exigencies of the sinner's case. It is neither obedience to the law, nor to the gospel; neither love to God, nor faith in Christ. It is in its loveliest form only the cobweb covering of a fair exterior, and wrapped only in this covering, the soul shudders at the thought of death, and falls back in dismay at the sight of the great tribune.

The Apostle enjoyed great peace in the near prospect of death; but it was derived not from a moral life, but from faith in Christ, from evidence felt within that he had a personal interest in the great salvation, and was clothed in His righteousness who had loved him and given Himself to die for him. This is the only sure ground of peace in the hour of death. Every other is then found to be insufficient, and trusted in, ends in destruction. It is not giving up the breath, said the nobleman before referred to, it is not being forever insensible, that is the thought at which I shrink; it is the terrible hereafter, the something beyond the grave, at which I recoil. Those great realities which in the hours of mirth and vanity I have treated as phantoms, as the idle dreams of superstitious beings, these start forth and dare me now in their most terrible demonstrations. "O, my friends," exclaimed the pious Janeway, "we little think what Christ is worth on a death-bed. I would not now for a world, nay, for millions of worlds, be without Christ and pardon." "God might justly condemn me," said Richard Baxter, "for the best deeds I ever did, and all my hopes are from the free mercy of God in Christ."

Said the meek and learned Hooker, as he approached his end, "Though I have by His grace loved God in my youth and feared Him in my age, and labored to have a conscience void of offence to Him and to all men, yet, if Thou, O Lord, be extreme to mark what I have done amiss, who can abide it? And, therefore, where I have failed, show mercy to me, for I plead not my righteousness, but the forgiveness of my unrighteousness, for His merits who died to purchase pardon for penitent sinners." Such too were the feelings of our own venerated Hooker* in his dying hour. To a friend who said to him, "Sir, you are going to receive the reward of your labors," he replied, "Brother, I am going to receive mercy." And not to mention other examples under this head, let me refer to the case of Dr. Johnson. He was a moral man; but his morality could not soften the terrors of a death-bed, nor give him the least peace in prospect of meeting his Judge. When a friend, to calm his agitated mind, referred him to his correct morals and useful life for topics of consolation, he put them away as nothing worth, and in bitterness of soul exclaimed, "Shall I, who have been a teacher of others, be myself cast away?" This great man had not then fled for refuge to the blood of atonement, as he afterward did; and therefore, notwithstanding his moral and useful life, he was afraid to die, and all beyond the grave looked dark and gloomy to him. And so must it look to all who come to the dying hour with no better preparation than is furnished in a moral life.

IV. Men, at the hour of death, are constrained to acknowledge the folly and guilt of an irreligious life, and the supreme importance of a saving interest in the Lord Jesus Christ. Whatever apologies are made in the days of health and prosperity for the neglect of religion, those apologies are found utterly worthless on a death-bed, and are renounced as vain and delusive. All excuses vanish in the presence of the king of terrors, and the sinner looks back with self-reproach and astonishment upon the presump-

---

* First pastor of the First Church in Hartford—died 1647.

tion and folly which led him to disregard God and neglect the concerns of His eternity. Religion is then felt to be indeed the one thing needful, and the whole earth too poor to be given in exchange for the soul. I have attended many death-beds in the course of my ministry, but I recollect no instance where reason was in exercise, in which this acknowledgment was not ready to be made. All are then ready to exclaim—O, that I had been wise, that I had understood and considered my latter end. And even Christians, as much as they love and prize religion in life, feel, when they come to die, that their highest and best views of its importance were far below the reality. They see then that it is the only true wisdom to live for God and eternity, and they are amazed to think that they have lived at so poor a rate, and have done so little for the honor of Christ and the advancement of His cause on earth. However men may differ respecting the value and importance of religion in health, there is but one opinion on the subject when they come to lie upon the bed of death. The great question which then absorbs all others and presses with overwhelming weight on the soul, is : Have I a saving interest in the Lord Jesus Christ? Have I been born of the Spirit? Am I pardoned through the blood of atonement, and prepared to appear before my Judge in peace? The world, with all its pomp, pleasures, and interests, then appears infinitely too light to engage a single thought in comparison with the great question, Am I a Christian, and may I hope on good ground to enter into the joy of my Lord on leaving this earthly abode? None find peace and hope in that hour but those who have fled for refuge to lay hold on the hope set before them in the Gospel. The world retires then, and leaves its wretched votaries in poverty and despair. But heaven comes near to sustain and comfort the faithful servants of God, and they feel that an interest in Christ is of more value than a thousand worlds like this. Look at Enoch walking with God, and through faith exempted from death, and who was not for God took him ; at David comforting himself in the close of life in the assurance that God had made an everlasting covenant with him, ordered in all things and sure ; at Paul joyfully declaring in the near view of death, "I know in whom I have believed ;" at the dying missionary, Ziegenbalger, exclaiming, "Washed from my sins in the blood of Christ, and clothed with

His righteousness, I shall enter into His eternal kingdom;" at Swartz sweetly singing his soul away to everlasting bliss; at Baxter, saying, amid the sinkings of nature, "I am almost well;" at Owen, lifting up his eyes and his hands as if in a kind of rapture, and exclaiming to a friend, "O, brother, the long-looked-for day has come at last, in which I shall see the glory of Christ in another manner than I have ever yet done;" at Edwards, comforting his family, as they stood around his dying bed, with the memorable words, "Trust in God, and you have nothing to fear;" at Martyn, in the solitudes of Persia, writing thus a few days before his death, "I sat alone, and thought with sweet comfort and peace of God, in solitude my company, my friend, and comforter;" at Dwight, exclaiming, when the seventeenth chapter of John was read to him, "O, what triumphant truths;" at Evarts, shouting "Glory! Jesus reigns!" as he closed his eyes on death; at Payson, uttering the language of assurance, as he grappled with the last enemy, "The battle is fought! the battle is fought! and the victory is won forever!" In a word, look at the great cloud of witnesses, who, in the faith of Jesus, have triumphed over death and the grave, and peacefully closed their eyes on the world in a joyful hope of opening them in another and a better, and you will learn in what estimation religion is held, when the scenes of earth are retiring, and those of eternity are opening upon the vision of dying men.

When men are laid upon the bed of death and know that they must go hence to be seen here no more, they always feel that it is indeed a solemn thing to die and pass into eternity. If there be exceptions, they are very rare, and occur only in cases of extreme scepticism, or of profound stupidity. Hume could amuse himself with playing chess when death was at the door; and Rousseau could lightly talk of giving back to God his soul as pure as when it came from His hand. But conduct like this is the extreme of infatuation, and can be regarded in no other light than as a part of the accursedness of those who are reprobate of God. Think of it as we may, while the event is viewed as future and distant, we shall all find, when the last hour comes, that it is indeed a serious matter to die. To close all our connection with this world; to lie down upon the bed from which we shall never rise up; to have our bodies turned to dust, and our souls go into the world of spirits to appear before God, and pass the all-decisive trial, and enter upon a state of being that is never to change—these are events which may well make mortals tremble and shrink back at their approach. So the dying nobleman felt, whom I have more than once referred to, when he said, "A condemned wretch may, with as good a grace, go dancing to his execution, as the greatest part of mankind go on with such a thoughtless gayety to their graves." "A future state," said the Duke of Buckingham, dying in despair, "may well strike terror into a man who has not acted well in life ; and he must have an uncommon share of courage indeed who does not shrink at the presence of God." And when Lord Chesterfield, sceptic and devotee of pleasure as he was, was compelled to acknowledge, as the closing scene drew on, "When one does see death near, let the best or the worst people say what they please, it is a serious consideration." "Remorse for the past," exclaimed the dying Altamont, "throws my thoughts on the future. Worse dread of the future strikes them back on the past. I turn and turn, and find no ray. Death is knocking at my doors ; in a few hours more I shall draw my last gasp ; and then the judgment, the tremendous judgment ! How shall I appear, all unprepared as I am, before the all-knowing and omnipotent God ?" "O eternity, eternity !" cried the distracted Newport, as he lay upon his death-bed, contemplating the solemn scenes before him, "who can paraphrase on the words for ever and ever ?"

Such are the confessions that are wont to be made by dying men ; such the feelings and thoughts that crowd upon the mind as the last hour approaches. And in view of them we may remark—

1. They are founded in truth ; there is just cause for them. It is *true* that life is short, and that time is of infinite value. It is *true* that this world contains nothing which can satisfy the wants of the immortal mind. It is *true* that a moral life is utterly insufficient as a preparation for death and the judgment. It is *true* that an irreligious life is a life of extreme folly and presumption, and that a saving interest in Christ is a matter of supreme importance to every living man. It is *true* that it is a solemn thing to die and go into eternity, to appear before a holy God. And the wonder is, not that dying men should feel these things to be true,

and be deeply affected by them, but that living men should treat them with indifference, and go through the world contradicting the feelings and views which are sure to crowd upon them with overwhelming interest in the day of death. Here is just matter of astonishment ; and of all the strange things that are witnessed in the conduct of our fallen race, this is the strangest, that men should walk in the midst of graves, convey their own friends and acquaintances to the house of silence, and meet every day and in every path of life with the most solemn monitions of their own approaching end, and still live as though they were never to die, and shut their eyes on scenes which must soon burst upon them in all the weight and solemnity of a present eternity. I remark—

2. That many of my hearers will, in a short time, view this subject in a very different light from that in which they now contemplate it. Some of you are young, and in the buoyant feelings of youth and health scarcely think it possible that you may soon be called to death and the judgment. Some of you are profoundly careless of your immortal well-being, and are so enamored of the things of the world that you seldom think of your latter end, or of what you need to prepare you to die. Others of you are perhaps sceptical as to the reality of a change of heart to fit you for the closing scene, and are trusting to a moral life as a foundation of hope in the coming day of trial ; others of you still, who bear the Christian name, are probably deceived as to the ground of your hope, or are living in a state of backsliding from God, awfully unprepared for His summons to leave the world. To all such the Son of Man is likely to come in an hour they think not of ; and when He comes, they will be thrown into fearful consternation, and the dreams with which they are now deluded will vanish forever. You have heard what is the testimony of dying men on some points of infinite moment to yourselves, but which you at present regard with little feeling, and treat with great neglect. But the time is not distant when you shall join your testimony with those that have gone before you into the invisible world ; when the scene of life shall close, and your eternal state commence. And whatever be your present views and feelings, it is not in the least doubtful what they will be then. Should you die in the exercise of your reason, you will look back with amazement on your present course of life, and wonder how

you could be so infatuated as to neglect God and your souls, and make no preparation for the solemn scenes of a dying hour. Those of you who are now young will then learn that you are not too young to die; and those of you who are living securely in sin, that it is indeed a fearful thing to fall into the hands of the living God; and those of you who are trusting to a moral life, that you are trusting to a foundation of sand; and those of you who are cold and formal in religion, that in such a state of mind you are sadly unprepared to die, and render up your account unto God. Death will bring your hearts and lives to a new and severe test, and draw from all of you the confession that to fear God and keep His commandments is the first duty and the highest wisdom and happiness of every living man. I remark—

3. It is the part of true wisdom to cherish those views and feelings now, which we know we shall regard as of supreme importance when we come to die. Why should any spend life in treasuring materials for sorrow, disappointment, and despair in the dying hour? Why should any gather food for the worm that never dies, or fuel for the fire that is never quenched? If, as we draw near to death, we shall regard life as very short, and time as infinitely valuable, let us regard them so now, and be quickened to do with our might whatsoever our hands find to do. If we shall then feel that this world is a poor thing, considered as a portion for the soul, let us view it in that light now, and choose God as our portion, and heaven as our home. If a hope of acceptance with God, built on a mere moral life, will then perish as a spider's web and leave us in despair, let us renounce that vain confidence now, and build our hope on that sure corner-stone which God has laid in Zion, and which will never disappoint us. If an impenitent, irreligious life will then appear to us the greatest folly, and a saving interest in Christ the one thing needful, let us not pursue such a life any longer, but close at once with the Saviour, and follow Him as our Lord and Master unto the end of our days. And if when the end comes we shall find it indeed a solemn thing to die and go into eternity to appear before God, let us regard it so now, and make that preparation which will sustain us in the last conflict, and give us peace in the day of final decision.

Look forward, then, immortal man, and endeavor to realize what will be your feelings and views in the dying hour, and if you would be wise, begin without delay to cherish those sentiments and pursue that course of life which you will then wish you had; which will save you from remorse and self-reproach and bitter despair in the great day of the Lord.

> "Nothing is worth a thought beneath,
> But how we may escape that death
> That never, never dies;
> How make our own election sure,
> And when we fail on earth, secure
> A mansion in the skies."

4. The confessions of dying men are of no avail, only as they indicate the folly of sin and the value of religion. They do not change the character—they do not fit the soul for death or for heaven. Of the many instances mentioned in this discourse of wicked men being awakened at the close of life to some just view of their character and state, there is not one in which there is any evidence that they repented and embraced the salvation of the Gospel. Their groans, like those of the damned, come up to proclaim the miseries of sin, and to warn the living to avoid their wretched end. It is not the remorse and fear of a dying hour; it is not the shudderings of guilt, and the confusions and tears which are wrung from sinners when they find they can enjoy the world no longer, but must go and give an account of themselves unto God, that can avail to change the heart and prepare the soul for the inheritance of the saints in light. The strong bands of sin are not so dissolved, nor is it so that the love of God and Christ is inspired in the bosom, and meetness acquired for a place among the redeemed in heaven. No, dear hearer; if you put off religion till you come to a death-bed, you will probably be left to put it off forever. You will not find it so easy as you suppose to cast off the habits of sin, to believe in Christ, and make your peace with God. You may be awakened to see your sin and misery; you may bewail the stupidity and folly of your past life; your misspent time, your abuse of privileges, your neglects of calls and warnings; the terrors of death and the pains of hell may get hold upon you, and you may cry in agony of spirit for help; but God may leave you, as He has other despisers of mercy, awful monuments to warn those who survive you of the danger of trifling with the claims of religion and the high concerns of eternity. Be

wise, then, in this your day, to attend to the things which belong to your peace, lest they be hid forever from your eyes. Go learn the value of religion in the peaceful and triumphant death of those that die in the Lord; go learn its value in the remorse and despair of those that die in neglect of Christ and His salvation. Then look to the end of life, and remember that with one or the other of these two classes of persons you are to terminate your mortal career: that with the friends of God, the followers of Jesus, you are to bear your testimony to the value of religion, in the joy and hope that will then fill your bosom; or with the enemies of God and the neglecters of the Saviour, you are to bear your testimony to the guilt and misery of an irreligious, prayerless life, in the remorse and fear that will then agitate and corrode the soul. Which, then, will you do?—which does conscience admonish you to do?—which will you wish you had done in the day when you shall bid adieu to the scenes of earth, and go to dwell among the dead? Decide now, and let your life be regulated accordingly. Decide now, and let no day or hour of the year on which you have just entered find you unprepared to meet the summons, should it come, that is to call you out of time into eternity. Hear the voices of those who, during the year past, departed from this congregation into the world of spirits—eleven in all, ten of whom were members of the church, and died, I trust, in good hope of eternal life. Would you die like them, and have your last end like theirs? Then, as you stand upon the threshold of this new year, with its unknown events before you, retreat a while from the snares and delusions of the world; shut your eyes upon the scenes of time, upon which they must soon be closed forever, and converse with the world to come—with death, judgment, and eternity. Go stand upon the shores of that dark, vast ocean you must sail so soon, and listen to the sound of its waves till you are deaf to every sound besides, and then with those solemn scenes around and before you, endeavor, with all earnestness and diligence, to gather about you those resources of faith and piety which you will assuredly need in the day when you shall be called to meet that enemy whom you must conquer, or die forever.

A MOTHER'S DEATH.

BY REV. ALBERT BARNES,[*] PHILADELPHIA.

I bowed down heavily, as one that mourneth for his mother.
—PSALM XXXV. 14.

There is a peculiarity in every kind of bereavement. There is enough to separate it from all other modes of trial, to produce a peculiar state of feeling, and to convey its own lessons to the soul, distinct from those imparted by any other divine dispensation. The loss of a wife, a friend, a companion, a sympathizer in trials, a fellow-heir of the grace of life, a sharer of the joys and a divider of the sorrows of our pilgrimage ; of a son who we hoped would be our stay and staff in old age, and perpetuate our name when we are dead ; of a daughter whom we have tenderly nourished and tenderly loved ; of a sister, the companion of the playful days of childhood, and a kind friend as she advanced with us to the maturity of life ; of a father, the counsellor and guide of our youth—each one of these bereavements has its own sad lesson to convey to the soul ; each one touches a chord in the heart which vibrates only then. It is a part of our duty and discipline here carefully to gather up these lessons and apply them to our own souls.

In the text it is supposed that the death of a mother affects those who are bereaved by her loss in a peculiar manner, and that such a loss is among the heaviest of sorrows. " I bowed down heavily, as one that mourneth for his mother." To see the force of this text it is not necessary to suppose that this is the heaviest of all the sorrows which we can experience, nor is it necessary to make any comparison between this and the other forms of bereavement which we may be called to endure. All that is necessary to say is, that there are chords of the soul touched then which have not been touched before, and which will not be again. A man has but one mother to love ; and when such an event occurs it is well for him to endeavor to learn the lessons which God once in his life designs to teach him.

[*] On the occasion of his mother's death.

It is the duty of a minister of the Gospel to adapt his teaching to all the relations of life, and to apply the lessons of religion to the various circumstances in which his hearers may be placed. At no one time indeed can it be supposed that any considerable part of his audience will feel an immediate interest in a topic of this kind ; but there are usually enough who have been recently afflicted in this manner to make such a topic of public discourse proper. Besides, how large a portion in a congregation is there who have at some time been thus bereaved ! How many are there here to-day who at some period of their lives have known what it was to lose a mother ! It will be no injury to recall the memory of that scene—not for the purpose of opening wounds again which time and religion may have healed—but to make more fresh in the recollection the lessons which God designed to convey by the living virtues, and by the death of a mother. It may be useful, too, to those who have mothers from whom they may soon be called to part, to contemplate this relation, and to be told of the kind of emotions which spring up in the soul when a parent is taken away to be seen no more. It may teach you to prize their counsels and their friendship more ; it may make you more careful not to pain their hearts by unkindness or disobedience.

I shall make no comparison between this relation and that of a father. *That* is in many respects as important and as influential as this ; and when that is sundered, the bereavement as much demands the tribute of our tears, and conveys as important lessons to the soul. Perhaps in some cases there may be more to affect the heart in such a loss, for some of us may owe more to the inherited mental characteristics, and the example and the direct teaching of a father, than we do to a mother. But though this may be so, the remarks which I propose to submit to you now, will, I trust, be seen to be founded in truth. Without any very exact order, yet with such a general distribution of my thoughts as will be adapted, I hope, to make a distinct impression on the mind, I shall submit to you a few reflections on such a relation, and such a loss, which I trust may be fitted to be useful.

I. I need hardly say that the relation of a mother is a peculiar relation, and has features which are found in no other. The tie is one which exists nowhere else ; which can never be renewed ;

which, when it is sundered, is sundered forever, unless it is cemented by religion, and grows up into eternal affection in the heavens.

Her affection for us began at a period of which we have no recollection, and when we were not conscious that any being loved us. It was laid far back in her nature, by a benignant Providence, to anticipate our helplessness and our wants as we came into the world. It began when as yet we had manifested no qualities of mind or heart to deserve affection; when we were incapable of returning the tokens of her love; when we could not give back the kiss that was tenderly impressed upon us, and when it was certain that the expressions of her lavished affection could not be remembered by us should we ever reach a period when we would be capable of repaying appreciated kindness. It existed in her heart whatever we were to be, or whatever was to be our fortune in this world, and was so strong that even could she have foreseen all our ingratitude, and all that we might yet do to pain her, she would still have loved us, and perhaps her caresses would have been only the more tender while we were yet innocent, and our souls were uncontaminated by contact with evil. She met us as we entered on life already prepared to do us good. Her first emotion toward us was that of love; and even then, when we had no character, and no claim for services rendered; when we had furnished no evidence that we ever would be worthy of her love, or repay her kindness with anything but ingratitude, she was ready to do for us what we may have even now scarcely secured a friend to do by all our virtues. Not a friend have we now who would watch more patiently by our sick-bed than she would have done by our cradle then, nor have we one who would sorrow more sincerely over our grave. This care we owed primarily to God, and under Him to that affection which He had created in her heart.

> "Unnumbered comforts on my soul,
>   Thy tender care bestowed,
> Before my infant heart conceived
>   From whom those comforts flowed."

The affection thus laid in her heart to anticipate our necessities was strengthened on her part by all her own toil, and care, and watchfulness, and sacrifices on our behalf. Whatever might be the effect on us, the effect on her was to make her love us more.

Her own solicitude and toil became thus a measure of her augmented affection; for God has instructed us to love much that which is the fruit of sacrifice and toil. Her love for us was measured far more by her own sacrifices than by our own worth, or by any developed traits of character which seemed to justify her ardor of affection, though it was also strengthened on her part by everything in us—then estimated perhaps at more than twice its value—which seemed to reward her care. On our part the attachment formed is not that which grows out of favors rendered, but favors received. It is laid indeed in nature; but it grows up and expands because we receive so many benefits; because there is such an obligation of gratitude; because we learn more and more, as we advance in years, how much we owe to a mother.

The attachment for a mother is different from that which we have for a brother or sister. That may be exceedingly tender and pure. Indeed, there is nothing more pure in our relations than love for a sister. But it is formed in a different way. When the tie which binds us to her is severed, it cannot indeed be renewed; it makes a sad desolation in the soul; but it is not precisely the sorrow which we have when we "bow down heavily, mourning for a mother." We love a sister, for we began life together, under the same roof, under the fostering care of the same parents. We played together in childhood; we shared the same gentle amusements; we went to the same school; we had the same father to counsel and guide us; and had the same mother to teach us to pray, and to give us the parting kiss at night. We grew up equally beloved by our parents, and we have learned to love each other much by mutual acts of affection and kindness.

The attachment is different from those friendships which we form as we advance in life. Those may be dear, and they may be stronger than that which binds to a mother, but they are not the same. A man leaves father and mother and cleaves to his wife with an affection more tender and strong than that formed by any natural relation, but it is not the same. He forms strong friendships in life, like that which bound the heart of David and Jonathan, but such friendships did not begin as we entered on life, nor imbed themselves in the soft heart of infancy and childhood, nor are they cemented by so many acts of kindness.

The attachment to a mother is different from that which we

form for our children. It is what we expect of them, rather than what we feel for them. We love them much—even as she did us. But it is a love for them as our children ; as dependent on us ; as helpless ; as needing our care and counsel ; as a part of ourselves ; as those who we hope will do us honor when we are dead. These attachments which we form in after life, of nature and affection, are strong and tender ; they may be more immediatley tender than those which we bear for a parent ; grief may be more poignant when they are sundered by death, and when we follow wife or child to the grave, but it has its own features, distinct from that when a venerable and much loved parent is conveyed to the tomb. As there was a peculiarity of attachment, so there will be a peculiarity of sorrow such as we are not to experience again.

II. I notice a second peculiarity of feature in this kind of bereavement. It is in the change which is produced in our ideas of home—the home of our childhood and youth. When she lived there, there was always a home—a place which in every situation of life we felt was such, and which we regarded as such.

In our childhood and youth there was in that home where she was, one who always cared for us, and for all that appertained to us. There was one who we were sure would take an interest in everything that we took an interest in, and whose ear we were certain would be open to listen to all our tales of childish success or of childish trouble. We were sure that she would take the same interest in it which we did, and we expected confidently that whoever might be against us, she would be for us. We never had a doubt that she would listen to our tale of fright, of disappointment, of calamity ; nor that she would feel just as we did about it. The matter might be in itself important or unimportant ; it might be dignified or undignified, yet we never doubted that she would regard it as important, and as sufficiently momentous to claim her attention. We might have felt that it was not grave enough to tell a father about ; we might have doubted whether he would suspend his more weighty employments to interest himself in our affairs ; but we never had such a doubt for a moment about a mother. No matter what her employments, or her cares, or what she might be interested in, we were sure that she would be interested in us, and that, in all our troubles, we should find her our friend. We had our difficulties in the little world of childhood. Bigger and older boys struck us, or laughed at us, or reviled us, or surpassed us in learning, in running, or in skill, and in that little world we might have found no sympathy, and there was no one there to whom we could unburden an aching heart. But we were sure that there was one who would sympathize with us, and who would be on our side. Our playmates derided us, and laughed at us because we said, in our simplicity, that we would "tell mother." And yet it was philosophy deep and pure to do so—like the pure crystal spring that breaks out of the side of a hill in the uncultivated forest. It was what nature prompted to—for nature designed that she should know our troubles, and nature had formed for us such a friend there, that, whoever was against us, we might know she would be on our side; whoever wronged us, she would not; whoever exulted over us, she would not join in the exultation. You may say that this is childish philosophy. So it may be; and the nearer our philosophy comes back to simple nature as developed there, the nearer we shall be to truth. In our troubles we have always needed a friend who would sympathize with us, and to whom we might unburden all the sorrows of the soul. The disciples of John's Redeemer "came, and took up his murdered body, and buried it, and went and told Jesus" (Matt. xiv. 12). In Him they had a friend--tender and delicate above all a mother's feelings—who they were sure would sympathize with their sorrows; and what was more natural than that they should go and tell Him? So in the home of our childhood, it was dear to us as a home, for there was not a sorrow of our heart that we might not tell our mother.

Many of us—most of us who are advanced beyond the period of childhood—went out from that home to embark on the stormy sea of life. Of the feelings of a father, and of his interest in our welfare, we have never entertained a doubt, and our home was dear because he was there; but there was a peculiarity in the feeling that it was the home of our mother. While she lived there, there was a place that we felt was home. There was one place where we would always be welcome; one place where we would be met with a smile; one place where we would be sure of a friend. The world might be indifferent to us. We might be unsuccessful in our studies or our business. The new friends which we supposed we had made, might prove to be false. The honor which we thought we deserved, might be withheld from us. We might be chagrined and mortified by seeing a rival outstrip us, and bear away the prize which we sought ; but there was a place where no feelings of rivalry were found, and where those whom the world overlooked would be sure of a friendly greeting. Whether pale and wan by study, care, or sickness, or flushed with health and flattering success, we were sure that we should be welcome there. Though the world was cold toward us, yet there was one who always rejoiced in our success, and always was affected in our reverses—and there was a place to which we might go back from the storm which began to pelt us, where we might rest, and become encouraged and invigorated for a new conflict. So have I seen a bird in its first efforts to fly, leave its nest, and stretch its wings and go forth to the wide world. But the wind blew it back and the rain began to fall, and the darkness of night began to draw on, and there was no shelter abroad, and it sought its way back to its nest, to take shelter beneath its mother's wings, and to be refreshed for the struggles of a new day ; but then it flew away to think of its nest and its mother no more. But not thus did we leave our home when we bade adieu to it to go forth alone to the manly duties of life. Even amid the storms that then beat upon us, and the disappointments that we met with, and the coldness of the world, we felt still that there was one there who sympathized in our troubles as well as rejoiced in our success, and that, whatever might be abroad, when we entered the door of her dwelling, we should be met with a smile. We expected that a mother, like the mother of Sisera, as she " looked out at her window" waiting for the coming of her son laden with the spoils of victory, would look out for our coming, and that our return would renew her joy and ours in our earlier days.

> " Oh ! in our sterner manhood, when no ray
> Of earlier sunshine glimmers on our way ;
> When girt with sin, and sorrow, and the toil
> Of cares, which tear the bosom that they soil ;
> Oh ! if there be in restrospection's chain
> One link that knits us with young dreams again,
> One thought so sweet, we scarcely dare to muse
> On all the hoarded raptures it reviews,
> Which seems each instant, in its backward range,
> The heart to soften, and its ties to change,
> And every spring untouched for years, to move,
> It is—THE MEMORY OF A MOTHER'S LOVE !"

It makes a sad desolation when from such a place a mother is taken away—and when, whatever may be the sorrows or the successes in life, she is to greet the returning son or daughter no more. The home of our childhood may be still lovely. The old family mansion; the green fields; the running stream; the moss-covered well; the trees; the lawn; the rose; the sweet-brier, may be there. Perchance, too, there may be an aged father, with venerable locks, sitting in his loneliness, with everything to command respect and love; but she is not there. Her familiar voice is not heard. The mother has been borne forth to sleep by the side of her children who went before her, and the place is not what it was. There may be those whom we much love, but she is not there. We may have formed new relations in life—tender and strong as they can be; we may have another home dear to us as was the home of our childhood, where there is all in affection, kindness, and religion to make us happy; but that home is not what it was, and it will never be what it was again. There is a loosening of one of the cords which bound us to earth—designed to prepare us for our eternal flight from everything dear here below, and to teach us that there is no place here that is to be our permanent home.

III. I notice a third thing in such an event which is found to convey a lesson to the soul such as we always feel in bereavement, but which, like the other things adverted to, has a peculiarity of its own. I refer to a class of emotions often not less painful, and of a much more admonitory character, than those which I have adverted to, and which, such are our imperfections in all the relations of life, we are always destined to feel when a friend is removed by death. I mean the quickened recollection of our neglects, of our acts of unkindness, of our ingratitude, of our improper feelings in our intercourse with those whom we have lost.

What I now advert to is one of the most beautiful and benignant laws of our nature—one of the most delicate arrangements to bring our guilt to remembrance in order that we may exercise true repentance, and to prompt us to kindness and fidelity in the remaining relations of life.

This law of our nature, which cannot well be explained except on the supposition that there is a moral government, and that God designs that all our sins shall be brought to our remembrance, is this—that in the death of a friend we instinctively recall the wrongs that we may have done him; for some mysterious power seems to summon them up from the land of forgetfulness, and to cause them to pass in solemn procession before us. Things which we had forgotten; words which we long since uttered but which had passed from the memory; expressions of irritated feeling; unjust suspicions; jealousies; neglect of the respect or the courtesies due in that relation of life; a want of attention when the heart of the friend was sad; want of sympathy in his successes or reverses—all seem to revive as we stand around the open grave, and as the coffin of the friend descends there, they are quickened into life—as the dead man was by the bones of Elisha. How this is so, as a matter of moral administration, we may not be able to explain. Perhaps it is because, though conscious in general that we had erred in that relation, we still hoped that the friend would somehow forgive us—but now he has gone to the grave, and now we can never ask him to pardon us. Perhaps it is that we look on him now as a sufferer—and pity his condition—and all his sources of sorrow seem summoned to aggravate his condition, and among others the wrongs that we have done arise to our view as a bitter ingredient in his cup of woes. Perhaps it is that God meant so to make the conscience that it would not always slumber, and designed that once at least it should do its appropriate work.

This law of our nature has been so beautifully described by one of our best American writers, that I can do nothing so well as to copy his words: "Oh the grave! the grave! It buries every error, covers every defect, extinguishes every resentment. From this peaceful bosom spring none but fond regrets and tender recollections. Who can look down even upon the grave of an enemy, and not feel a compunctious throb that he ever should have warred with the poor handful of earth that lies mouldering before him? But the grave of those we loved—what a place for meditation! There it is that we call up in long review the whole history of the truth and gentleness, and the thousand endearments lavished upon us, almost unheard in the daily course of intimacy; there it is we dwell upon the tenderness of the parting scene, the bed of death with all its stifled grief, its noiseless attendants, its most watchful assiduities—the last testimonies of expiring love, the feeble, fluttering, thrilling—oh how thrilling is the fluttering pulse —the last fond look of the glazing eye, turning upon us from the threshold of existence—the faint, faltering accent, struggling in death to give one more assurance of affection. Oh, go to the grave of buried love, and there meditate. There settle the account with thy conscience of every past endearment unregarded of that departed being who never, never can be soothed by contrition. If thou art a child, and hast ever added a sorrow to the soul, or a furrow to the silvered brow of an affectionate parent—if thou art a husband, and hast ever caused the fond bosom that ventured its whole happiness in thy arms to doubt one moment of thy kindness or thy truth—or if thou art a friend, and hast injured by thought, by word, or deed, the spirit that generously confided in thee—if thou art a lover, and hast ever given one unmerited pang to the true heart that now lies cold beneath thy feet, then be sure that every unkind look, every ungracious word, every ungentle action will come thronging back upon thy memory, and knock dolefully at thy soul ; be sure that thou wilt lie down sorrowing and repenting on the grave, and utter the unheard groan, and pour the unavailing tear, bitter because unheard and unavailing."

Who, I may add, ever saw an endeared friend die, and did not feel that there were things in his intercourse with him to regret, and for which he would now desire to ask forgiveness? Who ever saw a man die of whom he had said hard hings, or thought hard things, who did not lament that he had given indulgence to such words and feelings? Who ever attended one to the grave—friend or foe, partner or rival, with whom he had been at variance, who did not now wish to have it all buried in oblivion? Who can carry his enmity to the grave? There, when a rival or a foe is laid " earth to earth, ashes to ashes, dust to dust," we lay our animosities aside. There we feel, that whatever may be true of him whom we commit to the tomb, there was much in us that was wrong. And there we regret every unkind word, feel pained at the remembrance of every unkind thought, and mourn that we have done no more to impart happiness to the cold sleeper whom we are to see no more.

I said that this was a beautiful and benignant law of our nature, and though attended like other laws when violated, with pain, the design is as apparent as it is beautiful. It has two objects as a part of the divine moral administration. One is to lead us to repentance for our errors and faults, that we may obtain pardon of our God before it be too late. True, the sleeper there cannot now utter the word of forgiveness. Those lips are forever sealed in death—and how much would we give now could we ask that friend to forgive us! How much would we rejoice could we have the assurance from those lips that the faults that now come thronging on our memory were forgiven and forgotten, and that they did not add a pang to his last sorrows! But if we cannot now confess the fault in the ear of that friend; if we cannot now hope that those lips will open to declare us forgiven, we may confess the fault to God, and may be assured that He will blot the remembrance of it from His book. Around each grave of a friend, therefore, He summons up groups of our past offences that we may be humbled and penitent, and may not go unpardoned to eternity. The other design of this benignant law is, to keep us from offending hereafter; to teach us to manifest kindness in the remaining relations of life. True, we cannot again injure, or offend, or pain the sleeper there. Whatever may be his condition now, he is where our unkindness or neglect will not reach or affect him. But we have other relations in life, perhaps equally tender and equally important. There are other hearts that may be made to bleed by ingratitude, or coldness, or neglect, or mercy, and we may be assured that what has happened in the case of the friend that we have now lost, will happen also in theirs. The design of the law is, to teach us to indulge no thought, to speak no word, to evince no feeling which we would regret when they too are removed. And what a restraint would this be on our temper, our words, our whole deportment!

In each bereavement there is a peculiar group of these painful thoughts that come thronging to the recollection. They are those which are revived by that bereavement, but would be unaffected by any other. How many such things there are laid away in the chambers of the soul, now slumbering there like torpid adders, perhaps hereafter to be quickened into life to be our tormentors! The occasion requires me only to allude to that class of emotions which is thus summoned to our recollection on the death of a mother. And who is there of us that can see a mother die without many such painful and disquieting thoughts—greatly embittering the natural grief of parting? Even while we were conscious of having had for her strong and tender love; even when in the main we desired to respect her and to make her happy; even when we knew that our general character has been approved by her, and that in life thus far we had not disappointed her fond anticipations, yet how many times in childhood have we been disobedient, how often have we spoken disrespectfully, how often have we disregarded her wishes, how often have we uttered sentiments peevishly that we knew differed from hers; how often have we failed in rendering that prompt and ready obedience which was due to her as a mother, and to her kindness to us; how many times by our perverseness, our self-will, our pride, our obstinacy, have we discouraged her in her efforts to do us good; how often have we done that which would weary out the patience of any one but a parent—and God. Could we hear her speak again, how many things are there which we would wish to confess, and which we would desire her to forgive!

There are lessons flowing from this subject adapted to those who are more particularly interested from having recently been called to this trial—lessons requiring us to submit to God; to be grateful for the example, and counsels, and toils in our behalf of those who have been removed; to imitate them as they imitated their Saviour, and to be prepared to follow them to the world of glory. But on these I will not dwell. There are two thoughts, however, which, in conclusion, I will suggest, addressed to two classes of my hearers.

1. The first relates to those who have had pious mothers, who are now removed to heaven, but whose prayers and counsels they have disregarded. I refer to those who have thus far withheld their hearts from that Saviour whom their mother loved, and with whom she now dwells; who have embraced sentiments such as they know she would not approve; who have made choice of companions such as she lived to warn them against; or who indulge in scenes of revelry and sin such as, if she were living, you know would break her heart. Go, young man, and walk in the stillness of the evening among the graves. Beneath your feet, in the sacred slumbers of a Christian death, lies a much-loved mother. How calm her slumbers! How sweet the spot! How lovely a mother's grave! How the memory delights to go back

to the nursery, the fireside, the sick-bed, the anxious care of a mother! How it loves to recall her gentle look, her eye of love, her kiss at night! At that grave, thoughtless young man, think of thy revels, thy neglect of God, thy forgetfulness of the prayer that she taught thee, thy friendship now for those against whom she warned thee! She sleeps now in death; but from that grave is it fancy that we hear a voice: "My beloved son! Is this the life that I taught thee to lead? Are these the pleasures which I taught thee to pursue? Did I bear thee, and toil for thee, and wear out my life, that I might train thee for sin, and death, and hell?"

2. The other thought relates to those who now have a Christian mother—and who yet disregard her living counsels and prayers. I have adverted to a law of our being, beautiful in its nature, but painful in its inflictions. The day is coming when that mother will die. You may see her die; or far away, you may hear of her death, and may return and visit her grave. Be thou sure that every unkind look, every disobedient action, every harsh word, will come back and visit thy soul. Be sure you will remember everything that ever gave pain to her heart, and remember it with unavailing regret when too late to recall it, or to ask forgiveness. Be sure if you are unkind and disobedient; if you are an infidel or a scoffer; if you slight her counsels and neglect the God and Saviour to whom she would conduct you, there are laid up in the chambers of your soul the sources of bitter repentance hereafter—and that you cannot find forgiveness of her whose heart you broke, though you seek it carefully with tears. And be sure that the sweetest of all consolations when she dies, will be found in such love of her Saviour that you will appreciate what is meant when it is said she has gone to Heaven; and in evidence in your own heart that you will be prepared when the summons comes, to rejoin her in the realms of bliss.

> Into the eternal shadow that girds our life around,
> Into the infinite silence wherewith Death's shore is bound,
> Thou hast gone forth, belovèd! and I were mean to weep
> That thou hast left life's shallows, and dost possess the deep.
>
> LOWELL.

AN OVERCOMING FAITH.*

BY RICHARD FULLER, D.D., BALTIMORE, MD.

But none of these things move me, neither count I my life dear unto myself, so that I might finish my course with joy.—ACTS xx. 24.

To adopt this sentiment and act upon it unshrinkingly, is the noblest achievement of Christian heroism. And if the conflicts and sacrifices which Paul had to encounter were far more fearful than ours, it must be acknowledged that he seems to have possessed one vast advantage over us and all other men. We, in our trials and combats and sufferings, have to be sustained by faith. But what is this faith? How dim its light! How seldom is it a steady illumination! If the Son of Man should now come, how much faith would He find upon earth? At best, how very inadequate its discoveries, how very feeble its anticipations of eternal things!

Now, those eternal realities our apostle had seen. He had been "caught up to the third heaven," and favored with an open vision of the celestial glory; seeing and hearing things inexplicable to man. No wonder he was ardent. I am not surprised that he was fired with quenchless zeal and tireless ambition; that toil, and pain, and shipwreck, and want, and stripes were all despised, and death and martyrdom thrice welcome.

Let us not, however, envy him this advantage. "Blessed are they that have not seen, and yet have believed." Faith honors God more than sight (as it is written of Abraham, that he "was strong in faith, giving glory to God") and will, therefore, be more nobly rewarded. Nor only so. Although the apprehensions of faith are less vivid than those of the senses, its influence is not less stringent; and, if it be genuine, what motives does it not furnish to elevate us above all the trials of life, and make us—in view of the joyful termination of our course—superior to death, even the most appalling death. . . .

I. The first infinitely important truth taught by our text is, that

---

* Preached on the death of William T. Brantly, D.D.

to each of us a course has been prescribed, which each may call *his* course, and which *each is to finish.* "My course," says the apostle; but how forgetful are we all here, and from this forgetfulness have flowed the most lamentable mischiefs. How constantly do we find Christians pleading something in their present condition as an excuse for their unfaithfulness, and persuading themselves that in other circumstances they would be more holy and devoted. "Had I but other talents," says the slothful servant, "I would be useful." "For my part," argues a second, "were I only free from these embarrassments, nothing would interrupt my zeal and charity." While a third—the representative of almost the whole church so called—in spite of reason, and Scripture, and his own experience, is ever promising himself some more auspicious season, and thus year after year mocking God and wronging his own soul. Pernicious errors! Fatal heresies! Let us avoid them; let us comprehend our religion better. And, that we may do so, let us never forget what I am now urging; let us settle in our minds and always recollect the following propositions, which are practical axioms of universal application.

Let us settle in our minds this proposition, that *to each individual God assigns his own course,* and that his piety, and happiness, and acceptance, depend not on the course itself, but on his fulfilling it—not on the sphere in which the Christian moves, but on his glorifying God in it. An angel, sent to live on this earth, would not be at all concerned whether he were seated on a throne of diamond, or toiled as a scavenger sweeping the streets. His only solicitude would be about occupying the place designated for him, and glorifying God there. And we, if we would be useful or happy, must cultivate the temper of that angel. We must remember that every age, every calling, every condition, has its peculiar trials and duties; and that the trials and duties we meet are those which are assigned to us—which have been accurately adjusted so as to constitute our probation, and be the ordeals of our faith, and love, and patience. This affliction cometh not forth of the dust, neither doth this trouble spring out of the ground; they are paternal chastisements for my good. This besetting sin is permitted, that I may be kept ever prayerful and watchful; it is the thorn in the flesh, to make me always humble.

These losses, these sad reverses, are designed to try my confidence and resignation, and to fix my treacherous heart on things above. This sphere of action, however humble or arduous, is my sphere—that which I am to fill to the honor of Christ and the advancement of His cause.

It is recorded of John the Baptist, that he "fulfilled his course." Paul says, "I have finished my course." How different the courses of these remarkable men I need not tell you; each, however, completed his course, and this constituted his piety. And just so now; how diversified are our circumstances, our trials, and duties, and difficulties. Are we meeting them all with sustained piety, and prompt, unshrinking consecration to our Father's will? If we would obey "the high calling of God," we must have done with our illusions about the future—that future will bring its own trials and duties; "sufficient unto the day is the evil thereof." If we are to be Christians at all, we must not be repining at our lot, nor indolently sighing after chimerical advantages, nor flattering ourselves with the nobleness we should display under imaginary difficulties. Our happiness and our salvation depend on our serving God in the condition in which He has placed us, not in another; we are required to improve the talents we have, not those we want; and if our present trials be too great for our faith and love, what transparent folly is it to be amusing ourselves with fanciful and fictitious dreams of martyrdom. Our actual, real trials and sacrifices are the martyrdom to which we are called; these are the way the Lord our God is leading us, "to humble us, and prove us, and see whether we will keep His commandments or no;" these are our probation—the obstacles to be surmounted in "the race set before us"—our courses, and to every man is assigned his own course.

To every man a certain and definite *time* is given in which to finish his course; "His days are determined, the number of his months is with Thee, Thou hast appointed his bounds that he cannot pass." We all die, say the Scriptures, and are as water sinking into the ground and returning no more. Our lives roll on like rivers. We may be renowned or obscure; we may become benefactors or scourges of our race; our existence may be calm and bright, or dark and turbulent; but to each a period is allotted, after which we are confounded in the tomb—even as rivers, the most celebrated and the unknown, the tranquil and the impetuous, those which desolate and those which bless the earth, all traverse spaces accurately prescribed, and then mingle their waters and lose their names and distinctions in the ocean.

Such are our lives. Ah, my hearers, if Almighty God should this moment reveal to us the future, what startling discoveries might we not make ; what alterations in a few months ; how many graves ready and opening under our feet! Here the youngest and giddiest might stand aghast at finding themselves already touching the fatal limit. There the votary of mirth, and the eager aspirant after honor, and the man all absorbed in business, might be seen pale and terrified at that message, "This year thou shalt die." All around us, and at our very sides—in these pews—in the circles where we move—in our families—how many unexpected and melancholy changes might we not behold, if God should disclose what even a year shall bring forth. My brethren, God hath not revealed to us the future, nor do we require any such knowledge. Use the reason which has been vouchsafed you. Look at the scene in the midst of which you daily live, and at what is hourly passing about you. Open your eyes to the spectacle now exhibited. Listen to the voice which now speaks from the tomb. Be warned, be wise, reflect, meditate on the truth I am now urging, that to each of us there is prescribed a time in which to finish our course, a period fixed and definite, and that cannot be passed.

"The time is short," says the apostle ; and of all the admonitions of the Bible, this is that which seems least to require a preacher to make us feel it. "What," indeed, "is your life?" The longest human life—what is it ? Compare our life with that of the generations before the flood—men who reckoned not by years, but centuries—and what is it ? What is it when compared with the duration even of inanimate objects—these venerable walls —those seats—this pulpit ? Why, the very pages of this old Bible—so frail that a rude touch would rend them—how many eyes which have rested on these pages are now quenched in death ; how many lips which have expounded these pages are now sealed in the tomb ! And what if I could go on and compare our life with eternity. What if we could comprehend the incomprehensible, and measure the infinite, and fathom the fathomless, and then compare our little, shrivelled handbreadth with eternity, with the boundless abysses of the future, with myriads upon myriads of ages accumulating for ever and ever—ah! imperceptible atom, grass cut down in a moment, flower, smoke, vapor, shadow, dream, nothing.

Yes, "Man that is born of a woman is of few days," and these days pass rapidly away. "The world passeth away, and the lust thereof." "The fashion of this world passeth away"—the "*fashion*," the vain pageant, of this world passeth away. The image here is that of a procession marching before our eyes. It may be surmounted by gay banners, and be decked in every brilliant hue, and move to all the pomp of festive or martial music blown from reed, and shell, and metal—but it is soon gone. It is yonder, and scarcely can you hear the faint notes of its coming—it approaches—it is before you in its imposing array—it has passed—it disappears forever, and again you are left in solitude and silence.

"It passeth away," is written upon everything here. We look, we love, we desire, we possess—but no matter how dear and cherished the object, we soon trace upon its fragile form this melancholy inscription, "It passeth away." Our pleasures, what are they doing? Passing away. Our afflictions, what are they doing? Passing away; they are, says the apostle, "but for a moment." Where are the companions of our childhood? Where are the associates of our youth? "Our fathers, where are they?" Where are those who once inhabited the houses in which you dwell, and occupied the chambers in which you will sleep tonight? Where are those who once trod these hallowed courts, and filled this sacred desk? WHERE?—Gone! They have finished their course; they have passed away. And we are following them. We, too, are "accomplishing as an hireling our day." "Our days are swifter than a weaver's shuttle;" and everything around us is changing, consuming, vanishing "as a cloud"—passing away. This young year is passing away. This Sabbath is passing away. These seasons, these songs, these prayers, these opportunities—all, all, are fleeting, passing away, hasting to be gone.

> "Time rolls his ceaseless course ;—
> The race of yore that danced our infancy upon the knee,
> How are they blotted from the things that be ;
> How few, all weak and withered of their force,
> Wait, on the verge of dark eternity,
> > Like stranded wrecks, the tide returning hoarse,
> > To waft them from our sight !"

My brethren, children of an hour, have you any just conceptions of a life so brief and transient as ours? "He fleeth as a shadow and continueth not." "Behold thou hast made my days as an handbreadth, and my years are as nothing before thee." "Lord, make me to know mine end, and the measure of my days, what it is ; that I may know how frail I am." "So teach us to number our days, that we may apply our hearts unto wisdom."

II. What effect the truths I have been urging may have on your minds, I, of course, cannot tell. Upon Paul, their influence was constant and powerful, as you see in the text. They filled him with ardor ; they armed him for every event of life. They caused him to forget the past, to rise above the present, to fix his eye with an eagle gaze and from an eagle station on the future, and to feel that the only object worthy of his cares, and toils, and sacrifices, was the glorious consummation, the joyful termination of his course. "And now behold I go bound in the spirit unto Jerusalem, not knowing the things that shall befall me there. Save only that the Holy Ghost witnesseth in every city, saying that bonds and afflictions abide me. But none of these things move me." Let us enter into this noble language. It was not peculiar to the apostle, but is the sentiment of all who are bound in spirit for the New Jerusalem.

What, then, is the import of the language before us ? I answer, it denotes plainly, that in the Christian's estate, *the finishing his course with joy is the great concern of life.* Other and indispensable duties engage his hands ; but they are only by-work, they are not the grand object. Never perhaps did there live a man whose occupations were more diversified than those of Paul—now compassing the earth by land—now ploughing the deep—now working as a tentmaker—now thundering before kings—in a word, doing everything, and seeming almost to possess ubiquity ; yet, amidst all, he says, "One thing I do." And such is the language of the Christian I am describing. He can say, "One thing I do"—*one* great absorbing wish monopolizes my heart. He can, with the Psalmist, exclaim, "One thing have I desired of the Lord."

> "My first, my last, my chief requests
> Are all comprised in this;
> To follow where thy saints have led,
> And then possess their bliss."

This is one import of the words we are now analyzing. This, however, is not all their meaning. It is not enough to feel that the finishing our course joyfully is our grand work—or to pray importunately for this. An ungodly Balaam could say, "Let me die the death of the righteous;" and that man is assuredly deceived who prays, but contradicts his prayers by his life. The text denotes, farther, that the Christian is directly and earnestly *occupied* about finishing his course with joy. Many *mean* to be engaged, but he *is* engaged. Not only in his aspirations, but in his efforts, he presses toward the mark for the prize of the high calling of God in Christ Jesus. His face is "set as a flint," and he answers all resisting strokes, as the flint does, with fire. Forgetting those things which are behind, he reaches forth unto those that are before, that he may apprehend that for which also he is apprehended of Christ Jesus. An irresolute spirit is destroying more souls among us than any form of open sin. But his spirit is not irresolute. "My heart is fixed, O God, my heart is fixed"—such is the felt consecration and concentration of his soul to its work. He is busy about eternity; striving to enter in at the strait gate; actually employed in vanquishing difficulties, and subduing corruptions, and surmounting obstacles. And he is intent upon this very thing. No soldier bent upon carrying a citadel, was ever more engrossed by a single object. No mariner on the open sea, struggling with winds and waves, and longing for port, was ever more tenacious of a single purpose. "That I may finish my course with joy"—this is the all-animating thought, the sublime anticipation, which girds him for toil, and cheers him on amidst discouragements; nor for this is any sacrifice deemed too costly. What, indeed, are we to understand, when Paul declares that none of all the sufferings he might endure could move him? Was he a stoic? Was he invulnerable to persecution, and affliction, and shame? Not at all. He felt, and felt keenly—for piety does not dull, it refines, our sensibilities. Our apostle meant that nothing deterred, nothing impeded, nothing diverted him. "None of these things move me"—such was the exclamation of this heroical man; and how much is there in this exclamation for us all!

Sensual souls, the lesson of this passage is for you; you whose passions and appetites are so many chains with which Satan draws you back from God, and binds you to his chariot. It is for you, worldly souls, you, who, instead of laying aside every weight, are only anxious to entangle yourselves with fresh cares. It is for those temporizing spirits who are always projecting, but never performing; always admiring the firmness of the Christian, but never possessing courage to imitate it. It is for the slothful servant. It is for that man whose piety is fruitful only in excuses for doing nothing. It is for that woman whose wishes and pride control her as much in the Church as they had done in the world. It is—in short, it is, as I said, for ALL—all of us who are forever indulging in effeminacy and inglorious repose, and saying we do not commit any sin, we are only a little indolent. As if indolence were not one of the greatest sins; as if all ages and conditions did not require action; as if poverty and wealth, sickness and health, life and death, are not parts of our probation; as if, in fine, each day is not ushered in by a herald announcing new conflicts, summoning to fresh victories, and publishing the heavenly proclamation, "To him that overcometh will I grant to sit with me in my throne, even as I also overcame and am set down with my father in His throne."

This is another import of the language of the text. It expresses the earnestness and intentness of the Christian's application to the course before him; and, once more, the words denote the *constancy* of that application. Would, my brethren, there were less need to press this part of our subject upon you. Would there were not too much reason to fear that most of you are deplorably wanting here. Am I wrong?

Then answer me a single question, solve this problem: Why is it that sudden death appears so formidable? Surely protracted disease is not desirable; and there is no one who would not wish to escape the pains and nauseating appliances and miseries of a sick-room. Why then do we all stand appalled at a sudden death in our midst? I will tell you. All feel how unprepared they are for such a stroke. Each trembles as he thinks, What if it had been I—what if I had been thus hurried to the foot of the dread tribunal!

Not so the man who possesses the unshaken steadiness of which I speak. No, he holds on his way not only with singleness of aim, and intensity of application, but with unfaltering perseverance. The thought of finishing his course with joy, accompanies him everywhere, and thither all his solicitudes tend with unremitted energy of impulse. "I am now ready to be offered"—such was the frame in which the closing hour found our apostle; and such is the frame which the Christian before us maintains. His constant care is to keep his soul prepared, with outstretched wings, plumed and ready for the skies; and still, when danger threatens, and disease assails, and death approaches, his language is, "I am now ready to be offered." Others rest in present attainments; he counts not himself to have apprehended. Others show too plainly that their hearts are on rewards and possessions here; they resemble those tribes who said to Joshua, Give us our inheritance on this side of the river. He rejoices that his possessions and rewards are not here. His affections are set on things above. His affinities are with eternity. His soul glows with the illapses, the first gushes of heaven, and feels the resistless attractions of God Himself. He resembles old Paulinus, who, when his friends told him that the Goths had sacked the city and burned all his treasures, looked up smilingly and said, "Lord, Thou knowest where my treasures are!"

What, indeed, is there in this earthly life to satisfy the Christian? What is the world? The world! it is a scene of agitation, disquietude, and restlessness—a stormy ocean, allowing at best only a momentary and treacherous calm. The world! it is an abode of vanity, a land of sorrow, a valley strewed with thorns and watered with tears; a tomb where we are every day burying hopes that can know no resurrection. Renouncing forever such a world, I fly to Him who calls the weary and the heavy-laden. I obey the gospel. I cling to the cross. And I find, it is true, in the service of Christ, a peace the world never gave; joys —oh how much sweeter the memory of those joys than the possession of all besides! But still, religion exempts me not from afflictions and sorrows. Religion brings sorrows of its own, trials, sacrifices, enmities, bitter separations, unkindnesses too often from those to whom we are linked by the tenderest ties, and to whose hearts our hearts have long been wont to leap in kindness back. Even "the cup of thanksgiving is mingled with tears," and through much tribulation we must enter the Kingdom of God. And what do I learn from all this? I learn that not in this world, not in this economy, but in another world, another economy, I am to find my felicity. I learn daily to turn my eyes to that other world, that other economy; I learn to listen to that voice which is forever crying to me, "Arise, depart; for this is not your rest, because it is polluted." Happy we, if the vanity and disappointments of this world cause us to close our eyes on it forever, and fix them on a world which will not defraud our hearts. Happy he who, by the brevity and misery of life, is taught the true purpose of his being; and who, regarding an immortality of bliss as the goal to be won, and "striving to enter into that rest which remains," keeps ever before him the crown, the end, the joyful consummation of his course. Happy, thrice happy, such a man. And why? Why, for reasons most plain; reasons which you must already feel. Because such a man will be kept calm, unmoved, intrepid, amidst all the events of life; calm, unmoved, intrepid (nay, joyful and full of holy triumphing) amidst the last conflict, the struggles with death itself, even the most appalling death.

III. I place such a man, for example, amidst the temptations and allurements of the world; but for him how impotent their assaults and solicitations!

Maxims of this world, how false are ye all in his eyes! Examples of this world, how pernicious do your unsearchable seductions appear! Pleasures, riches, grandeurs—a Christian—a Christian who is athirst for God, whose heart is warmed by habitual contemplations of God, such a Christian is incapable of that debasement which degrades an immortal mind in a vortex of sensual pleasures; that meanness of soul which is dazzled by a little human parade, and prostrates itself before a little gold, a little pomp, a little tinsel splendor. No, the world is unmasked. The pleasures he seeks are pure and celestial. Eternal riches inflame his avarice. True glory is the object of his competition.

I place this man, again, amidst the fears and discouragements of the believer. Fears, discouragements, how many, and from how many sources! Sometimes from our conscious weakness; and David despondingly says, "I shall now perish one day by the hand of Saul." Sometimes from the small number who are devoted to Christ; and even the lion-hearted Elijah wishes for death as he exclaims, "I, even I only, am left." Too often (alas that it should be so) these fears and discouragements arise from the reproach of the cross. "I know not the man!" What, Peter, know not Jesus Christ? You knew Him once. You knew Him when, sinking in the waves, you cried, "Lord, save or I perish." You knew Him when you said, "Lord, to whom shall we go but unto Thee," and protested, "Though all shall be offended, yet will not I;" "If I should die with Thee, I will not deny Thee." You knew the Man then, Peter, and why not know Him now?

Ah! see, He is now exposed to shame. He is persecuted and seized and forsaken. He is about to be condemned. He is despised and smitten and derided; and Peter knows not the Man now. But how do these fears vanish when, over all, the Christian lifts his eye to heaven, and hears that assurance, "I am Almighty God, walk thou before Me and be thou perfect." Then how does he scorn this unworthy timidity. Then with what magnanimity does he defy every discouragement, and despise the shame, and exultingly cry, "God forbid that I should glory save in the cross of our Lord Jesus Christ." If the world despise him, he knows how to despise the world in return. And he sternly pursues his career with a courage only strengthened by opposition.

And what more shall I add? In his afflictions, in all his trials and conflicts and sufferings, what ineffable consolations does not such a man taste; with what holy firmness is he not armed? "I reckon" (such are his thoughts, such the arguments by which he "encourages himself in the Lord his God")—"I reckon that the sufferings of this present time are not worthy to be compared with the glory which shall be revealed in us." These trials are the road which all have trod who are gone to that place where trials are unknown; and for them as for me the path hath been lined with fire. My light affliction, which is but for a moment, is now working for me a far more exceeding and eternal weight of glory.

> "Though painful at present,
> 'Twill cease before long.
> And, then, O how pleasant
> The conqueror's song!"

Such are his thoughts, and what thoughts these! What can they not do, what have they not done, to fortify and animate the Christian hero, and to cause even the feeblest to brave misfortune, and persecution, and pain, and all the sternest vicissitudes of wretchedness. Ye martyrs, I appeal to you, for you can answer. I appeal to you, cloud of witnesses which compass us about, for you can testify. *Them*—and many of them the most timid and delicate women—*them*, "of whom the world was not worthy"—what powerful principle inspired them? By what were they sustained when they "had trials of cruel mockings and scourgings, yea of bonds and imprisonment;" when they "wandered about in sheepskins and goatskins, being destitute, afflicted, tormented;" when they "wandered in deserts and in mountains, and in dens and caves of the earth;" when they were tracked and hunted down like wild beasts by that tiger Nero; when their way was obstructed by racks, and scaffolds, and gibbets, and flames; but when they still pressed on, the cruelty of their tormentors only surpassed by their constancy in defying it;—amidst scenes like these, what was it that supported the heroes and martyrs of the faith? It was, my brethren, the prospect, the joy set before them. It was the recompense of the reward. It was the good land burning in the sun to which, as from Pisgah tops, they looked over. It was the glory, the exceeding glory, the far more exceeding and eternal weight of glory.

I was right, then, when I affirmed that in view of the joyful termination of his course, the Christian can be prepared for every event of life. And I was equally right in saying that such a prospect can do more; that it can make the Christian intrepid, nay triumphant, in the last hour, the trying conflict with death itself. Lose nothing of these concluding remarks, my dear hearers, for they concern you deeply. You must soon die, and you will then require no common supports. Many fine things have been written about the pleasures of the good man's death-bed; but death is still the king of terrors for all that. I know there have been those who affected to regard death as annihilation, and thus to be elevated above the fear of it. But what were these men? Even supposing they were sincere—supposing that they did not assume an air and tone to impose on others while they could not impose on themselves—what were such men? They were idiots and madmen. They "died as the fool dieth." But to know what death is, and yet to meet it calmly and triumphantly, this, this is a noble conquest, a sublime victory. And this victory, the Christian before us, the man who is ever contemplating the end of his course, can achieve. Death is not to him what it is to all others. And this you will at once feel, if you just glance at three truths which I only indicate in so many words.

In the first place, *such a man has formed a correct estimate of life.* What is the design of life? Apart from his immortality, what a failure is man; nay, he is an enigma baffling all our conceptions of the Deity. Did God mean man to be happy here— why then so much misery? Did He design him to be miserable —but how can I reconcile this with all my sentiments of God? Oh man, who hath misplaced thee thus? The Christian of whom I am now speaking has his ideas rectified on this subject. This span, this handbreadth, this dream, this vapor, these few dozen years, these fleeting moments, are not life. They are but a harsh probation, and shall we repine when this probation is over? They are but the portico of our being, and shall we wish to remain there, where the wind, and rain, and storm can beat upon us? Disgusted with the condition of his country, Cato the Younger, we are told, shut himself up and applied his mind to Plato's book on the immortality of the soul. "I am still Cæsar's superior," he said, and, after reading that treatise through twice, he fell eagerly upon his sword. In that very work Plato condemns suicide; yet, once convinced of a life hereafter, nothing could restrain the ardors of Cato's soul. He wooed death as a bride, and embraced joyfully the tomb with immortality for a dower. What, then, should be the emotions of a Christian; a man for whom life and immortality—and such a life, such an immortality—have been brought to light in the Gospel!

In the next place, *the very life which the Christian I am describing leads, must prepare him for death by weaning him from all earthly things.* He dies daily to the world. He becomes daily more crucified to the world; and death can separate him from nothing, because faith has before separated him from all. To the lovers of this world death is indeed a melancholy, a cruel shipwreck—a shipwreck of hopes, and wishes, and projects, and treasures, and affections, and hearts, and everything. But the Christian who lives the life of faith, and is ever refreshing his eyes with heaven, loses, and can lose, nothing. Sweeping, scourging, crushing, the tempest comes; but he is calm. His heart and his treasure are high above the storm. His hope survives the shock, and shines brighter and brighter amidst the desolation. What to such a man are those objects which enslave the hearts of the multitude, and make death the greatest of calamities? They are, say the Scriptures, "lying vanities;" nay, fuel for the fire. And the whole world—that world which so fills and intoxicates its votaries—what is it to such a Christian? A grand impertinence—a magnificent funeral pile awaiting the last conflagration. Yes, ye worshippers, ye martyrs of the world, behold your idol! As the Jews—after collecting their treasures, and "the ornaments of their wives and sons and daughters," and fashioning a calf of gold—cried, "these be your gods, O Israel;" so would I say of those idols on which you are desecrating your passions, and your wives, and sons, and daughters, lavishing affections formed for Christ. These be your gods. Behold your deity! To-morrow, you shall be stretched upon beds of anguish and death, and be torn, all pale and trembling, from your idols, your lands, your houses, your silver and gold. Then (as the Lord formerly said), "Cry unto the gods to whom you have offered incense, and see if they will help you in your trouble." But this is not all. To-morrow, those idols themselves—those lands, those houses, this silver and gold—shall be burnt up, and become a heap of white ashes. These are the objects of your insane homage. What objects to engross the immortal mind! Sinners, you who are also finishing your course, but with a sorrow which it will require eternity to deplore; presumptuous mortals, who, by some strange infatuation, are still deluding yourselves while all around you and within you is decaying, see your folly and madness. Let death, let the fires of the judgment, preach to you. Behold the true character of that world for which you are forfeiting heaven, and plunging your souls in the lake that burneth with fire and brimstone.

The Christian's heart is on a very different world. "Seeing

that all these things shall be dissolved, what manner of persons ought ye to be?" He is one of this manner of persons. His affections are not on these, but on very different things. They are on an inheritance which is incorruptible—a kingdom that cannot be moved; on riches, honors, pleasures, undefiled and unfading. These, these have long been his meditation and his desire, *and death* (this is our last reflection) *death puts him in possession of them.* Death rends the veil, and throws open the barriers between him and that salvation for which he has long waited. I am thinking of an old hermit of whom I have read. He was just dying, when, with a broken, faltering voice, he began to sing. They asked him why he sang? "I sing," he replied, "because I feel that the old walls are tumbling down at last." Ah! fall, fall, ye walls of partition; be rent in twain, interposing curtains; down, down with time, and flesh, and sin, and all that separates the soul of the Christian from the bosom of its loving Redeemer.

Yes, my brethren, what is death, even the most excruciating death, to him who, over all its terrors, fixes his gaze upon the glory that shall be revealed? Replenishing their souls with that view, how often have believers found their strength redoubled in the closing agony, and displayed a fortitude which filled even their enemies with amazement! Witness Stephen, piercing the cloud of stones, and beholding the heavens open, and Jesus waiting to receive him home. Witness that woman who said, as she ran to join a company of martyrs going to execution, "Crowns are about to be distributed this day, and I am hastening for mine." Witness the noble Blandina, who, though delicately brought up, defied all the tortures which the malice of fiends could invent; and from the rack, the iron chair, the very jaws of the beasts that were tearing her, still exclaimed, "I am a Christian! I am a Christian!" and exhorted those who had been condemned with her to suffer cheerfully for Christ. Witness these! Death was not only disarmed of its terrors to their minds, but it conducted them to the summit of their intensest aspirations, their devoutest wishes. And what is death to any Christian—a Christian, I mean, who is Christ's not only in name, but in his choice and life; who can say, "Living or dying, I am the Lord's;" who is constantly proposing to himself the prize that endureth forever, and whose faith is thus daily ripening into full assurance—what is death to such a

Christian? I die—I depart—but it is to be with Christ. I die, I depart, the world recedes, it disappears; but I am going to an eternal world—to that world which has long been the object of all my wishes, my prayers, my toils, my most exalted aspirations. I die, I depart; thick darkness wraps my vision; I can no longer see my friends, my brethren, my weeping family around me; I can no longer hear the farewell words they are speaking to me. But I see Jesus Christ. There He is beckoning me to come up. But I hear Jesus Christ. I hear the voice of the Son of God calling me, encouraging me, saying to me, "It is I, be not afraid"— "To him that overcometh will I give to eat of the tree of life which is in the midst of the Paradise of God, and he shall be clothed in white raiment, and I will confess his name before My Father and before His angels." Ah! Lord, and shall I be afraid of this? Shall I shrink back from this? No, I count not my life dear unto me. I have a desire to depart and be with Christ, which is far better. Lord, I beseech Thee show me Thy glory. "Thou canst not see my face and live." Let me die, then, O God, for I do long to see Thy face, I long to behold Thy face in righteousness, and to be satisfied, when I awake, with Thy likeness.

THE NATIONAL BEREAVEMENT.

BY REV. HENRY WARD BEECHER, BROOKLYN.

1. *And Moses went up from the plains of Moab, unto the mountain of Nebo, to the top of Pisgah, that is over against Jericho: and the Lord showed him all the land of Gilead, unto Dan.*

2. *And all Naphtali, and the land of Ephraim and Manasseh, and all the land of Judah, unto the utmost sea.*

3. *And the South, and the plain of the valley of Jericho, the city of palm trees, unto Zoar.*

4. *And the Lord said unto him, This is the land which I sware unto Abraham, unto Isaac, and unto Jacob, saying, I will give it unto thy seed: I have caused thee to see it with thine eyes, but thou shalt not go over thither.*

5. *So Moses, the servant of the Lord, died there in the land of Moab, according to the word of the Lord.*—DEUTERONOMY xxxiv. 1–5.

THERE is no historic figure more noble than that of the Jewish lawgiver. After many thousand years, the figure of Moses is not diminished, but stands up against the background of early days, distinct and individual as if he lived but yesterday. There is scarcely another event in history more touching than his death. He had borne the great burdens of state for forty years, shaped the Jews to a nation, filled out their civil and religious polity, administered their laws, and guided their steps, or dwelt with them in all their sojourning in the wilderness, had mourned in their punishment, kept step with their marches and led them in wars, until the end of their labors drew nigh, the last stages were reached, and Jordan only lay between them and the promised land. The Promised Land! Oh, what yearnings had heaved his breast for that divinely promised place! He had dreamed of it by night, and mused by day; it was holy, and endeared as God's favored spot; it was to be the cradle of an illustrious history. All along his laborious and now weary life, he had aimed at this as the consummation of every desire, the reward of every toil and pain. Then came the word of the Lord to him, "Thou must not go over. Get thee up into the mountain, look upon it, and die." From that silent summit the hoary leader gazed to the north, to the south, to the west, with hungry eyes. The dim outlines rose up, the hazy recesses spoke of quiet valleys. With eager longing, with sad resignation, he looked upon the promised land, that was now the forbidden land. It was a moment's anguish. He forgot all his personal wants, and drank in the vision of his people's home. His work was done. There lay God's promise fulfilled. There was the seat of coming Jerusalem—there the city of Jehovah's King, the sphere of judges and prophets, the mount of sorrow and salvation, the country whence were to flow blessings to all mankind. Joy chased sadness from every feature, and the prophet laid him down and died.

Again a great leader of the people has passed through toil, sorrow, battle and war, and come near to the promised land of peace, into which he might not pass over. Who shall recount our martyr's sufferings for this people? Since the November of 1860, his horizon has been black with storms. By day and by night he trod the way of danger and darkness. On his shoulders rested a government dearer to him than his own life. At its life millions were striking at home; upon it foreign eyes were lowered, and it stood like a lone island in a sea full of storms, and every tide and wave seemed eager to devour it. Upon thousands of hearts great sorrows and anxieties have rested, but upon not one such, and in such measure, as upon that simple, truthful, noble soul, our faithful and sainted Lincoln. Never rising to the enthusiasm of more impassioned natures in hours of hope, and never sinking with the mercurial in hours of defeat to the depths of despondency, he held on with unmovable patience and fortitude, putting caution against hope that it might not be premature, and hope against caution that it might not yield to dread and danger. He wrestled ceaselessly through four black and dreadful purgatorial years, when God was cleansing the sins of this people as by fire. At last the watchman beheld the gray dawn. The mountains began to give forth their forms from out of the darkness, and the East came rushing toward us with arms full of joy for all our sorrows. Then it was for him to be glad exceedingly that had sorrowed immeasurably. Peace could bring to no other heart such joy, such rest, such honor, such trust, such gratitude. He but looked upon it as Moses looked upon the promised land. Then the wail of a nation proclaimed that he had gone from among us.

Not thine the sorrow, but ours. Sainted soul, thou hast indeed entered the promised rest, while we are yet on the march. To us remains the rocking of the deep, the storm upon the land, days of duty and nights of watching; but thou art sphered high above all darkness and fear, beyond all sorrow or weariness. Rest, oh weary heart! Rejoice exceedingly, thou that hast enough suffered. Thou hast beheld Him who invariably led thee in this great wilderness. Thou standest among the elect; around thee are the royal men that have ennobled human life in every age; kingly art thou with glory on thy brow as a diadem, and joy is upon thee for evermore! Over all this land, over all the little cloud of years that now from thine infinite horizon waver back from thee as a spark, thou art lifted up as high as the star is above the clouds that hide *us*, but never reach *it*. In the goodly company on Mount Zion thou shalt find that rest which so many have sought in vain, and thy name, an everlasting name in heaven, shall flourish in fragrance and beauty as long as men shall last upon the earth, or hearts remain to revere Truth, Fidelity, and Goodness.

Never did two such orbs of experience meet in one hemisphere as the joy and sorrow of the same week in this land. The joy was as sudden as if no man had expected it, and as entrancing as if it had fallen from heaven. It rose up over sobriety, and swept business from its moorings, and ran down through the land in irresistible course. Men wept and embraced each other; they sang or prayed, or, deeper yet, could only think thanksgiving and weep gladness. That peace was sure; that government was firmer than ever; that the land was cleansed of plague; that ages were opening to our footsteps and we were to begin a march of blessings; that blood was stanched and scowling enmities sinking like spent storms beneath the horizon; that the dear fatherland, nothing lost, much gained, was to rise in unexampled honor among the nations of the earth—these thoughts, and that undistinguishable throng of fancies, and hopes, and desires, and yearnings, that filled the soul with tremblings like the heated air of midsummer days—all these kindled up such a surge of joy as no words may describe. In an hour, joy lay without a pulse, without a gleam or breath. A sorrow came that swept through the land, as huge storms sweep through the forest and field, rolling thunder along the skies, dishevelling the flames and daunting every singer in the thicket or forest, and pouring blackness and darkness across the land and up the mountains. Did ever so many hearts in so brief a time touch two such boundless feelings? It was the uttermost of joy and the uttermost of sorrow —noon and midnight without space between. The blow brought not a sharp pang. It was so terrible that at first it stunned sensibility. Citizens were like men awakened at midnight by an earthquake, and bewildered to find everything that they were accustomed to trust wavering and falling. The very earth was no longer solid. The first feeling was the least. Men waited to get strength to feel. They wandered in the street as if groping after some impending dread or undeveloped sorrow. They met each other as if each would ask the other, "Am I awake, or do I dream?" There was a piteous helplessness. Strong men bowed down and wept. Other and common griefs belong to some one in chief, they are private property; but this was each man's, and every man's. Every virtuous household in the land felt as if its firstborn were gone. Men took their grief home. They were bereaved, and walked for days as if a corpse lay unburied in their dwellings.

There was nothing else to think of ; they could speak of nothing but that, and yet of that they could speak only falteringly. All business was laid aside ; pleasure forgot to smile. The city for nearly a week ceased to roar, and great Leviathan laid down and was still. Even Avarice stood still, and Greed was strangely moved to generous sympathy with universal sorrow. Rear to his name monuments, found charitable institutions, and with his name above their heights ; but no monument will ever equal the universal, spontaneous, and sublime sorrow that in a moment swept down lines and parties, and covered up animosities, and in an hour brought a divided people into unity of grief and indivisible fellowship of anguish ! For myself, I cannot yet command that quietness of spirit needed for a just and temperate delineation of a man whom goodness has made great.

Reserving that for a future occasion, I pass, then, to some considerations aside from the martyr President's character, which are appropriate to this time and place.

I. Let us not mourn that his departure was so sudden, nor fill our imagination with horror at its method. When good men pray for deliverance from sudden death, it is only that they may not be plunged, without preparation and all disrobed, into the presence of the Judge. Men long eluding and evading sorrow, when suddenly overtaken, seem enchanted to make it great to the uttermost —a habit which is not Christian, although it is doubtless natural. When one is ready to depart, suddenness is a blessing. It is a painful sight to see a tree overthrown by a tornado, wrenched from its foundation and broken down like a reed ; but it is yet more painful to see a vast and venerable tree lingering with vain strife, when age and infirmity have marked it for destruction. The process of decay is a spectacle humiliating and painful ; but it seems good and grand for one to go from duty done with pulse high, with strength full and nerve strong, terminating a noble life in a fitting manner. Nor are we without Scripture warrant for these thoughts : '' Let your loins be girded about. . . . Blessed are those servants whom the Lord, when He cometh, shall find watching.'' Not those who die in a stupor are blessed, but they who go with all their powers about them, and wide awake, as to a wedding. He died watching. He died with armor on. In the midst of hours of labor, in the very heart of patriotic consultations, just returned from camps and council, he was stricken down. No fever dried his blood—no slow waste consumed him. All at once, in full strength and manhood, with his girdle tight about him, he departed and walks with God. Nor was the manner of his death more shocking, if we will surround it with higher associations. Have not thousands of soldiers fallen on the field of battle by the bullets of an enemy, and did not he? All soldiers that fall, ask to depart in the hour of victory, and at such an hour he fell. There was not a poor drummer-boy in all this war that has fallen, for whom the great heart of Lincoln would not have bled ; there is not one private soldier without note or name, slain among thousands and hid in the pit among hundreds, without even the memorial of a separate burial, for whom the President would not have wept. He was a man from and of the people, and now that he who might not bear the march, the toil and battle, with these humble citizens, has been called to die by the bullet, as they were, do you not feel that there is a peculiar fitness to his nature and life, that he should in death be joined with them in a final common experience ? For myself, when any event is susceptible of a nobler garnishing, I cannot understand the nature or character of those who seek to drag it down, degrading and debasing, rather than ennobling and sanctifying it.

II. This blow was but the last of the expiring rebellion ; and as a miniature gives all the form and features of its subject, so, epitomized in this foul act, we find the whole nature and disposition of slavery. It begins in a wanton destruction of all human rights, and in the desecration of all the sanctities of heart and home. It can be maintained only at the sacrifice of every right moral feeling in its abettors and upholders. It is a two-edged sword, cutting both ways, desolating alike the oppressed and the oppressor ; and violently destroying manhood in the victim, it insidiously destroys manhood in the master. No man born and bred under the influence of the accursed thing can possibly maintain his manhood, and I would as soon look for a saint in the darkness of perdition, as for a man of honor in this hot-bed of iniquity. The problem is solved, its demonstration is complete. Slavery wastes its victims, it wastes estates. It destroys public morality, it corrupts manhood in its centre. Communities in which it exists are not to be trusted. Its products are rotten. No timber grown in its cursed soil is fit for the ribs of our ship of state or for our household homes. The people are selfish in their patriotism, and brittle, and whoever leans on them for support is pierced in his hand. Their honor is not honor, but a bastard quality which disgraces the name of honor, and for all time the honor of the supporters of slavery will be throughout the earth a byword and a hissing. Their whole moral nature is death-smitten. The needless rebellion, the treachery of its leaders to oaths and truths, their violations of the commonest principles of fidelity, sitting in senates, councils, and places of trust, only to betray them—the long, general, and unparalleled cruelty to prisoners, without provocation or excuse—their unreasoning malignity and fierceness—all mark the symptoms of the disease of slavery, that is a deadly poison to soul and body. There may be exceptions, of course; but as a rule, malignity is the nature and the essence. Slavery is itself barbarous, and the nation which upholds and protects it is likewise barbarous. It is fit that its expiring blow should be made to take away from men the last forbearance, the last pity, and fire the soul with invincible determination that the breeding ground of such mischiefs and monsters shall be utterly and forever destroyed! It needed not that the assassin should put on paper his belief in slavery. He was but the sting of the monster slavery which has struck this blow, and as long as this nation lasts, it will not be forgotten that we have had our "Martyr President," nor while Heaven holds high court or Hell rots beneath, will it be forgotten that slavery murdered him.

III. This blow was aimed at the life of the government and of the nation. Abraham Lincoln was slain, but America was meant. The man was cast down, but the government was smitten at. The President was killed, but national life-breathing freedom and benignity were sought. He of Illinois, as a private man, might have been detested, but it was because he represented the cause of just government, liberty, and kindness, he was slain. It was a crime against universal government, and was aimed at all. Not more was it at us than at England or France, or any well-compacted government. It was aimed at mankind. The whole world will repudiate it and stigmatize it as a deed without a redeeming feature. It was not the deed of the oppressed, stung to madness by the cruelty of the oppressor; it was not the avenging hand against the heart of a despot ; it was the exponent of a venomous hatred of liberty, and the avowed advocacy of slavery.

IV. But the blow has signally failed. The cause is not stricken, but strengthened ; men hate slavery the more and love liberty better. The nation is dissolved, but only in tears, and stands more square and solid to-day than any pyramid in Egypt. The government is not weakened, it is strengthened. How readily and easily the ranks closed up ! We shall be more true to every instinct of liberty, to the Constitution, and to the principles of universal freedom. Where, in any other community, the crowned head being stricken by the hand of an assassin, would the funds have stood firm as did ours, not wavering the half of one per cent.? After four years of drastic war, of heavy drafts upon the people, on top of all, the very head of the nation is stricken down, and the funds never quiver, but stand as firm as the granite ribs in the mountains. Republican institutions have been vindicated in this very experience. God has said, by the voice of His Providence, that republican liberty based upon universal freedom shall be as firm as the foundations of the globe.

V. I observe lastly : Even he who now sleeps has by this event been clothed with new influence. Dead, he speaks to men who now willingly hear what before they shut their ears to. Like the words of Washington, will his simple, mighty words be pondered on by your children and children's children. Men will receive a new accession to their love of patriotism, and will for his sake guard with more zeal the welfare of the whole country. On the altar of this martyred patriot I swear you to be more faithful to your country. They will, as they follow his hearse, swear a new hatred to that slavery which has made him a martyr. By this solemn spectacle I swear you to renewed hostility to slavery, and to a never-ending pursuit of it to its grave. They will admire and imitate his firmness in justice, his inflexible conscience for the right, his gentleness and moderation of spirit, and I swear you to a faithful copy of his justice, his mercy, and his gentleness.

You I can comfort, but how can I speak to the twilight millions who revere his name as the name of God ? Oh, there will be wailing for him in hamlet and cottage, in woods and wilds, and the fields of the South. Her dusky children looked on him as on a Moses come to lead them out from the land of bondage. To whom can we direct them but to the Shepherd of Israel, and to His care commit them for help, for comfort and protection? And now the martyr is moving in triumphal march, mightier than when alive. The nation rises up at his coming. Cities and States are his pallbearers, and cannon beat the hours with solemn procession. Dead! dead! dead! he yet speaketh! Is Washington dead? Is Hampden dead? Is David dead? Now, disenthralled of flesh, and risen to the unobstructed sphere where passion never comes, he begins his illimitable work. His life is grafted upon the Infinite, and will be fruitful now as no earthly life can be. Pass on, thou that hast overcome! Your sorrows, oh people, are his pæan! Your bells, and bands, and muffled drums sound in his ear a triumph. You wail and weep here; God makes it triumph there. Four years ago, oh Illinois, we took him from your midst, an untried man from among the people. Behold, we return him a mighty conqueror. Not thine, but the nation's; not ours, but the world's! Give him place, ye prairies! In the midst of this great continent his dust shall rest, a sacred treasure to myriads who shall pilgrim to that shrine, to kindle anew their zeal and patriotism. Ye winds that move over the mighty spaces of the West, chant his requiem! Ye people, behold a martyr, whose blood, as articulate words, pleads for fidelity, for law, for liberty.

SORROW FOR THE DEATH OF FRIENDS.

BY I. S. SPENCER, D.D., BROOKLYN.

But I would not have you to be ignorant, brethren, concerning them which are asleep, that ye sorrow not even as others which have no hope.—1 THESS. iv. 13.

AT the death of the pious, Christians should not sorrow *as* those do who are not Christians. This, I suppose, is the meaning of the text, and this the single thought which solicits your attention during this sermon.

I. We will restrict the application of this principle. Some sorrows of the irreligious are not to be condemned or shunned. We will maintain that part of the sorrow of those who have no hope is not improper for a believer.

II. We will apply the principle, and show what *kind* of sorrow common among unbelievers, is improper for pious people.

When unbelievers are called to part with Christian friends by death, their hearts are affected with grief ; and *some* of their sorrow is not to be considered as improper for those who have hope in Christ. Let us see : we name three particular ideas.

1. There is a sorrow arising from the recollection of past *endearments*.

Persons without piety are affected with it when their friends die : and the text would not forbid this sorrow to them or to believers. On such an occasion, how natural it is for the mind to turn back upon the past ! We recall the benefits of our departed friend. Our mind wanders back upon the years we have lived together. We remember the instances of kindness, the days of intimacy, the times in which the cares and counsels of our friend aided us. We recall the seasons of fear, of perplexity and discouragement, when our friend took us to his bosom, and we learned to know there was one spot on earth where we could weep and be comforted. We recollect how our distresses melted away under the soothings that fell from those lips, and the kindness that beamed on us from those eyes. But that bosom is cold, those lips are silent, those eyes are sealed up in death ! One for whom our labors were endured, and round whom our hearts hung, is gone— he will meet us no more ! And now we turn our thoughts down to the future, and are sadly reminded that we have met with a loss never to be retrieved ! We are to go abroad : and amid trouble, toil, and unkindness, our heart cannot turn back for its solace to the friend who used to cheer us when we came home ! We are to come home : there is a voice wanting in the circle ! there is a seat vacant at the table ! there is a heart that once opened to us, now gone—gone forever ! We are compelled to have sorrowful recollections of the changes that have passed upon our lot ! Midnight has settled down upon our soul !

This is a kind of sorrow which belongs to those *which have no hope*, and this sorrow is not to be censured in a Christian. It is proper to dwell on the endearments of the past ; to remember the fidelity of our friend ; the counsels he gave us, the conversations of frankness, and the hints of delicacy so tenderly flung out, lest our sensibilities should be wounded. It is right to remember the language of the death-bed—those tears, those prayers, those anxieties of expiring nature !' Yes, Jesus may weep at the grave of Lazarus : her friends may weep when they *show the coats and garments which Dorcas made while she was with them.* David may go up to his chamber, weeping as he goes : "Oh ! my son Absalom ! my son, my son Absalom ! would God I had died for thee, oh, Absalom, my son, my son !" This is one kind of sorrow which the text would not censure.

2. There is a sorrow arising from the recollection of our past *failures.* It is sometimes a very bitter sorrow. When we are parting with our friends we are prone to think how little we prized them, and how very improperly we requited their kindnesses while they were living. Even if we did not blame ourselves for lack of tenderness and affection while they were alive, we are very apt to find good reasons for doing it when they are dead. Then, how every unkind word, every ungracious look, every emotion of indulged resentment, will come thronging over our memory, and deepening the poignancy of our anguish ! Oh, how we wish we could live those days over again, when our ingratitude or unkindness wounded the heart which will bleed for us no more ! Oh, if we could put hearing into the ears of the dead, how we would confess our faults, and beg forgiveness for the errors which our thoughtlessness committed ! This is a kind of sorrow which children often feel when they lose their parents. They bitterly remember their disobedience, their petulance, their unkindness, and the lack of gratitude for those favors and that love which flowed out in such numerous instances of tenderness from the heart of the parent that never will bleed at their unkindness again. That heart has ceased to beat. It is cold and dead. Ah ! if they could bring back its love, and put its wonted sensibility into it for a single hour, what tears of penitence they would shed ! how fondly they would ask forgiveness ! and with what diminished sorrow they would resign again to insensibility in death the heart that had forgiven them !

This kind of sorrow is common with those *who have no hope,* and it is allowable for believers. It is nothing more than a tender and affectionate justice. It is due to the dead. It is not one of the deceptions of grief, but it arises from mournful deficiencies which affliction brings to our mind, and compels us to weep over, and weep the more bitterly because now we can do nothing else : the dead are beyond our confessions and our unkindness forever. This sorrow arises from the honesty of grief. It is profitable for the living. It tends to humble us, and tends to make us more careful and affectionate to our surviving friends, when our heart bleeds at the remembrance of our cruelty to those who are now dead.

3. There is a sorrow concerning them which are asleep, connected with the consideration of *our loss*. You will excuse me for not attempting to sketch it. I cannot describe it. I remember my father ! And I am sure no words could give any idea of the feelings of desolation that came over me when I came back from his funeral and found myself fatherless, young, unbefriended, and poor. Oh, what a dark wilderness the world was ! Who should take care of me ? Who should defend me against the injustice of a cold world ? Who should educate me, and fit me for the conflicts of life ? Who should soothe me when I should be sick ? Who should gently counsel me any longer, and let me pour my young sorrows into his bosom ? No, no ! language has no terms to tell the sorrows that came on my heart. There is something that cannot be described, when we realize the loss we have met with by the death of our friends. Some of you do not need any description. The wounds are fresh and bleeding in the hearts of not a few who are here.

And if you have any doubt whether religion allows of sorrow on account of such a loss, look at bereaved families, and you will doubt it no more. You shall see little children fatherless, stripped ! But here again I must stop. I cannot speak of it. Let the *facts* preach to you.

These considerations (and we might add to them) are enough to show that there is a kind of sorrow for the death of friends which affects those who *have no hope*, and which is not disallowed to those who have hope in God. This is the *restriction* in the application of the text.

II. We proposed, in the second place, to show what kind of sorrow, very common with them who *have no hope*, is improper for believers. Five items will include all we mean.

1. With those *who have no hope, sorrow concerning them which are asleep* sometimes becomes *unsubmissive*. In the freshness of

our affections it is very difficult for us to tell (and no one can tell for us) whether our sorrow is tinctured with rebellion or not. Certainly, no one in such sorrow *intends* to be rebellious. But when the full sense of trial comes over the heart, we are exposed to feel that God is dealing hardly with us. Persons without faith do sometimes feel so. The text reproves *them*, and admonishes *you* that ye sorrow not like them.

Submission under such strokes may be a most difficult thing, but it is a Christian duty. Sorrow and submission should go together; not that we should be willing to be miserable, but that we should be willing that God should reign; and if His dispensations cause us sorrow, we should be willing that our tears should flow. Two considerations especially ought to restrain us from a murmuring and unsubmissive sorrow. One is the righteous sovereignty of God. We are His, and our friends are His. We live by His sufferance, and die at His bidding. "The Lord killeth and maketh alive, He bringeth down to the grave and bringeth up." The other consideration is, that we are unable to penetrate His designs; and the things which seem to us most severe are often to be numbered among our most remarkable mercies. Let us take them submissively at His hand. If there is goodness anywhere, it is to be found in God. Let us trust Him. Let us trust Him in the dark. Let us resign up our friends to death like old Eli, and say over their coffins and their graves: "It is the Lord, let Him do what seemeth Him good." Let us receive the cup of bitterness out of His hand like Jesus Christ: "The cup which my Father giveth me, shall I not drink it?"

I am not going to undervalue the sentiments of grief or the feelings of submission which often dwell in unsanctified hearts when friends die. I am sure that in such cases there are sensibilities and sentiments deserving of all respect. And it would be contrary alike to the tenderness of humanity and of God to insult the wretchedness of the weeping unbeliever in such cases. But we must honor religion. It deserves honor. Here, not less than on every other point, it surpasses any ordinary measure of humanity. We must not undervalue the sentiments which grace implants. And it is a truth—it is a blessed truth—that faith in God produces a *kind* of submission which unbelief knows nothing about. Unbelief submits at best *because it must*. The time has come. An inexorable destiny has taken away a friend ; and the power, the right, the wisdom of God in doing it, are not to be called in question. The heart bows before the majesty of a throne which the eyes cannot gaze upon, and which the arms cannot embrace. But it may—it ought to be different with a believer. While his heart bleeds under the stroke, he looks up to the God that smote him : "Though He slay me, yet will I trust in Him." He turns from the fresh grave of his parents : "When my father and my mother forsake me, the Lord will take me up." He submits, not merely because he *must*, not because it is *right*, but because he *loves* to submit ; and never does he cling to the throne of God with such a willing and submissive embrace as when his dearest friends have dropped from his arms.

Sometimes it takes repeated bereavements to bring a believer to this sweet submission. A Christian of Florida, of whom I have some knowledge, once said : "After my husband died, and I had mourned bitterly and long, my heart turned to my children. When my first child died, all my grief came back upon me. The second died, and I murmured ! The third died, and I was entirely rebellious ; I thought God was cruelly and improperly severe upon me ! But now, the fourth and *last one* is taken away, and I am satisfied. I *know* that the rod with which my heavenly Father hath smitten me was cut from the tree of life." Grief ought to be submissive. To make it so, sometimes stroke follows stroke.

At the funeral of President Davies, just as the people were about to take up the coffin to remove it to the burial, his mother, an aged widow, came to take the last look of her son. She gazed intently upon him—the tears fell upon the face of the corpse as she bent over it, and then, retiring a single step as she still gazed upon him, she exclaimed, "There lies my only son ; my only earthly comfort and earthly support. But there lies the will of God, and I am satisfied." Sorrow, tearful though it be, ought to be submissive.

2. Under such afflictions as the text mentions, those *who have no hope* are sometimes inconsolable. They feel their loss. They cannot but feel it. The heart is robbed and desolate. Indeed, they seem to think it due to their departed friend to resemble Rachel, and *refuse to be comforted*. And their consolation comes

only from the fact that the lapse of time wears out the traces of grief. It would be easy to apologize for this, and justify it too, if we had no Bible and no Christ. Situated as we are in this world, all our blessings seem to be wrapped up in a single point. That point is—the father of a family—is an only child—or the wife of one's bosom. On this point we rest. We have nothing earthly without it. We are compelled to feel so. And when we have seen surviving parents committing their only child to its little grave ; or seen the mother bedewing with her tears the coffin of a mature daughter, who had become companion as well as child ; or seen the strong man robbed of the wife of his bosom ; or seen the widow and her children turn away from the grave where they had just buried their father and their friend, who has not felt, that if Heaven could excuse any sin, it must be the sin of that heart which should refuse to be comforted ?

But after all, the believer ought not to mourn as those *who have no hope*. His sorrow ought not to be inconsolable. Child, wife, and father, should not be such heart-idols to us that we cannot give them up. God, the blessed God, should be the object of our warmest attachment and our firmest confidence. We ought to have only a submissive attachment to the objects of earthly and transient good. They that "use this world ought to be as though they used it not, for the fashion of this world passeth away. Put not your trust in princes, nor in great men, in whom there is no help : his soul goeth forth, he returneth to the earth, and in that very day his thoughts perish." A believer may be consoled. He ought not to sorrow as those *who have no hope*. His best friend can never be taken from him ; his firmest support can never be laid in the grave. His God liveth, and he may pour his sorrows into His bosom and be comforted.

3. The sorrow of those *who have no hope* has a character and depth which arise from their own unbelief and the false estimates they put upon the world. They judge of the happiness of others very much as they judge of their own. And since their own felicity is found in the world, they sorrow for those who are taken out of it as if they were deprived at once of all their enjoyments. They think of the dead very much as if stripped of every comfort and consigned to the dark and cheerless tomb. This is common. Go out with me, and I will lead you to a desolated habitation,

where the widow weeps with her fatherless children, and bemoans the lot which has taken the husband and father away from the comforts of life. Draw near. Listen. What is she saying? "Alas," says she, "that dear companion of my life has gone! That friend on whom I leaned, that father of my children, that tender husband who sought to do me good, has gone from all the enjoyments I hoped he would have shared with me! He sleeps in the cold grave! No comfort can reach him; no voice of friendship breaks the eternal silence of the tomb!" Turn again to another habitation. Here is a mother, but she is childless. Fresh tears flow unbidden at the recollection of her babe. "Poor babe," she is saying, "he sleeps in his little grave! No mother's kindness can reach him! I can never do him good; he has gone to his cheerless and lonely tomb!"

Sorrow like this is the sorrow of those *who have no hope*. In such cases the Christian should not be like them. He need not: no, he need *not*. That little babe is in heaven. That pious husband would gladly have remained to comfort the partner of his life, support her children, and aim to lead them all to salvation; but grace has taken him to glory. As Christians we are extremely liable to forget that which, as Christians, we rejoice to believe. We believe the immortality of the soul. We believe at the moment of death the soul of the Christian takes its flight to heaven. To die is gain. Jesus Christ verifies His promise, "I will come again and receive you to myself, that where I am there ye may be also." The departed babe and the departed believer have gone to the bosom of God. We ought not to sorrow as those *who have no hope*. We ought rather to rejoice that our pious friends have died on earth to live in heaven. Death has done that for them which our affection tried in vain to do. Many, many times we saw them "tossed with tempest and not comforted." But now they have entered into a haven of rest. Would we wish them back again to be lashed with the storms of life? Many times we were unable to dry up their tears and make them happy, but now God hath wiped all tears from their faces. While they were with us we heard them often lamenting their sin, and expressing many a bitter fear that they should never reach heaven. But now they are afflicted no more. Now they fear hell no more. Now they see God face to face. "They are come unto Mount

Zion, and unto the city of the living God, the heavenly Jerusalem, and to an innumerable company of angels, to the general assembly and church of the first-born, which are written in heaven." They are now like God in perfect holiness; the measure of their bliss is full. "Blessed are the dead that die in the Lord, for they rest from their labors."

Our feelings do dishonor our faith when we think of death as a loss to the pious. It is gain. It may be loss to us; but it is gain, it is all gain to them.

4. Those who have no hope, yield up their friends to death, with—(I am sorry to be compelled to say this, but it is true, it is greatly true; I must say it)—they yield up their friends to death, with the sorrow of an *eternal separation*. It is so commonly—not always, perhaps, but ordinarily it is just this. Unbelievers seldom joyfully think of meeting their pious friends in heaven. Dearly as they prized them, they think little of meeting them again. They do sometimes rejoice that their departed friend has left behind him evidences of piety, and is now happy in heaven. But they have no pious hopes of their own which assure them that they shall yet meet him and be united with him forever in bonds more endearing and tender than any which death has broken. At the mouth of the tomb they give up their friend *forever!* They resign the parent, the brother, the child, in the sadness of an eternal separation! Their sorrow is not assuaged with the assurance that that parent shall own them in heaven—that that brother shall take them by the hand on the hills of the heavenly city—that that child, with more than an angel's bliss and glory, shall come back to their bosom in the eternal kingdom of God.

But believers sorrow not so over the death of saints. They look forward to a happy meeting. Their friend is "not lost, but gone before." When *they* shall be released from the body and take their flight, that friend perhaps will rush to welcome them into heaven, and lead them up to the embrace of the blood-stained Redeemer that brought them there. Heart shall again open to heart, and love mingle with love in the bliss and glory of the city of God. And when the scenes of this earth shall be no more, and the time of the resurrection of the dead shall be sounded by the voice of the archangel and the trump of God, these blessed souls shall come back again to enter into spiritual bodies, "made like unto

Christ's own glorious body, not having spot or wrinkle or any such thing." Communicants, friends separated by death, shall see one another again. Pious ministers and pious people shall meet at the mouth of the opened tomb. Pious parents shall see their pious children. Friend shall greet friend, and brother shall greet brother, as graveyards are broken up in the day of the resurrection. They shall be caught up together in the clouds to meet their Lord in the air ; so shall they ever be with the Lord. Comfort one another with these words. Sorrow not as those who have no hope.

Death and the grave are dreadful realities. We shudder at dissolution. We fear the judgment of the Most High God, and are overwhelmed when we stand just on the entrance of eternity. We know the world is little to us. We shall soon leave it! Covered with crape, we are travelling toward the resting-place of the dust of our fathers. Our sins, our deathless souls, our God—oh, what amazing anxieties crowd on our aching hearts! But in the Gospel we see everything provided for us that sin, and death, and the grave, and the judgment, and eternity can make us need. If we are to die, Jesus Christ can sympathize with us : He has died before us ; He has died for us. Oh death, where is thy sting? Death may be a terror to nature ; but death is the servant of the Christian. Death is yours. Ye are not death's. He shall not hurt you. All he can do is to take up the trembling believer, and put him into the arms of Jesus Christ, when He comes again to receive him to Himself. If we are to give our bodies to the grave, we know who owns it, who has conquered it, and robbed it of its victory. Ah, more : we know *how* he robbed it. Our best Friend, our Almighty Saviour, has been down into its bosom. He has softened, sweetened, sanctified that bed of sleep. Oh ! if I am a Christian, I would rather go by that dark path to heaven, than go like Elijah with his chariot and horses of fire ! It will be more like Christ. I shall lie where He lay. I shall prove His love. I shall experience His power. This dead body shall rise ; and in heaven, a sinner saved, redeemed, loved, raised from the dead and taken into the family of God—in heaven, I shall love to tell what Jesus Christ hath done for me. Angels shall hear it! I will tell it to the old prophets ! I will hunt up my fathers who go there before me, and tell it to them ! I will wait for my children to die, and, as they come there, I will tell it to them ! Oh, my God, my God! this is enough! I will praise Thee for it forever! Oh! I am comforted now. I can bury my friends, my minister, my father, my daughter; I can set my foot upon the grave; and, with a heart filled with comfort from the God of heaven, I can wait the day when that stilled heart shall beat again, and those dumb lips shall speak from the opened coffin, and we shall be caught up together in the air. "For our conversation is in heaven, whence also we look for the Saviour, the Lord Jesus Christ, who shall change our vile body, that it may be fashioned like unto His glorious body, according to the working whereby He is able to subdue all things unto Himself."

5. Those who have no hope are exercised in such cases of affliction (I am ashamed to say it as much as I was sorry to say the other, but it is true; I am compelled to say it)—those without hope are exercised with a very *ineffectual* sorrow. How few of them make any good use of the affliction. We see them afflicted often. Where is the sinner without hope who has lived in the world twenty years and not had his heart torn and forced to bleed at the death of some loved and valued friend? But what is the result? We see those without hope, then downcast and troubled. We go to the funeral of their friends; we bear them to the tomb; we come to sympathize with them and beseech them to lay it to heart, for such is the end of all flesh. But such persons —these same persons so afflicted, so tender and heart-stricken— do not come at the next communion to the Lord's Supper. They mourned their friends, they remembered for a little while that the way he had gone was the way of all the earth. And they believed, too, that such an affliction would not be lost upon them— that the counsels and entreaties of the dying would not be to them a vain lesson. But they do not come to repentance. And while their happy friend is in the bosom of God, they continue the same rejection which gave the last and the deepest pang to the heart of that friend in his hour of death. The grass has not sprung green upon the turf that covers him before they are embarked again in the world as eager as ever, dishonoring his memory by their transient impressions, and his anxiety by forgetfulness of God.

Christians ought not to sorrow like them. Such sorrow dishonors the dead. It pours contempt upon the anxieties and prayers of the dying, and insults by neglect the grace of God which enabled them to die in peace. No, no! let your afflictions make you better. If you are Christians, let your sorrows lead you to mourn the sin which brought death into the world, and trust more firmly in Christ who vanquished death for you. Make due improvement of your afflictions—solemn improvement. God means something by it when He afflicts you. Ask Him what He means. Let not the affliction sit lightly upon you, and for a mere transient week. You do not sorrow in a proper manner if your sorrows do not make you better Christians. They ought to make you better. They ought to make you love prayer more, love Christ more, love one another more. They ought to bring you to the communion-table on next Lord's day in a more tender, and holy, and happy frame. Death is doing up his work in this communion. And, my brethren, shall we not make haste and get ready to die? Where the next blow shall fall, God only knows. This father, this mother, this child, this minister, may fall next. Oh, God! take none of us away unprepared! Plunge none of us into hell! Lead us by our warnings to our Saviour; and then come—come when thou wilt—and take us from the pains of our death-bed home to the bosom of our God.

THE PURPOSE OF DIVINE CHASTISEMENTS.

BY ARTHUR T. PIERSON, D.D., PHILADELPHIA.

For they verily for a few days chastened us after their own pleasure; but he for our profit, that we might be partakers of his holiness.—HEB. xii. 10.

IN nothing, perhaps, is it so hard to feel for ourselves and to help others to feel that God is good, as in life's great afflictions. We are so prone to look only at the present sorrow and forget the future joy; so apt to dwell on the aggravations of grief rather than its alleviations; so inclined to interpret God's dealings by our sinful deserts rather than His pitying love, that, under the burden of some severe and sudden calamity, we feel more like Job's wife, tempted to "curse God and die," than like that Old Testament saint himself, prompted to say, "Blessed be the name of the Lord." Nor can it be thought very strange if, when one stands and looks upon what De Quincey calls a "household wreck," in which are brought to ruin not only all one's bright hopes, but one's best joys and purest loves, so that the very heart itself seems crushed and buried beneath the fragments of its idols—it is not altogether strange, if, looking upon what to all human sight is wanton waste, unmingled woe, one cannot, under the sudden paralysis of the shock, feel that such a blow was from a hand guided only by love. Is it strange, too, if they who behold such ruin of joy and hope and love and life itself, are struck dumb—if words of solace or even of sympathy die on our lips, and we who would fain comfort and console, stand speechless and, looking upon these earthly wrecks of happiness and hope, ask, "Why is this so? Can it be that there is mercy in such seeming wrath?" But if we *are* speechless, there is this comfort even to our dumbness: we need not speak, for God has spoken. In ways without number, under every variety of figure, by every mode of speech and form of illustration, He assures us that "He doth not afflict willingly nor grieve the children of men;" that whatever sorrow He sends upon us is "solely for our good." In the text, the climax of all possible representations of this truth is reached. If this do not convince our understanding and appeal to our hearts, nothing can. God condescends to reason with us, from the analogy of parental affection, drawing both argument and illustration. We have often felt the beauty of the methods elsewhere used for presenting the same essential truth, as, for example, where God compares himself to the refiner of silver, melting His people down in the crucible of affliction to "purge away their dross;" but in *this* comparison is couched the beauty of an unutterable tenderness. You know how a father feels toward a son—how he yearns over him; how he loves him; how he lives for him. You know how a father shrinks from the necessity of chastising the son, yet nerves himself to the duty of correcting his faults, lest sparing the rod he may spoil the child. You know with what an agony of reluctance a father surrenders his son to the surgeon's hand, to save him from death, or the living death of a distorted and crippled form; how he would fain himself lie down and submit to be bound with cords and probed by keen blades to save his boy the pain and peril of such an operation; how his father-heart sickens and his face grows ashy pale as he witnesses the suffering by which alone the child may be saved from death or deformity. Do you understand that? God can then speak intelligibly to you. "Like as a father pitieth his children, so the Lord pitieth them that fear him." If you murmur at God in the time of your calamity, He says to you, "Ye have forgotten the exhortation which speaketh unto you as unto children: *My son*, despise not thou the chastening of the Lord, nor faint when thou art rebuked of him: For whom the Lord loveth he chasteneth."

He addresses our parental instincts, and asks us whether we do not ourselves know that love and chastening are not contradictory or inconsistent. Even so, says God, do I love whom I chasten, and scourge my every son. Nay, He presses the analogy further, and says to us that we are to regard chastening as an evidence of love, a confirmation of our sonship, and because all true sons are partakers of this fatherly discipline, its absence in our case would bring into doubt the legitimacy of our very claim to be called God's children.

Then, as this fatherly argument proceeds, He appeals to our best judgment whether, if we yield submission and reverence to our fathers in the flesh, we shall not be in subjection to Him who represents the perfection of all fatherhood and fatherliness.

I need not say that this doctrine of *Love* as the impulse and interpreter of *affliction* is peculiarly Biblical. When calamity befell a pagan he beheld in it a mark of divine displeasure, and at once set himself at work to appease the wrath of Deity. There is a tradition which accounts for the existence of an "altar to the unknown God" at Athens, upon the ground of an attempt to remove the scourge of pestilence. It is said that when offerings to every known deity had been offered in vain, it was suggested that some yet unknown god might be the author of their calamities, and hence the altar with its inscription. Even the ancient people of God were very slow to accept the right view of God's chastisements. It is true many of God's severer dealings were *in His displeasure*, yet still not in wrath to destroy, so much as in love to reclaim His erring people; and only assuming a destructive form when the sacrifice of some seemed to be essential to the salvation of the rest. It was very proper then, that in this epistle to the *Hebrews*, the apostle should inculcate the Christian doctrine of God's fatherly chastisements, teaching us to regard trial as a discipline of love and not a visitation of wrath : a discipline of parental love, a pitying love, and not to the cold attachment of a mere educator or disciplinarian.

And this is the Scriptural introduction to the exact thought of the text. God has shewn us by a glimpse into the father's heart what is *His motive* or impulse in our chastening, illustrating this love by a familiar comparison ; in the text He shows us His *object*, and now the comparison becomes contrast. Our earthly parents "for a few days" and "after their own pleasure chasten us ;" our heavenly Father, with eternal results in view and for *our good*, that we may "share His own holiness," corrects us. The perfect Parent, the faultless Father above, bids us reason from the imperfection of parent love and wisdom and knowledge up to the Father of all, that in His infinite insight and foresight and affection we may find solace and comfort.

I. The first element of contrast suggested by the text is this Our human parents punish passionately, and not always deliberately. Without meaning to, without, perhaps, being conscious of it, they are sometimes simply giving vent to impatient, excited, or even angry feeling, in chastising their offspring. Brethren, these things ought not so to be ; yet but few parents who have any force of character can truly say that they have never allowed passion to gratify itself through the parent's rod of correction. Were it not for separating too widely the offense and its punishment, would it not be well always to defer the correction till it can be calmly, dispassionately administered ? It may seem harsh even for the word of God to hint to parents that they in any measure chasten their children "for their own pleasure." Yet we cannot but think, after giving this passage careful study, that there is here a divine rebuke of a great wrong which we cover up from ourselves. We too often chastise our children in anger, and from anger. Without deliberate malice or conscious indulgence of our bad passions, we undoubtedly do inflict many punishments of more or less severity that would not be inflicted at all had we ourselves under perfect control. The impatient impulse, the caprice of the moment, rules us and puts into the correction the sharpness and severity, it may be violence, of an indignation by no means wholly righteous. The text literally reads, "they indeed for a few days chastened us according to what seemed good to them," and will bear the interpretation which we have given, and which seems to have been in the mind of our English translators when they rendered, "After their own pleasure"—that is, according to what seemed good to their caprice or impulse. There is no doubt some of us can recall instances in which it still seems to us, after the lapse of many years, that in perhaps a deserved chastisement our parents were unconsciously gratifying their own bad temper quite as much as they were seeking our good ; and rare as it is to be hoped such cases are, they are not so infrequent as not to need an admonition and to justify the divine contrast.

God never acts from impulse, in haste, or in a passion, and all representations in the Bible that so impress us do that injustice to His character which cannot be avoided while terms which strictly apply only to *man* are the only terms by which the idea of God *can* be conveyed to us. Yet while using human language, drawn from human experience and limited by human consciousness in representing God to man, let us remember that these terms really have an entirely different significance applied to Him. God is not susceptible of anything like passion as we understand it— either in its impulsiveness, impetuosity, malice, or malignity. Even God's anger, mighty and terrible as it is, is the unchanging, invariable hatred of evil—the anger of principle, not of passion— calm even in its fury, slow even in its haste, cool even in its heat. Our anger is like the agitation of a shallow lake, rippled with every breeze, lashed into foaming fury by every wind and tempest, yet falling into calmness when the exciting causes are removed. God's anger is like the great sea heaving its unfathomable depths, moving with solemn majesty in mountain waves. Nay, rather like that sea itself, which in its most perfect calm has a mighty undercurrent that eternally and uninterruptedly sways with resistless momentum against every obstacle, and makes the very mountains abandon their footing and the rocks crumble.

All this is our assurance in affliction that God can not deal harshly, severely, or unjustly with us. His anger is not " slow to rise ;" it never *rises*, it never gathers, not even from all eternity, for that would imply change in God. No, it is the law of His very being that He hates evil and with an unchanging anger abhors sin. His anger is never greater at one moment than another, though its manifestation may vary. If, therefore, a blow from His rod fall quick and sudden upon us, let us not feel that God is in a passion—that does Him injustice. He is a tender father, infinitely loving, yet dispassionately dealing with us. With the calmness of eternal patience, the steadfastness of eternal love, He afflicts us solely for our good.

II. Again, our earthly parents chastise us *punitively and not correctively*. They aim more to punish the offence than to correct the evil and reform the evil-doer. Here is another way in which passion often inflicts chastisement. An earthly father is justly indignant at the wrong done—not angry for the act as implying disrespect for his own authority, but disregard of the right. He is grieved and rightly angry because the son has offended against truth, virtue, honesty, integrity. This is a far nobler passion than the caprices of ill temper, yet it is doubtful whether a parent can be sure of inflicting profitable correction under its influence. It hurries one into a method of punishment which hardens rather than softens—which is ill adapted to the peculiar temperament of the child, which may restrain from similar offences, if at all, only from fear of the rod, and not at all from love of the right. It should ever be borne in mind that the highest purpose of all punishment is not the vindication of a principle, but the reformation of an offender, or at least the salvation of others from similar sins. A principle is a cold, abstract truth ; every man represents an immortal soul. To contend for a principle is noble, but oh, how insignificant all else in comparison with the welfare of a soul ! Now there can be no doubt that earthly parents too often think more of giving the offence its due than of making the offender hate it. Sometimes, should we patiently but lovingly exhibit the wrong, showing to the child its hatefulness and deformity, it might make all punishment unnecessary, or it might make a milder form equally and even more effectual. We should study more the differences between children, and adapt our discipline to their individual education in right living. What if a punishment, inflicted for anger, only provokes them to anger ; what if the severity of our correction for dishonesty only prompts to slyness and concealment ! What if chastisement for disobedience only makes them hate our authority and despise our restraints ! Oh, let us not forget that true love of the parent may help to kindle that true love of the right which is stronger than any fear of correction. The word here rendered "chasten," means educate. All *God's* chastening is meant to *educate* His children; His dealings are designed as a discipline. He must punish our offences against natural and moral laws; but the grand end He proposes to Himself is to secure our sanctification and salvation. We do our heavenly Father great wrong in our hearts when we complain of His dealings as severe. This is to charge God foolishly. Because we are greater sufferers than many others, because we are visited with greater calamities than they, it does not follow that we are greater sinners than they, or that God is simply punishing us —or as we sometimes think, persecuting us—with harsher judgments! This may do for a pagan, but never for a Christian! God teaches us that with Him fatherly *pity* prompts His chastisements. Even where he visits overwhelming punishment, sweeping the offender from earth, it is that the exhibition of His just displeasure against sin may serve to deter others. In all his chastening He dealeth with us as with sons. He aims to produce in us a higher life—to elevate our affections, to purify our purposes, to produce in our hearts and lives some great and grand result. If He deals with us less gently than others, it is not because He feels less loving, but because our natures, differently constituted, demand different treatment. For in all God's afflictions He consults the exact temperament of His children. He knoweth our frame. Our secret habits of thought and feeling are all familiar to Him: even where we are deceived, He cannot be. He never inflicts an unnecessary blow, nor twice afflicts where once will suffice, nor uses one method or means when another will answer better or even so well. The whole tendency of Scripture teaching is to instil in us confidence in God's wisdom and love. We are to accept His afflictive dealings as designed not to punish our sins, but to purify our souls, and prayerfully seek to know what in our hearts He would change, what in our habits He would reform, what in our lives He would remove or remodel, and instead of complaining of His severity, confide in His affection, and co-operate with Him in producing every good result. Our first question in affliction should be reverently, "Why is this? Lord, what wilt thou have me to do?" In this way we may make further chastisement unnecessary for the same result, and although what God does we know not now, we shall know hereafter. It is one of the most palpable facts of history that the men who have wielded the mightiest moral influence have been prepared for it by the severest divine discipline. The reason is plain. Only from a strong nature can we expect the moral power which is to mould other men and work great results; yet in order that a strong nature be subjected to Christ, disciplinary measures are necessary which would not be needed for those of milder and weaker native character. Look at the long, hard course of suffering which fitted Martin Luther to lead the armies of the Reformation ! No less means would have subdued that great will and made its stubbornness an element of steadfastness and stability. A degree of heat that must melt down the harder metals is far more intense than that which melts the softest ; yet when made into vessels, that which it took the hotter fire to fuse is far the stronger and more enduring and serviceable ; while you can bend and twist the other, this is unaffected by hard usage. So does God use the chastening rod with tender consideration for our temperament and constitution, adapting His discipline to our need. If we desire the largest fitness for service, we must submit to His wise chastening.

III. Again, our earthly parents chasten us *imperfectly, not infallibly ;* according to their own fallible judgment of right and wrong. This thought is suggested in the text by the phrase, "according to their own pleasure," literally according to what *seemed* good or right to them. The most conscientious and careful parents may sometimes commit a great wrong, punishing with unnecessary severity, or, it may be, unjustly and mistakenly. They may exaggerate the guilt of the offence, or fail to adapt the correction to the nature of the wrong and the temperament of the evil-doer. In a word, all our parental training is necessarily imperfect and fallible at best. Parental love is imperfect, and so is parental wisdom, so that with the best possible intentions grave mistakes may be committed in a child's discipline.

Here appears perhaps the principal emphasis of the text : They, according to what *seemed* good ; He, according to what *is good* for us. God reminds us that He cannot err. The chastening he inflicts is for our profit—and let us grasp the *full* meaning—not only for our profit is it *designed*, but *adapted*. Not what *seems* best, but what *is* best. Joseph said to his brethren with regard to God's strange permission of their crime in selling him into Egyptian slavery, "God meant it unto good." What He does is "for our good always." Even while, like Jacob, human weakness is crying out in despair, "all these things are against me," the answer of the Holy Ghost is, through the pen of St. Paul, "All things work together for good." Yet how weak our faith! When God sends suffering upon us we begin to ask, What have we done that we should be singled out as the objects of God's displeasure? But God Himself says, "not in wrath but in love have I rebuked thee," and "for thy profit." What if we ourselves cannot see that we *need* such discipline, or even feel that it is working us harm and not good, shall we trust our own judgment rather than divine wisdom? shall we cultivate a morbid gloomy complaining or indifferent spirit while infinite *love* is unwillingly afflicting us, that under the chastening influence of sorrow we may grow into a more Christlike beauty of character? Oh, let us remember the perfect fatherhood and fatherliness of God! Divine knowledge of our character and needs, divine wisdom in foreseeing results, divine love for His dear children—these are our guaranty that in nature, measure, and frequency, God will adapt and apportion to the temperament of His children all His afflictive dealing.

As to the exact result He proposes in our chastisement—the profit He would secure—it is not any merely human virtue of patience, or any single grace or virtue He would add to our character, but a transformation of our whole self. This is *the profit* for which He chastens us, as He himself defines it, "that we might be partakers of the divine holiness."

Think of the stainless purity of Him in whose sight the heavens are not clean; as, in comparison with the perfect whiteness of snow, nothing else seems white. What must it be to share such purity! to partake of such holiness! There is no conceivable good to be compared with that. It is better than heaven, for it makes heaven. Will not such a result repay the patient endurance of sorrow? Will it not be a privilege to come up out of great tribulation and wash our robes thus, so that they shall be forever gloriously white and glistening? The highest glory of our religion is that it holds out to us something to be! The most the world offers is something to have, or rather to hold, for we can *possess* nothing save what we have in ourselves; what we have most truly is what we are—what we become. The unspeakable promise which invites us onward and upward is not then, we shall "*have*" —even heaven—that is too small a reward for a God of infinite love to offer those who share His perfect bliss and glory; but we "*shall be*"—shall be "*like Him.*" That is the only thing that represents infinite riches! God is rich, not because of what He *has*, but of what He is; if it were conceivable that the universe were annihilated, He could not be poor, because of what He is : and therefore He cannot promise His beloved any higher bliss than to be like Him. He does promise we shall share as sons the father's property; our patrimony, however, is not a partaking of the universe, but "of His holiness!"

IV. Once more, our earthly parents chasten us *temporarily, not permanently*, as the text says, "for a *few* days." This phrase means more than it seems to imply. It probably refers to the fact that much of our parental training looks to immediate results, not remote ones—it is with reference to a few days, or at most to our short earthly life. Not only do a few days limit the period during which we endure their chastening, but they limit also its ordinary results. The effect is transient, not permanent. It is true that there are times when parental correction looks with foresightedness into a remoter future, and with pious anxiety seeks to prepare the soul for another life, looking beyond the immediate present, these few days, to the unnumbered years of the great Forever. But how seldom is the chastisement of a child regulated by *such* calm, earnest, prayerful reference to an immortal future! How careful is the parent then to make the child see the real guilt of sin, its peril, its hatefulness—to adapt the correction to these remote results of everlasting well-being!

Now, God's chastening always looks to eternal results. That which is near at hand impresses *us* most vividly; the future seems far off and uncertain; we are therefore always emphasizing present good and undervaluing the more precious things of the hereafter; we feel our present ills to be almost too heavy to be borne, while the great results which lie in the future seem vague and shadowy. How different must all this appear to God, whose omniscient eye sees the end from the beginning, and to whom the remotest future is as vivid as the present, the remotest result as real as the present process! The life that may seem long to us is nothing to Him who sees a thousand years as a day. Hence God speaks to us of "our light affliction, which is but for a moment." If some human being should dare to call some of our earthly afflictions light and momentary, we should esteem it heartless mockery of our grief. *Light!* Is that blow *light* that knocks a strong man to earth and buries him beneath the wreck of his dearest joys and hopes, and seems to overwhelm him in a general ruin? Is that sorrow *for a moment* which darkens every future earthly hour, covers every prospect with a funeral pall, and through years and years haunts the heart with mocking shadows of former happiness, and as in the old Egyptian feasts, sets a ghastly skeleton at every table of festivity? To us, affliction is heavy and of crushing weight! To us, it is life-long burden and sorrow. Why does a pitying Father above call it light and momentary? He sees the glorious results; to His eye the future is unveiled; the few days of our earthly pilgrimage are over, the endless cycles of eternity begun. All sorrow and sighing have hushed their plaintive wail, every tear is wiped away. We have come up out of great tribulation.

GOD'S VOICE TO THE NATION.*

BY TRYON EDWARDS, D.D.

Know ye not that there is a prince and a great man fallen this day in Israel?—2 SAMUEL iii. 38.

This matter is by the decree of the watchers, and the demand by the word of the holy ones, to the intent that the living may know that the Most High ruleth in the kingdom of men.—DANIEL iv. 17.

THIS world is a place where God is ever present—walking about it as He did of old in Eden. In various ways He is ever addressing us, as there He did our first parents—now in the lessons of instruction and kindness, now in the tones of solemn monition and reproof, and now in the accents of terror. He comes to us in the morning light and the gathering darkness—in the bud, the

---

* Preached in Rochester, N. Y., the Sabbath after the death of President Harrison.

leaf, the flower—in the summer's breeze and the whirlwind's voice —in the gurgling of the streamlet and the roar of the cataract; now, as to Adam, in stillness in the cool of the day, and now, as in some flaming sword, waving with its burning sweep around the tree of our richest blessings and fondest hopes. But though God is ever about us, and ever addressing us, there are times when He does this in more than the ordinary sense—when we almost hear His voice in audible accents. There *are* times when the tones that come to us are almost startling—seasons that are echoing points—reverberating stations, where *God* arrests us, that He may pour His appeals in all their fulness upon our ears; seasons every one of which is as a burning bush to us, to which God compels us to look, that from it we may hear His voice. Such, for example, was the day of the assertion of our national independence, when the noble declaration of our fathers broke in upon the stillness and security of a king-trodden world, unfolding the great principles of human dignity and right, and that man is the hereditary subject of none but God; sending doubt and paleness and fear to the thrones of despots, and in calm decision proclaiming those great principles which are yet to revolutionize the world, and perhaps to prepare the way for the universal spread and triumph of the Gospel of Christ. Such, again, was the season when two of our ex-Presidents, in a single day, and that the jubilee of our country, passed to their final account—when the pealings of a nation's joy were exchanged for the tollings of grief, and the sun that rose in gladness went down in sorrow. Such, again, would be the case, if war should now burst in upon us, with startling crash, like a thunderbolt from heaven, blighting our commerce, and cutting off and eating up our wealth, and desecrating, not to say ending, our Sabbaths, and spreading its almost numberless vices, and devouring our sons and fathers and husbands, and filling the land with fear and violence and blood. Every such event, whether past or possible, is as a sermon to a people, *where God is the preacher*— calling them to repent of their sins, and to remember and bow to His rule.

And such an event, my hearers, is that which so lately and sadly has sounded to your ears, and through the land, sinking deep into the nation's heart, and sending thoughtfulness to the brows, and seriousness to the hearts of millions. I refer to the death of the

President of these United States. He has gone from the highest station of earthly greatness—gone, as in a moment—torn from the summit to which he had but just ascended, and while the plaudits were still sounding in his ears. As the warrior, the scholar, the statesman, the Christian, I stop not to dwell upon his character, or to estimate his merits. Standing upon higher ground, as God's ambassador, I turn to his removal as a national event in which the Lord is speaking to us as a people. I say it is *a national event;* for the party views that favored or opposed the *man* are forgotten at the grave of the *ruler.* Death has pushed them aside for a season, and the nation, like one family afflicted, bows like one family around the grave of its head. And to us as members of that family sound the lessons that God is sending—lessons to which we should bow with reverence—lessons designed for our monition, for our good. To us as individuals, to us as citizens, in all our public relations, God is speaking. Let us then dismiss every other thought, that we may listen to His voice, that we may ask for and ascertain the meaning of His Providence.

I. *God, by this event, is reminding us of His own supremacy—of His overruling Providence.* Prone as we are, whether as individuals or as nations, to forget God, His sovereignty and our dependence, we need something ever to keep them in our view, something that, like the miracles to Israel in the desert, or the handwriting on the walls of Belshazzar's palace, shall ever keep the Almighty before us. And God sees this, and He is ever sending sickness and sorrow, and trial, and death, His visible and terrible ministers, to impress them upon us—ever to make us feel His providence and His rule. Every pang that racks our frame; every sorrow that crushes the heart to the world's eye, or that gnaws it with keener tooth in secret; every sickness that points with meaning finger to the grave, all whisper to us of the divine supremacy. But pre-eminently is this true of death. The agonizing throes of dissolution, as they send their pulsations through the world, are ever and loudly speaking of God. If there be a place on earth where we are impressed with His overruling sovereignty and providence—where we feel that His will is supreme, and that ever and steadily He will carry forward His purposes, it is in the chamber, and by the bed of death. There we see the nothingness of earthly might, of human strength. Disease comes on with silent steps and unsuspected progress, and soon so fixes its grasp as to set at naught human wishes and defy the skill of the wisest physicians. And as it presses onward with relentless power, laughing to scorn every opposition, and crushing in its grasp the mightiest strength almost visibly, we can see that its step is the step of God, as in calm but resistless might it bears onward to its end. O ! how weak, how impotent, is all that man can do, when death, as God's messenger, tears from us the friends of earth, to whom we would fain cling a little longer, but find in anguish that we cannot. How intensely, in such an hour, do we feel that it is *God* that " turneth man to destruction," and that *His* rule is constant and supreme ! Far more deeply, then, should we feel this, when the Almighty thus appears, not merely in the social circle, but in the great family of nations—not in some remote and obscure apartment, but in a dying chamber to which a country is gathered, and at a dying bed on which the eyes of the world are fixed ; and when there with the same resistless might, in calmness, in stillness, in terror, he bears onward with His work ! Here, as we gaze, we feel it, almost tangibly we feel it, that *God* rules, that He does " His will, in the army of heaven, and among the inhabitants of the earth, and that none can stay His hand, or say unto Him, what doest Thou ?" It is God that hath done it, and as we gather around the sepulchre which He hath opened, we hear a voice echoing from it, " Be still, and know that I am God !" Again, I remark, that in the sad dispensation upon which we are dwelling—

II. *God is pouring contempt upon all human greatness.* We have all read of the Roman Emperor who, to reclaim a miser, marked around him with a spear a space of ground large enough for his body, and then said to him, " Now go on, and add wealth to wealth and riches to riches, and yet in a few short days this is all that will be yours !" And often, too, have we heard of the memorable monarch who, after almost superhuman conquests, commanded with his dying breath that his shroud should be borne aloft, through his armies, with the solemn and affecting message, " This is all that remains of Saladin the Great !" And the same thing God is doing—doing with almighty authority and power ; the same message He is echoing, not merely to a solitary individual, not merely to the gathered armies of a monarch, but to the millions of this nation, and to the very ends of the earth. If there be any station which of all is the highest, the loftiest of earth, as lofty, from the character of our nation, as the throne of any earthly ruler, and far loftier because it is not an inheritance, but the free gift of a free people, it is that which but lately was filled by the one who has now gone from it forever! And yet God has no more regarded it than if it were the abode of the moth, the dwelling of an insect. It has no more stayed His progress or kept Him back from His purposes, than the atom in the air could stay the progress of some rolling world. And by all this He is pouring contempt upon the honors, and stations, and glories of the earth. But a few months since and our entire nation was shaken by the struggle for this very place that death has now so fearfully made vacant. Strong convulsions seemed upon us, and deep heavings of excitement, like the coming throes of some moral earthquake. And now when that excitement is over, and all our plans seemed fixed, God has blown upon them, and they are withered in a moment. Lofty as was that station, and high as were the hopes, and bright as were the prospects of its possessor, death dashed on as madly and as gladly to riot in them all, as though his victim had been the veriest outcast upon earth. Where but a few weeks since those heart-strings were vibrating to the breath of millions, they are now still forever. Where was the shout, and the plaudit, and the gathering throng, and the heedless and giddy dance, there is now the stillness and sadness of the chamber of death, and the funeral procession, and the desolate home, and the silent grave. So ends all human greatness!

> "The boast of heraldry, the pomp of power,
>   And all that beauty, all that wealth e'er gave,
> Await alike the inevitable hour;
>   The path of glory leads but to the grave."

> "The riches, glories, honors of the earth,
>   And they who hold them, all are speeding there;
> There shall the worm feed on them—that's their end!"

Oh! how vain, what utter nothingness, seem all the pomp, the glory, the greatness of earth, when the shadow of the grave is upon it, when death has unmasked it, and shown it to us as God beholds it, as eternity will reveal it! Again, I remark, that the dispensation before us—

III. *May well rebuke the violence of party strifes, and soften the temper of party feelings.* Somewhere I have seen the story of two brothers who in bitter enmity had hated each other for years, but who, as they met at their father's opening grave, were humbled, and melted, and subdued, and there rushed in tears to each other's arms and were reconciled forever. Would that such an effect might here be produced on the parties that exist, and ever must exist in our land; that here at "the reconciling grave" all violence and bitterness might cease; that here their asperities might end, and their prejudices die away; and that here, if like Abram and Lot they must be separate, in the kind language of the former they might say to each other, "Let there be no strife between us, for we are brethren." By the side of the grave shall we not, do we not, feel our brotherhood? Here shall not the prejudice, and the unkindness, and the narrowness of party wilfulness and vehemence be forgotten amid the touching and hallowed lessons of the narrow house? Here shall not the voice of God be heard, saying to every surge of party bitterness, "Peace, be still"? Here shall not our great opposing parties, like the members of some family, who while living in enmity are summoned to some common grave, hear the voice that sounds to them from above, calling them to renounce their alienation forever? Honest party differences we must expect will exist; and thorough and frequent scrutiny of opposing principles, we must expect will ever be made; and both are deeply to be respected and desired, *for they are the pledge of our safety.* But there is too often a disingenuousness of party perversion, and a personality of party suspicion and attack, and a littleness and loathsomeness of party abuse, that "defiles the whole body" politic, and "sets on fire the course of nature, and is set on fire of hell!" It regards not the sacredness of private character, or of domestic life. It hurls its poisoned shafts at the highest because they are exalted, and, if possible, to cast them down from their elevation. Regardless of God's command that we honor our rulers, it treats them, because they are our representatives, as though they were the basest of menials and slaves. With the spirit of the slanderer and the assassin, it hews down the *individual,* where with the manliness of the statesman, it should discuss the *principle.* It is inconsistent with self-respect, with the kindly feelings of social life, and with the courtesies that are ever due from man to man; and it should humble us in our own estimation, as it disgraces us in the eyes of the civilized world. Would that one grave were deep enough to swallow it up forever! And by this grave which God hath opened, is He not calling us to lay it aside, to do all in our power to discountenance and destroy it, reminding us that that which we feel should cease at the tomb, *at once* should cease forever!

IV. *God, by the dispensation before us, is rebuking us for our national sins, and calling us to repent of and forsake them.* As when He comes to a family by affliction, He is often chastising them for their sins, and calling them to search out and ponder their transgressions, and to forsake them by deep and humble repentance, so it is with nations. And by the chastisement with which He has now come to us, tearing from us, as a nation, our chosen ruler and head, loudly is He calling upon us to forsake our sins, lest a deeper and a darker judgment be sent upon us. Man-worship, and party recklessness, and, ambition, and worldliness, and pride, and profaneness, and intemperance, and then those deeper and darker crimes, legalized Sabbath-breaking, and slavery, crushing in its grasp the bodies, and what is far more, the souls of millions and trampling, in them, on God's image—these are some of the many sins that rise up from our land in dark clouds of guilt, threatening to descend in storms of curses upon us. Long have they been calling with iron voice, with deathless peal, to Heaven for vengeance. Amid the bustle and tumult of the world, we may not have heard their cry. But God has heard it, and the vials of His wrath have been filled, and He has been ready to pour them out, in their fury, upon us. And yet, *as is like Himself*, He is still waiting for our repentance. Already He has warned us by many and startling monitions. He has sent the pestilence to ravage our borders, and, the flame to consume our cities, and fearful disasters to our seas and rivers, to make them the theatres of suffering and death. He has prostrated our commerce, and blighted the plans and swept away the wealth of individuals, and given our states to embarrassment, and hung out the portents of war in the heavens. And as all these were not enough, He has now sent *this* national affliction—this deep and humbling and monitory judgment, again to call us to repent, lest He come out in deeper and darker and desolating wrath. And if we fail to do it, other visitations may be upon us; and we may yet feel, in our own experience, the full meaning of that fearful declaration, that "The nation that will not serve Him shall perish!" If we refuse to humble ourselves before Him, though no voice of inspired prediction should declare it, "our own sins shall be the sure prophets of our coming woes." In them we may read God's fiat, as palpably as though it were written on every cloud of the heavens in letters of living flame. God may let loose upon us the furies of war from without, or He may develop the elements of ruin from within. In the fearful thought of Burke, He may leave "our own passions to forge our fetters," or slavery, in some deep and providential upheavings, to pour out ruin upon us, or political volcanoes to disgorge their fires to consume us. In the strong language of Milton, "God," in indignation, may "become weary of protecting us, so that after we have passed through the fire He may leave us to perish in the smoke." He may give us up to desolation from abroad, or to faction and violence in our own midst, or He may destroy us by gradual and lingering decay —by giving us up to moral degradation ("for a nation dies when the spirit of all that is noble and good dies within it"), leaving our sins to eat out our very life, and His abused and perverted mercies to work out their own revenge and our destruction. And then, over us, as over the mouldering ruins of the once splendid but now heaven-stricken cities of the plain or the desert, the travellers of future ages may wander in sadness, and over us, as over them, may be written the striking and fearful inquest, "Died by the visitation of God!" Let us then be warned by this the first stroke of God, before He shall follow it with deeper and darker judgments. Let us "humble ourselves, under the mighty hand of God," in view of our guilt, lest He be compelled to humble us. Let us humble ourselves as individuals, and as a people—deploring our sins as a nation—turning from them by deep and sincere repentance, that the anger of the Lord may be averted, and that He may return in mercy to dwell with us, sanctifying us through all His gifts, leading us to humble and reverent submission to His will, and to a wise improvement of all His mercies, that thus He may be "a wall of fire round about us, and a glory in our midst," ever making us "that happy people whose God is the Lord."

V. *God by the dispensation before us, is coming personally to ourselves, warning us of the uncertainty of life, and calling upon us ever to be prepared for death.* This world is a world of death. The march of time, like some vast and endless funeral procession, is bearing us all onward to the tomb. If we look to the past, nation after nation is moving to eternity, as wave follows wave to dash and die upon the shore. Their untold millions flit, like graveyard shadows before us, and even while we gaze upon them they are gone from our view forever. And if from the past we turn to the present, here too the king of terrors is ever at his work. All around us graves are opening; monuments are rising; friends are departing to the world of spirits. Even while we cling to them, a mighty and unseen hand tears them from us, and their faces are seen and their voices are heard no more. In all the past, in all the present, generation after generation passes in silent and spectral march before us, warning us by *their* shadowy forms, " what shades *we* are, what shadows we pursue," and solemnly beckoning us after themselves, on to the judgment. Of every death it is true that it unmasks the world to us—that it shows us the uncertainty of life, and the frailty of all human hopes. Of every grave it is true that

> " 'Tis the pulpit of departed man,
>   From which he speaks—his text and doctrine both,
>   ' Thou too must die, and come to judgment!' "

But when God, as now, sends the warning from the high places of the earth, it comes to us, though with the same lesson, yet with a deeper and more monitory tone. When we think what were the hopes and prospects of the departed—how the future spread out in brightness before him—how he had just laid his hand on the prize that had been hoped for for years; and then when we think how, after four short weeks, he is torn from it forever—how the garland has withered in his grasp, and the joy has crumbled as he touched it, and the pomp of life is exchanged for the stillness of the grave, and the admiring gaze of men for the searching glance of God, and the estimates of earth for the just judgment of Jehovah—in the light of all these things, oh, how little, how as nothing does this world appear compared with that to which he is gone and we are hastening! Could the heavens be rent, and the voice of the departed now be heard from the world of spirits, first of all would he not warn us that we too are to die and to pass to the judgment—that heaven or hell is before us—that the grave, which is but the passway to the one or the other, will soon open beneath our feet, and that we, as in a moment, may sink to it, no more to rise but to life or death eternal? Gone, as he has gone, from the pomp and pageantry of earth to the realities of an endless state, and having gazed upon the blessedness of the redeemed— hearing the harping of their harps, and witnessing their joys and rapture which no tongue can tell, and there, too, having looked down upon the horrors of the bottomless gulf, where their worm dieth not, and their fire is not quenched, and the wrath of God burns forever, if now he could come back, would not his first warnings be of the soul, and of God, and the judgment, and heaven, and hell? Would not earth, with all its glories, now seem as nothing to him—its wealth as but glittering dust—its pleasures but as the empty wind—its honors but as a fading flower, a flitting dream, blown by a breath away forever? The soul, the soul, the never-dying soul—would not this be his only and his burning theme, and would he not warn you in God's name, and by the realities that he has witnessed, "to work out your salvation with fear and trembling" before it be forever too late? In his last, and as now we may almost call it, his dying message, from the station where God had placed him, he earnestly commends *Christianity*—not some vague and indefinite religion, but *the religion of the cross—the atoning system of a crucified Redeemer*—to this widely extended people, and among them to ourselves. And now may we not imagine him bending from another world, and as a preacher from eternity reiterating to us, by all the sanctions of the unseen state, that in the cross, *in the cross*, is our only hope, and asking, with solemn earnestness, of each one of us, "What shall it profit a man if he shall gain the whole world and lose his own soul, and what shall a man give in exchange for his soul?" Yes—we may—we may; and what is far more, we may hear God's voice sounding to us from this opening grave and this departed spirit, warning us to prepare—to prepare! As by every death, so pre-eminently by this, He warns us that our time is short, that our salvation is at hazard, and that if we would ever be saved, we must "do with our might what our hands find to do"—"working out our salvation with fear and trembling"—laying hold on life while yet it may be ours. This is the great end of all God's dealings, the solemn and personal close of every appeal and warning and truth, whether from His providence or Word or Spirit—that you, too, are to die, and that you *prepare* for it now, while yet you may. Look not away then from this solemn truth, when it is thus written on the heavens above, and echoed from the earth beneath, and when ere-long it shall gleam upon you from the flaming heavens, and the convulsed and dissolving world, and the burning throne of judgment. Look not away from the thought that die you must, and when, you cannot tell. Here in this house of prayer—around this grave which God has opened—by the coming hour of your own death—by our meeting at the judgment seat, I entreat you to listen to these warnings, to prepare for the coming of the Son of Man. Speeding as you are to the dying chamber, and the winding-sheet, and the final hour, hurried as you soon may be, as in a moment, to the bar of God, and the retributions of an eternal state, again I entreat you to prepare, before your probation is forever wasted, and your soul forever lost!

THE FUNERAL OF THE SOUL.

BY H. B. HOOKER, D.D., FALMOUTH, MASS.

And these shall go away into everlasting punishment.—MATT. xxv. 46.

As we are all familiar with the event of death, so are we also with its usual accompaniment, a funeral. We associate these events together, as the one naturally and necessarily follows the other.

But while we recognize the fact, and often think of the funeral of the body, is there not also what may be called the funeral of the soul? If natural death occasions a necessity for one of these events, why may we not believe spiritual death creates a like necessity for the other? If it be a fact, that natural death causes such a change in the state of the body, that funeral rites must be performed, and that the body must be removed from all connection with the living, is it anything unreasonble to believe that spiritual death produces such a state of the soul that funeral solemnities should be performed over that, and that there should be a removal of it from the society of all the holy and the happy?

In proof of such a fact, the text and context are clear and decisive. Hence, my present topic is THE FUNERAL OF THE SOUL.

I. VARIOUS FACTS ARE IMPLICATED IN SUCH AN EVENT, IMPORTANT TO BE NOTICED.

1. That the kindest efforts have been made to *prevent the necessity of such a funeral.* Who does not strive to arrest the hand of temporal death? Had you ever a departed friend whose funeral you would not have prevented had it been in your power?

And has there not been much done in the kindest way, to prevent the funeral of the soul? Was there not an atoning sacrifice, of astonishing value, once offered for the very purpose of preventing this melancholy event? Has not the Holy Spirit, the Heavenly Dove, been spreading his wings in all directions to stay such a catastrophe? Has there not been sent to the human race a whole volume of every variety of dissuasives from such courses as would lead to such an event? And has there been, anywhere in a Christian land, a human soul that has not been surrounded by kind friends who have been deeply interested in preventing its funeral? Was there not warning, and entreaty, and prayer? And could that benevolence have prevailed in leading the sinner from his sins, would there have been the funeral of the soul?

2. It is implied in the funeral of the soul, that all the efforts of kindness to prevent it have *failed.* So we judge when we attend the funeral of the body. As we look upon the wreck and ruin of death, we see that all the tenderness of love, and all the assiduity and self-denial of kindness have been baffled, and that disease and death have had their triumphant way.

So the idea of the funeral of the soul carries with it the idea that, whatever have been the offices of Christian kindness to prevent that dreadful event, they have all failed. The love of Christ, as a dissuasive from its sins, has been set before it in vain. The gracious Spirit has striven without success. All the rebukes of conscience availed not. And Christian admonitions were wasted on unyielding hardness of heart.

3. The funeral of the soul is most decisive of the fact, *that it is*

actually dead! We do not bury the living body, but only the dead. The smallest degree of life stays us. The pulsations may be so feeble as to require the closest and most delicate scrutiny to detect them. But, if they exist at all, there will be no burial. The procedure of the burial is founded on the most perfect assurance of death.

So it is because the *soul is dead* that there is a funeral of it. No such solemnity would occur if there were the least spark of spiritual life. The slightest pulsation of such life would save it from that awful solemnity. Never was there the burial of a soul that was not dead. No such event could possibly occur under the government of God.

4. With the funeral of a soul *we cannot avoid associations of sorrow*. It is always so in reference to the body. Its burial! How often it implies the burial of sweetest happiness and fondest hopes! That scene pours a tide of bitterness through bereaved bosoms. How many sighs! How many tears!

But before there can be the funeral of a soul, what sadness there has been over it! Over its spiritual death were there not the tears of a compassionate Saviour? And have not the true people of God, in all ages, mourned over those around them whose sinful courses were hastening them to a burial in the bottomless pit? Every association of thought with the funeral of a soul is one of sadness. Tears, more bitter, have never been shed in this world, than those of pious friends over those dear to them, who, by persistence in sin, were wrapping themselves in the winding-sheet of moral death, and making the funeral solemnities at the Great Day a dreadful certainty!

5. The funeral of a soul suggests itself *as an inevitable consequence of its spiritual death*. It is so with the body. The rites we perform, in connection with burial, are associated with the unavoidable necessity of committing it to the grave. The state of natural death is at war with the health and life of survivors, and there must be a separation of the dead from us. We obey this law as imperious beyond question or resistance.

So of the funeral of the soul. The event of spiritual death having occurred, there is no alternative. The funeral of a soul implies its removal from the society of all the pure and the good in the universe. *It must be removed.* It has no more elements of harmony with the holy and happy servants of God, than dead bodies have with living ones. The burial of dead souls is an act of holy justice which the Infinite owes to His own character, and owes to the happiness of those holy beings whose bliss would be marred by the presence of those so utterly discordant in character.

II. I NOW PASS TO THE VARIOUS CIRCUMSTANCES ATTENDING THE FUNERAL OF THE SOUL.

1. *Vast numbers* of souls will have the rites of burial performed for them *at the same time*. All that finally remain dead in trespasses and sins will be buried. All the fallen angels belong to that number, together with every member of the human family who has lived and died in sin. We have no means of knowing the number, but we have melancholy reasons for believing it will be very great. What vast multitudes, in all generations past, have passed into the grave unreconciled to God ! How many are now living in that growing blindness of mind and hardness of heart, which affords sad presage that they will perish ! The Great Day will be the funeral day of innumerable millions !

2. There will be an immense assembly convened as witnesses of that great funeral. At the rites of burial in this world, in cases of distinguished persons, or when the mode of death has been extraordinary, great numbers of people are gathered. But the greatest scene, as respects numbers present, ever witnessed on earth, is as a drop to the ocean, compared with the one now in contemplation. How striking the language of one competent to inform us : "When the Son of Man shall come in His glory and all the holy angels with Him." *All* the angels ! What a congregation ! An apostle speaks of the angels as "an innumerable company." And we read of different ranks, as Archangels, Thrones, Dominions, Potentates, and Powers, and there are immense numbers, doubtless, in each rank. And we cannot but rationally suppose that what would summon these orders of holy beings together would summon all others, if indeed these orders do not include the whole intelligent universe. We cannot therefore doubt that so extraordinary an event as such a solemnity will draw together the whole rational creation of God.

That, in addition to the *holy* angels, all the *fallen* angels will be present, is evident from two facts :

a. The direct assertion of Scripture : "And the angels that kept not their first estate, but left their own habitation, He hath reserved in everlasting chains under darkness, unto the judgment of the great day."

b. The funeral rites will embrace these very beings; for they are "reserved" now in reference to the performance of that very solemnity over them. They of course will be there.

And, in respect to attendance on that scene from *our world*, the context expressly affirms, that before the Judge "shall be gathered *all nations.*" And elsewhere it is said, "And I saw the dead, small and great, stand before God; and the dead were judged out of those things which were written in the books according to their works."

If, then, all the angels of God, and all nations, and all the dead, both small and great, are to be present at the great funeral day of souls, then what a congregation, what a funeral solemnity! So important is it, that God summons His whole rational universe to witness it. Surely He must be in earnest when He appoints and prepares such a solemnity. What an event that burial! Whose soul should not have troubled thoughts concerning it!

No wonder this is called the GREAT DAY! How proper to call it the GREAT FUNERAL! If the greatness of the number of spectators can impart awful grandeur and deep solemnity, this fact is not wanting here.

3. The funeral of souls will be attended with an exhibition of their characters. This is sometimes done at the burial of the body in this world. But it is a settled part of that great solemnity now under discussion. The funeral of souls is an event of such overwhelming magnitude and importance—it will be followed by consequences so terrible—it will be an act of the government of God so awful and so impressive upon the whole witnessing universe, that the Infinite Ruler designs to unfold the reasons fully for treating, as He then will, fallen angels and fallen men. He is about to bury them in the bottomless pit! But he will show, as a reason, that they are DEAD! As the testimony that a human *body* was dead would be the complete vindication of its burial, so the testimony that the soul is dead in trespasses and sins, will be the vindication of its burial in perdition! This great fact, the spiritual death of the soul, will be made known, for its moral

character shall be fully disclosed. "For God will bring every secret thing into judgment." And such will be the disclosure of iniquity, that "every mouth shall be stopped and the whole world found guilty before God." Then it will be seen that such was the sinner's enmity against His character, and opposition to His government, and resistance to His will, as to proclaim His spiritual death, and therefore the glorious justice of His burial. The Judge will not declare, "These shall go away into everlasting punishment," till He has shown to the witnessing universe that the guilty had totally disqualified themselves for heaven, and that their characters had fitted them for no other place than the regions of woe. So startling and awful will be the display of human guilt, that there can be but one sentiment among all the holy myriads who witness the scene, expressed in the Amen that all shall give as the funeral sentence shall be pronounced!

4. *Consciousness* on the part of the condemned of the awful nature of the transaction will be also one of the circumstances attending the funeral of souls.

Burial solemnities in this world are for the inanimate and the unconscious. Not so in the great funeral day of souls. Those in that day about to be buried, are fully aware of what is transpiring about them. They know where they are, and all the terrible facts of their position. They can *see* the Infinite Judge as He "comes in the clouds of heaven with power and great glory." The great white throne is in sight, and all the holy beings who compose that vast assembly. The opened volume—the language of accusation—the map of earthly life—the guilt with which they are defiled—the frowning face of Eternal Justice—they are conscious of all! Not one of the awful solemnities of the occasion is undiscerned, and not one but has a response of the soul's emotions in their utmost intensity.

We have read of the terrible emotions with which the supposed dead have been conscious of their own funeral solemnities; but here is that consciousness in circumstances infinitely more awful. Here are intelligent minds, in all the sensitiveness of rational existence, beholding their own funeral rites, and conscious of the tremendous fact that the grave is nothing less than the bottomless pit!

5. In the world *men* execute the funeral solemnities of the de-

parted, but in the funeral of souls *God Himself is the Great Executor.* It is His voice that summons death and hell to give up their dead. It is He that charges the guilty with their rebellion. It is His voice that closes the scene with the sentence, "Depart ye cursed into everlasting fire!" This is a solemnity so momentous that He commits it to no created hands—He presides Himself.

6. One other circumstance: There will be no *resurrection* of buried souls! We stand by the grave of the *body* and see it lowered to that resting-place. But it will come forth. At the sound of the trump of God it will arise.

But with the funeral of souls there can be no such associations. Here is a burial without a resurrection. "He that is unjust shall be unjust still." "These shall go away"—no voice will ever recall them. No being will stand by the side of that awful sepulchre, and penetrating its horrible midnight, cry, "Come forth!" Every spectator of that solemnity will recognize the *unchangeable* decision of the divine government. The burial of a guilty soul in perdition is a *final* transaction. Just as the funeral solemnities of the body in this world suggest and imply no return of the departed, so does the funeral of the soul imply no return. All the spectators will retire from that mighty sepulchre in the conviction that the buried are wrapped in the shroud of everlasting death!

Now let us take home to the deepest ponderings of our hearts two facts:

a. That each of us will be *personally present* at the great funeral day of souls. What there will be of awful grandeur, and terror, and glory, in that day, will be before *our* eyes. The Judge, the throne, the book of life, the angels, holy and fallen, men redeemed and unredeemed—*we* shall *see* all this. And all that is to be *heard* that day, *we* shall hear—the voice of the Infinite Judge, the anthems of angels and saints, the wailings of the lost!

b. There is *danger* that then shall be performed the funeral solemnities *of our own souls.* Have *we* not sinned? And is not the penalty death and consequent burial? Do we say we have escaped it by "repentance toward God, and faith in our Lord Jesus Christ?" These are elements of salvation; but how many have fallen into deadly delusion concerning them—have taken up with the form without the spirit; and, though confessors of Christ and numbered in Zion, are in as great danger as ever of final ruin! By the very side of that dreadful sepulchre, and on the funeral day, many will hear—many that thought all was well—will hear the startling announcement: "I NEVER KNEW YOU!" Who of us has not occasion to search his heart, to inquire after the grounds of his hope, and to seek with all possible earnestness to escape so terrible a disappointment!

But have not the topics of this discourse met the eyes of some, in the consciousness of total unfitness for eternity, since nothing effectual has yet been done for the safety of the soul? Bear with the kindness and plainness that tells you every sin you are indulging is aiding to weave the winding-sheet that will be used in the Great Funeral Day! You are making yourself ready for the solemnities of an everlasting burial! Indulged sin is bringing your soul into such a moral state that there can be nothing done with it but to bury it.

Think too of this: you do not walk in darkness in reference to this great matter. God has sent you word about the great Funeral Day. He has drawn, in awful brightness, a picture of it, and made to stand out before you the prominent circumstances of that fearful scene. And all for the express purpose of so instructing and alarming you, as to prevent its becoming your own funeral day.

Oh, mariner on the sea of life, the beacon blazes before you, clear and bright, kindled by God's own hand. Will you not heed it? Will you go on to deal so unworthily with your Infinite Benefactor and Judge, that He can do nothing with your guilty soul but to call the universe to see the justice of its being buried in perdition?

OBITUARY ADDRESSES.

RESPONSIBILITIES OF THE LIVING.*

BY C. F. DEEMS, D.D., NEW YORK.

My brethren, it would seem to be a happy thing that the custom of the pastor of this church at funerals should be in such perfect accord with the explicit wishes of our deceased friend. It is almost never appropriate to speak about a dead man at his obsequies. No man would desire to allude to any of his human frailties and faults, and no man can make the dead man's friends love him more than they do when they surround his remains. And so when he charged, that at his funeral not many words should be said, and that those words should be said deliberately, and that there should be no attempt to set forth any supposed virtue he might possess, the request was in accordance with my own feelings. And it is all the better because an occasion is to come when he who held the position of pastor toward him will have an opportunity to state deliberately his own estimate of this character and this career. I have therefore prepared no note of sermon, no note of address. I have come to talk, not about the dead, but to the living. I have come to seize this occasion, when you are all solemn, when you are all arrested by the fact that another death—the death of a most conspicuous man—has occurred, to bring you for a few moments to the consideration of this blessed Christian faith of ours by which men can best live. I have not come to talk to you about death; living men have nothing to do with dying. I am not come to exhort you to prepare for death, as if such preparation could be made apart from holy living; I do not believe in wasting men's lives that way. You and I have no time

* At the funeral of Cornelius Vanderbilt.

so to prepare for death. Our lives are packed and crowded too closely with responsibilities to be wasting one minute in thinking of dying. That is not the Christian faith, and yet there are many men who seem to regard religion as simply an arrangement for a happy and safe passage over the river of death into a land of immortal life. That is not the religion set forth in New Testament Scripture. Life and immortality are all that concern us. What have you to do with dying? God takes care of that. What had you to do with being born? God took care of that, and you have no more to do with preparing for dying than you had to do with preparing for being born. Those are the two inevitables of human existence, and God Almighty alone manages the inevitable. But this thing God has given to you and me: He has given us bodies that are to be the temples of the Holy Ghost. He has given us intellects capable of indefinite expansion. He has given us influence over our fellow-men, influence so that there is not a day we live in which we do not make some man or some woman better or worse. Men talk of dying; women faint at the thought of dying. Dying! It is but an instantaneous physical experience—over as quickly as one winks. Dying is solemn, but living is awful. It is not that you and I may die at five o'clock this evening—it is not that which ought to concern us; but we may live until five o'clock, and there is no man who lives until that time who will not have grown into a greater ripeness for the everlasting life or have commenced that decay which goes down into spiritual rottenness.

It is awful to live, for in our jokes, in our witticisms, in our addresses from the pulpit, in our intercourse in mercantile and domestic life, we are constantly exerting an influence that is to go on forever. It is that which makes living such an awful thing. Therefore, Christianity comes to men for living, not for dying. The conclusion of the 15th chapter of Corinthians is one of the most powerful internal proofs of the divine origin of the Bible. If a philosopher or man of the world had written a peroration to what seems to be a sublime oration on life and immortality, he would never have written that with which the apostle concludes his address. He says this mortal *must* put on immortality, and this corruptible *must* put on incorruption, and then says, "Therefore, my beloved brethren, be ye steadfast, immovable."

That is not the conclusion of a man of the world, or a mystic, or a philosopher.

They would say: "Call in the children from their play; call down the women from their toilets; call up the men from the markets. If this mortal must put on immortality, why should one care for this present life? Why should beauty seek adornments, or power a field of exercise? One would send the world to the cloister; another to the closet; another to the wilderness. As the generations of men are passing so rapidly away, why should we spend our brief time here in toil?" They would say, "What is the use of living? Strong men like Cornelius Vanderbilt are stricken down. What is the use of climbing? He was a mighty climber and ascended above all others, yet, on the summit, he was stricken down in such a way that if he had piled $20,000,000 of gold upon his chamber floor his physicians could not have given him twenty minutes of perfect ease." We are told to be steadfast, to be immovable, and to work. Christianity says, men may come and men may go, and whole generations be swept off by war, and flood, and flames, and pestilence; but "be steadfast." Steadfastness is an element of Christianity, if exercised in a legitimate and honorable business; stand right, and do not be swept away by fanaticism or false enthusiasm. And what more? Work. What! work in the presence of impending death? Yes, work. Work, even in the presence of impending death, and never think of retiring. I have seen too many young men retire in their prime and die before their full ripening. Now let me charge you, as a minister of the Gospel of the Son of God, never retire. Look around such an assemblage as this, and see men who, according to the idea of laying off the harness before one dies, might have retired twenty years ago, and they are still, thank God, examples of earnest work.

The Holy Spirit says, "Be steadfast and work!" If you are founding a bank, or constructing a railway, or preparing a brief for the courts, or studying the case of a patient, or ploughing your field into furrows—whatever be your employment—"keep steadfast" to it to the last minute of life, and "work." Are you driving toward a goal, don't leap from your chariot; don't check your horses. Hold your reins tightly and send the forces of life which is in you down to your spirited steeds, and drive till your chariot leaps over the line at the goal. Your business is to drive; there will be those at the barriers to arrest the steeds.

The Holy Spirit says, "Always abounding in the work of the Lord." And what does that mean? I humbly venture to think it is this, that if I have done anything on Sunday, I must do more on Monday, and increase the amount of labor day by day, up to the last, making the last hour of life the fullest of thought, love, and action, possible to our perpetually cultivated powers. The last thoughts of his (Mr. Vanderbilt's) life were business thoughts conducted through his own mind, religiously, for the honor and glory of God. But our work must be the work of the Lord. Whatsoever our beloved and revered friend did from selfishness, whatsoever he did from vanity, whatsoever he did from pride, or from worldliness, might have grown to be large and brilliant things, and yet each one of them as it strikes his tombstone will burst like a bubble. What of him remains? Only that which he did "in the Lord." That has everlasting permanence.

I think it will be a soft pillow for my dying hour that I have one remembrance—which I may venture to state, even here—of our beloved friend. One day he took my hand and looked me in the face; the tears started to his eyes, and he said, "Dear Doctor, you never crowded your religion on me, but you have been faithful to me." "Yes," I said, "Commodore, I have held back nothing of the counsel of God which I thought needful to say to you for your salvation." And shall I here, in the presence of this people, and in the presence of his precious remains, fail to be faithful to his memory and to you? What gave him his comfort at last? That there was not a civilized nation on the face of the earth that did not know his name? That there was not a king, or an emperor, or other ruler of men upon earth, that did not know his name? That the lustre of his deeds shone like sunlight among the nations? What gave him his comfort at the last? That he could count up millions to be left to his children? No! It was this: that Jesus Christ, by the grace of God, had tasted death for him; that there was in the Godhead not simply his Creator, but his Redeemer, and that, coming as a little child, he could lay his head in the lap of Jesus and feel that he had a Saviour there.

Oh, you and I may speculate as we please about Christianity, but here is the solemn fact of Christianity, and here is the solemn fact that when men do come to the Lord Jesus Christ with simple trust, having repentance toward God, they find peace and everlasting rest. There is no other name given among men whereby we can be saved. God gave His only begotten Son, that whoso believeth in Him should have everlasting life. The blood of Jesus Christ, His Son, cleanseth us from all sin.

This is the gospel of Christianity — the gospel of salvation through Jesus Christ. To those who have heard nothing about the Redeemer I have nothing to say; but you who have listened to the Gospel of Jesus, I charge as you shall come to the judgment-seat of Christ, that you be prepared to answer this question: What did you do with Jesus? What have you done with all that came to you through His death? For remember, that you are not to be judged as cultivated pagans, but by the Gospel of Jesus you shall be judged.

You may have lived as though you had nothing to do with Jesus, saying, that "do as ye would be done by" is enough religion for you. Cornelius Vanderbilt once saw all in that, but he lived long enough to consider that precept in the light of this question which I now urge upon you: Have you done by Jesus as you would have Him do by you, if your places were changed? If you have millions, what are they worth compared with the wealth of Jesus before the world began? If each of you were a crowned monarch I would ask you, What is your bauble compared to the eternal crown of glory? Yet He laid them all down to save you. Suppose you were to empty yourself of all glory and take on you the form of a servant, and die for Jesus; and then suppose He was so engrossed in selfish pursuits, or so mad with the greed of gain, that He cared nothing for your death, what would you think of Jesus? If you reject or neglect this great salvation, and will not be saved in God's way, He will judge you by your own rule, and you must answer at the judgment of the great day this question, Did you do unto Jesus what you would have Him do for you?

There were two things our beloved friend lacked. One was the advantages of early scholastic culture; another was intimate religious associations through his middle life and the main part of his career; and those two wants of his life, as he has solemnly said to me, were the only great regrets he had. But remember, that while Cornelius Vanderbilt had not the advantages of the schools, that great lack was compensated for in a large measure by the extraordinary intellectual endowments with which God had gifted him. And then, and above all, remember this, that what saved him was the fact that never in any part of his life did he for one single instant doubt that this sacred book was the Word of God and the rule of faith and practice. That was his sheet-anchor, and his love for his mother was his sheet-cable. I must now say what he charged me to say, if ever I spoke of him in public: "Say to all men that you did not have the slightest influence in the world in persuading me to believe in the Bible; that you could not, nor all the angels, nor ministers, for I have never had a minute when I did not believe it was the Word of God, whether I kept it or not." Have you that faith? If he had gone through life without that faith and come to this great battle, this eight months' campaign, fighting for life, fighting on the outskirts, fighting in the intrenchments, fighting in the citadel to the last—if he had come without that wonderful faith in the Word of God, who could have helped him? Let us not attach undue value to the things of this world, but let us not underrate ourselves. That man lying there never owned one single dime. He never possessed one single foot of ground in his own right. He was bound to hold these things as a steward of God. That is the state of the case with us, and we must give an account at the last, as he has gone to render his account of his stewardship, to the only One who has a right to judge him, Jesus Christ our Lord.

My friends, I might have made these remarks briefer; but nature is nature; and I am not—God knows I am not—discharging in a perfunctory manner the duties of a pastor toward a parishioner. I have made no preparation for this occasion, because I knew that at the moment when I was to speak over his remains I might not be able to control my feelings, and I have been talking as far away from him as I could upon these general topics. I felt, if I spoke of him at all, I should not be able to speak of him as befitted the love I bore him. And oh, how he was loved! Money can never buy love—you know it cannot. We never shed tears over a rich man just because he is a rich man. But look at these men in these galleries that have wrought with him, and what a body-guard of affection do they not present? Better than ten thousand Swiss with halberds, hired for a funeral, is one simple, manly soul, that looks lovingly upon the remains of his friend.

If one grain of love is worth ten thousand tons of admiration, then Cornelius Vanderbilt died rich. This I say as one who, with the solicitude of a pastor and a friend, watched all his spiritual motions through the last year of his life, and say it as if he were alive, and that lid were open, and he had those eagle eyes turned on me; I will say I believe that this man, at the last, had true repentance toward God—had simple, childlike faith in the Lord Jesus Christ as his personal and divine Saviour, and did yield himself to the operations of the Holy Ghost; and that, having thus yielded, and in such repentance, in such faith, and in such submission died, we may confidently trust that He who is able to save to the uttermost did fulfil His promises to our beloved friend, and that he is numbered with the saints in glory everlasting.

LIFE'S REVIEW.

BY THEODOR CHRISTLIEB, D.D., UNIVERSITY OF BONN.

[From the German.]

1. *What am I gathering?*

Let me ask *childhood*, so often overtaken by death, what hast thou gathered into thy short span of existence? Nothing but play and amusement; or also loving obedience to parents? Have thy lips learned the sweet accents of prayer, and is there within thee a growing attachment to Him who so gently suffered the little children to come unto Him and promised them "the kingdom of heaven"?

And thou, *young man or maiden*, what would pass before thine eye as the sum of thy life? If the Lord should break the fresh and blooming shell of thy life and lay open the inner kernel of thy being, what would come to view? What has accumulated within the shrine of thy heart? Hopes and wishes, acquirements and skill for this life only, an insane thirst simply to please men and attain their approbation? Or, with all thy gladsome ardor and youthful enthusiasm, hast thou also cultivated a serious aspect of life, which has early taught thee to keep in view its exalted destiny, and with spiritual weapons to contend "against youthful lusts which war against the soul"? Hast thou, through the humility of an earnest faith, conquered the vanity of knowledge and the idolatry of man-worship? Or art thou still in Egypt—still hankering after the flesh-pots of this world? Have ye " escaped the corruption that is in the world through lust"? As ye cast a glance upon the recent past, know ye something of fidelity in little things? If ye take your measurement according to Christ's word, " He that is faithful in that which is least is faithful also in much," are ye not probably lacking in both? Do not countless neglects already accuse your short lives? How many are ready to strike their sails before serious obstacles! Whatever glides not along easily and smoothly, but requires earnest thought and persevering application, is by multitudes at once dismissed. Is not this also unfaithfulness and culpable weakness?

And we, *of riper years and greater age*, how is it with us? Our lives are indeed full of God's numberless mercies and blessings, yet "the cup of thanksgiving is mingled with saddening tears." For how many temptations, dangers, and storms of life have left their stings behind! How many divine commands have either been wholly neglected or but partially executed, our conduct being determined more by a regard for our own situation than the honor and glory of God! How many a dissension, even with our nearest kindred, casts its gloomy shadow over our lives! How often has our deference to others' views and wishes betrayed us into a wrong course or made others to sin! When confronted with a clamorous tumult, have we bravely stemmed the storm, or like Aaron suffered ourselves to be swept along with the stream? Ah! how many humbling recollections of sins like or even worse than Aaron's have we gathered! He saw only the morning's dawn of God's kingdom; we live in the full blaze of its noonday sun. Has now the more glorious revelation of God in Christ Jesus influenced us so as to walk always in its light, to devote our energies to its extension, and, prompted by the love of Christ and the will of God, so to serve our own generation that when the summons comes: " Thou shalt be gathered unto thy people and die,' we can hear that summons without alarm?

Or have our aims and wishes, our words and deeds, been only from and for beneath, so that when the final reckoning comes we could wish that most of them had never been or were greatly different? Will what you have gathered be a memorial to your honor or to your everlasting disgrace? Have you with the Lord gathered, or without Him only scattered?

Look once more upon Aaron. Moses shall lead him and his son Eleazar to Mount Hor: "And strip Aaron of his garments and put them upon Eleazar his son, and Aaron shall be gathered unto his people and shall die there. And Moses did as the Lord commanded; and they went up into Mount Hor in the sight of all the congregation. And Moses stripped Aaron of his garments and put them upon Eleazar his son." Behold this little group in the awe-inspiring stillness on the mountain's summit. For miles no soul is near; only the eye of God is upon them. Moses, the younger, but, as God's prophet, now more honorable brother, begins to take the mitre from the elder brother's brow, the breastplate from his bosom, the ephod from his shoulders, and the white surplice from his body, and puts them all on Eleazar. Increasingly poorer and humbler becomes the dying man, until he stands there at last, externally, like every other mortal. How death levels all earthly distinctions and makes high and low alike!

And when, dear hearer, thou shalt at last arrive at eternity's portals, and there perceive that before the holy Judge nothing merely human shall stand which our only Mediator has not consecrated, cleansed, and sanctified by His Spirit, then will the mitre of wisdom drop from thy brow, the honors of the world and the frontlets of genius sink into the dust as nothing worth, if tainted with selfishness or corroded with pride; then will the glittering breastplate of human ambition with which the carnal heart girded itself for so many years be untied, and its delusive dreams, so fondly cherished, vanish into air; then will the surplice of good works, upon which the eye so confidently lingered, be stripped off, if wrought only for the pleasement of men and not from love to the Master. Yea, then will every fruit of life sink irrecoverably out of sight whose root is not found in genuine faith "and love unfeigned" as the product of the Holy Ghost; then will be made manifest to many a one who had hoped to have gathered a great deal, that "Whosoever gathereth not with Me scattereth abroad."

Oh, poor soul that then finds nothing else at life's final revision but what must remain behind—and accuse it!

Thus, then, our first question, *What am I gathering?* naturally leads to—

2. *What should I have gathered when life's final revision comes?*

This too we learn from the dying priest's history on Hor's summit. Now, what God demanded of him and of all His people was *uncompromising fidelity to his covenant with the Almighty.* This one point includes all others. And despite the many weaknesses and sins Aaron had always, through the divine mercies and discipline, returned to the Lord, and had yielded such fruits that heaven's benedictions could abidingly rest on them. He had never refused to accompany Moses to the vacillating Pharaoh; had with prayer upheld his brother's hand in the battle with the Amalekites; had retained and executed the office into which God's free choice had placed him and his house unto the end; and when, after the destruction of Korah and his band, the people murmured against him and Moses, and the plague broke out among them and thousands had already perished, then Aaron, like a true priest, with the atoning censer in hand, flung himself into the breach and nobly used his prerogatives as High Priest in his intercessory prayers for the rebellious people, standing like a breastwork of protection "between the living and the dead until the plague was stayed." Yes, his life contained imperishable fruits—deeds of faith, of love, and of trust in God.

He can, therefore, at life's final review gather from it not only the memorials of God's fidelity and of his own failings, but *that* also which, through God's grace and discipline, he has become; gather the fruits of his faith, his love, his hope and his trust in God. And leaning on the divine promises—perhaps his mind's eye glancing upward to that greater High Priest who should atone for the sins of the whole world, and whose office his own had but prefigured—*he can close his eyes in peace.* Upward, not downward, does he go in his death. Though privileged to see the promised land only at a distance, his end was assuredly in peace and reconciliation with God—albeit that his life-history had been a stormy one, full of toils, sufferings, and chastisements. Calmly submissive to God's holy but most gracious decree, deprived of his outward priestly robes, yet retaining the inward priestly adornments of peace and hope, of trust and humble resignation to the divine will—thus is he gathered to his fathers, and permitted, without a protracted struggle, to pass away. He had not lived in vain; following the wise guidance of God he had brought forth fruit, and therefore his name was held in blessed remembrance among the people. "And Aaron died there in the top of the mount: and Moses and Eleazar came down from the mount. And when all the congregation saw that Aaron was dead, they mourned for him thirty days, even all the house of Israel."

Here, then, you too may learn what you ought to gather for life's final revision. Before all else, certainly *that one and only support and comfort* in life and death, which the first answer of a well-known catechism holds up to us, "That with body and soul . . . we should not be our own, but belong to our faithful Saviour, Jesus Christ." That is the *sure foundation*, the high rock of faith on which we ought to stand when life draws to its close. There should we be clothed with the priestly garments of salvation, which will forever cover our nakedness, even with the righteousness of that High Priest who changes no more, since "by one offering He hath perfected forever them that are sanctified."

And with this divine power—this new life-power of faith, mercy, and peace in God—you ought to labor and *gather fruit* from works wrought in God, which aid, amid the various positions and vocations, in the upbuilding of the future of God's people who, by word and deed, prayer and example, co-operate in the development of Christ's kingdom; and which works, therefore, follow those who die in the Lord, in order that at the judgment day they may be revealed to the honor of God and His children.

You ought to gather fruits, too, from all the experiences of your lives, whether elevating or depressing, and hold them fast in your last hour with that calm submission to God which grows out of a humble trust in the Almighty and a careful observance of all the leadings and changes of your lives, since, as disciplinary and merciful, they are always designed to confirm this one great truth, "God doeth all things well."

And, finally, you ought to gather from all these things a *sure hope, a happy prospect* of your future inheritance, of reunion with all the fathers and brethren in Christ; of those "green pastures" where the Chief Shepherd leads His flock, where there is neither a

Red Sea nor a Dead Sea, but "a sea clear as crystal;" where flows the river of life, on whose margin grow the trees of life; where beckon you, not the black surface of the wilderness, but the lightsome plains of immortality; not the burning desert, but the bowers of Eden; not the bleak and barren wastes of Paran, but the fields of living green of Paradise. You ought to be able to say, "I know that my Redeemer liveth;" "I have fought a good fight"—have gathered for the hour of my departure mercy and peace, faith and hope; "henceforth there is laid up for me a crown of righteousness."

Oh, dear brethren, whoever of you desires at last to depart in peace, and calmly to review not only this or that division of concluded labor, but his whole life, let him diligently and frequently institute such reckoning days, and work while it is day, sowing and gathering in faith what in that solemn hour he will wish that he could gather. We all, as it were, step by step, with the seeds of death in our bosom, ascend the mountain for life's last revision—some farther advanced, others farther back. Life's way leads to death's summit. The higher the ascent, the farther the outlook. But not all obtain the blessed view, like Moses on Mount Nebo, of the promised land. If we have gathered nothing abiding, nothing satisfying, then will thick mist, or even black thunder-clouds, veil our goal. If, however, on the other hand, we have gathered with Christ, then "at evening time it shall be light" for us.

Blessed is that soul at whose review of life *faith issues into vision*, which suffers itself willingly to be stripped of all earthly things, since it desires to depart and be with Christ and be gathered to the people of the Lord, and which can say on the confines of the wilderness and Canaan, of life and death, "I am both thy pilgrim and thy citizen."

DEATH OF AN ONLY DAUGHTER.*

BY WILLIAM M. TAYLOR, D.D., NEW YORK.

DEATH always comes veiled in mystery and draped in sadness, but in the dispensation which has gathered us together here this afternoon, there are some elements of peculiar sorrow. A brief, bright earthly life, radiant while it lasted with sunshine and joy for all around, and to human view full of promise for the future, has come to a close. The daughter, after having reached that stage where the filial has been merged, if I should not rather say exalted, into the sisterly, has been removed from the parent's embrace, and a glory and gladness have gone out of the home. Scripture has emphasized the bitterness of the sorrow that is caused by the death of an only son ; but that has its parallel at least, if not its superior, in the grief that is occasioned by the removal of an only daughter. I may not dwell on all that this loved one was to all in the household to which she belonged, lest in my well-meant effort to administer consolation, I should after all do little more than aggravate the grief which I desire to soothe. But as in this case, the magnitude of the loss is also, blessed be God for it ! the measure of the consolation, it is meet that I should say a word or two on her character and disposition. Over and above the natural buoyancy of youth, there was in her the bright sparkle and effervescence of a mind which was singularly quick in its apprehension, and peculiarly active and alert in its movements. The constitutional animation of her temperament was modified and subdued in her by the discipline of affliction. For years she had been very much of an invalid, but that, while it did not mar her cheerfulness, gave it only a finer and more sensitive quality, so that, mature beyond her years, she had been fitted by her affliction for companionship with those who were a long way her seniors. Hence it is that to-day her loss is mourned with equal intensity by her youthful schoolfellows to whom she was allied by that buoyancy to which I have referred, and by her elder friends who found in her a ripeness of experience that was unusual in one

---

* At the funeral of the only daughter of Dr. Ormiston.

of her tender age. As was to be expected, considering the household in which she was reared, she came early under the influence of the Gospel of Christ, and connected herself publicly with the membership of the Church. Her piety, however, was more pervasive in its influence over all her conduct, than given to express itself in any one form. She did not say much of it in words, but it spoke through her cheerfulness, her purity, her truthfulness, and above all, through that affection which embraced all who loved the Lord Jesus Christ. In her last illness she spoke but little directly of her own religious experience. At first she was slightly perplexed with the question, why she should have been so greatly afflicted, but having received a kind and wise answer from her father, she put the difficulty from her and resigned herself entirely to the will of God. Two sayings of hers in the closing days of her illness will be ever treasured by those who were dearest to her, and I mention them here as indicative of the current of her unspoken thoughts throughout her sickness. After her father had prayed with her, she asked, "Papa, why is it that we get so much nearer to God when we are in affliction? Is He not equally accessible to us at all times?" A question which shows how the cross that she was called to bear was raising her into closer fellowship with her Lord. Asking again from what text her father had preached on the afternoon of last Lord's day, she received for her answer, "If I may but touch His garment I shall be whole," whereupon she replied, "I can touch His garment now," and it is our consolation to know that now she is made whole. So we cannot weep for her. Our sorrow is for ourselves, and the day is coming when by happy reunion in the presence of the Lord our sorrow shall be turned into joy.

It is not unusual to speak and think of the death of a maiden like this as premature, and of the life as unfinished. In our cemeteries we often see a broken shaft over a young person's grave, as an emblem of this view of the case, and I will not deny that there is both poetry and pathos in the symbol. But after all, is not every human life from one point of view unfinished? Which of the sons of men has done all that he designed to do in life? The historian is called away, leaving his great work a fragment; the novelist is stricken down, leaving his tale half told; the artist is removed, while yet the work on which he is engaged is only begun. There never was a finished life upon this earth, excepting one, and that was the life of One who was more than man—even Jesus Christ the Incarnate God. We are stopped in our work, and at the best it is very far from finished work, but He fully filled in the ideal which He designed. In this aspect, therefore, the death of a young person does not materially differ from that of another; and a broken pillar may fitly symbolize even the longest life of mere man upon the earth.

But in the case of the Christian, is any life unfinished? We may not forget here that our present existence is the root from which our immortality will spring, and that what seems unfinished here will be perfected above. Wandering once up the side of a mountain in my native land, I came in sight of a monument in the shape of a tall pillar, which crowned its summit. I resolved to go and examine it, but as I ascended, the mist came down; and when I came to the base of the shaft, I could read the inscription on the pediment, but the top was concealed from me in the cloud. So I think it is in a case like this. The pillar is not broken; but its finished capital is concealed from our eyes by the misty veil that hides the future from the present, and when that is removed we shall see not only that the shaft is unbroken, but that the symmetry and beauty of the top are in perfect keeping with its early earthly foundation.

I am aware, indeed, that so far as we have any knowledge of heaven, we may say that it is certain that there shall not be there the same relationships and occupations we have here; but there is no doubt that there shall be need there for the qualities of character which were developed by our training and experience here, and we shall then understand, as we cannot here, not only why we were each brought, through his own personal history, but also why our dear ones were taken from us at the time they were. The Lord had need of them just then, and their removal was necessary not only to the symmetry but to the finish of their immortal excellence.

Sometimes, again, when we are brought face to face with a dispensation like this, we are disturbed by the mystery of the question, why there was so much promise in a young life that came, to human view, to no maturity. We cannot answer that question fully, but we can point to a parallel mystery in which the contrast might have seemed yet greater, and by the contemplation of which we may be consoled. We cannot forget here that our Saviour Himself died while yet He was but a young man. For four thousand years, from the date of the primal prophecy, preparations were being made for His appearance. The whole Mosaic system and the entire history of the Jews was in order to His manifestation. One would have thought, therefore, that when He came His life would have been greatly prolonged. But instead, He died at the age of thirty-three, after little more than three years of public life. What a poor outcome for such preparations! one might say, speaking after the manner of men; but now, recalling His resurrection and ascension—behold what that life has done for humanity, and with the history of the past eighteen centuries behind us, who dare say that the result has not been worthy of the preparation?

Now I know that is a peculiar case. But still the dead in Christ have a participation in the ascension life of Christ, and no matter how brief the earthly existence may have been, no Christian life has ever been in vain. There have been influences, we may be sure, on the companions of this beloved girl, which shall tell many days hence, and in the outcome of which she will, so to say, live anew. And there will be influences on those to whom she was dearest, which will affect them all their days. That is a true and deep word of the poet to his friend in a similar sorrow to this:

> "God gives us love; something to love
> He lends us; then when love is grown
> To ripeness, that on which it throve
> Falls off, and love is left alone."

There has been left by this young life a deposit of blessing on the heart of every member of her household, and in the fertility which that will give to their after lives, she will still be operative in the world. This is true of personal character, but I cannot forbear from adding, for the sake of my beloved brother, the pastor of this church, that it is true also of public usefulness. Ezekiel was made a sign to the people to whom he was sent, by the loss of his wife, when "the desire of his eyes" was cut off by a stroke; and through the personal discipline of His ministers yet, God often begins to give a special blessing to their people. It is a terrible ordeal. Yet when souls are born again through it, and saints are built up as the result, we may see a little of the purpose of God in our trial. This trial will give, I am sure, new power and pathos to my brother's teachings and influence here, powerful as his ministry has been in the past, and he will be able to comfort others with the comfort wherewith he himself was comforted of God. Years ago, when first I looked upon the face of my loved friend in the old country, it pleased God, as he well remembers, to come into my home and take within a week two of my children to Himself. It was a dreadful experience. Yet at evening time it was light, and when within two years after that there were no fewer than six families in my church similarly afflicted, I saw something at least of God's design. I learned that He had sent me on before these friends that I might explore the nature of the path, and might be the better able to help them through. So it comes that these darkest experiences blossom up into higher usefulness. "Out of the eater comes forth meat, and out of the bitter sweetness;" and we may not doubt that the influences of this sore trial to the minister will fall in blessing on the people.

For the rest we know whither Clara has gone. She is with Jesus. Safe, happy, pure, and perfect. Far better than she ever was or even could be on earth. Shall we wish her back again, then? Nay;

> "What here we call our life is such
> So little to be loved, and she so much,
> That we would ill requite her to constrain
> Her unbound spirit into bonds again."

No. We wish not to have her back. We shall go to her; she shall not return to us. We shall go to her, and so that which is a happy memory is made to give new power to a golden hope. The light has not gone out: it has only been transferred from earth to heaven to lighten us thither, and to bring us more than ever under the power of the world to come.

Blessed consolation of the Gospel! What should we do at such a time without it? Glorious triumph of the grace of God, that His comforts most abound when our sorrow is the darkest! The loved one is absent, but she is not distant. I have never been able to sing of the happy land as "far, far away." There is no place to which we are so near as heaven. We cannot cross the street without taking time in which to do it, but we may be in heaven in a moment. The veil between this and the heavenly life is not one of distance, but of nature. In this house of our Father there are more mansions than the visible abode in which now we dwell, and our dear one has but gone "from one room into the next." When you go down the street arm in arm with a friend, you are not far from him who is walking on his other side. Clara is "with Christ." But we, too, in a very real and true sense, are "with Christ," and as we go through life hand in hand with Him we cannot be far away from those who are on His other side. There is only one between us, and that one is Christ. Brother, let that thought be your comfort in this hour of sadness.

A MOTHER'S REMOVAL.

BY JOHN HALL, D.D., NEW YORK.

Death being universal, it might be supposed it would be without variety of aspect. The common lot might be expected to have a certain sameness. What happens alike to all might be thought to lack anything like variety.

But it is far otherwise. No two lives are absolutely identical, any more than any two bodies. And no two deaths are identical. Each has something distinctive and peculiar about it. This occasion, for example, if you will consider it, has something that renders it unlike other funerals you have attended.

A mother has gone from her home and household cares into the Master's presence. A wife has been called from the duties of this life into the dwelling-place of the Most High. Her children are not in absolute infancy; but at a time of life when the body does not require, the mind and character do need care and oversight. There has been a close and tender and happy married life, but when does the time come to either party in such a union when it is felt that either can be spared? And, as has happened to mothers with startling and mournful frequency this past winter, the stroke has descended with only brief foregoing warning. All this is displeasing to us naturally. It shocks our sense of the fitness of things. It seems to us as if benevolence would lengthen out such a life, protract such tenderness, and give to the young the benefits of maternal supervision, and the comfort of a mother's kindly, constant, loving guidance.

But it is by such lessons that God is constantly showing our wisdom to be foolishness, throwing us off from human calculations and back upon Himself. It is by such lessons, that make their appeal to our deepest and our best natural feelings, that He is saying to us, "Be still, and know that I am God." Did we live in a sinless world, where the exercise of benevolence alone is needed, and were we sinless ourselves, like the angels, taking in heavenly wisdom as we take the air into our lungs, it might not be needed to teach us this acquiescence. But we are slow of heart to believe. Lessons of truth have to be beaten into us with many stripes. We are members of a fallen race, and in a world where God is owned only where He compels attention. The seed of life has to be planted in uncongenial soil, and the breaking up of the fallow ground is accomplished only by forcible and persistent application. We are, besides, all bound together, as families and communities. "No man liveth to himself, and no man dieth to himself." While God does no injustice to the individual, we may be sure, He makes the providences that affect the individual a discipline to the family, an instruction to the community. So the sufferer is often an unconscious benefactor, and God's children, I think, often resemble the Master, who, while His hands were lifted up in blessing, departed from the disciples, and whose choicest gift came to them when He Himself was gone! General considerations like these go a certain length to silence objections, and enforce patient acquiescence in God's will.

We can be helped a little farther in the same direction, if we will try to suppose an opposite course pursued by the Almighty, to that which He adopts, and which is here illustrated. Suppose, for a moment, that parents were uniformly permitted to survive to see their children mature and settled in life; suppose no such violent rending of the tenderest ties ever to occur as we witness; what, on general principles, might we expect to see?

Is not one of the most impressive reflections in the mind of a thoughtful husband or wife founded on the possibility of separation? and is not this the very healthiest check on all tendency to impatience, or undesirable self-assertion under the inevitable petty troubles of life? "We may be parted at any time—let there be nothing but tenderness to sweeten the present. Let there be no bitterness to make sad recollections in the future." So the thought of possible and even abrupt separation is a continual and quite necessary motive to mutual forbearance and tenderness.

How easy it is—as a second consideration—in our natural indolence to defer the careful training and restraining of children! Not many parents mean to mislead their offspring. But too many put off the hard and unpalatable tasks of commanding them in the right way and enforcing compliance. But if parents uniformly lived to see them grow up to maturity, how much more powerful would this temptation become! As it is, a thoughtful parent will say, "I may not be long over these dear ones—let me make the right impressions while here; by my words, by my spirit, by my life with them, let me give the right direction to their young lives; for soon I may be to them nothing but a name and a memory." And you and I will miss something we should gain from these painful removals, if we do not on this principle count home-life more sacred, and home responsibilities greater. An error of the tenth part of an inch where the bullet leaves the gun is a divergence of many yards where it is meant to strike. And so slight error at the point where we are in immediate contact with our children, giving direction to their commencing career, may be an irreparable mistake in their lives.

But we need not—cannot perhaps profitably—exercise reason to a great extent in a case like this—certainly not when our hearts are full and our eyes dim with tears. We do better when we fall back on God's word and believe it: "This is the victory that overcometh the world, even your faith." Our sister, lately the light and joy of this house, combined in an unusual degree a cheerful, playful spirit, and a bright and rapidly working fancy, with great penetration and sound judgment. She was independent in mind, averse to artificial and superficial life. She was of warm, strong feelings, and gave, where she gave, her whole confidence. She was this by nature—would have been this, I presume, had nothing greater or deeper ever come to her. But from early life she was under the influence of that religion which she heard preached by her father, and saw in her home. For years before professing her faith, according to Church appointment, she gave evidence of a true spiritual life, and her course throughout has been in consistency with that profession. The Lord Jesus was real to her in the cares and duties of her course; He was real to her in hours of anxiety and pain, and if there be a great blank in this home, it is not because a life has been extinguished forever, but transferred to another sphere, to an elevation, and purity, and perfection, of which we see here but the germs and promises.

So we bury our believing dead out of our sight, in submission to the divine will; in loving recognition of the Redeemer who has brought life to us by His own death; in confidence that even their dust shall not lack His affectionate care; in the assurance that He shall come again bringing His people with Him, and reunite His people in imperishable bonds in a glorious and a deathless kingdom. Let it be our main care that we be of His people; that, joined to Him, our natural affinities be with them; for death neither regenerates nor sanctifies. The bent and direction of our life while here must be the bent and direction of it forever. "If we live after the flesh we shall die; but if we, through the Spirit, do mortify the deeds of the body, we shall live."

LIVING AFTER DEATH.

BY J. M. SHERWOOD, D.D., BROOKLYN.

THE influence which mind exerts upon mind is a mysterious and powerful characteristic of our being. It enters into every act, relation, and circumstance of life. It begins with moral agency, and extends along the entire line of existence. It is ever flowing out from us through a thousand channels and agencies, over the surface of society. No man can divest himself of this power, or refrain from exercising it; it is a condition of moral existence; we must exert a deep and lasting influence on the world, for good or for evil. A link, unseen, yet real, connects us all with the past and with the future. Those influences which are moulding our character, and working out our destiny, took their rise far up the stream of time ; we did not create them, and we cannot arrest or escape them. And we, in turn, are living for coming ages ; souls yet unborn will feel our influence, and be saved or damned by it. The good man little knows the extent of that blessed power which he will silently wield over human minds and hearts when he has ceased to be ; the fruit of it all gathered to heaven will fill him with adoring wonder. And the sinner knows not how fearfully his influence will accumulate in after ages, nor how many souls will charge their sins upon him in the judgment-day.

"We are fearfully and wonderfully made." Such are the elements of our own being, and such our relations to others, that we cannot die in this world or the next. How numberless are our actions !—and not one of them will ever find a grave, or live an idle life, or prove false to its parentage. They may be unwise, and regretted by us—the work of a moment's folly or passion ; no matter, we have given them life and we cannot take it away ; and they will live on in their consequences when the occasion which called them into being, and the remembrance of the deeds themselves, have perished—live still to fasten impressions on human character, and control the destiny of souls immortal.

The wicked Cain is alive still on the earth ; his type of character is manifest, and his footprints are seen along the pathway of the living world. The man who hates goodness and sheds innocent blood, copies the example and acts out the spirit of the first murderer. Abel is not dead. He belongs to living piety, as well as to history. By his recorded example of obedience and faith, and by the memory of all that he was, he is present with the child of God in every land and age of the world, declaring the necessity of faith in Jesus, the mercy and favor shown to the penitent and believing, and the treatment which the good are to expect in this world of enmity and death. All the great and good of past ages are speaking to us—with united voice crying to us to press on in the race and seize the immortal crown ; their influence, in letters of light and purity, is recorded on every page of the world's history ; it is embodied in a thousand forms of living truth, and freedom, and piety. The Voltaires, and Paines, and Byrons of past days are still leading actors in the great drama of life. Their monuments stand thick along the road we are travelling to immortality. They live to-day in all those sentiments and movements which are hostile to Christianity, and operate, through a corrupt literature, a false philosophy, and an infidel creed, along all the channels of human intellect, affection, and enterprise. On their mission of madness and death, they are travelling round the world. The missionary encounters them in the very heart of heathendom. They are breeding a moral pestilence amid the altars of Christianity. The press is wielding its giant power to give them a yet wider and deeper influence. What a harvest of ruin and damnation will such men reap! What a legacy to leave to posterity! What a curse to entail upon untold generations!

Not less certainly, indeed, does the life of *every sinner* reach into the future. His influence corrupts and destroys beyond his death-bed. It rolls onward from his grave with a cumulative sweep and strength. His example ruins his children; a whole community is infected by it; the poison courses through all the veins of living men, and flows down the ever-widening channels of human thought and life. And should not every *good* man, therefore, treasure up for posterity a holy influence, to counteract the many examples of wickedness, and perpetuate goodness, and truth, and piety in the earth? Should it not be the strenuous aim of every living man to leave a *good* influence to come after him, since he must leave one of some kind—either a saving or a ruining one? We cannot gather up our influence when we come to die, and take it with us. We cannot bury our example with our bones in the grave, so as to prevent its breeding a moral pestilence. We cannot take back our words, call in our sentiments, blot out our deeds, and so put an end to our moral being on earth. Many a dying man would give worlds if he could but do this. If he could drag with him into the darkness and oblivion of the grave, his infidelity, his wicked example, and all the evil influences which he has originated and set a-going, that they might not live after him, to curse his memory, and blast the hopes of his family and friends, and entail misery on the world, he might die in peace. But no: the dying man cannot do it. He has no power over his influence; he cannot stay the waters which he has let out. He has sown the seed, and the harvest is sure to follow. The grave shall receive his body only—the living world will retain his character, example, and principles. Death cannot arrest our influence; it may but augment and diffuse it. It will live and yield its fruit when our names have perished from the earth. It may speak for us in praise or blasphemy, in life or death, while time endures. It may go on producing impressions on the living world, which no man or angel can ever efface.

There is a thought here which the minister of Christ, the professional man, and the man of wealth, the Sabbath-school teacher, and above all, the parent, may bring home to his heart with salutary and impressive force. There is a light of *warning* and a light of *encouragement* in it. Each of us may so live as that our very grave shall bloom until the resurrection morn. The good we do is not to be measured by the length of our days, but by our stamp of character, the piety of our purposes, the grandeur of our aspirations and conceptions. Then up and be doing, ye children of light! Every prayer, every charity, every effort for Christ, every tear shed over sinners, will yield a revenue of reward and glory.

A TIME TO DIE.

ANONYMOUS.

> "Death! 'tis a melancholy day
> To those who have no God,
> When the poor soul is forced away
> To seek her last abode!"

"A TIME to die!" Only one time. In seeking a fortune we may make new trials when we fail in one; but dying is one solemn, final, eternal experiment! The voyager launches upon a shoreless sea, and returns no more forever to the land he leaves. "Man dieth, and wasteth away; yea, man giveth up the ghost, and where is he? As the waters fail from the sea, and the flood decayeth and drieth up, so man lieth down and riseth not: till the heavens be no more, they shall not awake, nor be raised out of their sleep!" The tide of life will roll on; the bustle of the world will continue; friends will meet in smiles, and part in tears, as before; flowers will bloom, and stars will shine; empires will arise and fall; the sower will walk forth and scatter in hope ; the reaper will gather the sheaf to his bosom ; autumn winds will moan, and fierce wintry storms will drive in anger past ; the cheerful hearth will chime its crackling notes of comfort, with glad music of fireside joys ; but by all this the dead are not disturbed, for " they have no more a portion forever in anything that is done under the sun." They die, and are laid into the grave, and there all is to them alike.

> " The storm that wreaks the wintry sky
> No more disturbs their calm repose,
> Than summer evening's latest sigh
> That shuts the rose."

It is somewhat strange that the truth of our mortality is so often repeated in the Bible. "A time to die" is echoed into our ears again and again. It is because we are so prone to put the thought of dying away from us. Every day's experience teaches this truth. The tolling bell, the long funeral train, the garments of mourning, the new-made grave, are daily testimonies that it is appointed unto man once to die. And yet how soon is all forgotten ! Scarce has the grass grown upon the grave of the departed, before even many of the relatives have ceased to feel that death is solemn. As when we throw a stone into a stream it causes a momentary sound and agitation of the surface, and then the stone lies silently below while the stream glides on as before, so when one falls by death, it causes a short groan, a tear, and a few thoughts of death and dying ; but the sod is closed over, the sleeper lies in silence beneath, and the tide of life and human folly flows madly on !

The world around is also full of admonitory voices. The fading flower, the falling leaf, and the autumnal moans of the dying year all speak of death. We all do fade as a leaf, and as for man, he cometh forth like a flower, and is cut down ! But man, bent upon the chase of wealth and honor, heeds not, though the tide of life ebbs fast from his heart.

Let us but step forward a little way in life and our death scenes will be around us. They will surely come. All the solemnity which we have witnessed in the death of others will be experienced by us. Who can realize fully the dread anxiety of the last moment? Solemn twilight, in which the dying rays of earth and the new-born light of heaven are blended ! The world and life are full of changes, but there is no change like dying. How far is that moment from us? The answer is, "man also knoweth not his time." A step, as thy soul liveth, is between thee and the grave ! "As the fishes that are taken in an evil net, and as the birds that are caught in the snare, so are the sons of men snared in an evil time, when it falleth suddenly upon them." These figures are expressive. The fish *in the net*, while it is yet in the water, thinks he is still at liberty, and while the net is drawn toward the shore he knows not that he is snared ; even while he is at the edge of the water he feels still in his element, when lo ! at once he is raised above the surface and he is caught. He was in the net before, and was in reality caught, but now he feels it ; so man swims in the midst of influences and tendencies which are preparing his dissolution, and when he is thus led to the very shore of eternity, he is suddenly snared and carried away. So also the bird walks upon the snare, and knoweth not that it is for its life, when at once it is caught. So also a blind man walks up to a precipice, and knows not that the next step will dash him upon the rocks below. Great God ! how solemn thus to walk on the earth hollow with the caverns of the dead, and not know at what moment the frail shell upon which we stand may break down into eternal burnings ! How knowest thou, O man, how far before thee stands the stake which is to bound the days of thy pilgrimage ! Who has numbered your days and told you their sum ? If you know not, why do you boast yourself of to-morrow, and say it shall be as this day. Why does vain man walk so proudly, so carelessly, and so madly forward, not knowing whether the next foot he puts down will be on earth, in heaven, or in hell ! "Seeing his days are determined, the number of his months are with thee, thou hast appointed his bounds that he cannot pass."

> "How shocking must thy summons be, O death !
> To him that is at ease in his possessions ;
> Who, counting on long years of pleasure here,
> Is quite unfurnished for that world to come !"

There must be some painful things in the death of a wicked man. Many untold horrors must gather around him in that fearful crisis. Of this the countenance of the corpse the moment after death bears awful witness. Who has not observed the difference in the countenance of the recently dead? The infant gathers a smile upon its face in the moment of death, which it retains for days. Perhaps that smile is a response to the friendly greetings of angels who are waiting with friendly wing to bear the disembodied spirit to its God. Or it is caused by the sweet presence of the Saviour, who stands by, as if kindly to reprove the weeping parents with those blessed words, "Suffer little children to come unto Me." Not only in children, but in aged Christians who died ripe for glory, is the same phenomenon often witnessed. The smile of the spirit when it breaks through into glory is left behind impressed upon the lineaments of the face. But who has not witnessed the haggard and gloomy horror that death leaves behind it on the countenance of the man of sin who dies in despair? It seems, as if by some deep convulsion, the soul were expelled in shattered fragments from the body! The half-opened mouth and the eyes fixed in wild astonishment denote that the soul at the moment of its exit had been fearfully surprised. And why should it not, when perhaps at the moment it realized the thrilling truth, "Thou art weighed in the balance and art found wanting!" O man of sin, in your life's last twilight hour, you will find around you images ill boding and fearful, and dark floating phantoms relieved in lurid fire, will be the landscape sketched out before your dying eyes!

THE MASTER'S SHEPHERD DOG.*

BY JUSTIN D. FULTON, D.D., BROOKLYN.

UNCLE JOHN VASSAR, the eminent lay evangelist, the poor man's friend, the soldier's preacher, could say with the apostle (2 Cor. ii. 14): "Now, thanks be unto God who always causeth us to triumph in Christ." It was in Christ he triumphed, never apart from Him. The words of the apostle were written while he held in his thoughts the triumphal procession in which all the paraphernalia of war, all the glories of success, all the manifesta-

* At the funeral of John Vassar, Poughkeepsie, N. Y.

tions of joy should be employed publicly to express thanks to some honored chieftain whose wisdom, whose prowess, and whose leadership had won victories for the army and glory for the nation.

On such occasions the victorious commander was usually preceded by the spoils of war, among which were the most valuable and magnificent trophies which had been obtained by the princes, nobles, generals, and representatives of the people whom he had captured. On the platform of a car drawn by milk-white steeds was an altar on which were burning aromatics, whose cloud of incense and fragrance pavilioned the multitude and spread through the capital the information that a wonderful triumph had been declared.

It was review day with Paul. He has in his mind's eye Damascus, where he was let down the wall in the basket; Troas, where he was disappointed in not seeing Titus; Philippi, where he found no place to worship and so went to the river bank; he thinks of the town where he was beaten and dragged through the street as one dead, where he had revelations he dare not disclose; of his night in the prison, where the jailer was converted after the earthquake's throes, after a night had been given up to singing praises to God; he thinks of being before Felix and Agrippa, of being sent to Rome, of his shipwreck and disasters, and yet exclaims, "Now, God be thanked who always causeth me to triumph in Christ."

Paul triumphed in Christ because Christ his Lord found it always possible to triumph in him. He lived for Christ and not for self. His business consisted in doing the will of God; he had no other desire but to glorify Christ, on shipboard, in tent-making, in marching, in prison and in palace. The victories were won for him, not by him, and before the world he desired to place the testimonials of gratitude to Christ, who triumphed in him in every place.

This is review day. In this life now closed methinks I hear the echoes of the same shout of triumph. Uncle John Vassar took no glory to himself. From the day when the Spirit of God wrestled with him in the brewery, causing him to give up position, business, thoughts of opulence and independence, our brother found in Christ the source of power and the earnest of victory.

. Though he is mourned to-day from Maine to California; though he will be remembered in the palaces of the great and in the cabins of the humble as few men ever were or will be, yet he was distinguished for winning victories on fields which by the majority would be neglected, or turned from in contempt. He began as a colporteur. He grew to be a master in Israel, and was the companion, the brother beloved, of the noblest of the land. He sought not his own, but was everywhere as He that served. It was in Boston I first saw him. The war was over. He had been working in some one of the churches, when on one occasion he came into a meeting at Tremont Temple. God was there. I seem to see Uncle John's eyes now as they flashed with joy. I hear his voice in song. I seem to see him all on fire, rolling from side to side, and, half laughing and half crying, overflowing with love. He did not speak, he did not pray; he revelled in bliss. When at the close of the meeting I took his hand and asked his name, he said, "I am *Uncle John Vassar*, the Master's shepherd dog! I have been helping so-and-so, and I am just through, and as I had a spare hour, I came into your meeting to get a little honey from the rock. It is good to be here, brother; it is good to be here."

"Can't you stay a week and help?"

"You must ask so-and-so, who has charge of me." I obtained his help. How he took hold. I hardly saw him; but how he did pull sinners out of the fire day after day! He brought trophies and laid them at his Master's feet. He has often been with my people, never much with me. He was a worker. He was not much in sight; and yet I hold in my memory a sermon he delivered in Tremont Temple, which was one of the most impressive to which I ever listened. He had immense power on the platform. He plowed in the closet and could reap everywhere.

His characteristics were: (1) Piety; Christ lived in him. (2) Consecration. Harlan Page did not surpass him. (3) Self-forgetfulness. He lived for his family next to Christ. This church and that home in Poughkeepsie were always in his thought. (4) Tact—unbounded tact. (5) Wisdom, which came from God. (6) Love, love, love! (7) Devotion to friends. (8) Capabilities to win favor for Christ. Among the poorest he was one of them, entered into all their sorrows; and among the rich he was a brother beloved.

Few men will be more tenderly mourned, for few were more tenderly beloved. In the schoolhouses and country churches of New England his face has been seen. Over its bleak hills and through its valleys his feet have carried him as he sought the wandering sheep. In villages and cities no form is more familiar, no face was more tenderly beloved. In his life was the romance of John Bunyan, the simplicity and the earnestness of John Vine Hall. One wrote, "Come to Jesus!" the other illustrated it. Both are with Jesus and are crowned heroes evermore.

INFIDELITY AND THE GRAVE.

BY ROBERT G. INGERSOLL.*

[The title is our own. We give this address by way of *contrast*. No beauty of language or wealth of natural affection can hide the utter dreariness and darkness of the picture here drawn. If unbelief has no word of hope or comfort in life's supreme hour and in the presence of death, we turn with relief and rejoicing to the teachings of Him who is the Resurrection and the Life.—EDITOR.]

My friends, I am going to do that which the dead oft promised he would do for me. The lovely and loving brother, husband, father, friend, died where manhood's morning almost touches noon, and while the shadows still were falling toward the west. He had not passed on life's highway the stone that marks the highest point; but being weary for a moment he laid down by the wayside, and, using his burden for a pillow, fell into that dreamless sleep that kisses down his eyelids still. While yet in love with life and raptured with the world, he passed to silence and pathetic dust.

Yet, after all, it may be best, just in the happiest, sunniest hour of all the voyage, while eager winds are kissing every sail, to dash against the unseen rock, and in an instant hear the billows roar above a sunken ship. For whether in mid sea or 'mong the breakers of the farther shore, a wreck must mark at

* At the funeral of his brother.

last the end of each and all ; and every life, no matter if its every hour is rich with love and every moment jewelled with a joy, will, at its close, become a tragedy as sad and deep and dark as can be woven of the warp and woof of mystery and death.

This brave and tender man in every storm of life was oak and rock, but in the sunshine he was vine and flower. He was the friend of all heroic souls. He climbed the heights and left all superstitions far below, while on his forehead fell the golden dawning of a grander day. He loved the beautiful, and was with color, form, and music touched to tears. He sided with the weak, and with a willing hand gave alms ; with loyal heart, and with the purest hands he faithfully discharged all public trusts. He was a worshipper of liberty, a friend of the oppressed. A thousand times I have heard him quote these words : "For justice all places a temple, and all seasons summer." He believed that happiness was the only good, reason the only torch, justice the only worship, humanity the only religion, and love the only priest. He added to the sum of human joy, and were every one for whom he did some loving service to bring a blossom to his grave he would sleep to-night beneath a wilderness of flowers.

Life is a narrow vale between the cold and barren peaks of two eternities. We strive in vain to look beyond the heights. We cry aloud, and the only answer is the echo of our wailing cry. From the voiceless lips of the unreplying dead there comes no word ; but in the night of death hope sees a star, and listening love can hear the rustle of a wing. He who sleeps here, when dying, mistaking the approach of death for the return of health, whispered with his latest breath, "I am better now." Let us believe, in spite of doubts and dogmas and tears and fears, that these dear words are true of all the countless dead. And now to you who have been chosen from among the many men he loved to do the last sad office for the dead, we give his sacred dust. Speech cannot contain our love. There was, there is, no gentler, stronger, manlier man.

FUNERAL ORATION FOR THE PRINCE OF CONDÉ.*

BY JAMES BENIGNÉ BOSSUET.

[From the French.]

Peroration.

COME, ye people, come now—or rather ye Princes and Lords, ye judges of the earth, and ye who open to man the portals of heaven; and more than all others, ye Princes and Princesses, nobles descended from a long line of kings, lights of France, but to-day in gloom, and covered with your grief as with a cloud, come and see how little remains of a birth so august, a grandeur so high, a glory so dazzling. Look around on all sides, and see all that magnificence and devotion can do to honor so great a hero: titles and inscriptions, vain signs of that which is no more; shadows which weep around a tomb, fragile images of a grief which time sweeps away with everything else; columns which appear as if they would bear to heaven the magnificent evidence of our emptiness; nothing, indeed, is wanting in all these honors but the one to whom they are rendered! Weep then over these feeble remains of human life; weep over that mournful immortality we give to heroes. But draw near especially ye who run, with such ardor, the career of glory, intrepid and warrior spirits! Who was more worthy to command you, and in whom did ye find command more honorable? Mourn then that great Captain, and weeping, say, "Here is the man that led us through all hazards, under whom were formed so many renowned captains, raised by his example to the highest honors of war; his shadow might yet gain battles, and lo! in his silence, his very name animates us, and at the same time warns us that to find, at death, some rest from our toils, and not arrive unprepared at our eternal dwelling, we must, with an earthly king, yet serve the King of Heaven." Serve then that immortal and ever-merciful King, who will value a sigh or a cup of cold water, given in His name, more than all others will value the shedding of your blood. And begin to

---

* Delivered before Louis XIV., of France.

reckon the time of your useful services from the day on which you gave yourselves to so beneficent a Master. Will not ye too come, ye whom he honored by making you his friends? To whatever extent you enjoyed his confidence, come all of you, and surround this tomb. Mingle your prayers with your tears; and while admiring, in so great a prince, a friendship so excellent, an intercourse so sweet, preserve the remembrance of a hero whose goodness equalled his courage. Thus may he ever prove your cherished instructor; thus may you profit by his virtues; and may his death, which you deplore, serve you at once for consolation and example. For myself, if permitted, after all others, to render the last offices at this tomb, O prince, the worthy subject of our praises and regrets, thou wilt live forever in my memory. There will thy image be traced, but not with that bold aspect which promises victory. No, I would see in you nothing which death can efface. You will have in that image only immortal traits. I shall behold you such as you were in your last hours under the hand of God, when His glory began to dawn upon you. There shall I see you more triumphant than at Fribourg and at Rocroy; and ravished by so glorious a triumph, I shall give thanks in the beautiful words of the well-beloved disciple, "This is the victory that overcometh the world, even our faith." Enjoy, O prince, this victory, enjoy it forever, through the everlasting efficacy of that sacrifice.* Accept these last efforts of a voice once familiar to you. With you these discourses shall end. Instead of deploring the death of others, great prince, I would henceforth learn from you to render my own holy; happy, if reminded by these white locks of the account which I must give of my ministry; I reserve for the flock which I have to feed with the word of life, the remnants of a voice which falters, and an ardor which is fading away.

* The sacrifice of the mass, which concluded the funeral ceremony.

FUNERAL ORATION ON LOUIS THE GREAT.

BY JEAN BAPTISTE MASSILLON.

[From the French.]

Peroration.

RETURN then to the bosom of thy God, whence thou didst come, O heroic and Christian soul! Your heart is already where your treasure is. Break these feeble ties of mortality, which prolong your desires and retard your hope; the day of our grief is the day of your glory and your triumph. May the guardian angels of France go before you to conduct you with pomp upon the throne which is appointed unto you in the heavens at the side of your ancestors, the royal saints Charlemagne and Saint Louis. Go and meet Theresa, Louis, and Adelaide, who await you, and with them, in your immortal sojourn, dry the tears which you have shed over their ashes. And if, as we hope, the sanctity and uprightness of your intentions have made good before God that which during the course of so long a reign was wanting in the merit of your works and the integrity of your justice, then, from the heights of your celestial domain, watch over a kingdom which you leave in affliction, over an infant king who has not had the leisure to grow and ripen under your eyes and example, and secure the end of the evils which overwhelm us, and of the crimes which seem to multiply with our disasters.

And Thou, great God, from the height of heaven, cast down thine eyes of pity upon this desolate monarchy, where the glory of thy name is better known than among other nations, where faith is as old as the crown, and where it has ever been upon the throne as pure as the very blood of our kings that occupied it. Defend us from the troubles and dissensions unto which Thou dost nearly always deliver the infancy of kings. Leave to us the consolation of at least peaceably bewailing our misfortunes and losses. Extend the wings of thy protecting care over the precious child that Thou hast put at the head of thy people—that august offspring of so many kings, that innocent victim, the only one saved from the blows of Thy wrath and from the extinction of the royal race. Give unto him a docile heart to receive the instructions which must be sustained by good example ; that piety, compassion, humanity, and many other virtues, which influenced his education, may be felt throughout the whole course of his reign. Be Thou his God and his Father, to teach him to be the father of his subjects ; and lead us altogether unto a blessed immortality.

SERMONS ABRIDGED.

SORROW FOR THE DEATH OF FRIENDS.

BY REV. JAMES SAURIN.

[From the French.]

But I would not have you to be ignorant, brethren, concerning them which are asleep, that ye sorrow not even as others which have no hope.—1 THESS. iv. 13.

ST. PAUL does not condemn all sorts of sorrow occasioned by the loss of those we love. He requires only that Christians should not be inconsolable in these circumstances as those which have no hope.

I. THE SORROW WHICH IS REPREHENSIBLE.

1. *That which proceeds from distrust.* Such is sometimes our situation on earth, that all our good devolves on a single point. A house rises to affluence. All its elevation proceeds from a single head. This head, the protector, the father, the friend, expires, and by that single stroke all our honors and pleasures seem to descend with him into the tomb. At this stroke nature groans, the flesh murmurs, the soul is wholly absorbed in its calamity, and concentrates itself in anguish. Now, when the loss of a temporal good casts into despair, it was obviously the object of our love—a capital crime in the eye of religion. The most innocent connections of life cease to be innocent when they become too strongly cemented. Whether it be a father, or a husband, or a child, which renders us idolaters, idolatry is not the less odious in the eyes of God. These strokes of God's hand are the tests whereby He tries our faith, according to the Apostle's idea (1 Peter 1 : 7). In prosperity it is difficult to determine whether it be love for the gift or the Giver which excites our devotion. It is in the midst

of tribulation that we can recognize a genuine zeal and a conscious piety. The example of Abraham here occurs to our view. If ever a mortal had cause to fix his hopes on any object, it was Abraham on his son Isaac. Yet when commanded to sacrifice that son, what did Abraham do? He submitted; yet in submitting, he hoped. How did he hope? He hoped against hope. Believers, here is your father. If ye are the children of Abraham, do the works of Abraham.

2. *That sorrow of which despondency is the principle.* A man judges of the happiness of others by the notion of his own happiness, and estimating life as the supreme good, he regards the person deprived of it as worthy of the tenderest compassion. The dead one seems to us to be stripped of all comforts. If he had lost his fortune, his sight, one of his limbs, we should have sympathized in his affliction; how much more so when he has been by a stroke deprived of all these things! This sorrow is appropriate to those who are destitute of hope; but for Christians nothing is more directly contrary to the faith they profess. For we believe the soul to be immortal; we believe the deceased who were here upon earth subject to so much of trial and temptation, are now afflicted no more, but are come to Mount Zion, and see God face to face.

3. *The sorrow which comes of a mistaken piety.* The foregoing remarks apply to those sorrowing over the Christian's death. But should not piety indulge her tears when we see die impenitent those who were closely bound to us by ties of nature? We answer, first, that nothing is more presumptive than to decide on the eternal loss of men. A contrite heart may be concealed under the exterior of reprobation. But often the lives we love afford us too just a ground of apprehension, and even doubt on such a matter is anguish. I confess it would be unreasonable to censure tears in such a case. An ordinary piety is inadequate to repress excess. Yet religion forbids, even in such a case, to sorrow above measure. Consider that (1) our grief really proceeds from a carnal principle. If the grief were altogether spiritual, if it were merely from the idea of a lost soul, whence is it that this one object should excite us so much more intensely than the multitude of unhappy men all around us rushing to destruction? (2) The love we have for the creature should always conform itself to the

love for the Creator. We should love our neighbors, but when a man becomes an avowed enemy of God, our love should return to its centre and associate itself with the love of the Creator (2 Cor. v. 16; Ps. cxxxix. 22; Matt. x. 37). This duty may be too exalted for the earth. The sentiments of nature may be too closely intertwined with those of religion to be so distinguished. But it is certain they shall be in heaven.

II. THE GRIEF WHICH IS INNOCENT.

1. *The grief of sympathy.* The submissive sorrow by which we feel our loss, without shutting our eyes to the resources of Providence; the sorrow which weeps at the sufferings of our friends in the road to glory, but confident of their having attained that glory —this sorrow, so far from being culpable, is an inseparable sentiment of nature and an indispensable duty of religion. Yes, it is allowed to recall the endearments which intimacy with the dead shed upon our life—those tender adieus at the final parting, the fervent prayers, the torrents of tears, the last efforts of expiring tenderness. It is allowed in weeping to show the garments which Dorcas had made. It is allowed the tender Joseph, coming to the tomb of his father, to make Canaan resound with the cries of his grief. It is allowed David to go weeping, and saying, "would to God I had died for thee, O Absalom, my son, my son!" (2 Sam. xviii. 33).

2. *Sorrow from the dictates of nature.* The first reflection which the sight of a corpse should make is that we also must die. This is a reflection every one seems to make, while in reality we generally avoid the particular application to our hearts. We follow the dead to their burial, we return home to divide their riches and enter upon their estates, just as the presumptuous mariner, who, seeing a ship upon the shore driven by the tempest, takes his bark and braves the billows to share in the spoils of the wreck. A prudent man contemplates the death of his friends with other eyes. He clothes himself in their shroud; he extends himself in their coffin; he regards his body as about to become like their corpse, and the duty he owes to himself inspires him with a gracious sorrow on seeing in the fate of his lamented friends an image of his own.

3. *The sorrow which brings repentance.* Seeing Jesus Christ has satisfied the justice of the Father for the sins of Christians, why

should they still die? To this it is commonly replied that death is now no longer a punishment for our sins, but a tempest that rolls us into port. This is a solid reply, but we still may ask, Why does God lead us by so strait a way; for, say all we can, dying is still a terrible thing, and death a formidable foe. Why do not God's chariots carry us up to heaven as they once carried Elijah? I answer, that the death of the righteous is a portrait of the divine justice which we should have constantly in view. It is an awful monument of the horror God has of sin, which should teach us to avoid it. "If the righteous be saved with difficulty, where shall the wicked appear? If the judgment of God begin at His house, where shall the end be of those that obey not the Gospel?" (1 Pet. iv. 17, 18).

These are the three sorts of sorrow that the death of our friends should excite in our breast. And so far are we from repressing this kind of grief, that we would wish you to feel it in all its force. Go to the tombs of the dead; open their coffins; look on their remains; let each there recognize a husband, or a parent, or children, or brethren; but instead of regarding them as surrounding him alive, let him suppose himself as lodged in the subterraneous abode with the persons to whom he has been closely united. Look at them deliberately, hear what they say: death seems to have condemned him to an eternal silence; meanwhile they speak; they preach with a voice far more eloquent than ours.

We have taught you to shed upon their tombs tears of tenderness. Hear the dead; they preach with a voice more eloquent than ours: "Have you forgotten the relations we formed and the ties that united us? Is it with games and diversions that you lament our loss? Is it in the circles of gayety and in public places that you commemorate our exit?"

We have exhorted you to shed upon their tomb tears of duty to yourselves. "Hear the dead;" they preach with a voice more eloquent than ours. They cry, "Vanity of vanities. All flesh is grass, and all the godliness thereof is as the flower of the field. The world passeth away, and the lusts thereof. Surely man walketh in a vain shadow." (Eccles. i. 2; Isa. xl. 6; 1 John ii. 17; Ps. xxxix. 6.) They recall to your mind the afflictions they have endured, the troubles which assailed their mind, and the deliriums that affected their brain. They recall those objects, that you may contemplate in their situation an image of your own; that you may be apprised how imperfectly qualified a man is in his last moments for recollection and the work of his salvation. They tell you that they once had the same health, the same strength, the same fortune, and the same honors as you; notwithstanding, the torrent which bore them away is doing the same with you.

We have exhorted you to shed upon their tombs the tears of repentance. Hear the dead; they preach with an eloquence greater than ours; they say that "sin has brought death into the world—death which separates the father from the son, and the son from the father; which disunites hearts the most closely attached, and dissolves the most intimate and tender ties." They say more. Hear the dead—hear some of them, who, from the abyss of eternal flames, into which they are plunged for impenitency, exhort you to repentance.

O terrific preachers, preachers of despair, may your voice break the hearts of those hearers on whom our ministry is destitute of energy and effect. Hear those dead; they speak with a voice more eloquent than ours from the depths of the abyss, from the deep caverns of hell; they cry, "Who among us shall dwell with devouring fire? Who among us shall dwell with everlasting burnings? Ye mountains, fall on us; ye hills, cover us. It is a fearful thing to fall into the hands of the living God, when He is angry." (Isa. xxxiii. 14; Luke xxiii. 30; Heb. x. 31.)

Hear the father who is suffering in hell for the bad education given to the family he left on earth. Hear him, by the despair of his condition, by the chains which oppress him, by the fire which devours him, and by the remorse, the torments, and the anguish which gnaw him, entreat you not to follow him to the abyss. Hear the impure, the accomplice of your pleasure, who says that if God had called you the first, you would have been substituted in his place, and who entreats to let your eyes become as fountains of repentant tears.

This is the sort of sorrow with which we should be affected for the death of those with whom it has pleased God to connect us by the bonds of society and of nature. May it penetrate our hearts, and forever banish the sorrow which confounds us with those who have no hope.

VICTORY OVER DEATH.

BY REV. FREDERICK W. ROBERTSON, BRIGHTON, ENGLAND.

The sting of death is sin ; and the strength of sin is the law. But thanks be to God, which giveth us the victory through our Lord Jesus Christ.—1 CORINTHIANS xv. 56, 57.

I. THE TERRORS OF THE DYING HOUR.

That which makes it peculiarly terrible to die is asserted here to be guilt. It is not the only sting of death, but it contains the venom of the most exquisite torture. It is no mark of courage to speak lightly of dying. There is a world of untold sensations crowded into that moment when a man puts his hand to his forehead and feels the damp upon it which tells him his hour is come. He has been looking for death all his life, and now it is come ; it is all over ; his chance is past, and his eternity is settled. It is a mockery to speak lightly of that which we cannot know till it comes.

1. *Every living thing instinctively cleaves to its own existence.* It is the first and intensest desire of living things *to be.* It is in virtue of this unquenchable impulse that the world, in spite of all the misery that is in it, continues to struggle on. What are war and trade and labor and professions ? Are they the result of struggling to be great ? No ; they are the result of the struggle *to be.* Reduce the nation or the man to the last resources, and only see what marvellous energy of contrivance the love of being arms them with. Read back the pauper's history at the end of seventy years, and learn what he has done to hold his being where everything is against him, and the only conceivable charm of whose existence is that it *is* existence. Talk as we will of immortality, there is an obstinate feeling that we end in death ; and *that* may be felt together with the firmest belief in resurrection. Our faith tells us one thing ; our sensations, another.

2. *It is the parting from all around which are twined the heart's best affections.* We become wedded to the sights and sounds of this lovely world more and more closely as years go on. When Lot quitted Sodom, the younger members of the family went on gladly ; it was the aged one who looked behind to the home which

had so many recollections connected with it. Every time the sun sets, every time the old man sees his children gathering around him, there is a filling of the eye with an emotion we can understand.

3. *The sensation of loneliness attaches to death.* Have we ever seen a ship preparing to sail, with its load of pauper emigrants, to a distant colony? All beyond the seas, to the ignorant poor man is an unknown land. There comes upon him a sensation new and inexpressibly miserable—the feeling of being alone in the world. So we go on our dark, mysterious journey, for the first time in all our existence, without one to accompany us. Friends are beside our bed: they must stay behind. We die alone. Grant that the Christian has something like a familiarity with the Most High— that breaks this solitary feeling. But for the mass of men there is no one point in all eternity on which the eye can fix distinctly and rest gladly.

4. *The sting of death is sin.* There are two ways in which this truth applies itself. Some carry about with them the dreadful secret of certain sin that has been committed, guilt that has a name. They have injured some one, made money by unfair means, been unchaste, or done some one of the thousand things which leave a dark spot upon the heart. They shut them out, but it will not do. When a guilty man begins to think of dying, it is like a vision of the Son of Man calling out all the voices of the unclean spirits: "Art thou come to torment us before the time?"

But with most men it is not guilty acts, but *guiltiness of heart* that weighs the heaviest. It is just this feeling: "God is not my friend; I am going on to my grave, and no *man* can say aught against me, but my heart is not right. It is not so much what I have done; it is what I am. Who shall save me from myself?" But let us bear in mind that this sting of sin is not constant. We may live many years before a death in our family forces the thought of death personally home—many years before the quick, short cough, lassitude, emaciation, pain, come upon us in our young vigor and make us feel what it is to be here with death inevitable. And when these symptoms become habitual, habit makes delicacy the same forgetful thing as health.

The Apostle traces this power of sin to torment, to the law.

He means any law and all law. Law is what forbids and
threatens; law bears gallingly on those who wish to break it. St.
Paul declares that no law, not even God's, can make man
righteous in heart. It can only force out into rebellion the sin
that is in them. It is so with a nation's law. If against the
spirit of the whole people, there is first the murmur of disapproba-
tion, then transgression, and then the bursting asunder of that
law in national revolution. So with God's law. It will never
long control a man who does not love it. First comes the sense
of constraint, then a murmuring of the heart, and last the rising
of passion in its giant might, made desperate by restraint. That
is the law giving strength to sin.

II. FAITH CONQUERING IN DEATH.

There is nothing in all this world that ever led a man on to real
victory but faith. Faith is that looking forward to a future with
something like certainty, that raises man above the narrow feelings of the present. Even in this life he who is steadily pursuing
a plan that requires some years to accomplish, is a man of more
elevated character than he who is living by the day. And
therefore it is that faith, and nothing but faith, gives victory in
death. It is that elevation of character we get from looking
steadily and forever forward till eternity becomes a real home to us;
that enables us to look upon the grave, not as the great end of
all, but only as something that stands between us and the end.
We are conquerors of death when we are able to look beyond it.

This victory is to be *through Christ*. Mere victory over death
is no unearthly thing. Only let a man sin desperately and long
enough to shut judgment out of his creed, and he can bid defiance
to death. An infidel may be, in this sense, a conqueror over
death. Or mere manhood may give us a victory. We have steel
and nerve enough in our hearts to dare anything. Felons die on
the scaffold like men; soldiers can be hired for a few pence a day,
to front death every day. Then, again, necessity makes a man the
conqueror. When a man feels that he must go, he lays him
down to die as a tired traveller wraps himself in his cloak to sleep.
But the Christian's victory over death is different from all these.

1. *He is a conqueror over doubt.* There are some men who have
never believed enough to doubt; some who have never thrown
their hopes with such earnestness on the world to come as to feel

any anxiety for fear it should not all be true. But every one who knows what faith is knows too what the desolation of doubt is. We pray till we begin to ask, Is there any one who hears, or am I whispering to myself? We hear the consolation administered to the bereaved, and we see the coffin lowered into the grave, and the thought comes, What if all this doctrine of a life to come be but a dream of man's imaginative mind, carried on from age to age, and so believed because it is a venerable superstition? Now Christ gives us victory over that doubt by His own resurrection. The grave has once, and more than once, given up its dead at His bidding. It is a world-fact that all the metaphysics about impossibility cannot rob us of. It means that we shall live again. Then we get the victory over doubt by living in Christ. All doubt comes from living out of habits of affectionate obedience to God. By idleness, by neglected prayer, we lose our power of realizing things not seen. Doubts can only be dispelled by that kind of active life that realizes Christ. When such a man comes near the vault, it is no world of sorrows he is entering. He is only going to see things that he has felt, for he has been living in heaven. He has his grasp on things other men are only groping after, and touching now and then.

2. *He is a conqueror over fear.* Let us understand what really is the victory over the fear of death. It may be rapture, or it may not. That depends very much on the temperament; and, after all, the broken words of a dying man are a very poor index of his real state before God. Rapturous hope has been granted to martyrs in peculiar moments. But it fosters a dangerous feeling to take such cases as precedents. Christian bravery is a deep, calm thing, unconscious of itself. There are more triumphant death-beds than we think, if we only remember this: true fearlessness makes no parade. Oh! it is not only in those passionate effusions in which the ancient martyrs spoke sometimes of panting for the crushing of their limbs by the lions in the amphitheatre, or of holding out their arms to embrace the flames that were to curl around them—it is not then only that Christ has stood by His servants and made them more than conquerors. There may be something of earthly excitement in all that. Every day His servants are dying modestly and peacefully, not a word of victory on their lips, but Christ's deep triumph in their hearts, watching the

slow progress of their decay, yet so far emancipated from personal anxiety that they are still able to think and plan for others, not knowing that they are doing any great thing. They come to the battle-field to which they have been looking forward all their lives, and there is no foe with which to fight.

3. *He gains the victory by his resurrection.* It is a rhetorical expression rather than sober truth when we call anything but the resurrection victory over death. We may conquer doubt and fear, but that is not conquering dying. It is like a warrior crushed to death by a superior antagonist, refusing to yield a groan, and bearing the glance of defiance to the last. And when you see flesh melting away, and mental power becoming infantine in its feebleness, and lips scarcely able to articulate, is there left for a moment a doubt as to who is the conqueror?

Bear in mind what this world would be without the thought of a resurrection. If we could conceive an unselfish man looking on this world of desolation with that infinite compassion which all the brave and good feel, what conception could he have but that of defeat, failure—the sons of man mounting into a bright existence, and one after another falling back into darkness and nothingness, like soldiers trying to mount an impracticable breach, and falling back crushed and mangled into the ditch before the bayonets and rattling fire of their conquerors. Until a man looks on evil till it seems like a real personal enemy rejoicing over the destruction it has made, he can scarcely conceive Paul's rapture when he remembered all this is to be reversed, when this sad world is to put off *forever* its changefulness and misery, the grave is to be robbed of its victory, and the bodies are to come forth purified by their long sleep. One battle has been fought by Christ, and another battle, most real and difficult, but a conquering one, is to be fought by us.

THE CHRISTIAN'S FINAL TRIUMPH.

BY GEORGE W. BETHUNE, D.D., BROOKLYN.

O death, where is thy sting? O grave, where is thy victory? The sting of death is sin; and the strength of sin is the law; but thanks be to God, which giveth us the victory through our Lord Jesus Christ.—1 COR. xv. 55-57.

I. THE CHALLENGE.

1. *Where is the sting of death?* Alas! and is it nothing to die? Is it nothing to leave this fair earth, our pleasant homes, our loving friends, and become as dust beneath the sod, and under the gloomy cypresses? Is it nothing to have the sad certainty before us at all times, in the midst of our best successes, that the hour is coming when the cold, ignominious grave shall hide us from them all? That our plans of ambition, gain, knowledge, service to those who are dear, zeal for our country and for the welfare of mankind, must be broken off, and the brain which projected, the hand which wrought, the heart which beat strong, must become still as the clod, and the luxury of worms? Is it nothing that the first tottering step of the child, the spring of youth, the firm tread of adult vigor, and the halt of the old man leaning on his staff, are to the same vile end? Is it nothing that the blood shall be chilled at its fountain, the clammy sweat-drops start out on the forehead, the breath come slowly and in agony, and the life, clinging desperately, be torn away and cast forth by fierce convulsion? Has death no sting when we hold the beloved, who made life precious and the world beautiful, by so frail a tenure? Has it no sting for the yearning bosom from which the little one has been taken, never again to nestle sweetly there? Has it no sting in that "life-long pang a widowed spirit bears?" Has it no sting when we follow the good man, the generous, the just, the friend of the sorrowful and the poor, the champion of the weak, to his last resting-place? No sting in death! Is there one among us such a miracle of uninterrupted happiness, so insensible to others' grief, as not to have felt its keen and lingering sharpness?

2. *Where is the victory of the grave?* Where is it not? The kings of the earth lie in " the desolate places they built for them-

selves." Riches can purchase no allies skilful to avert the blow. Obscurity affords us no refuge. The slave falls by the side of the master, and the beggar is slain by the wayside. What conqueror is so mighty, when all conquerors fight in its battles and then bow themselves in death with their victims? The track of its march is cumbered with the wreck of fairest symmetry and beauty and vigor. The generations of past ages are all crumbled into dust; all the living are following in one vast funeral; all posterity shall follow us. Were all the cries of those who have perished, and the shrieks of the bereaved over their dead crowded into one, the shriek would shake the earth to its centre. Where is the victory of the grave? The silence of the dead, the anguish of the surviving, the mortality of all that shall be born of mortals, confess it to be universal.

Yet were there nothing but this, the calamity would be light. A few tears, a sharp pang, and all would be over. We should sleep, and dream not. But there is more than this. How came there to be graves upon this decorated earth, which God looked down upon and pronounced good? My fellow-children of the dust, God is angry with us. God has armed death and sent him forth, the executioner of a divine sentence, the avenger of a broken law. The victory of the grave is the victory of justice over rebellion. Here is the sharpness of death's sting. It is the evidence and punishment of sin. It is the lowering darkness of the storm of wrath which is eternal. The bitterness of death is that, pleasant as sins may be now, death will soon and surely come, and after death the judgment, when every sin shall find us out, and the sinner shall stand with no excuse, or plea, or refuge; and after the judgment, eternal woe for all the condemned. Here we see the Apostle's boldness, the valor of Christian faith. For knowing he must surely die and the grave cover him, he stands up bravely and flings defiance in its face.

II. THE THANKSGIVING.

1. *Whence is our victory?* God gives death its sting, the grave its victory. So long as He arms and strengthens them, it is impossible to resist them. He alone can give us the victory by becoming our friend. Then His ministers, which were our enemies, must be our friends.

2. *How is the victory given?* Will the sting still remain with

death, or strength with the grave? Will God still arm the believer's enemies and yet fight for him? Will mercy deliver the sinner whom justice holds bound? Does sin cease to be guilty or law to lose its force? Hear the Apostle: "Thanks be to God, which giveth us the victory *through our Lord Jesus Christ.*" For this the Son of God became incarnate, that, as man, in the place of man the sinner, He might be capable of suffering the penalty of the law, which is death. He became man that He might suffer; He died that man might live. He stood forth in our stead to answer all the demands of the law; and the sovereign Lawgiver accepted the Substitute, and laid upon Him the iniquity of us all. More than this, He demonstrated His victory over the grave. For though He was buried, and the grave and the powers of darkness struggled mightily to hold Him fast, He dragged them forth, captivity captive, openly triumphing. But the full manifestation of His triumph and ours is kept for that day when the voice of the archangel and the trump of God shall proclaim His final coming to judgment, and all the dead, the countless dead, shall start to life. Thus will God vindicate His conquest over death and the grave, by compelling them to give liberty to the bodies of the redeemed.

3. *Wherein does our victory consist?* The believer triumphs in Christ's perfect atonement. By faith he obeys in Christ, walks with Christ in His holy life, and through Christ honors the divine law which before he had broken. By faith he is crucified with Christ (Gal. ii. 20). Death with its precursors, pain and infirmity, remains; but their mastery over him exists no longer. Pain and sickness are now God's faithful chastenings, and death is no more death, but life eternal.

The believer triumphs in Christ's resurrection. "I am crucified in Christ, nevertheless I live, yet not I, but Christ liveth in me." For this is the office and power of Christ to give eternal life to as many as receive Him; and this is the privilege of the Christian even while on earth, to have his conversation in heaven. Death has lost its power to divide him from God. He soars upon the wings of faith far above the gloomy barrier, enters the company of the Church of the first-born, and listens to the harpings of innumerable angels. Is not this a victory over death and the **grave?**

The believer triumphs in the final resurrection. Christ not only arose, but ascended on high. There the body which was here bent by sorrow has been made glorious in divine beauty; and the countenance here channeled by tears, buffeted and spit upon, is altogether lovely, its smile the fairest light of heaven; and heaven rolls up its waves of hallelujahs at His feet, in which the print of the nails perpetuate the memory of the cross. As the Redeemer is glorified in His flesh, so shall the believer be raised up to glory. What then to him whose faith can grasp things unseen, are all the passing ignominies, and pangs, and insults, which now afflict him? Every revolution of the earth rolls on to that fulness of adoption "when this mortal shall put on immortality."

"Thanks be to God, who giveth *us* the victory!" And who are included in that? "Not to me only," says the Apostle, "but unto all them also who love His appearing" (2 Tim. iv. 8). Ye shall share it, ancient believers, who from Adam to Christ worshipped by figure and under the shadow. Ye shall share it, ye prophets, who wondered at the mysterious promises of glory following suffering. Ye shall share it, ye mighty apostles, though ye doubted when ye heard of the broken tomb. Ye martyrs, whose howling enemies execrated you, as they slew you by sword and cross, and famine and rack, and wild beast and flame. And ye, God's humble poor, whom men despised, but of whom the world was not worthy. God's angels are watching, as they watched the sepulchre in the garden, over your obscure graves, keeping your sacred dust till the morning break, when it shall be crowned with princely splendor. Yes, thou weak one, who yet hast strength to embrace thy Master's cross; thou sorrowing one, whose tears fall like rain over the grave of thy beloved; thou tempted one, who, through much tribulation, art struggling on to the Kingdom of God—ye all shall be there, and ten thousand times ten thousand more. Hark! the trumpet! The earth groans and rocks herself as if in travail! They rise, the sheeted dead, but how lustrously white are their garments! How dazzling their beautiful holiness! What a mighty host! They fill the air; they acclaim hallelujahs; the heavens bend with shouts of harmony; the Lord comes down, and His angels are about Him. He owns His chosen, and they rise to meet Him, and they mingle with cherubim and seraphim, and the shoutings are like thunders from the throne of God—thunderings of joy: "O death, where is thy sting? O grave, where is thy victory? Thanks be to God, who giveth us the victory through our Lord Jesus Christ!"

Christians, death is before us. The graves are thick around us. I do not say, suffer not: Jesus suffered. But suffer like men valiant in battle, whose wounds are incentives to new valor, earnests of future honor.

I do not say, weep not: Jesus wept. But sorrow not for the Christian dead. They are safe and blest. Weep for the sins that unfit you to follow them.

I do not say, shudder not: Jesus trembled when He took the cup into his hand, dropping with bloody sweat. But I do say, fear not. Now it is your duty to live. When death comes, you shall have grace to die. But oh! be sure you are in Christ; that you are covered by His atonement. Then may you be sure of the victory.

But Oh! my God, what shall I say to those who have no faith in thee, no repentance, no consideration? They are going down to death and the grave, yet they live and laugh on as though they were to live here forever. How shall I tell them of the sting of death—of eternal death? Of the victory of the grave—the grave of everlasting fire? Speak thou to them, O Holy Spirit! Turn them, draw them, compel them to come under the wings of thy pardoning love.

THE CHARACTER AND DEATH OF WASHINGTON IRVING.

BY JOHN A. TODD, D.D., TARRYTOWN, N. Y.

For behold the Lord, the Lord of hosts, doth take away from Jerusalem and from Judah the stay and staff, the whole stay of bread, and the whole stay of water, the mighty man, and the man of war, the judge, and the prophet, and the prudent and the ancient, the captain of fifty, and the honorable man, and the counsellor, and the cunning artificer, and the eloquent orator.—ISAIAH iii. 1–3.

THE prophet does not allow the thoughts of those he is addressing to rest upon the Chaldeans as the primary cause of the events he predicts; but he leads their contemplations upward and onward along the narrow channel through which the divine energy rolled forward to its effect, until they find themselves in the presence of the Lord Jehovah Himself. In the preceding chapter the people had been called upon "to cease from man, whose breath is in his nostrils,"—that is, to cease from reposing their trust in any human protection. And in the text is presented the argument by which the prophet sought to persuade them into compliance. Thus does he teach them that there is a Power above all human power, upon which they are dependent, and in which they ought to put their trust ; that man, whatever may be his prowess in battle or his wisdom in counsel, whatever may be the resistless enchantment of his genius, whether revealed in thoughts transferred to the written page or breathed by the living voice in tones of eloquence—that man is after all but a *creature*, whose breath is in his nostrils, and whose heart is exposed to the shafts of death.

But your thoughts, my hearers, have already outstripped my words, and gathered in solemn silence around the event which has cast a shadow of gloom over the whole nation, and especially upon this community. Not that death is unfamiliar to our minds. Every day, and often in many places at one and the same moment, is death exerting his solemn power upon the race of man. But when the men who walk upon the loftier heights of place and power are laid prostrate, the event impresses itself more vividly upon the minds of men and calls forth a profounder sentiment of sorrow. I know not what may be done or spoken elsewhere of the illustrious and beloved citizen whom we were so proud to call our friend and neighbor ; but I cannot believe that you are willing that his dust should be laid in the tomb without some words of heartfelt sorrow, some expressions of love and reverence, some offerings of praise to God for the gifts with which He was pleased to endow him. His name is to be revered and cherished. Its glory shines upon our country's annals. A country's glory is the collected glory of her great men, and it is right they should have their monuments not merely in the mute and icy marble, but in the warm, living hearts of all her sons. When we thus give our offerings of love and admiration to that which God has made so fair, so wonderful in capacity, we praise God in His works, and glorify His infinite skill. It is a solemn event when God removes from a nation the mind He has most highly endowed. Insensible must be the heart that fails to receive, with reverent humility, the lessons such an event is designed to teach.

Washington Irving—the patriarch of American literature, the accomplished scholar, the admirable historian, the elegant writer, the wonderful magician, who evoked from the realms of thought the spirit of romance and beauty, and breathed it upon every hill and valley, upon every shady retreat, upon every wandering brook, ay, upon the very air that fans the summer verdure, or whistles through the wintry wood around us; the pure patriot, the diplomatist, watchful of his country's honor, yet skilful in the arts of preserving peace; the kind neighbor, the faithful friend; and, what is better than all, the sincere disciple of the Lord Jesus Christ—*Washington Irving is dead.* Dead, did I say? No! He has just begun to live. God has given to him a twofold life—the life eternal of the glorified in heaven, and the life of an undying memory in the hearts of men.

Born in New York, April 3d, 1783, and dying in his quiet home on the Hudson, November 28th, 1859, he received the fulfilment of the promise, "Thou shalt come to thy grave in a full age, like as a shock of corn cometh in his season." The record of his life has been carried to the remotest corners of the civilized world. It is enough to say that, beginning his literary career at the age of nineteen, and sending forth the first of his principal works at the age of twenty-six, his progress to the end was but the continued repetition of success. Of him it may be said,

> "He kept Victory on the run,
> Till Fame was out of breath."

His last and perhaps greatest work, the "Life of Washington," was completed but a few months before his death, and as long as the English language shall express the thoughts of men, that work will perpetuate the names of George Washington and Washington Irving. To him we can apply the sentiment which, it has been affirmed, applied to none but Milton, that "he was the only man who ever eclipsed his own fame by a higher and brighter noon; who, after winning an immortality for his youth, gave it back to oblivion by the achievements of his age."

But he was something more than the man of genius. Honored

as he was the world over, he was yet loved as well. The one word which expresses his character as a man is the word *peace*. For the struggle of intellectual warfare he had no taste. On more than one occasion, when questions of ecclesiastical order or subjects of a kindred nature were debated, he has interposed, saying : " Let us live in love. We are all striving for the same object and going to the same place of rest ; and why should there be contentions by the way ?" He had a broad and catholic spirit, which he manifested not only in words, but in deeds. In quiet simplicity, with a heart overflowing with kindness toward all men, and filled with humility before God, with a mild and amiable nature rendered more lovely by the religion of Jesus Christ, which he firmly believed and consistently professed, he passed his days among us till they closed with the closing year. It is delightful to think that the same Providence which smiled upon his life gave to the time of his death the placid beauty of unclouded skies, the brightness of warm and golden sunshine. It is more delightful to think of the love and veneration that swelled the hearts of the thousands congregated to pay homage to his genius and worth. But it is most delightful to think that the patriarch's work was done, and he was waiting for the call of the blessed Master. We have nothing, my friends, to mourn but our own loss.

And now, what are the lessons we are to learn from this solemn dispensation ? Is not God teaching us individually, and as a nation, that every earthly staff is frail at best ? One by one the great lights of a nation are extinguished by death. Who shall fight the battles, stand at the helm of government, record the march of history, sing the song of joy, chant the dirge of sorrow, explore the mysteries of science, defend the cause of truth and righteousness, and plead with men in the accents of persuasion, and with God in the accents of prayer ? Ah ! we know that none but God can give the arms of strength, the hearts of courage, the intellects of power. Let us, therefore, take refuge in Him, and pray that our whole country may go with us, and then " the place of her defence shall be the munitions of rocks."

Let me entreat you also to be admonished that life is short and death is certain. Rank, wealth, learning, genius—they are all nothing to the stern regard of death. True, death does sometimes come in the vesture of friendship and gladness, and smile upon the suffering, the heart-broken, and the weary; but oftener far does he come to men in stern and appalling aspect. When the bud of enterprise is unfolding itself into the flower of success; when hope stands with sparkling eye to greet the approaching fulfilment; when victory, like an eagle, comes sailing down the heavens to perch upon the banner that has been upborne with heroic courage through a long and weary struggle—then, then, suddenly there is a flash like a bolt from heaven, and the noontide brightness is changed to midnight gloom. The man is dead. His hands are folded across his icy breast. Oh! how true are those words which burst from the agonized heart of Edmund Burke when he contemplated the death of his only son : " What shadows we are, and what shadows we pursue !"

To-day, then, with the vision of a new-made grave before you, let me come to you in the name of Christ, with the offer of everlasting life. He gives freely, abundantly. Oh! love Him, trust Him, follow Him. Then, when the spirit is about to depart from the falling tabernacle of the body, it may pour itself into that triumphant shout of God's redeemed : " O death ! where is thy sting ? O grave ! where is thy victory ?"

THE SPEED OF LIFE IMPRESSING PROBATION.

BY TRYON EDWARDS, D.D., NEW LONDON, CONN.

O Lord, by these things men live, and in all these things is the life of my spirit.—ISAIAH xxxviii. 16.

THESE are the words of Hezekiah after his miraculous restoration from sickness, when the fifteen years had been added to his life. Going back in imagination to the hours of suffering, he cries out : " In the cutting off of my days I shall go to the gates of the grave, and be deprived of the residue of my years. No more shall I see God in the land of the living ; I shall behold no more the inhabitants of the world. Mine earthly dwelling is plucked up and removed from me as a shepherd's tent ; and my life is cut off as a weaver's thread. He is wearing me away with pining sickness ; from morning to night he is making an end of me

Mine eyes fail with looking upward. O Lord, I am oppressed ; I am weighed down with my sorrows. Do thou—O do *thou* undertake for me."* And when his prayer is answered and he learns that he shall still live for fifteen years, he turns from a plaintive to a joyous strain. Then passing in thought from the divine healings to their intended spiritual influence, he utters the words of our text. That our afflictions are intended for spiritual profit, every Christian has felt. But Hezekiah's thought seems chiefly, not of his afflictions, but of the brevity of his days which they emphasize. In endeavoring to illustrate this thought, notice—

I. THE FACT THAT LIFE IS FAST SPEEDING AWAY.

Every one has felt with Hezekiah that he is going to the gates of the grave ; or, with Moses, that he is carried away as with a flood ; or, with Job, that his days are swifter than the weaver's shuttle. In early youth, as we looked onward to the future, time did indeed seem long. But the longer we live, the swifter appears its flight. The time when you were but a child engaging in childish sports ; when you entered on the instructions of school ; when you lost a father or mother ; when you left the dear home of childhood to engage in active life ; when this joy first lightened your days or that sorrow first shadowed your path—does it not seem but a moment since that time was passing ? Where once you were busy with the prattle of childhood, it may have been exchanged for the hopes of youth. Where you were buoyant with the hopes of youth, these may have given place to the anxieties of opening manhood. Where you were exultant in the vigor of manhood, the feeble step and furrowed cheek may have taken its place. And where once the laugh rang loudly from your lips, the sobered, perhaps saddened, smile may now slowly creep, while the hoary head, the stiffened limbs, and feebler pulse are whispering of the narrow house !

And yet, whether joy has brightened your onward course or sorrow been doing its wearing work upon your heart, swift and still swifter has been the flight of the hours. Other wings may weary and droop in their course, but the wings of time, with their calm, steady beat, seem but to gather strength with exertion and to bear us with a mightier sweep the nearer we are to eternity. This, I believe, is the experience of every one who is thoughtful.

* Paraphrased from the Hebrew.

II. It deeply impresses our probation.

The speed of life is not needed to establish the fact of our probation, for it is written, as with the finger of God and in letters of fire, on all the arrangements of our earthly state, and is clearly revealed in Holy Writ. But there are few things that more strongly impress it on the thoughtful mind than the speed of time, and this because,

1. *It rarely allows us to complete the plans in which we are engaged.* We are torn from object after object and from plan after plan, by the rapid flight of time, leaving them, like structures we may build in dreams, unfinished in reality. Who has not felt that

> " To will is ours, but not to execute.
> We map our future like some unknown coast,
> And say, Here is a harbor, there a rock.
> The one we will attain, the other shun !
> And we do neither ! Some chance gale springs up,
> And bears us far o'er some unfathomed sea.
> Our efforts all are vain ; at length we yield
> To winds and waves that laugh at man's control.
> . . . Upon each beckoning scheme
> No sooner do we fix our hope, than still
> Time bears us on, leaving each still undone,
> Adjourned forever !"

2. *By the rapidity of its flight it keeps us always in effort.* Not only are we allowed to complete few, if any, of our schemes, but we are forced to constant labor to effect even the little we actually do. "All things," says Solomon, "are full of labor." But this ever-living struggle would not be ours were it not for the speed of life, which compels us to be constantly active if we would save even the least of time's floating treasures from the rolling flood.

3. *It gathers more thickly about us the changes and trials and admonitions of life.* If the changes of the world were the incidents only of centuries ; if the trials and sorrows of our short life were spread out over thousands of years ; if warnings and startling providences burst upon us like the explosions of long buried volcanoes, only at intervals of ages ; if friends were cut down and graves were opened only at long distant periods, easily might we forget our probation, rarely feeling its discipline.

4. *It so soon hurries us away from earthly scenes, and while in full*

vigor of all our powers. How often is the statesman cast down in the full maturity of his talents and influence; and the man of business just as he is qualified by long success to enter on the largest plans; and the Christian minister just when with polished intellect and ripened piety he promises richly to serve his generation! The votaries of honor, the servants of usefulness, the idols of affection, are cast down, and those who stand as pillars of the state totter and fall in their full strength. And thus we are pointed to another state where all these faculties shall tell on endless duties and results in the paradise of God.

III. APPLICATION.

Considering the subject further, a few more reflections arise.

1. *The speed of life should admonish us of our coming retribution.* Every day that passes, every beating pulse, and heaving breath, and ticking moment should be speaking to us of those endless states of joy or woe on which so soon we must enter. And so with every unfinished plan, and toiling effort, and passing change: every one of them, as the commissioned messenger of God, should speak to us of eternity and its results, leading us, at every hour, to live as though it might be the very crisis of our existence. Every one of us on earth is doing an amazing work, and its final results in eternity will be of our own procuring. In all that work, it is true, God shows us our position, surrounds us with motives, and offers us His truth, His sympathy, and the aid of His Holy Spirit. But there He leaves us. The work is ours, and He will not perform it. The warfare is ours, and only we can fight it. The seed we now sow we are sure to reap, and to ourselves He is leaving whether it shall be a harvest of glory or of death.

2. *The speed of life should lead each one of us seriously and habitually to prepare for death.* The whole of probation is the season of preparation for retribution, and what is to follow death depends, not on the act of dying, but on the life lived before we come to it. It is true that some, as the dying thief, may find grace in the dying hour. But such cases are exceptions, *a single one* being given in the entire Gospel, that none may despair, and *but one* that we may not presume. The only truly wise or safe preparation for death is to be always living a faithful Christian life.

3. *It is no wonder this world does not satisfy the soul.* Away from

Christ and holiness, you must, from the very structure of your nature, be wretched—like one forever dying of famine, but never dead. Here in this world, I grant you, you may keep from utter starvation by feeding on the husks of time and sense; or in part slake your thirst at the impure fountains of sin, though it will be like drinking from a poisoned cup, which satisfies for the moment, to destroy in the end. But when you pass to eternity, and there find even these streams cut off, and these husks torn from you, will not these desires, ever gathering strength and never, *never* satisfied, be the unquenchable flame and undying worm to you?

4. *Probation will soon be ended, and retribution soon begun.* Now you have Sabbaths, and sermons, and communion seasons, and all the means of grace, each, by the love of Christ, appealing to you, and waiting like some commissioned angel of mercy to bear you to Christ. Soon will all these means be gone. Then results—*results*—RESULTS will be all that remain to you forever. See to it, through the offered grace of Jesus, that they are such that in them you shall rejoice and not mourn to endless ages.

THE DARKNESS OF PROVIDENCE.

BY B. M. PALMER, D.D., NEW ORLEANS.

Jesus answered and said unto him, What I do thou knowest not now; but thou shalt know hereafter.—JOHN xiii. 7.

I. REASONS FOR THE MYSTERY OF GOD'S DISPENSATIONS.

1. *It is necessary in order to the assertion of God's absolute supremacy.* The mightiest despot that ever sat upon a throne never could gain control of the heart of a single subject. His power was limited to the external, the fortunes and acts of men; but to constrain the thoughts and affections was beyond his power. But when God claims supremacy, it is a supremacy over the whole nature of man. His wisdom, justice, power, and holiness are infinite, and all that is, exists by virtue of His creative will. This attribute of sovereignty is that which, in the Scriptures, God guards with the greatest jealousy. And the reason lies in the possibility of man's rebelling from that power. When God endowed man

with a free will, He made him the supreme work of the universe; but at the same time He rendered possible the thwarting of His own will. To secure the interests of His government at large, it is necessary for God to guard His supremacy over all His creatures. It is necessary that we should learn to bow to what God does, not because we perceive that it is best or wisest, but simply *because He does it.*

2. *This darkness rests upon Providence because of its complexity.* Even if God's dealings with us had reference but to ourselves, they would be hard enough to understand. What man can tell the uses to which God means to put him, the glory to which He means to exalt him, even in this world; how much less that in the world to come! These threads of the earthly life, how they stretch beyond the chasm of death and are woven into a new web above the stars! But the problem is rendered vastly more complex for us by the interdependence of all our lives. Each thread is necessary to the integrity of the fabric, and has its relation to all other threads. It is in life as in the diagrams of the mathematician, where the same line may represent the side of many different figures. Our personal history touches that of many another, and our influence ramifies through the society in which we move.

3. *The violence of our emotions renders us incompetent to understand.* How often does the bolt fall upon us from a perfectly clear sky! And how our afflictions seem to link to each other, or, like our mercies, grow together like a bunch of grapes! One sorrow is succeeded by another and another, until we are overwhelmed. In such a condition, how can we calmly estimate the influence of this or that affliction upon us? We can only exclaim with the Psalmist: "Deep calleth unto deep at the noise of thy waterspouts; all thy waves and thy billows are gone over me." We are as a man wrecked at sea—now borne upon a mountain wave so high that it seems he shall be dashed against the stars, then as suddenly plunged into the depths as if to be swallowed up in the womb of the earth. No, it is not when the instinct of love is going out in its wild cry after that which the grave has seized that we can interpret the meaning of the bereavement.

4. *Our spiritual state is often inadequate to receive the explanation.* "I have yet many things to say unto you, but ye cannot bear them now," said Christ to His disciples, and so He taught them in

parables containing the seeds of truth which should spring up in the fulness of Christian knowledge. It is the great art of the human educator to know how to proportion the knowledge conveyed, to the ability of the one receiving, lest by overcommunication the very faculties it is desired to strengthen be overloaded and stunted. Now God, in His infinite wisdom, is adjusting His providences to our spiritual condition. And thus it happens that we are often able, partially at least, to understand what was, in a less mature state of our spiritual nature, altogether inexplicable.

5. *The great law of faith renders this mystery indispensable.* Faith is the law of this probationary dispensation, just as knowledge is the law of the dispensation of reward. If a man says that the doctrines of God's word are incomprehensible, the answer is twofold. God is infinite, and cannot be perfectly apprehended by finite minds. His truths, like the mountains, lift their gray heads and hide themselves in the clouds of heaven; and though we pass around the base, and partly take their measure, we must ourselves enter the world in which these mysteries are lost to sight, before we can take their altitude. Then another answer may be returned, that this intellect of ours must, along with the affections and the will, be put upon probation. It is *the whole man* that God is now proving, educating, training. Does not God in this world put the intellect of the creature upon its trial before Him, so that he shall see the reasonableness of accepting all the high mysteries of grace, simply by the testimony upon which they rest? This law of faith extends no less to the conscience, inasmuch as the divine law is made the sole standard of rectitude to man, and he is not permitted to guide himself by his natural conscience except as that conscience is enlightened by God's infallible rule of right.

This law of faith extends to the affections, since we are to yield a cordial and loving trust, though God himself is wrapped in clouds. This law extends to the will, since we must defer to the naked authority of God's commands. Now, if God explains this sickness or that bankruptcy, this bereavement or that sorrow, there could be no exercise of faith, and the law of the whole economy under which we are placed would be completely reversed.

II. THIS MYSTERY OF GOD'S PROVIDENCES WILL BE TEMPORARY.

This is declared in our text. In Peter's case the promise was soon, in part at least, fulfilled by Christ's explanation; yet how far short did his understanding fall even then, to that he gained on the day of Pentecost! So with us: many a dispensation is dark until God takes us by the hand and brings us into higher views of Himself and of His grace.

1. *There is a strong presumption that this revelation will be made, in the known connection between the two worlds.* The two worlds are united in man. He has "a true body and a reasonable soul." As "fire ascending seeks the sun," as the balloon strains at the cords that impede its flight, so the unconquerable instincts of man's spiritual nature leap upward. The very principle of ambition is but the finger upon the dial-plate of his spiritual nature, pointing to hopes and rewards which can be realized only in the spiritual world. And when the soul is renewed from sin, the spiritual apprehension is clearer, the spiritual longing stronger. I need not speak of this to those familiar with the privileges of prayer. And at the border line of death, what strange overlappings we sometimes see! How shall the two worlds thus touch each other in us, all through our earthly career, and their relations not be disclosed at last? I have no idea that at death we are to lose all individuality, like drops in the sea. Our career there will be distinctly personal, colored by our history here. At every moment we touch wires that vibrate in eternity.

2. *All limitations of sense will be removed.* We shall possess the spiritual body, with spiritual organs which, as our senses now apprehend material things, shall apprehend spiritual things. All truth, whether of nature or grace, we shall be able to read in its unity. The lesson which science is teaching us is the lesson of humility. As she uncovers one mystery, there opens another. We feel in the very height and glory of her revelations, how the spirit is fettered by sense. Ah! in the world where these limitations are thrown aside, we shall survey God's providence, and the darkness will disappear.

3. *God's plans there will be complete.*

4. *The removal of this obscurity is necessary to God's vindication.* Do we ever reflect that this obscurity is as great a hardship upon God as upon us; that it exposes Him to constant misconstruction and suspicion on our part? But God will not always lie under suspicion.

5. *Heaven is the state and place of reward and praise.* In order

that we may apprehend its joys as the rewards bestowed upon us by the Master, we must survey our earthly life in all its connections. And the word *praise* indispensably requires that we embalm in song our whole experience.

THOUGHTS ON IMMORTALITY.

BY THE RIGHT REV. SAMUEL FALLOWS, D. D., CHICAGO.

If a man die, shall he live again?—JOB xiv. 14.

WE are met on the threshold of our theme with the fact, that among all the nations of the earth the idea of Immortality has been held. This is a signal proof that the idea is true. It does not affect the validity of the position taken, that the ideas of these various nations were incorrect as regards the nature of the future state. The clearing up of all doubts, the dispelling of all mists, depends upon revelation. The function of God's revealed truth is not to discover new and fundamental ideas to the universal intelligence of man. It is to clarify them of all error in their application, to bring them out into fulness and prominence; to make them nutritive and determinative in the moral and spiritual life.

While holding to the transmigration of the soul, the ancient Hindoos believed in its essential immortality. It was taught by them, "As a man throweth away his old garment and putteth on new, so the soul, having quitted its old mortal frames, entereth into others which are new. The weapon divideth it not. The water corrupteth it not. The wind drieth it not away. It is indivisible, inconsumable, incorruptible."

Herodotus says of the Egyptians: "They were the first of mankind who had defended the immortality of the soul."

Lord Bolingbroke, freethinker though he was, declares that "the doctrine of the immortality of the soul and a future state of rewards and punishments began to be taught before we have any light into antiquity. And when we begin to have any, we find it established that it was strongly inculcated from time immemorial."

Volney admits that all the earliest nations taught that the soul survived the body, and was immortal.

It has been the belief of earlier and later peoples. The nations of Northern Europe, the fierce, restless hordes who forced the gates of the Eternal City and crushed the Roman power, believed that the slothful and cowardly, at death, went into dark caves under ground, full of noisome creatures, and there they grovelled in endless stench and misery. But those who died in battle went immediately to the vast palace of Odin, their god of war, where they were entertained in perpetual feasts and mirth.

Among civilized and uncivilized nations, on continents and islands in every quarter of the globe, the belief in immortality has been retained. Whence came the idea? Some of the deniers of the soul's inherent immortality have attempted to answer the question. Philosophers and statesmen, they allege, "practising a pious fraud upon the people, foisted it upon them. It was found necessary to bring in the idea of a future life, to hold the masses in subjection, to secure their allegiance to the State, and uphold the dignity of philosophy." Plato is represented as quoting a Pythagorean philosopher, who taught that, "as we sometimes cure the body by unwholesome remedies, when such as are most wholesome have no effect, so we restrain those minds by false relations which will not be persuaded by the truth." In like manner, it is claimed, the philosophers and statesmen reasoned, and so invented the idea of immortality to compass their ends.

We have only one question to ask. *What* philosopher, or *what* statesman invented it? When his name is ascertained, we may entertain such an unfounded assertion. He will be found closely akin to the one who invented the love of the beautiful, the sentiment of harmony, the love of children, the fact of conscience, and the idea of God. If the historical argument for immortal existence were pressed no further than the admitted position that it is congenial to the universal mind of man, a strong presumption would be created in favor of the doctrine. But it goes much further, and proves that the idea of continued being is *native* to the human soul. The consent of all nations is the grandest affirmation possible of what the consciousness of man teaches. The philosopher, the statesman, and the priest may have played upon the credulity of the people, and held them fast in dire superstitious bondage; but it was through a perversion of the instincts and principles God had implanted in the constitution of man himself.

I may adduce the metaphysical and moral argument.

In the Kensington Museum, in England, I saw some of the sketches from the master-hand of Turner. Rough and rude they were, but yet such only as his hand could draw. Over against them were the finished pictures, with all their faithfulness of detail, accuracy of expression, and magnificence of execution. So the best human life here, with its marvellousness of inventive powers, its royal reach of reason, its sublime daring of genius, its amplitude of affection, its deeds of goodness, is but an imperfect sketch, and yet a sketch that the hand of God only could draw. It is but the alphabet out of which the stately, glowing, and immortal epic of a Paradise regained shall spring from a Paradise lost. It is but the wail of a new-born child compared with the symphonies of angels.

No clearer truth does the open book of Nature unfold to the wise and reverent reader than the existence of a plan in the development of the animal kingdom. No St. Peter's or St. Paul's can more clearly indicate the idea of Michael Angelo or Sir Christopher Wren than the *four* great types on which organic life is built, the *idea* of the Great Architect of the universe. This plan, in its fourfold manifestations, implies predetermination, and involves consummation. Every organ, however rudimentary at any particular stage of the unfolding, becomes a function somewhere on the line of development. It is sure to be employed down in the scale of existence. Some animals have fingers which are never used. They are given them by the Being who unvaryingly adheres to His plan. They are there, because when man, the lord and head of the kingdom, comes to the throne, bringing forward and *completing* all the lower and preceding types, he *must* and does possess five fingers on each hand, of varying length and strength. Those rough and rigid protuberances, in the structure of his inferior relations, prophesied the free, facile, and flexible use of the most perfect instruments for carrying out the thought of the brain and the love of the heart. If there be no immortal life, all the prophecies of Nature fail—suddenly and unaccountably fail.

In the splendid make and mechanism of the body, compared with which the most cunning piece of man's workmanship is a bungling performance, every promise has been redeemed, and every prophecy fulfilled. It is correlated to the world about it.

Light has been made for the eye, sound for the ear, food for the palate. Nay, in the very constitution of the mind, axioms have been given to the reason, truth to the intellect, and beauty to the æsthetic taste. Still further the conscience has asked for light and cleansing, and they have been given; the soul has cried out for God, for the living God, and "the invisible appeared in sight, and God was seen by mortal eye."

We have the instinctive fear of death—the unutterable dread of annihilation—the passionate longing for continued existence. We have powers capable of endless progression; faculties which find no appropriate sphere on earth, which are caged and confined, as the panting bird aspiring after liberty beats its breast against the restraining bars. We *feel*, we *know* our kinship with the skies. This world *now* cannot bound our intellect; burning worlds and burned-out worlds, swinging in their brilliant and gloomy orbits, throw up no barriers against the swift feet of our soaring imaginations. Beyond the uttermost limits of creation, we send our thoughts, our adoring love; beyond prostrate cherubim and seraphim, above the very throne itself, to Him that sitteth upon the throne, God over all, blessed for ever more. This light of intellect to be quenched in oblivion's waters! These powers to be stamped out by annihilation! These longings to be unsatisfied, these hopes to be mocked! Oh, what a superb farce is this!

The God of Nature is the father of the immortal soul. The brute attains its ends. Man would be a little lower than the brute if he did not attain his. There is no annihilation of a single *substance* in Nature, though the *form* may be endlessly changed. There is no annihilation of spirit. The body may wax and wane. "I call it *mine*, not me." Connected with it, I yet know that from it "I am distinct, as is the swimmer from the flood." My thought, emotion, and will are not acids and phosphates. Our essential instincts are not a supreme forgery. Our faith in the God of Nature and man is not in vain.

> "'Tis the Divinity that stirs within us,
> 'Tis heaven itself that points out an hereafter
> And intimates eternity to man."

You cannot sail upon the ocean, out of sight of land, without calling upon the heaven and its orbs of light to aid you. You must rectify your compass and your course by its central sun. You cannot sail life's sea without life's heaven. Your compass of philosophy, history, of political economy, of statesmanship, of civilization, must have the rectification of the skies, or you never can reach the heaven of humanity's hopes. Break away from the Heaven-Father, and you are plunged in the blackness of darkness, and the horrors of chaotic ruin. You have read that poem on Darkness, by one of the most gifted but sadly erring writers this earth has ever held. It was

> "A dream which was not all a dream.
> The bright sun was extinguished, and the stars
> Did wander darkling in the eternal space,
> Rayless and pathless, and the icy earth
> Swung blind and blackening in the moonless air."

You know the rest. The prayer for light; the watch-fires of thrones, and palaces, and huts; the burning cities, the blazing homes, the crackling trunks of forest fires; the crouching of the freezing multitudes before their ineffectual flames; the looking up with mad, disquiet awe on the dull sky, the pall of a past world; the cursing, the gnashing of teeth, the howling of despair in the dust; the shrieking of the wild birds, and the flapping of their useless wings; the wildest brutes becoming tame and tremulous; the crawling vipers, hissing, but stingless; the glut of war, the gorging with blood; the death of love; the pang of famine, the dropping dead; the last two who survived—enemies, "scraping with their cold, skeleton hands the feeble ashes;" the gaze of each upon the other; their shriek, and death from mutual hideousness!

Extinguish those greater and lesser lights of God and immortality from our sky, and you make the poet's dream a fearful reality on our earth. In that awful winter which shall bring icy death to man's religious nature, and to his instincts and aspirations for the life to come, all else that we hold dear below—government, home, social order, civilization, faith, hope, love, shall perish with eternal frost. And the horrors of the vision of atheism, seen by the philosophic Jean Paul, shall be added to those of the poet Byron: "Raising his eyes toward the heavenly vault, he beheld a deep, black, bottomless void! Eternity, resting on chaos, was slowly devouring itself!"

The end of the life of that greatest of American statesmen, foremost of American lawyers, and most commanding of American orators, Daniel Webster, came in the course of time. Too feeble to hold his pen, he said in a whisper to Mr. Curtis, his biographer, "I had intended to prepare a work for the press, to bear my testimony to Christianity; but it is now too late. Still, I would like to bear witness to the Gospel before I die. Writing materials were brought, and he dictated: "Lord, I believe; help thou my unbelief. Philosophical objections have often shaken my reason with regard to Christianity, especially the objections drawn from the magnitude of the universe contrasted with the littleness of this planet; but my *heart* has always assured me, and reassured me, that the Gospel of Jesus Christ is a divine reality;" and these words are carved on the marble that rests over his sacred dust at Marshfield. But, as that brilliant orb was going down behind the western hills, he asked, as if still intently anxious to preserve his consciousness to the last, and to watch for the moment and act of his departure, so as to comprehend it, whether he were alive or not. On being assured he was, he said, as if assenting to what had been told him, because he himself perceived it was true, "*I still live!*"—his last words. The sunset had come; but it was a sunrise to know no more setting. "His earnest soul repeated, I think, the last words he spoke on earth as his first in heaven—"*I still live!*"

LESSONS FROM LIFE'S BREVITY.

BY W. W. RAMSAY, D.D., DETROIT, MICH.

So teach us to number our days that we may apply our hearts unto wisdom.—PSALM XC. 12.

No difference is so wide as that existing between life and death. In the activities of the one and the stillness of the other, the familiar tones of life and the unnatural hush of death, is manifest an incongruity more painful than is anywhere else observed. The stillness of death renders the occasion a time favorable for hearkening to those echoes which respond to the questionings of the heart. Death brings its sadness, if not its gloom; but even this reveals a light precious and cheering.

The questionings of the intellect are important, yet its responses at such a time are necessarily evasive. The giants of thought can be observed then but as gladiators which struggle in the arena for the mastery. From such curious displays men turn away to listen to the heart's throbs. They are not cold and distant, nor abstruse and evasive. The schools of philosophy may hide their evidences in the alcoves of learning beyond the reach of the masses, but the heart writes, in lines of light and shadings of sorrow, a vernacular which can be read by all. The masses may not be able to define life, but they feel its throbs. They may not trace the threads of its intricate logic, but they can feel the assurance of its unmistakable impressions, as Mrs. Browning says:

> "Like a white soul tossed out to eternity
> With the thrills of time upon it."

It is then, when the death shadow has fallen about our path, that we are impressed with

1. *The brevity of life.* Brevity is a relative term. To the child who anticipates a coming pleasure, the lagging hours are torture with their delay. To the child who has entered into the possession of the coveted delight, the hour is gone as though its minutes were but moments. To the aged man, boyhood is crowded into a distant perspective, while to the same, life yesterday was as the flight of time. But if the heart is caught in the cruel cogs of sorrow, the moment is as an hour, and the hour becomes an age. But when the soul stands where it surveys in dread or hope the vast stretches of the future, time is relegated to its appropriate brief curve in the swift current of being.

Time is but a speck, the merest dot along the ages. What is the age of a man compared with that of the race, and this with the vast stretch of world-building which stretches from Eden back to "the beginning"? It was such a retrospect which moved Jacob to declare in the presence of Egypt's King: "The days of the years of my pilgrimage are an hundred and thirty years: few and evil have the days of the years of my life been."

The brevity of life is forcibly suggested by Moses in this ninetieth Psalm. It is as a flood which rises upon the impulse of weeping skies, which threatens to be a permanent devastation, and yet in a single night retires within its banks and promises obediently to minister to the beauty of nature and the welfare of man. It is also as a sleep. Who does not know the sweetness of sleep in the years preceding the weight of care? The child weary with play sinks to his pillow, and is only aroused by the advance of the brightening morning, to question the assertion that the night is equal in length to the day. And so is life, a brief, dreamless sleep.

Again, says the Psalmist, "We spend our years as a tale that is told." From parental lips we heard the recital of childish story. It was the delight of only the fraction of an hour, and the tale was told. And such is life. Notwithstanding its engrossing interests of business and amusement, soon it is gone, even as a tale that is told. The moment refuses to stay, and rushes with its impress of virtue or of sin into the unchangeable past. The grass, too, in its fragile beauty, is made to illustrate this same all-important truth. Mark its tender growth and speedy maturity. "In the morning it flourisheth and groweth up," but the instruction is in its speedy decay; for "in the evening it is cut down and withereth. For the sun is no sooner risen with a burning heat, but it withereth the grass, and the flower thereof falleth, and the grace of the fashion of it perisheth." "All flesh is grass, and all the goodliness thereof is as the flower of the field." So whether we wake or sleep, work or pray, we grow in days and in years, and—then die.

2. *The vanity of earthly pursuits.* The masses by their action seem to indicate that they expect to live here forever. The foundations of their mansions of pleasure are deep and strong, the walls thick and high, as though they were to shelter the millenarian instead of the man of threescore years and ten.

One large part of humanity are busy with the effort to accumulate riches, as though this were the chief end of man. They heap up riches as though they knew who should gather them. Another part, goaded by a conscienceless ambition, are reaching after worldly distinction. The most tender and fragrant vines of the soul are ruthlessly trampled under foot, that they may send a sounding name abroad, only to make at the last the fearful discovery that ambition's highest success is the soul's deepest delusion. Wolsey said: "If I had served my God with half the zeal that I have served my king, He would not in mine age have left me naked to mine enemies." Napoleon in bitterness of spirit saw the walls of his empire crumbling about him, though they had cost the sacrifice of myriads of lives. It were assuredly wiser to sing with a man who wore honors forced upon him :

"O why should the spirit of mortal be proud?"

Then worldly pleasures make sensuous appeals for the devotion of immortals. The world's actors are numerous and talented, its scenes brilliant and attractive, as though to be amused were the highest purpose of life. But it is only a repetition of the same mistake. The soul, true to its heavenly origin, refuses to be satisfied with the unreal fictions of the stage and the intoxicating maze of the dance. Over all may be inscribed the character, Unsatisfying. A Roman emperor offered a reward to the inventor of a new pleasure. His was the poet's experience :

"I have sought round this verdant earth,
For unfading joy ;
I have tried every source of mirth,
But all, all will cloy."

Can such persons have numbered the brief moments which will so soon introduce them to that unfamiliar future, from whose bourn no traveller ever returns? If the Epicurean sentiment be true, such surrender to the waves of sensual pleasure is consistent and desirable ; but if "the soul, immortal as its Sire, can never die," such indifference is reckless and reprehensible.

3. *How can we apply our hearts unto wisdom?* The chief end of man is not amusement and pleasure-seeking. These are selfish and narrowing. God places before the race a broader and more enlarging mission, in which there is a brighter glory and a truer happiness. "The chief end of man is to honor and glorify God, and to enjoy Him forever." Living is full of terrible responsibilities. No wonder they overawed the majestic minds of Kant and Webster ! It is the mind unable or disinclined to sweep the wide vista of destiny that drifts aimlessly, as though a bright destiny were without conditions. But everywhere success attends studied preparation, while failure follows in the wake of indifference. Life has placed its secular prizes beyond reach of the listless and indifferent. Appreciation of good pays the price of effort for its

attainment. This means a hand on the helm, an arm at the oar, an eye on the chart, while the anchor awaits an emergency. God very wisely placed the glory of mind at the goal of intelligent investigation. Study is the mind's stimulus, and achievement its greatest joy. And the same divine goodness would reveal any essential truth, which by its nature was beyond man's powers of discovery. And yet with all their studying, ancient sages only guessed at moral truth. Here they needed that one who knew its influence, without the delays and disappointments of experiment, should announce what was beyond, and how, if desirable, it might be attained. David felt the need. Destiny was crowding him, and he knew not in the darkness where to place his feet, till the wave of a mysterious wand made a rift in the overshadowing mist. Then in his joy he cried out, "Thou wilt guide me with thy counsel, and afterward receive me to glory." God's counsel expresses His will, and is therefore good, perfect, and acceptable. This life with its varied experiences cannot disclose the wisdom of this will ; but as the soul among the possible ten thousand plans finds the one which shines brighter and brighter even to the perfect day ; as from the eternal heights it regards the wisdom of God's plan disclosed, it will join a chorus of the saved in ascribing wisdom to Him whom we should serve. Moore caught a glimpse of this peerless wisdom :

> "Go wing your flight from star to star,
> From world to shining world, as far
>   As the universe spreads its flaming wall.
> Count all the pleasures of all the spheres,
> And multiply each by thousands of years :
>   One moment in heaven is worth them all."

TRANSITION TO THE LIFE BEYOND.

BY LYMAN ABBOTT, D.D., NEW YORK.

It is appointed unto men once to die, but after this the judgment.—HEB. ix. 27.

1. It is very clear that the New Testament teaches that *there is a future state*, and that this world is not all, nor the greater part, of our existence. We are here standing in the vestibule of life. We

are the seed in the ground, just beginning to sprout. There are possibilities in us which eye hath not seen, nor ear heard, nor the heart conceived. It is true of man that, when the Spirit of God is playing upon him, he comes into a certain sense of what it is to be a son of God; but it is also true that "we know not what we shall be;" there is a future larger, grander, more glorious than we can conceive of—transcendent above all knowledge. We cannot comprehend it: our thought of heaven must seem to God as the Indian child's thought of a palace seems to us. If you undertake to give to the little child a conception of the pleasure that comes through literature, or through the study of language or science or philosophy, what conception can you give him? We are like the little child; we know not, nor can we know, what God hath in store for those that love Him.

2. We may know from the New Testament teaching that *the future state is a spiritual life.* It is not a state in which the enjoyments of this life are to be reproduced in larger measure. It is not a state in which the skies are brighter, the flowers sweeter, and the music more ecstatic. That was the Mohammedan notion, and it is the notion of a great many Christian people to-day; but it is not the New Testament notion. The New Testament teaching is, I think, that, when we die, we have done with the body. We lay it away in the grave, and that is the end of it; it is a cast-off garment. The old pagan notion was that there could be no future life of the soul without a future life of the body as well; they accordingly embalmed the bodies of their dead—buried the horse with its rider. When they thought of the departed, they connected him altogether with a physical organization, and imagined that the body must enter the future state, or the soul could not. This pagan notion has been engrafted in the Christian creed, but it is not to be found in the New Testament. Men say, Cannot God gather back again the various particles of the human body that have been scattered after burial, here and there, over the earth? Is He not able to gather these particles together and make out of them the same old body? Yes! I do not know that God cannot do this. But is God shut up to do this? Is there no recreative power in God to give the spirit a more glorious body for the larger and grander existence of the future?

3. *Christ has already passed through the door into which His dis-*

ciples are to enter. The New Testament does not speak of a Christ that is to enter by and by into glory ; it does not recognize Christ as existing in an intermediate state ; it declares that Christ has already entered into His glory. After Christ had risen and was walking on the way to Emmaus, He met some of His disciples : they were talking of His crucifixion, death, and burial, and were disheartened because of what had occurred. Jesus said : " Ought not Christ to have suffered these things, *and to enter into glory ?*" He was not, by and by, to enter in ; but, through suffering, He had already entered in. When Stephen was about to be stoned, he lifted up his eyes and beheld the Son of God standing at the right hand of His Father. He was not asleep ; He was not in some mysterious prison-house, waiting till His release should come ; He was already standing on the right hand of God.

It is a common notion that the dead lie in an unconscious state until the centuries have rolled away, or that they enter, half-clothed, half-prepared for the future life ; that they remain in their prison-house waiting for the time when the final judgment shall be made known. I do not think this is Scriptural teaching. I think the New Testament teaches that they that die in Christ follow their Christ and enter into glory with their Christ. The old Jews, in Old Testament times, believed as the pagans believed. Life seemed to them full of exultation and joy, but they who died went down into Hades, in which there was no joy, no life, there to await the final judgment-day. But the New Testament repudiates this idea of an intermediate state, clearly and distinctly. When Jesus went to Bethany and found the sisters sorrowing over the death of Lazarus, and Martha said to Him, " If Thou hadst been here my brother had not died," He began to give them consolation by saying, " Thy brother shall rise again." Martha saith unto Him, " I know that he shall rise again in the resurrection at the last day." They held the faith that was common in their time, that there was to be a long state of unconsciousness. They had laid Lazarus away in the tomb, to sleep the last long sleep, and they thought that by and by he should rise again. Jesus said : " I am the resurrection and the life ; he that believeth in Me, though he were dead, yet shall he live ; and he that liveth and believeth in Me *shall never die.*" When one has this faith in Christ, there is no break in life ; no cessation of existence ; no long, dreary sleep ; life flows on in one continuous current into the great ocean of eternity.

Christ said to the thief who hung upon the cross near Him, "To-day shalt thou be with Me in paradise." Paul says, "To die is gain ;" and just before his execution, writing a letter to his friend Timothy, he says, "Henceforth there is laid up for me a crown." Not in the future is there to be one, but from that moment the crown awaits him. When he would stimulate the faith of those to whom he wrote, he said, "Ye are come to Mount Sion, to the heavenly Jerusalem, to an innumerable company of angels, . . . and to God, the judge of all, and to the spirits of *just men made perfect*"—men who have already entered into the presence of God. John, in his vision on the isle of Patmos, beheld men who had come out of every tongue and tribe and nation, standing around the throne of God in heaven, singing the song of Moses and the Lamb. The heaven of the Bible is always in the present tense. The music has begun ; they that have gone forth from us have entered into glory. "It is appointed unto men once to die, after this the judgment ;" not, after death a long, dreary, intermediate sleep, and after this the judgment. Men have been accustomed to picture a great judgment-day, in which the dead, numbering hundreds of thousands and thousands of thousands, rise and stand in their places before one great throne and are called up, one after another, and judged one by one. It is estimated that one birth and one death take place every moment—you cannot conceive of any judgment that would take less time ; accordingly the judgment-day would last as long as the human race lasted before it. What if that day has already dawned, even though its sunset hour has not yet come ? What if you and I are standing before the throne of God, being judged to-day just as much as we shall ever be judged ? What if Christ sits on His throne to-day, placing the sheep on His right hand, and the goats on His left ? What if Christ is to-day separating those who, by patient continuance in well-doing, seek for glory and honor and immortality, from those who are contentious and obey not the truth, but obey unrighteousness ?

It is a solemn thought to me that I am not far from my judgment-day ; nay, that I am in my judgment-day, and any moment I may step over the border line. That day is not in the far future: The friend gone from my side has already gone through his inquisition. Those that have gone—father, mother, beloved—they have not gone down into the grave to wait there; they are not in a prison-house, waiting there; if they were sons of God, they have gone to Christ to be sharers in His glory. They have not been taken away in the midst of their usefulness, but they have entered a broader field of activity; they have already entered into Christ's glory, and are kings and priests unto Him. And I, too, look up; I behold a great multitude which no man can number, not in graveyards and cemeteries and beneath the sea, not huddled together in some dreary prison-house waiting the hour of release and redemption, but standing before the throne and the Lamb, clothed with white robes and palms in their hands, and crying with a loud voice, Salvation to our God which sitteth upon the throne, and to the Lamb.

THE CHRISTIAN'S GAIN BY DEATH.

BY REV. ZEPHANIAH MEEK, CATLETTSBURG, KY.

For to me to live is Christ, and to die is gain.—PHILIPPIANS i. 21.

PAUL, a servant of Jesus Christ, stands up in his representative character and exclaims: "For to me to live is Christ, and to die is gain." His language, therefore, becomes the language of every true disciple of the Saviour. In this brief and pointed sentence the apostle recognizes the fact of a personal providential care and oversight, so much so that life, with all its blessings, its joys and its sorrows, depends upon the will of Christ. As much as if he should say: "As I have no power over my own life, and cannot determine its duration, neither have I a desire upon the subject; for whether I live I live unto the Lord, or whether I die I die unto the Lord. Therefore, whether I live or die, I am the Lord's."

1. *What is it to live?* The body, of itself, is pulseless, lifeless, and only has life and vigor in connection with the soul, which is the active, essential principle. This life, or rather this stage of life, is dependent upon this mysterious union of soul and body.

Whether the union of the soul with the body gives life, or whether this union is in consequence of the life, we shall not now attempt to determine. Suffice it to say, upon this point, that our present existence, being purely primary and preparatory, this mysteriously blended form of life, is under tutelage preparatory to the higher vocations, the sublimer realities of our real life—an eternal existence.

2. *What is it to die?* In the earliest ages death was represented under the idea of a tyrannical ruler, having vast power and great dominion. The Jews before the exile frequently represented death as a hunter, who lays snares for men, spoken of by the Psalmist as the snare of the fowler. But after the exile they represented death as an angel with a cup of poison in his hand, which he reaches to men, from which, doubtless, we have the expression in the New Testament, tasted death. In this age we represent death as a venerable man, with a scythe in his hand, or as a ghastly skeleton, the latter of which presents death in its most hideous form. But the question suggests itself to the thoughtful mind, What is death?—or, to be more specific, What dies? If, as we have before stated, whatever there is of life—the soul—is immortal, and its separation from the body results in the latter's dissolution—its return to dust—it will be seen that really nothing which has life in itself dies.

Again, death in itself may be as mysterious as life. We cannot, by the most careful analysis, tell just what one or the other is. But we know that it means something more than for the heart to cease its pulsations and all the wheels of motion to stand still. It is something more than to grow faint and weary and then cease to live. It is indeed the humiliation of the body, when all its proud honors are laid in the dust, and its beauty and strength dissolve like ashes. But death derives its awfulness from the fact that it introduces us into the presence-chamber of the Judge of the whole earth. It would be a most solemn and unwelcome thought if the physical pain felt in the agony of death should put an end to our being; if, when we die, we should cease to exist; if, like the falling meteor, which leaves its waning track along the heavens, our light is to be extinguished in the darkness of the sepulchre, never more to be kindled; if in the last hour we could only say with the dying atheist: "Crown me with flowers, cover me with perfume, that I may enter upon eternal sleep." But to all who believe in the holy Scriptures this question is forever settled. Death is not annihilation ; death is not an eternal sleep. Jesus Christ Himself has gone down into the shadowy regions of the dead, and from the gloom of the grave has brought life and immortality to light. And upon His authority we affirm : " It is appointed unto man once to die, and after death the judgment." "When the silver cord is loosened, and the golden bowl is broken, and the pitcher is broken at the fountain, and the wheel is broken at the cistern"—" then the dust returns to the earth as it was, and the spirit returns to God who gave it." Oh, it is this that makes death such an awful thing ! It closes our eyes upon this world, but opens them upon another. It puts an end to our time, but introduces us into eternity. It separates us from men, but it brings us face to face with God. It closes the term of our trial for life, and fixes our destiny unchangeably and forever ! In one moment after we have passed away we can answer the question, replete with the joys of heaven or the miseries of perdition, Am I saved or am I lost ?

Such is the meaning of death. Oh ! my friends, can you to-day, in view of the solemn and unchangeable realities of death, adopt the language of the text, and say, " For to me to live is Christ, and to die is gain ?"

3. *But is the Christian to have gain by death ?* Is there for me, for you, another and better state of being ? Is there a sphere of life and of being in which all the inequalities of this life shall be adjusted and its labors rewarded ? Does the evidence of my life and being, separate and independent from every one else, in what I do, experience and suffer, leave its impress upon my higher destiny, beyond the scenes and employments of time ? Yes, brethren, in the aggregate results of all these things in the glorious future shall be the grand fulfilment of the text, " to die is gain." The dealings of Almighty God have something more to do than make us rich, poor, noble or ignoble in the estimation of the world. They are further reaching than time itself. They look to that state of preparation which will enable us to joy even amid the conflagration of the world, and, if rightly improved, will enable us to grow fresh and green over the sepulchre of buried ages. Oh, how far-reaching and enduring are the results of this life, under the

plan and providence of God! Let the mountains be moved from their solid foundations; let the thrones, dominions, and governments of the earth crumble and fall in pieces; let the great and the honorable be lost and merged in untitled names; let the world be dead, and buried, and forgotten, as the silent ages of eternity look down upon its sepulchre, and still the issues of life will remain unchanged as the truth of God itself—and here we have the grand summary of it all—" to die is gain." Oh, what a promise, and what a prospect to the good is this!

Look at the mighty range of providence as it begins with creation and comes sweeping down the ages. Think of all creatures, and all that has been and will ever be. Think of the history of this world as it stands out written upon the pages of time, between the two eternities, and then remember God affirms that all together shall bring their contributions of good and lay them down at the Christian's feet. "All are yours, and ye are Christ's, and Christ is God's." Here is the state to which religion invites you—to thrones, to crowns, to palms of victory, to mansions, to all that heaven means.

4. *This gain is eternal.* To the Christian death is an end of probation, of sorrow, pain and affliction. It introduces him into the higher realities of life, into the presence of God, the society of angels and the company of the redeemed. Here, amid the bowers of the tree of life, upon the shores of the river which issues from beneath the throne of God, we shall find an eternal home. "To die is gain."

PREPARING FOR DEATH.

BY WILLIAM IVES BUDINGTON, D.D., CONNECTICUT.

So teach us to number our days, that we may apply our hearts unto wisdom.—PSALM XC. 12.

THIS ninetieth psalm was written by Moses. His prayer here was that God would teach us so to estimate the duration of human life that we would be prepared for its termination. At the time of writing this psalm Moses was an old man. He had seen his companions, one after another, die. His sister, his brother, thousands of the leaders, and hundreds of thousands of the people of Israel had perished since they had left Egypt. But two only remain. Caleb and Joshua, of all the early companions of Moses, still survive. Because of the certainty of death, Moses would have God to teach man to properly number his days. God alone can teach this wisdom.

I propose this prayer of Moses to the younger members of this congregation : you have need of it. The learning of this prayer is the beginning of wisdom. In the midst of your ardent hopes, in the heat of your blood, you are in danger of putting off a long way the termination of your life. You can scarcely believe that you are all as liable to early death as was that one whose decease has shot you through and through the past week. There is a numbering of days that does not lead to wisdom. The atheist thinks of the time when he is to die, and thinks of his death as but the blowing out of a candle. The sensualist partakes of new pleasures as the fatal hour approaches, like the sailors on board of a doomed vessel who rushed below and knocked in the casks of wine and waited, amid the revels of wildest dissipation, for the approach of death. All know how crime and excess abounded when the plague raged in Athens. So in the prisons at Paris, during the Reign of Terror, filled at night to be emptied in the morning by the guillotine, riot held sway. To them, death just at hand was an eternal sleep. A great emergency brings out what is deepest in man. The approach of death brings uppermost, without any cover of hypocrisy, the strongest, the controlling motives of our natures.

Let us consider how you can so number your days as to be wisely prepared for the ending of them.

1. *By considering the uncertainty of life.* No one can tell when death will come. It cannot be safely guarded against. This uncertainty should impress upon you the importance of preparing now to meet it.

2. *By considering the shortness of life.* The human language was exhausted by the ancients to express life's brevity. Life is spoken of as the mountain flood that comes suddenly and is gone ; as the grass in desert lands that springs up after the shower and then quickly withers ; as the tale that is told to while away the hours of the travellers crossing the wilderness, and then forgotten when

the journey is past ; a declining shadow ; a swift post, now coming, here, gone ; water spilt on the ground ; weaver's shuttle, etc.

Dr. Franklin said the longer he lived the more rapidly time seemed to pass away, until like the filing of ranks of soldiers before him the years from the sixtieth to seventieth, from seventieth to eightieth of his life passed. Ask God that you may know that you are not to be satisfied with time ; you were made to live for immortality—to live when the stars fail, to pass aloft and beyond forevermore when the temporal has dissolved. Ask God that you may consider His eternity. Some one has said that the light which sped from this earth when it was chaos and the light which has sped from it since, in its different stages, is speeding on in the universe for evermore, carrying with it the picture of each event of development that has transpired on earth. Think of an Omnipotent eye that can grasp all this endless stream of speeding light, carrying the separate pictures ; that eye will have the whole history of the world forever before it. God has the omnipotence of vision. Endeavor to grasp this, as it will help you to grasp the omnipotence of His duration. This eternity that He is to live you are to live ; you have been created immortal.

Above all, ask God to teach you to number your days, that you will believe on the Lord Jesus Christ. Put your hand in Christ's hand. There is life in the touch. A strong man breathes the breath of a dying child. There is poison in the breath. The strong frame weakens, quivers, dies. We are affected by coming into contact with others. Let but faith bring your hand to touch Christ's, and an immortal life will course through your veins. The touch of an affectionate faith can bring the dead to life. In the first instance it is an act, it may be but a feeble act ; but act after act will bring your soul into a constant, living contact with Christ.

Do you now hesitate ? Then have you come to the forking of the roads of your eternal destiny. Put forth this act of faith while I am now speaking to you. Put forth act after act until it becomes a habit, and your union with Christ will be perfect. What can be more important than this act of trust ? I urge you to it tonight. I beseech you in the name of Christ. I beseech you in view of eternity. I urge you to follow Him who made duty the law of His life, who marched to death to rescue you from death, and who has triumphed over death and is seated at the right hand of the power of God, making daily intercession for you.

Thus, Jesus is ready to lift you up to-night to Himself. Will you not stretch out a hand and grasp His outstretched hand, and feel the first pulse of eternal life throbbing in your heart?

ABIDING AND DEPARTING.

BY ALEXANDER M'KENZIE, D.D., CAMBRIDGE, MASS.

For I am in a strait betwixt two, having a desire to depart and to be with Christ; which is far better. Nevertheless to abide in the flesh is more needful for you.—PHILIPPIANS i. 23, 24.

I. EARTH AND ITS CLAIMS UPON US.

1. *The joys of life.* Without controversy, heaven is better than this world. The soul expands in freer air. Days of trial, of infirmity, are past. Conflict, discord, temptation are left behind. But we are now in a world that was made good, and, marred as it is, still has its sacred joys, its purity, its divine ministries, its blessed discipline, its dignity, and worth and beauty. Life is not so sad, so desolate, that we need be impatient to break with it.

2. *The needs of the world.* The poor are here asking our alms; the weeping whom we may comfort; the erring whom we may lead. The world is to be brought back to God, and how shall that be if the good make haste to desert it? Good men are so rare, and the world so large; the harvest so plenteous and the laborers so few! This father, beloved, revered—how essential his life! He looks up, and Christ waits, and the angels. He looks around, and trustful hearts cling to him. This mother, the heart of the home, so strong in her gentleness, so gentle in her strength —how fitting that she should make heaven more fragrant with her presence! But what shall be the home when she has ascended? Heaven is rich in saintly women. Is not this world more in need of those who remain? This aged saint—shall it not be given her now to glide into the freshness of youth, to range the sweet plains on the banks of the crystal river, in companionship with those who shared her life, in the presence of her loved Saviour? Ah! but

the world needs the old. We need to see every day the treasures which virtue may lay up for the time of age.

3. *The purpose of life.* Neither life here, nor life to come, is alone desirable. For a wise purpose, the existence which is never to end has its beginning amid these lowly scenes. Life here is to be esteemed of great value, to be guarded with care, and used with diligence. St. Paul showed his estimate of life by the pains he took to preserve it. This world is a field in which we are to do our first works for God. Here we are trained. While we are here we can honor God more by doing His will than by begging for release. Those are wise words written by Thomas Shepard : " A man that will needs to bed at noonday, before night comes, what needs he but a cudgel. So he that will die before his night comes."

II. HEAVEN AND ITS ATTRACTIONS.

We have presented one side of the case ; but there is another to be considered. The spiritual life awaiting the children of God is higher and surer than this. Our treasure is to be laid up in heaven, our hope to be within the veil. Home is to be above ; rest is there. The severed saints shall be united where the sadness of parting is never known, and the redeemed shall be forever with the Lord. The poor earth renders up its choicest treasures for the faint similitude of the celestial magnificence. Imagination soars on its strongest wing and is lost in the radiance of the supernal heights. If Socrates could discourse on death with calmness, and say, " I entertain a good hope that something awaits those who die, and that it will be far better for the good than the evil," what should be the confidence of one who can say : " For we know . . . we have a building of God, a house not made with hands, eternal in the heavens!"

Thinking thus that both worlds are good, and each the best for us in its own time, we have no call to be distressed if we are summoned speedily away or are bidden to remain.

III. DEATH AND ITS WORK UPON US.

" Earth to earth, ashes to ashes "—that is not death. Even what there is in that is not final, for the resurrection ransoms the body from the grave. Death is far more a going on than any going back. Yet it is too solemn an event to be sought. When it passes on the body, the time of making ready for another world is ended. The beginning of faith and penitence and life is in the world of spirits.

But if we are Christ's, death ushers us into such grand scenes that we should not be found reluctant to depart, or unsubmissive when our friends' enter the glory. The mariner finds the most perilous places near shore, yet is he glad of the sight of the headland. Even so could our Lord forget that His path lay through Gethsemane and over Calvary, hearing the welcome of angels, the greeting of divine affection.

But our sins—our poor life which shrivels before the judgment of God's great day! " Every one of us shall give account of himself to God." Yet, if we be Christ's, we bear not our sins with us to that reckoning. " Who shall lay anything to the charge of God's elect ?" The faithful disciple goes to be with Him who has been loved, trusted, served. The early Christians would not write death, or make its sign upon the tomb of the brotherhood. They wrote, " In Christ," " In peace," " Victorious in Christ," etc. Christ sends His messenger to bring us to Himself. He comes veiled, perhaps shrouded in black, but He will conduct us to the Lord.

AFFLICTIONS NOT ACCIDENTAL.

BY REV. JOHN BURTON, ENGLAND.

For the Lord will not cast off forever: but though He cause grief, yet will He have compassion according to the multitude of His mercies. For He doth not afflict willingly nor grieve the children of men.—LAMENTATIONS iii. 31-33.

THIS apparent contradiction between divine compassion and our human griefs has but one solution : man, as he actually is, is under providential training for what it is possible for him to become.

I. GRIEF THE HERITAGE OF MAN.

There are the peculiar troubles of each individual. All men, in whatever else they differ, agree in this, that they are alike born heirs to a patrimony of sorrow. " Man is born unto trouble as the sparks fly upward." Then there are the troubles which afflict the community, the pestilence, the famine, the war, the financial panic. And there are the troubles which overtake us in the form of sudden calamities, accidents, shipwrecks, fires, etc., the "terrible things of God." For more than sixty centuries this planet, at every turn of its axis, has spread before the eyes of the All-merciful a scene of universal suffering, an "Iliad of woes." If in this huge complex of human grief the guilty only suffered, one might at once suppose a natural Providence were guarding the rights of the virtuous. But "there is no discharge in this war." "There is one event to the righteous and to the wicked."

Let us bear in mind that we have been speaking of facts, not of causes or theories. To the sceptic or infidel and to the Christian philosopher they are equally facts, to be accounted for. They are not the coinage of the Christian faith. If thinking matter or materialized thought be God, still it is a God under whose creative auspices man is born into a world of trouble. The problem is not solved. In either view, man's life is a riddle sternly realistic—with, however, this stupendous difference, that on one view the key that unlocks this mystery is furnished; on the other view, no key exists.

II. THE DIVINE COMPASSION IN ITS RELATION TO SUFFERING.

1. *All human suffering comes within the foreknowledge and is under the control of God.* While suffering in its origin and affliction does always hinge on to secondary causes in the fatalities and falsities of man, those secondary causes do always, immediately or remotely, fasten on to the purpose of God. Somehow and somewhere and for some purpose, there is running all through this seething mass of what appears little else than a complexity of sorrowful accidents, the activity of a prescient forethought, a permissive providence, a governing will. "The curse causeless shall not come." The writers of the Old Testament are never more emphatic than in their assertion of this double parentage of human sorrow. They teach that the plan of Providence takes in the universe as a whole, and yet the individual is never forgotten. He "worketh all things." The sudden blow that takes away the life of my friend; the accidental slip or shot; the explosion, the shipwreck, the collision, the conflagration, are contingencies to us, but they may have a direct relation to the hidden purposes of God. "A certain man drew a bow at a venture, and it smote Ahab, the king of Israel, between the joints of his harness, so that he died." It was a chance shot, and yet the track of that arrow

was foreseen and its issue directed. There can be no accident in the scheme of infinite thought, no surprise to the intelligence that infinitely knows. We see only results. To God the beginning, with its antecedents all hidden and remote, is a presence.

2. *Many of our troubles have their causes in ourselves.* They come within the divine plan, not as visitations which God foreordains and directly inflicts, but as actualities which He foresees, emergent in the history of man. Providence is the action of God through law ; and as a rule, providential laws work best for him who works the best with them. They work, it may be, silently and secretly, but they work surely against him who works against them. A man is intemperate. Very well. Subsequent temperance may alleviate, but not exonerate from, the penalty of a long course of riotous living. The mind neglected in early youth can never afterward become what it would have been if properly trained. So in the ordinary visitations of affliction. In numberless instances they are a self-inflicted visitation. We not only drink the bitter cup, but we supply and mix all its ingredients.

2. *There are many afflictions which come as the punishment for sin.* There are moral statutes in the government of God over men, as there are physical laws in man's government over himself. And as infraction of the one class entails suffering, so infraction of the other class brings punishment. "Though hand join in hand, the wicked shall not go unpunished." "Remember that thou keep holy the Sabbath day." How far as a nation, how far as individuals, do we keep this law? Look at the sin of intemperance, and of open, unblushing ungodliness. And is not one of the crying sins of the age its intense worldliness, its utter absorption in the things of sense?

Reflections :

1. In view of these conclusions, is not the first sentiment which ought to fill our minds that of profound thankfulness for the revelation in which the origin and purpose of all human suffering are made known?

2. Let us always recollect this, that God's dealings with us are regulated and should be interpreted by the fact that we are a race of sinners. Man is at war with his Maker. In such a strife on the one side, there must be resistance on the other. God will not vacate His sovereignty because man rebels.

DEATH OF BELIEVERS.

BY B. M. PALMER, D.D., NEW ORLEANS.

And if Christ be in you, the body is dead because of sin; but the Spirit is life, because of righteousness. But if the Spirit of Him that raised up Jesus from the dead dwell in you, He that raised up Christ from the dead shall also quicken your mortal bodies by His Spirit that dwelleth in you.—ROMANS viii. 10, 11.

A PLAUSIBLE objection may be urged that, as the Apostle declares death to be the evidence of guilt, he cannot consistently say, in the case of the dying believer, "there is no condemnation." The answer is twofold : In the case of the believer there is death of the body alone ; and the dominion of death even over this is only temporary.

I. WHY DOES DEATH PASS UPON THE BODY OF THE CHRISTIAN?

1. *The body is the instrument through which we sin, and a provocative to sin.* If it were not for the eye leering with jealousy or flashing with revenge ; if it were not for the hand dealing with violence and fraud ; if it were not for the feet swift to shed blood ; if it were not for the tongue tripping with the vocables of the pit, the soul might be full of sin, but of sin never revealed to others to the dishonor of God. The body is thoroughly implicated in all the sin a man commits. It is fitting then that God should put upon it the mark of His displeasure.

2. *It is not the design of grace to remove evil out of the world, but to convert it into a means of discipline.* Poverty, pain, sickness, bereavement, are not removed from the Christian, but are made to minister to his spiritual growth. Death comes in the same category.

3. *The body must die that, by being sanctified, it may be fitted for the world of glory.* As under the old dispensation a house infected with leprosy was first dismantled, stone being taken from stone and beam from beam, and was not rebuilt until each part had been carefully scraped to remove the fretting disease, so God deals with these defiled bodies. (1 Cor. xv. 50, 53, 54 ; v. 44.)

4. *The sudden translation of believers would subvert the principle of grace.* All the succeeding steps of the Christian's course must be repetitions of the act of faith, until he reaches that step which

must be the last and severest test. It is the fundamental principle of the scheme of salvation. (Gal. ii. 20 ; Heb. xi. 6.) Suppose now every Christian were taken up bodily to heaven, would there not have to be a constant intervention of the supernatural, superseding the faith which God requires?

5. *The translation of believers would anticipate the judgment day.* Should God put this visible distinction between believers and unbelievers, we would all know, of course, in this world, the eternal destinies of both. Could we bear the knowledge? Would it not disintegrate society and unfit every human being for the duties of this life? Shall the glory of the resurrection day, the coronation day of our Lord, be given us piecemeal?

II. WHY IS THE BODY TO BE RAISED AGAIN?

It is remarkable, the stress laid in the New Testament upon the resurrection of the body. (See Acts xvii. 30, 32 ; ii. 23–32 ; Phil. iii. 20, 21 ; 1 Thess. iv. 14–18.)

1. *The body will be raised because equally with the soul redeemed by Christ and united to Him.*

a. The body, as a constituent part of us, must be as truly redeemed as the soul. Without the body man ceases to be man. The separation of soul and body is unnatural, and hence the horror of death instinctively felt by all men.

b. Christ assumed human nature, body as well as soul, and we are united to Him in both. (See Rom. vi. 5 ; 1 Cor. xv. 20 ; Eph. v. 30.)

c. The curse of sin has fallen upon the body as well as upon the soul, equally necessitating its redemption. (See Gen. iii. 16–18 ; Rom. viii. 23.)

d. The Scriptures bear special testimony to the redemption of the body, and to its union with Christ. (See Isa. xxvi. 19 ; Rom. i. 3, 4 ; viii. 19, 23 ; Eph. v. 30 ; 1 Cor. vi. 15.)

2. *The body will be raised because of the indwelling of the Holy Ghost.*

a. Because it is the Holy Ghost's prerogative to impart life. He is the author of physical life, from the atom floating in the sunbeam to the angel whom John saw standing in the sun. No less is he the author of intellectual life. All the strength of reason and brilliancy of imagination owe their triumphs to the actuating energy of the Spirit of God.

b. The Holy Ghost is the bond by which the believer is united with Jesus Christ.

c. The body of the saint is the temple of the Holy Ghost. (1 Cor. iii. 16, 17; vi. 19; 2 Cor. vi. 16.) The body dismantled and dissolving in the grave is a temple still, though a temple in ruins.

d. The Holy Spirit is the sanctifier, and by virtue of this office will raise the bodies of them that sleep in Jesus.

Remarks:

1. These moral grounds of the resurrection satisfy us of its certainty, and bear us over all the difficulties by which it is invested. All the objections ever urged against the resurrection are objections drawn from our ignorance.

2. The comfort is precious which flows from these truths in view of death, both to ourselves and to those we love.

THE CHRISTIAN'S VICTORY OVER DEATH.

BY REV. JOHN LOGAN, ENGLAND.

O death, where is thy sting? O grave, where is thy victory? . . . Thanks be to God, which giveth us the victory through our Lord Jesus Christ.—1 CORINTHIANS XV. 55, 57.

IT is the glory of the Christian religion that it abounds with consolations under all the evils of life; nor is its benign influence confined to the course of life, but even extends to death itself. It delivers us from the agony of the last hour, sets us free from the fears which then perplex the mind, from the horrors which haunt the offender, and from all the darkness which involves our mortal state. So complete is the victory we obtain that Jesus Christ is said in Scripture to have abolished death.

1. *Christ gives us victory over death by delivering us from the doubts and fears arising from uncertainty regarding the future state.*

Without divine revelation men wandered in the dark regarding an after-life. The light of nature shed but a feeble light on the region beyond the grave. For whence could reason derive any knowledge of immortality? Consult with nature, and destruction seems to be one of its great laws. The species remains, but the individuals perish. Everything you behold around you bears the marks of mortality. To the eye of sense, as the beast dies, so dies the man. (See Job xiv. 7-12.) But what a prospect does annihilation present! Man cannot support the thought. Are all the hopes of man come to this: to be taken into the counsels of the Almighty, to be admitted to behold part of the plans of Providence, and when his eyes are just opened to read the book, to have them shut forever! If such were to be our state, we should of all creatures be most miserable.

From this state we are delivered by the Gospel of Jesus. In the tomb of nature you see man return to the dust from whence he was taken; in the tomb of Jesus you see man restored to life. In the tomb of nature you see the shades of night fall over the weary traveller, and the darkness of the long night close over his head; in the tomb of Jesus you see the morning dawn on the night of the grave. In the tomb of nature you hear, "Dust thou art, and unto dust shalt thou return;" in the tomb of Jesus you hear, "I am the resurrection and the life. He that believeth in Me, though he were dead, yet shall he live."

2. *We are delivered from the apprehensions of wrath and the forebodings of punishment.*

So manifest is it that there is a God who governs the world, rewarding the righteous and punishing the guilty, that the belief n Him has obtained among all nations. Many of the attributes of God are visible in nature: His power, in creating the world; His wisdom, in superintending it; His goodness, in providing for the happiness of His creatures. But nowhere is there an answer to the inquiry, Is mercy an attribute of His nature to such an extent that He will forgive those who rebel against His authority, break His laws, and disobey His commands? For anything we know from the light of nature, repentance alone may not be sufficient to procure the remission of sins. If in calm reflection man could find no hope or consolation in such thoughts, how would he be overwhelmed with horror when his mind was disordered with a sense of guilt! If in the day of health and prosperity such reflections have power to embitter life, what must they be in the last hour, when conscience can no longer be stifled, and the sins of a lifetime pass in review! This is the sting of death. But, O Christian! the death of thy Redeemer is thy strong consolation.

He satisfied the law, blotted out the sentence of wrath, and the plea of His blood drowns the voice of thy offences.

3. *We are relieved of the fears naturally arising from the awful transition from this world to the next.*

Who ever left this life without casting a wishful look behind? We have affections, and delight to bestow them. Bad as the world is, we find in it objects of our tenderest attachment. And after years of communion with congenial minds, what pangs it causes to think of leaving them forever! The very fields and hills and groves with which we are familiar have a charm for us, and absence even from them brings sorrow. Then how must be the affliction to bid an eternal adieu to the friends whom we have long loved, and to part forever with all that is dear under the sun! But let not the Christian be disconsolate. He parts with the objects of his affection to meet them again where change and sorrow never come, and where love and joy will exist unsullied by earthly imperfections.

THE MASTER'S CALL IN AFFLICTION.

BY REV. WILLIAM COCHRANE, BRANTFORD, CANADA.

The Master is come, and calleth for thee.—JOHN xi. 28.

WHY not sooner? Mary might naturally have asked. Day after day she and Martha had awaited His approach. But now all was over. Lazarus was dead and buried. Of what avail Christ's coming now? The language was, "If thou hadst been here, my brother had not died." And so we reason in our moments of despair, when our prayers are not answered in the way we desired, when our friends are not restored to health, and God's presence is not felt. But not so Mary. She arose quickly and came unto Him, believing He had done all things well. God never sends bereavement into a Christian family without some special end in view. As in this case, the end may not at the time be apparent, but we may rest assured He doth not willingly afflict the children of men.

1. *The Master calls us to commune with Him.*

Mary had often before this sat at the feet of Christ; but that was in the days when no sickness or deep sorrow afflicted the household, when there was no special call to muse upon the lessons of mortality. All this is now changed. Alone with Christ, she must be taught the reasons of God's mysterious dealings with her, be taught to bow to His will. The Master called her to impart such knowledge as she had never yet learned, nor could learn but in the closest communion such as sorrow gives.

So it is with every Christian. While he enjoys communion with Christ in every season of existence, yet there are times when he must withdraw from the common surroundings, and be alone with Christ. Mary must leave Martha behind when she would commune with Jesus at such seasons. How often amid the cares of every-day life secret communion is neglected! Yet how we murmur at the sudden calamity that summons us to closer fellowship with God! How few of us take time to examine our hearts, and review our lives, except when laid on a sick-bed, or when beside the grave of a friend! And even then the lesson is soon forgot, as the world's cares again occupy our minds. But when death invades our own home, when the cradle is emptied, or the son or daughter of blessed promise is snatched from us, or the husband or wife is taken from the centre of the home, then we feel there is only one with whom we can converse. "The Master has come, and calleth for thee."

2. *The Master calls us to experience His sympathy and receive divine consolation.*

Mary and Martha were not without sympathizing friends; but there come times when any sympathy is an intrusion. Christ did not come at the moment of bereavement; he waited purposely till several days had elapsed. But a period comes when the heart yearns for companionship. We would not undervalue the real sympathies of Christian friends, but above all we would have the companionship of Jesus Himself. He knows us as no other can; His love surpasses all earthly love. And though we cannot hear Him face to face, as did Mary, He still speaks to us through the Comforter, and in the words of revelation.

3. *The Master calls us to behold greater revelations of His power and goodness.*

Martha looked forward with hope to the last resurrection; but Christ designs gifts of mercy for these sorrowing sisters far beyond their expectations. Such a manifestation of His power as He soon displayed, they had never, in all these years, before seen. Though for us He does not restore our dead, yet He teaches us to regard them as not dead but living. The mere possibility of eternal separation will haunt even the Christian's mind; but Christ aids us to overmaster all doubts and fears.

4. *To each of us it will be said some time, "The Master is come, and calleth for thee."*

To some that call will come at the hour of death, and it may come at any time. To some it may come at the Second Advent. But to all it will come at the Day of Judgment. To many, come whenever it may, it will be sudden and unexpected. Are we prepared for it? Are our calling and election sure? Business men at certain seasons balance their accounts, examine the true state of their affairs. Have we settled the accounts with our Maker? Have we during the past year improved the many privileges God has given us? Have we availed ourselves of the means of grace? Have we made attainments in holiness? What have we done for humanity, for God's glory, for advancing His cause during the year? To many families in this Church the Master's call has come this year; but it should be heard by all. We cannot tell who may next be called into the presence of the Judge.

RIPE FOR THE HARVEST.

BY REV. W. P. TIDDY, LONDON, ENGLAND.

Thou shalt come to thy grave in full age, like as a shock of corn cometh in in his season.—JOB v. 26.

THE teachings of the text are sevenfold:

1. To produce the shock of corn there must have been seed sown. Nature does not produce corn otherwise. (1) So man's heart by nature is unable to produce of itself any good thing. It is barren and unfruitful. (2) The seed of eternal life must be sown in the heart. Christ's Word is that seed, and He is the sower.

2. The seed must have contained the principle of coming life. God giveth to every seed its own body, a body as it hath pleased Him. We do not reap wheat from a field sown with barley. So

in spiritual husbandry. The seed must be the Word of God, which liveth and abideth forever.

3. There must be a prepared and proper soil. (1) The natural and unregenerate heart is bad soil. (2) The fallow ground of the heart must be ploughed up. (3) The stony ground must be cleared by His Word—the thorns rooted up and burned by fiery trials. (4) The heart must be renewed and prepared by the Holy Ghost.

4. The seed must have grown gradually. (1) Because the work of regeneration is perfect. (2) Because justification is complete through the blood of Christ. In these two there is no progress. (3) No child is made more human in constitution by increase of years, but the babe increases in strength, knowledge, and fitness for service as it grows toward manhood. The babe gradually becomes the ripe Christian.

5. The plant must be supplied with nourishment from the root inwardly, and air, rain, etc., outwardly. This is absolute in nature, or the plant will wither and die. It is the same in the kingdom of grace. The trees of righteousness must be sustained by sap from the root through the Word and ordinances.

6. In growing it must have been exposed to many vicissitudes. Cold, heat, drought, flood, and tempest are common between seed-time and harvest, and Jesus declared to His disciples that in this world they shall have tribulation.

7. It must have sunshine to ripen it. No harvest without sunshine. Nor can the soul ripen without the shinings in of the rays of the Sun of Righteousness. The Christian walks in the light of the truth of God's countenance and of heaven.

Conclusion: 1. The husbandman sows seed for the purpose of reaping a joyful harvest. He cuts down the corn when it is golden in the ear that it may not be lost, and when the Lord's time is fully come, He sends forth His reapers. 2. The husbandman separates the grain from the straw, so the Lord separates the spirit from the body, " The body is dead because of sin, the spirit is life because of righteousness." 3. The ingathering is profitable and joyous (1) to the husbandman. Christ sees the travail of his soul and is satisfied. (2) To the angels and church above, (3) to the glorified spirit. 4. Shall we then mourn and regret our loss, when the soul has been received up into glory, as a shock of corn cometh in its season?

THE APPROACH OF DEATH.*

BY ERSKINE MASON, D.D., NEW YORK.

Behold, I come quickly.—REVELATION iii. 11.

WHILE you are all filling up the prospect of the coming year with days of peace and prosperity, I shall bring to your attention the nearness of death only with a view to preparing you for a higher good than your earthly hopes can contemplate. I will not insult your understanding by endeavoring to convince you that we must all die. Yet while none of us will deny it, we are certainly apt to forget it. It is my business to remind you of it.

1. *Death is to separate us from this world, change our mode of existence, and break up all our present associations.*

Deep in the nature of all is implanted an unconquerable aversion to death. Reason cannot remove it, poverty cannot destroy it; even the hopes of heaven cannot reconcile us to death as death. Moreover every man, no matter how wretched, has some tie that binds him to life. With most of us these ties are many and strong, and their sundering forever is painful to contemplate. But these views of death fall into insignificance before the thought of the connection between the present and the future. Life is but the first stage of our being; the second is yet to come, for which we are now preparing ourselves, and in which is the judgment.

Again, death will bring to a close our opportunities of earthly usefulness. Every life has its lines of influence, invisible, it may be, but far-reaching and powerful. Religion does not break those lines, but strengthens and increases them. Death changes all this, by withdrawing us from personal contact with each and all.

But with the unbeliever death means still more. It means the termination of his hopes for salvation. It means that probation has ended. And whereas the Christian looks to life eternal as the perfection of all joy, the unbeliever can see in it but the termination of all joy. In this life even the wicked are often granted prosperity and many comforts. But death removes them all, and brings nothing but despair to take their place.

We are apt to look at death merely as an event of nature, and

---

* A New Year's sermon.

its coming as a lawless contingency. But reflection shows us that it is but the coming of the Lord, and the time thereof is regulated by His will. And here lies the strongest reason for our shrinking. It is the coming of the Lord, and before Him, the righteous and all-discerning Judge, our soul is to be presented in all its guilt.

2. *The coming of the Lord is not only certain, but it is close at hand.*

Yet how few believe that death is near to them! We count on many years to come, and live and plan as though long life were assured us. Yet have we not all during the past year had solemn warnings in the death of those whose prospects were as bright as ours? Yet how soon we forget the warning.

Moreover, death comes suddenly. Almost uniformly it takes men unawares. It waits for no plans, or pleasures, or tears, or arguments. How solemn it is to think of it, and how terrible to go tripping through life without a thought of anything but the present and its perishable joys!

WORDS OF COMFORT FOR AFFLICTED PARENTS.*

BY REV. LEWIS O. THOMPSON, PEORIA, ILL.

Now we see through a glass, darkly.—1 CORINTHIANS xiii. 12.

IN casting about for what might be suitable at such a time as this, and under such trying circumstances, there came the thought that the limitations of the present life are so great that we understand its meaning and destiny very imperfectly. For what is there that these parents would more earnestly desire than to have the children God gives them spared unto them, to the end that they may grow up to be useful men and honorable women—the joy and comfort of their hearts? I do not say that these Christian parents—now that Providence has taken from them their dear daughter—would wish to bring her back contrary to the will of God. They have, doubtless, received grace from God to pray: "Thy will be done."

But it is often the case that our hearts are so set upon our children that we desire, by all means, to retain them, and are quite

---

* At the funeral of a child.

unreconciled when they are taken from us. The number, perhaps, is rather small of those who are able sincerely to say: "The Lord gave, and the Lord hath taken away: blessed be the name of the Lord!" Now, murmurings arise from two sources: first, from our lack of grace; and, second, from defective means of vision. With more grace we should have more resignation. With clearer vision we should have more desire to depart and be with Jesus, and more cheerful submission to the will of God when He takes our dear ones to Himself.

I. DEFICIENCIES IN OUR VISION.

The Apostle declares that "now we see through a glass, darkly." These limitations of vision are both natural and spiritual. Organs of sight have been given us for seeing the natural world, and intelligence to enable us to look within material things, to discern what is underneath their surface and discover their meaning and philosophy. But notice how these which serve us best—the senses and reason—come far short of perfection; up to a certain extent they serve us all alike. We see, in common with all animals, what is upon the surface of things—and the outward world looks alike to all of us; but the moment we try to look within, one man sees one thing, another another, and we have almost as many philosophies as there are minds.

For spiritual things faith is given us. And yet even through this noble eye of the soul, "we see through a glass, darkly." We see darkly through the dispensations of Providence. Many are its unsolved mysteries. Those dispensations that are favorable, we gladly accept and question lightly; but those that are afflictive we sadly accept, would gladly thrust them from us, and are at a loss how to understand or interpret them. But we still further see darkly through the glories and realities of the heavenly life and the full happiness of those who are gathered there.

When we contemplate death and behold its masterpiece, the lifeless body of your dear child, we look almost entirely from the standpoint of what it has done for us. And what is this? Death has destroyed a wonderful organization, and broken up a copartnership between body, soul, and spirit. In doing all this it has separated from us a living form and loving presence. The dear daughter shall never return to us. Death never restores to us those upon whom he has laid his icy hand.

II. Is there any remedy for our heavy affliction?

1. *We should seek after larger measures of grace.* Thanks be to God, "we may come boldly unto the throne of grace, that we may obtain mercy, and find grace to help in time of need." If we so do, our grief shall last only through a night, and joy shall come in the morning. Is it nothing that you have a child in heaven? Are the consolations of God small with thee? God does not stint us in the bestowment of grace, but He gives no more than we use. To him that uses shall be given, and he shall have more abundantly.

2. *We should look at what death has been instrumental in accomplishing for the child.* And what is this? Death has removed her from all the uncertainty, sickness, pain, sorrow, and change that belong even to the brightest and happiest life here on earth. Through the gateway of death her spirit has ascended to God, who gave it. She is now a full sharer in the glorified bliss of heaven. She dwells where Jesus is, and in full possession of eternal life. Oh, if we could only see more clearly the place she occupies in heaven, the grand capacities and possibilities of life opened to her, her early removal from us would have in it less of anguish and more of consolation! To-day, clad in garments whiter than the snow, she sings with sweeter voice than has e'er been heard upon earth, and bears a vocal part in that grand symphony of heaven: "Unto Him that loved us, and washed us from our sins in His own blood, and hath made us kings and priests unto God and His Father: to Him be glory and dominion forever and ever. Amen."

THE TENT HOME AND THE ETERNAL HOME.

BY THEODORE L. CUYLER, D.D., BROOKLYN.

Therefore, we are always confident, knowing that whilst we are at home in the body we are absent from the Lord.—2 CORINTHIANS v. 6.

Our body is our tent home; heaven is our eternal home. Eighty years this may last—generally but thirty years. How many have patched up this tabernacle, and by close and careful watching preserved it a few years more! Dust-bound at sixty, it begins to decay. How old you are! How changed you look!

The tent is failing. Soon we will have notice to quit. Every day I see these deserted homes—the inhabitants gone forever to a higher habitation.

1. *These homes are itinerating.* I see few faces here which I saw fifteen years ago. Many have gone to other parts. We are always on the march. In the Orient the piles of ashes, the tent-poles, marking the place where some one has tented for a night, are frequently visible. One day some other pastor will come here and see the ashes and the tent-poles of my stay.

2. *The frailty of this earthly tent.* This but heightens the idea of the permanence of our home beyond. One could have said, "Paul, you are homesick; you have no home, no family, no one but Jesus." Old and gray-headed Apostle, no wonder your eye was fixed above, far over the Mediterranean Sea. Here was a hero going home, to a home God from the eternities built, an abiding home, an everlasting rest. It hath no sun, no moon. Jesus is its light.

3. *The soul-home is where Christ and the people meet.* Heaven is a place; I have no sympathy with the philosophy that makes it a condition. An abstraction is no home. I believe it is a place as definite in location as London or Paris. Bunyan dreamed, but John says, "I saw." The moment I let go the literal translation I let go my home. Is the soul degraded by dwelling in a local heaven? Is it degraded by dwelling in the body? Have you not kissed the frail home of clay, silent, beautiful in death, and felt confident that to leave that tent was to be at home with the Lord? That hope was as an anchor.

The many mansions show that elective affinities may exist there. Families may be together. Emmons desired to talk with Paul, and why not? Will we not be looking for old acquaintances? Happy will we be if we find some one we brought there.

4. *But our entrance is not yet.* We are still in the body. Is your name in that Lamb's Book of Life? Let us make ready to go to that home. The negro judged his master had not gone home to heaven because he never talked about it. We must learn something about it. How can we learn if we do not converse about it?

THE HEAVENLY WORLD.

BY J. M. SHERWOOD, D.D., BROOKLYN.

For there shall be no night there.—REVELATION xxi. 25.

THIS is said of heaven, the eternal home of the blessed. It is scarcely in the power of language to express in so few words a more vivid and comprehensive description of the characteristics of that life, both in its physical and spiritual aspects. The imagery is poetic, and yet appeals to our intensest experiences. "Light is sweet, and a pleasant thing it is for the eyes to behold the sun." Light is the Scripture emblem of God, of happiness, and glory; while darkness impersonates sin, death, hell, the very genius of evil, brooding over a world of sighs and desolation and chaos. Heaven and light, heaven and everlasting day; hell and outer darkness, hell and one eternal night of gloom, are the ultimate final states of the righteous and the wicked.

Amid the gloom and sadness natural to this occasion, we are invited to look up and beyond the confines of earth and behold the day everlasting flooding all the fields of immortality with celestial radiance. Let us view the contrast between this present world and that.

1. *There is no night of ignorance in heaven.* Darkness fittingly represents a state of mental and spiritual ignorance. Darkness is not a substance; only the absence of light. Can you conceive of a state more appalling to a rational creature than a state of ignorance, a mind unillumined with the rays of knowledge and wisdom, groping in gross darkness through probation down to death and eternity, and that, too, while sun and stars shine in the heavens? Even the Christian, in this life, sees but "in part." The vision is dim, imperfect; the revelation is not finished. But finished it will be *there!* Not a cloud will obscure the sky. The horizon of knowledge will be vastly enlarged. The dark things of this life will be cleared up. It will be twilight no longer, but perfect day.

2. *No night of error in heaven.* In the darkness we lose our way, wander we know not where, and peril life at every step. Now *error* is darkness, a worse darkness than ignorance, for it is a

blinding, perverting, misleading substance. It causes millions to go astray from the truth, from life, and to fall into sin, into perdition. None are exempt from error in this world. Where there is sin, imperfect knowledge, imperfect sanctification, error will assert its power. How many Christian characters are tarnished by error in one form or another! How many tears flow over the sins and wrongs and evils which errors work in the lives of the good! But there will be no error in heaven, no lurking seeds of evil in the soul, no doubt or uncertainty in any part of revelation. Absolute light will cover and fill and permeate every thought and feeling and experience.

3. *No night of sin in heaven.* Sin is darkness itself, midnight darkness, darkness that may be felt; darkness in the soul and darkness in the world; is the prelude to that "outer darkness," that "blackness of darkness" which is to be the portion of the ungodly. Is it any marvel that such multitudes who give themselves to a life of sin should "stumble on the dark mountain of sin and perish"? Not even the believer escapes all darkness here. Sin is brought under, but not eradicated. He aims at perfection, but alas, how far short does he come! He often has occasion to wet his couch with his tears of penitence; to exclaim with Paul, "O wretched man that I am, who shall deliver me from the body of this death"? The night is often dark and the soul travails in sorrow. But yonder on the other side of the river there is no night. There is no sin there, no moral imperfection. The heart is pure, the surroundings are pure, the atmosphere is purity itself, the very heavens reflect purity in the beams of divine effulgence. Blessed be God, the night is past, the day has come, and such a day! Such light and peace and joy and blessedness, unmixed, perpetual, abounding more and more eternally!

4. *No night of conflict in heaven.* Where there is ignorance, imperfection, sin, there must be a state of conflict on the part of the Christian. Hence this life is a severe, constant, painful warfare, even down to the gates of death. There is no rest in this warfare, no intermission, no cessation. "Watch and pray," ever striving against principalities and powers, ever with armor on facing the foe and contending for the prize. The strife of battle, the clash of arms, wounds and fears, are the conditions of this life. But in yonder world all this will be changed. Not one element of strife

or conflict can ever enter the celestial gates. The war will be ended and the victor will there be crowned. There will be nothing to hurt or molest. Those skies are never ruffled. No warring or jarring sound is ever heard. Infinite peace will pervade all that blessed world, and the rest of attained and eternal life will be experienced by all.

5. *No night of weariness in heaven.* We need the natural night here for sleep, rest, recuperation. But it is because we are weak and imperfect. Exercise tires, exhausts us. But in heaven there is no night and no need of any. The amazing activity of that world never wearies. Sleep is unknown there. The soul is tireless, ever fresh and vigorous, ever in service. No time is lost in sleep, in feebleness. Heaven is a world of ceaseless, wondrous activities. There is no stagnation of life, no faltering, no fainting, but one ceaseless, blessed, angelic round of service.

6. *No night of danger in heaven.* There is always danger in the dark. We fear it and instinctively shrink from it. The night season is a time of special perils and evils. The wicked choose it to do mischief, to rob and murder, and commit all sorts of crime. "The eye of the adulterer," says Job, "watches for the twilight." Virtue and innocence, property and life, are imperilled every time the sun retires from sight. But yonder world is free from this evil. Once past the gates of the celestial city, and perfect, eternal safety will attend your steps. Those gates are never "shut," for there is "no night there." There are "none to molest or make afraid." There are no evils lurking there to surprise, no concealment, no temptation, no fall possible. The light of "God and the Lamb" is there, an infinite, everlasting effulgence.

7. *No night of sorrow in heaven.* How much of this life is passed in darkness, caused by sorrow in its manifold forms! The night of sickness, of affliction, of bereavement, of disappointment, of trial, of spiritual desolation—what gloom and fear and wretchedness does it cause even the Christian! What sighs, what depression, what longings for deliverance, are connected with our sorrows! So long is this night in the experience of many that it seems as if the morning would never come; so intense the gloom that the soul, just ready to give over, cries out in anguish, "Hath God forgotten to be gracious?" So much of misery and darkness

and bitter experience mingles in this earthly state, that we give expression to the plaintive wail :

> "It is a weary way, and I am faint ;
>   I pant for purer air, and fresher springs ;
>   Oh Father ! take me home ; there is a taint,
>   A shadow on earth's purest, brightest things,
>   This world is but a wilderness to me ;
>   There is no rest, my God ! no peace apart from Thee."

Well, the night is far spent, the day cometh. "No night *there.*" The angel of sorrow shall not so much as cast a shadow over that bright world. It will be a universal scene of perpetual brightness and joy.

8. *No night of suffering in heaven.* Sin, darkness, conflict, ignorance, are only other names for suffering. We are born to this inheritance. There is no escape, no exemption. The curse, the blighting, terrible curse of a sin-hating God is here—rests on everything which sin has defiled ; and that curse pursues every man to the very confines of the grave. Oh, what is life under this righteous tremendous infliction, life in its best estate ! As one has well said, "life begins with a sigh and ends with a groan." But the morn will come, and come with a radiance so full, so joyous, so glorious, as to dispel forever and ever all fear and gloom from every mind, and mantle the skies with a radiance that shall eclipse the noonday sun !

9. *Finally, there is no night of death in heaven.* Death is the most dreaded and tremendous event in human experience. The fear of it is a lifelong bondage. Night is the Scripture emblem of death. There is a profound mysteriousness about the night. The day closes, work ceases, darkness covers the earth, a strange drowsiness steals over us, the eyes close, we pass into an oblivious state, and all is silent about us ! Is it death ? It is akin to it. But for the frequency of the event we could not look upon sleep but with a shudder. And yet death is a great deal more. But in the case of every believer Christ has taken away the sting of it and robbed the grave of its spoil. There are no death-fears in heaven, no death-pangs, no death-chamber partings ! There are no graves in heaven, no funeral processions, no habiliments of mourning ! Death has never gained entrance there, even though angels once

rebelled. Life, only life, perfect, glorious, immortal life, is there. No sickness, no tears, no dying. Oh, blessed world !

Application. This subject is full of consolation to these bereaved friends.* You have far less occasion to mourn to-day than to rejoice. She was a child of the day. By faith she discerned the blessed world where there is no night, and with hope and patience waited for the morning. It has now come. Hers was a long night : fourscore and six years few attain to. And what a breadth and experience of life was hers ! But the "Star of Bethlehem" rose early on her path. There were times when the night was very dark about her, and when her soul travailed in fear and sorrow, and she longed for the dawn. But the damps and fogs and darkness tended to nurse her faith and cause her virtues to bloom the sweeter and purer. Yes, the morning has come to her. It dawned with unearthly splendor in that serenity of spirit, and fulness of faith, and triumph of hope which characterized her last days ; it shone forth with celestial radiance in her soul while you watched the falling of the last sands of her life ; and as she passed the dark valley the Sun of Righteousness, full-orbed and resplendent with divine glory, broke upon her vision. She is now basking in the light of that Sun which never sets and before which all darkness flees away. While your eyes are bedimmed with tears, hers are gazing with unspeakable wonder and delight on the scenes of angelic life. Oh, with what thanksgiving does she recognize the fact that with her the night is past never to return—the night of ignorance and error and sin and conflict and weariness and sorrow and suffering and death—and the day is ushered in—the day of deliverance from sin, the day of the complete triumph of grace, the day of glorious realization, of hope and blessedness and life in the kingdom of God !

* Preached at the funeral of an aged saint ripe for heaven.

GLAD HOME-GOING.

BY REV. JOHN LOBB, LONDON.

Therefore the redeemed of the Lord shall return, and come with singing unto Zion; and everlasting joy shall be upon their head: they shall obtain gladness and joy; and sorrow and mourning shall flee away.—ISAIAH li. 11.

THE sweetness and preciousness of some words only disclose themselves in seasons of holy calm, when we are alone with God. Others are not understood until we have suffered deeply and been sorely bereaved. Others are left for death to interpret in the fulness of their grace and glory. Some glimpse of their meaning may come to us, as the first faint streak of light in the dawning of the morning. The children sing words of wonder, whose meaning they only dimly apprehend. Still gladness steals into their hearts because they have a dim consciousness of a glory to be revealed. Like the children, we of a larger growth sing words of sweet and heavenly forecast, and the common life is brightened with a diviner radiance, and there stirs within, in stronger pulsations, the "earnest expectation of the creature." The words of the text, fulfilled in the history of the return from captivity, are awaiting the richer, fuller interpretation of death in our case. Though all the fulness of the blessing may not be disclosed, our meditation may help to assuage the sorrow of earthly trial and to brighten Christian hopes.

I. THOSE DESTINED TO THIS GLORIOUS HOME-GOING.

The expression, "the redeemed of the Lord," is one which grows out of the Levitical law. The precise signification of the word redeemed is that of substitution. A man redeemed his firstborn by substituting an animal for him. This law of substitution, and painful substitution, runs through all human history. Mothers are immolated on the altar of love that their children may sing glad songs of exulting joy. We must live for others and die for others. God has placed Himself under the same law. "He hath borne our griefs and carried our sorrows." The Redeemer is a ransom for all who believe in His name. The old Church was redeemed through Him. Nations unborn are included in His gracious purpose. The children share in the benefits of His grace. Our loved ones who have tasted death swell the blood-washed throng. Christ is drawing all men to Him, and one day all will be His.

II. THEIR DESTINATION.

"They shall return and come to Zion." Two ideas are here suggested.

1. *The redeemed on high are brought into nearer fellowship with God.* There will be a vast increase of spiritual capacity. The acquaintance with God's purposes, the sense of His love, will be greater and more intense than any known on earth.

2. *The coming to Zion is expressive of personal association and fellowship.* Every spirit forms one of a glorious company. Heaven is a social state. Lost loves are found, broken relations are united. As the years pass on, how rich heaven becomes!

III. THE NEW CONDITIONS AND CIRCUMSTANCES OF THE REDEEMED.

The text labors to express the fulness of delight. The word everlasting has in it the idea of ages past as well as ages to come. Heavenly joy is one the sources of which were prepared in past ages of unfolding grace. There is no sorrow here which shall not there be found to be the beginning of a new blessedness. Tears shall be wiped away—the tears of impotent, baffled nature; the tears of regret; the tears of remembered sin; the tears of bereavement. There is, then, no loss in death. The future of the redeemed is assured by the Redeemer. Life is theirs; death is theirs; heaven is theirs.

THE DEATH OF A MOTHER.

BY REV. JOHN M. JOHNSON, HANOVER, N. J.

I behaved myself as though he had been my friend or brother: I bowed down heavily, as one that mourneth for his mother.—PSALM xxxv. 14.

No thoughtful man can look on the face of his mother cold in death, without such emotions and reflections being awakened as nothing else ever has produced or will produce. It is an experience that comes but once in life.

1. *A mother's death reminds us of the blessings conferred by God through the maternal relation.*

The mother's love is different from the father's, in being more particular and minute. It springs from her own nature, not from any excellence in the child, and survives ingratitude, sin, and shame in the latter's life. Her influence is the first felt, her care the first bestowed on us. The maternal relation has been peculiarly honored by God. It was made the means of uniting the divine and the human nature, and Christ at all times honored and obeyed His mother.

2. *The death of a mother occasions bitter recollections of filial disobedience and neglect.*

God has set our duty to parents next to that which we owe Him. Parents stand in the place of God to the infant child, but the mother first exercises this authority. Happy is he who has no cause for repentance over his neglect or disobedience to maternal love.

3. *It breaks up the home of our early days, and makes us feel we are only sojourners here.*

Who can name all the tender associations that cluster about our early home? Amid them all the mother is the centre of influence and happiness. Ever after, the recollection is a hallowed one, kindling virtue and restraining vice. The mother's death seems to remove all this, but it is henceforth a cord to bind us to heaven.

4. *The death of a mother, especially of an aged mother, makes us sensible of our nearness to another world.*

It seems to place us a generation nearer the grave. It brings us in the foremost rank of the travellers to eternity.

Upon these relations I would present a few practical suggestions.

1. *I appeal to fathers.* Teach your children that a mother's love is the most sacred thing in life. Teach them to honor her authority fully as much as your own. When they come to despise that, they are far on the way to despising God's.

2. *I appeal to mothers.* Your responsibility is a most momentous one. You cannot carry it without God's help. You cannot delegate it to any other person.

3. *I appeal to those whose mother is living.* You cannot be too solicitous to fulfil your duties to her. Boys are apt to think that to despise the mother's advice and appeals is a sign of manhood. That is a folly, cruel and guilty. The truest men are those who honor their mothers as Jesus honored His.

4. *I appeal to those whose mother is dead.* Cherish her precepts and honor her religion. Let her grave be a sanctuary where you shall draw near to God. So live that you shall meet her in heaven.

PREPARATIONS FOR MEETING GOD.

BY RICHARD S. STORRS, D.D., BRAINTREE, MASS.

Prepare to meet thy God.—AMOS iv. 12.

"GOD is not far from every one of us." "If we ascend into heaven, He is there; if we make our bed in hell, behold He is there." But with those who love and obey Him, He is present as a loving Father; while He meets as an adversary those who reject His authority; and to such a meeting Israel is summoned in the words of the text, and God recalls the sufferings He has inflicted upon them to impress them that He is a God of justice as well as of mercy. To such a meeting is every unrepentant sinner summoned.

I. GOD'S JUDICIAL CHARACTER.

1. *His righteousness.* Every law of God is righteous, both in principle and in penalty. No one will be punished beyond his demerits.

2. *His benevolence.* He is the source of all benevolence. Strict righteousness, acting alone, would consign men to despair at once; but blended with benevolence it distributes numberless blessings to our undeserving race. The punishment hereafter of sinners is no more inconsistent with God's benevolence than are their sufferings in the present. Divine goodness will bestow on us all the blessings we can receive without injustice being done to Himself and other holy intelligences.

3. *His knowledge.* "His eyes are on all the ways of men, and He seeth all their goings." Nothing can escape Him, no one can deceive Him.

4. *His power.* Behold Him measuring oceans in the hollow of His hand, meting out the heavens with a span, comprehending the dust of the earth in a measure, weighing the mountains in scales, and the hills in a balance, and doing according to His will in the army of heaven and among the inhabitants of the earth !

Remember He once swept the earth of every living thing, overthrew the cities of the plain, caused Babylon to drink the cup of His fury, overturned Jerusalem in anger. Before such a judge who shall stand?

II. PREPARATIONS FOR MEETING GOD IN PEACE

Some say no other preparation is necessary than sorrow for our sins. But Judas was afflicted with deepest remorse, yet "it had been better for him never to have been born." Who ever dreamed that law regards as atonement the criminal's sorrow? If tears will avail nothing, can sacrifice? God has said, "I will have mercy and not sacrifice." Two principles are here disclosed:

1. *The sinner has nothing of his own to offer God.*
2. *If he had anything, God would not need it.*

Preparation can be made to meet God in peace only by accepting of Christ as our Saviour. This act of acceptance is called faith. It is one thing to believe with the understanding, another thing to believe with the heart. Faith in Christ involves thorough regeneration, and constitutes a new and powerful principle of action.

HUMAN LIFE TRANSITORY.

BY EDWARD N. KIRK, D.D., BOSTON.

What is your life? It is even a vapor, that appeareth for a little time, and then vanisheth away.—JAMES iv. 14.

I. HOW MEN MAKE THE MISTAKE OF REGARDING THIS LIFE AS SOMETHING SOLID AND STABLE.

1. *Men count on the certain continuance of their strength.* Men's plans and hopes are generally built on the foundation of enduring health. All the pleasures of sense require health and vigor. Just so far, then, as life and happiness are made dependent on them, we count on continued strength. For such persons the thought of death is horrible, and they strive to banish it. The young can hardly realize that they are to become aged and infirm. Why do we dread advancing age? Because it shows the falseness of the life embracing only the pleasures that depend on health.

2. *Men count upon an indefinite prolongation of life.* Suppose that health is to continue as long as life, yet life itself is altogether

insecure. The eager pursuit of wealth, and power, and pleasure, appears vain and foolish when we consider that even if possession of the object desired be attained, how long such possession will continue is uncertain.

3. *Men count on the next life as resembling this.* Men fancy heaven as they wish it to be. The Indian's heaven is one of gross delights, but there are many in Christian lands whose views are not much more exalted.

II. THE UNIVERSAL UNCERTAINTY OF LIFE.

It is like the vapor, which a breeze or sunbeam may the next moment destroy. Look at it in reference to God. Before His eternal existence it is but a moment. Look at it in reference to nature. We call the hills everlasting, but even they shall vanish away. Look at it in reference to experience. Every day new illustrations crowd upon our attention. Our cemeteries vie with our cities. And this uncertainty is universal. No one, no matter what his plans or how important his life, can escape it.

III. HOW SHALL WE RECTIFY SUCH ERRORS IN OUR OWN MIND?

1. *We must understand the reality of the case.* "Teach me so to number my days that I may apply my heart unto wisdom." We must understand what life is given us for, and recognize fully that we must suffer pains and sorrows, and that earthly blessings are but transitory. Let us remember life is a scene of discipline.

2. *We should become reconciled to it.* If we come to look at life in the light of revelation and eternity, it is not thereby degraded, but rendered a thing of the utmost importance. It is exalted above all other views of life, and, rightly used, becomes the means of the highest good and fullest happiness to us.

3. *We must accommodate our feelings and plans to this view.* Make nothing that can perish the foundation of your hope. Lay up treasures in heaven. Let the heart find its chief joy, not in the vain pleasures and ambitions of earth, but in purity and self-sacrificing love.

STRENGTH AND BEAUTY IN CHARACTER.

BY REV. W. R. DAVIS, ALBANY, N. Y.

Upon the top of the pillars was lily-work.—1 KINGS vii. 22.

Him that overcometh will I make a pillar in the temple of my God.—REVELATION iii. 12.

OBSERVE that the strength was first and the beauty of lilies afterward. We have here those two qualities which are worshipped by the soul of man the world over. Power and beauty alike win his homage, but not unfrequently he yields himself to the sham of strength and the semblance of beauty—to power ungifted with love, to beauty unadorned by holiness. It is the lie of the world that the righteous must needs be the weak, and the pure the uncomely. God declares the right to be the only strong, and the good to be the only beautiful.

I cannot speak of the sudden darkness and inner pain that smote my heart when a messenger entered my room with the tidings, "Dr. Gregory is dead." I felt that a pillar in our temple had fallen, that a life on which leaned hundreds of lives was shattered. Yet looking forward beyond the finite I see a shining, stately shaft set up on high, and read, "Him that overcometh will I make a pillar in the temple of my God."

I. THE STRENGTH OF HIS CHARACTER.

1. *He was a man of convictions.* When he came to apprehend the realities of life illuminated by the realities of divine truth, it was in no negative mood, but with a vivid experience that made them his own. Faith was the substance standing under his personality.

2. *His fidelity.* He was not a rover or a shifter, playing fast and loose with duty, but an earnest man, who, having found truth, planted himself on it with a firmness invincible.

3. *He was sincere.* He could no more bear a sham than be a sham himself. He had no hiding-place even for his faults.

4. *He was self-sacrificing.*

5. *He sympathized with human life in every stage and experience.* The sorrows and struggles of others became his own. His consolations were swift to offer all his resources. Wherever his name was mentioned you seemed to hear the beat of a big heart. As

one upon a steamer's deck feels the throb of the engine and knows that he is near a force that helps him over the waves, so his friends were propelled by his power against adverse currents and over the crests of difficulties.

II. THE BEAUTY OF HIS CHARACTER.

1. *His cheerfulness.* This shone in his countenance, rang in his voice, was the elasticity of every movement. He believed mirth to be a real part of our moral nature, and he was one of its genial ministers.

2. *His appreciation of everything natural.* No matter how homely or insignificant, if it grew out of a legitimate germ he would give it due value. This directed his estimates, decided his tastes, and determined his criticism of art and character. It was not a weakness any more than it is a source of weakness to the oak to bear the foliage that elaborates strong roots and giant arms.

EMOTIONS OF A SAINT IN HEAVEN.

BY REV. A. S. GARDNER, NEW YORK.

In thy presence is fulness of joy.—PSALM xvi. 11.

HEAVEN is the Christian's goal. He feels more and more sensibly, as he advances toward it, that nowhere else is happiness in fulness to be found. And when he reaches it and enters upon his inheritance, then, and not till then, can he understand the full import of the words, "In thy presence is fulness of joy."

1. *He has been made the subject of a change that affects everything connected with him save his identity.*

The scene of his dissolution may be supposed to be vividly present. The bed of pain, the long hours of wasting sickness, the sorrowing friends that gathered around, will doubtless appear before him in sharp contrast with the rest and peace into which he has entered. He may have struggled with doubts and fears, but now all tremblings are at an end.

The body, with all its fevers and pains and fatigues, has been left behind. But it is left only that at the resurrection, purified, glorified, spiritualized, it may rise again to be the home of the spirit forever.

2. *The unencumbered action of the spirit.*

Circumscribed while upon earth by its habitation of clay, checked by the imperfections and depravities of the natural man, now its powers are brought into most vigorous action, and everything is exactly adapted to its nature. And one of the results will be the instant recognition of the redeemed. Parent will recognize child, and friend friend.

3. *The friendships of heaven will be of a higher order than those of earth.*

Doubts, suspicions, treacheries, will no longer endanger our friendships. Each may pour into the bosom of every other the most secret thoughts, and all will be worthy the same unbounded confidence. There will be no reserve, or pride, or selfishness. And, above all, the love of God will be realized in all its fulness, and His dealings with us upon earth, that sometimes caused belief to stagger, will now be seen in their true light.

4. *He will stand in the presence of Christ.*

The memories of all that Christ has suffered for him will mingle with exaltation at His unutterable glory. On earth he has followed Him through all the scenes of His earthly life, but at the ascension sight has become dim, and the longing to pierce the cloud which received Him out of sight is now for the first time gratified.

Such is a faint view of the joys of the redeemed. By it two reflections are inspired :

1. *That excessive grief over the departed is unwarranted.*

2. *That we should make sure of our inheritance with the saints in light.*

THE BLESSED DEAD.

BY REV. WILLIAM LLOYD, NEW YORK.

Blessed are the dead which die in the Lord from henceforth : yea, saith the Spirit, that they may rest from their labors ; and their works do follow them.
—REVELATION xiv. 13.

To read the Book of Revelation is like walking over a volcano, where here and there, on the very edge of the crater, surrounded by waste and fire, we find a beautiful flower. Amid the awful threatenings of the Revelation we find, strangely mingled in the Apostle's vision, the most beautiful flowers of promise. Amid the pictures of the divine wrath are glimpses through which we see the grand procession of the redeemed as, crowned, they stand before the throne of God. "Blessed are the dead that die in the Lord." What words could bring such sweet promise as these? They are like the sweetest wine, the Lachryma Christi, the grapes for which grow in the most desolate and sterile spots. They are as a star which breaks through the tempest at midnight to light the seaman home; as a chord of sweet music heard through dissonance. "Blessed are the dead that die in the Lord." These are words of divinest promise or mere mockery. Standing by the open grave, crushed with grief, the heart finds no comfort in them. It cannot understand how death can be blessed. There is no rainbow over the grave. Look at what was once a man, full of power. He was our tower of strength, and now he lies there more helpless than an infant. The mighty man that throbbed with life, and the eye that looked into ours and flashed with wisdom, are dull and dead. Can you find much comfort in death then?

Amid the wreck of human hopes these words come down to us like a benediction. Why are the dead blessed who die in the Lord? Because they live. Death is not descent; it is ascent. Death is not extinction; it is elevation to the highest life. Blessed are the dead, because they live. They are the living. It is not we that live. It is we who are dying; they are living. Blessed they are because they rest from anxiety and disappointment. And so these words have been woven into the burial service. We gaze after our loved ones who are taken from us as we watch a ship which sails away with our friends. We strain our eyes until the last flicker of the sail can be seen no more, and we know that until we take the same voyage we shall know nothing more of them.

But their work shall live after them. This life has in it immortality. There is an immortality in what we do here. True work has not mere personal aggrandizement for its end and aim. It is the helping of others—the being to the blind eyes and to the lame feet, the helping of the helpless. That is the definition of the work which lives after a man dies. The life of a true Christian will be spent in helping others, and this is the work that will bear fruit and live after him.

THE HIDINGS OF GOD'S PROVIDENCE.

BY M. W. HAMMA, D.D., BALTIMORE.

What I do thou knowest not now; but thou shalt know hereafter.—JOHN xiii. 7.

THESE words Christ spoke to Peter when Peter could not comprehend the meaning of His actions.

Most of the facts of Providence have their meanings veiled. We live in a world of mystery. The physical world has revealed very few of its secrets. This is equally true of the events of our lives. They come to us shrouded. Yet we may ever discover traces of intelligence, traces of wisdom. We see evidences of a plan. Let us pursue this thought:

1. *Every man's life is part of the great plan of God*—a plan that has many alternatives. All extremes of life are within the boundaries of this plan. The man who rises to the greatest height shows forth God's glory; he who sinks to the greatest depth serves as a warning.

2. *This plan of God is so great that you cannot judge of it by one event, or even by one life.* You go into the workshop of the artist who is framing a great structure. You see here a stone of a peculiar color; there a stone of another color; here one of this, and there one of that angle. You would not say to the artist, You had better take this stone or that stone next; you would submit to his superior wisdom. He sees the whole of the structure as it stands complete before his mind. What do you know of the whole plan? These few stones that you see can give you but the most imperfect conception of the cathedral in which they are to be placed. In God's providence I submit to the superior wisdom of the Great Architect. He takes from the earth one man and leaves another. We are amazed; we cannot understand it; we know not the plan that lies in God's mind.

   a. Sometimes God reveals in this life the reasons for His providences. This we see in Job. Jacob lived to see the reason for the strange providence that permitted Joseph to be taken from him. Years he walked in the shadow of that great sorrow before light came.

b. There are other sorrows, the explanation for which comes not in this life. This was true of the death of Rachel—Naomi fleeing from famine, losing her husband, and her daughters losing theirs. The triple sorrow was probably not revealed in life.

HOW CHRIST TAKES AWAY FEAR OF DEATH.

BY REV. R. S. STORRS DICKINSON, SCOTLAND.

And deliver them who through fear of death were all their lifetime subject to bondage.—HEBREWS ii. 15.

To remove the fear of death is here given as one of the reasons why Christ descended from glory, to suffer and die in shame. He removes this fear simply by making application to the individual, through the Spirit's agency, of the truths about death which He came to reveal.

1. *Christ teaches that death is not the end of our being.*

Nature has hints that point to immortality, but they are only hints. The longings of man's nature afford a presumption that the soul shall live forever, but nothing more than presumption. Philosophy, learning, science, all the resources of the human mind before the coming of Christ, failed to establish anything like certainty concerning immortality. And yet this is a subject concerning which a single doubt is agony. The bare possibility that the grave ends existence forever is a source of horror, and only the most emphatic proof to the contrary will satisfy the heart. Such proof Christ furnishes in His life, His teachings, and His resurrection.

2. *Christ teaches that the soul does not wait in the grave for the resurrection of the body.*

We are so accustomed to the association of the spirit and the body that we think of the person as lying in the grave. But the Bible tells us, "Then shall the dust return to the earth as it was, and the spirit shall return unto God, who gave it." (Eccl. xii. 7.) See also Luke xxiii. 43. He teaches us to fasten the mind, not upon the coffin, but upon heaven and the joy of the departed. At the same time we are not taught to despise the lifeless body. It is to rise at the resurrection and be transformed. But lest our interest in it become too absorbing, he often places obstacles in the way of its exercise. The sepulchre of Moses was revealed to no man. And how many mourn for those in unknown and in watery graves?

3. *Christ teaches how we may meet our Maker without fear in the judgment day.*

This fear is really the main cause of the dread of death. No one needs to be told that he is sinful in the sight of God. Conscience condemns us in advance, as far as our own merits are concerned. But Christ has borne our sins, and if we accept Him for a Saviour all is well. To one who may doubt the efficacy of so simple an arrangement, let me say, would it not take away all your fear of death to know of a surety that God is your friend? Consciousness of this is just what Christ seeks to impart.

CHRIST'S RESURRECTION THE PROMISE AND PROPHECY OF OUR OWN.

BY T. DE WITT TALMAGE, D.D., BROOKLYN.

But now is Christ risen from the dead, and become the first-fruits of them that slept.—I CORINTHIANS XV. 20.

I FIND in the text a prophecy of our own resurrection. Before I finish I hope to pass through every cemetery and drop a flower of hope on the tombs of all who have died in Christ. Rejoicing in Christ's resurrection we rejoice in the resurrection of all the good.

The greatest of all conquerors is not Alexander, or Cæsar, or Napoleon, but death. His throne is in the sepulchre. But his sceptre shall be broken, for the dead in Christ shall arise.

There are mysteries around this resurrection of the body which I can't explain. Who can unravel the mysteries of nature? Who can explain how this vast variety of flowers has come from seeds which look so nearly alike? Tell me how God can turn the chariot of His omnipotence on a rose leaf? Mystery meets us at every turn.

One objects: The body may be scattered—an arm in Africa, a

leg in Europe, the rest of the body here. How will it be gathered on the resurrection morn?

Another objects: The body changes every seven years. It is perishing continually. The blood-vessels are canals along which the breadstuff is conveyed to the wasted and hungry parts of our bodies. Says another: A man dies; plants take up parts of the body; animals eat the plants, and other men eat the animals. Now, to which body will belong these particles of matter?

Are these all the questions you can ask? If not, ask on. I do not pretend to answer them. I fall back on these words, "All that are in their graves shall come forth."

There are some things, however, we do know about the resurrected body.

1. It will be a glorious body. The body, as we now see it, is but a skeleton to what it would have been were it not marred by sin.
2. It will be an immortal body.
3. A powerful body—unconquerable for evermore—never tired.

CHRIST AND THE IMMORTAL LIFE.

BY W. J. TUCKER, D.D., NEW YORK.

Whither the forerunner is for us entered, even Jesus, made an high priest forever after the order of Melchisedec.—HEBREWS vi. 20.

THE doctrine of immortality was taught before Christ appeared, but in Him there was an assurance given of it such as was never before given. In an eminent sense, life and immortality were brought to light in Him. Before Him men reasoned ably on the subject, but still they were not satisfied—they felt the need of some higher evidence. Their thoughts were in a chaotic state—more light was needed.

What is there peculiar in the Bible in relation to this subject?

1. *The future, as revealed by Christ, is the continuance of that which is present.* He came from the other world, and presented the most convincing credentials of His character and mission. The evidence He gave was of a personal nature, and was on this account of the greater force. The believer is united to Him by

faith, and partakes of His life as the branch partakes of the life of the vine. Christ passed into the heavens and remains the same, but more highly glorified. The believer is conscious of partaking of His life and is assured of the pledge that he will live as Christ, his forerunner, lives, but in a more glorious state and sphere.

2. *That other life cannot be any less than this.* We have the assurance in Christ that it will be much more.

3. *We have the assurance of a complete life in Christ.* We feel that our powers are not fully developed here, and the most mature Christian does not represent the finished work of Christ. He knows only in part—he is only a babe. He who is the Master and Source of life will carry it on in a state higher than this. That is complete which answers the end for which it was originally designed and adapted. Christ has led the way into the most sacred things, and He will bring the redeemed soul into the state in which alone there can be an opportunity for its complete development. Through Christ we have an assurance of an introduction into a life that is pure, with a corresponding character. When on earth we sit by the side of an aged and devout saint, we often feel out of place, and almost as if we had no right to be there. The contrast is so great, that we do not feel at home. But what shall it be to enter into the society of a multitude of purified souls in heaven? Through Christ the purified saints of earth will enter the society of heaven without fear, and with a disposition and character that can make them feel entirely at home. They will be rightly introduced. Their Forerunner has gone there and prepared a place for them, as well as them for the place. He made them heirs and joint-heirs with Himself to the glorious inheritance. It is a blessed and consoling thought that, in the midst of sorrow and death, we have a Friend that has gone before who will soon receive us to Himself, where we shall see as we are seen, and know as we are known.

THE DEATH OF LAZARUS.

BY REV. HENRY BLUNT, ENGLAND.

Jesus saith unto her, I am the resurrection and the life: he that believeth in Me, though he were dead, yet shall he live.—JOHN xi. 25.

1. *The waiting.* It was while at Bethany that the Lord received the brief but affecting message, "He whom thou lovest is sick." Brief as it was, the message conveyed all that was needed—the brother's sufferings, the sisters' anxiety. How did they watch the return of the messenger! With what fluctuations of hope must they have scanned the face of the sufferer! But the messenger returns, and alone. Lazarus grows daily worse, and he whom they had vainly thought the Saviour loved, passes through every hour of human suffering, even to the last and darkest.

Thus we learn that the depth or length of any affliction is no evidence that God hath forgotten to be gracious; that a prayer unanswered is by no means a prayer unheard.

2. *The mourning.* Four days of mourning pass—hopeless, full of doubt, perhaps, regarding Christ's love or power. At length, but alas! too late, they hear of the approach of Jesus and His disciples. Martha meets Him with words expressive of the thought that had been uppermost during the mourning—"Lord, if thou hadst been here my brother had not died," implying almost a reproach for the Lord's delay. Jesus, to prepare her for the coming miracle, says, "Thy brother shall rise again." Now mark Martha's strange faith: "I know that he shall rise again at the last day." She could believe that distant miracle, that all the myriads of earth should be raised; but she staggered at the promise of a present miracle. How difficult it is for us to receive and act on the promise for to-day!

Mary meets Jesus with the very words of Martha. Probably that sentiment had formed the burden of conversation between Mary and Martha ever since the death of their brother. And as Mary fell weeping at the feet of Jesus, perhaps, humanly speaking, Jesus almost regretted that He had set their faith so severe a lesson. "Jesus wept." How full of comfort to many sorrowing at the new-made grave, to remember that Jesus had once wept as they weep!

3. *The rising.* As they roll away the stone, Martha's faith falters. Jesus mildly rebukes her, and with a brief prayer He speaks the word of command, which awakes the sleeper. It was no more effort for Christ to awaken the dead Lazarus than to awake the sleeping Peter in Gethsemane. But can we not dwell too long upon this one miracle of Christ? The day is coming when a miracle infinitely greater is to be wrought, when, the narrow graves unable to hold us down, the chains of death unable to restrain us, we must all come forth at the bidding of the mighty Judge. It is well for us often to realize this scene, as far as we may. I charge the worldly to carry from here some lasting impression of the solemnity of that scene. I charge the thoughtless to meditate upon its meaning. I charge those " troubled about many things," to remember the one thing needful.

THE YEARS FLEETING AND HEAVEN NEARING.

BY C. L. GOODELL, D.D., ST. LOUIS, MO.

Now is our salvation nearer than when we believed.—ROMANS xiii. 11.

THE Christian is advancing toward heaven. Every day brings him nearer home. This is the thought of the apostle. It was, no doubt, a joyous thought to Paul. Is it to you?

If you are truly Christians—those who have believed in Christ and accepted Him and strive to follow Him as a Saviour—you are going home to heaven. Heaven is nearer now than it ever was before. Life is a journey; the end is nearing. It is a race; the goal will soon be reached. It is a voyage; the port will soon be in sight.

How many of our friends have reached there before us! We have seen their departure, and are assured of it. We are following fast. It is a startling thought, that our business will soon be left behind; that our work will be done, and that we shall leave this stage of being—leave it forever—our homes and cares, and all the interests that engage us here, and never more come back. It is an amazing thought that we, if we are Christians, shall soon be in heaven. Think of it! Time and all its opportunities passed forever! The suns and moons and stars all behind us; springs and summers and autumns all gone; the sights and sounds of earth passed away! Soon—very soon—shall we be in heaven. We shall see God, we shall behold Christ in His glory, we shall look upon the angels. Mothers will be searching for their children, and husbands and wives shall find each other; and all hands, parted in Christ, will be clasped again. It is like coming into port after an ocean voyage. The shining shore-line, how it grows on the waiting eye! The joy will be like that with which the Crusaders first saw Jerusalem.

But a little while and all these things will be real to us. Time will be ended. Then unbelievers will believe, and skeptics doubt no more. But it will be too late. Now is the accepted time. They will call for the rocks and mountains to fall upon them.

What a change this will be! What an unveiling of the heart! What a disclosure in ourselves and others! All that is hidden shall be brought to light. Are we in sympathy with these things? Do we love to look forward to them, and long for the joy set before us?

The apostle says, in view of this: "Knowing the time, that now it is high time to awake out of sleep. The night is far spent. The day is at hand. Let us, therefore, cast off the works of darkness and put on the armor of light."

"Wake out of sleep," says the apostle, as if we do not realize these things, and are as those on a train coming in. How this thought should stimulate exertion! We should no longer be dreaming, but doing. It should lead us to redeem the time, to make up for the misspent past; giving our best thoughts and care to things that are worthy, and not to trifles. What preparations should we make for the companionships and enjoyments of heaven! Put on the wedding garment of salvation. You are to see the King in it.

It should induce men to leave sin and worldliness, and live for the great life beyond. Those who have no hope, how the nearing eternity should lead them to accept salvation! This nearing salvation—what a comfort to those in sorrow and affliction! What a world beyond opened to Bunyan in prison, and to all the weary and heavy-laden! If we could be shut up to thoughts of this nearing salvation, how soon should we be weaned from earth!

The sun grows large as it goes down, so ought the Christian's character to round and brighten. How quietly it sets, elsewhere to rise and shine! So should the Christian's going be.

To reach heaven there is, for the believer, no gulf to cross. The path that leads out of life leads to the presence-chamber of our Lord. Since heaven is so near, death is not loss.

THE LIFE AND DEATH OF A CHILD.

BY REV. WILLIAM VEENSCHOTEN, MINTZESHILL, N. Y.

For what purpose has this babe lived?

1. For God's sake. The universe seems, to some extent, a failure to carry out God's purpose; but not so the children. One third of the human race die in infancy—a demonstration of God's life-giving and saving power.

2. This babe has lived for its own sake. This short life has already achieved success. 1. Consider Matt. xviii. 3; xix. 14; Mark x. 14; Luke xviii. 16. 2. A human being has begun to live. 3. Eternity, with all its glorious possibilities, has been entered.

3. This babe has lived for its parents' sake. 1. It has occasioned anxiety, care and pain: these they can easily forget. It has also exercised their graces: this will be a lasting benefit. 2. The parents had a little one to love; a gift, around which their affections clustered, and for which God was praised. 3. The parents have a little one to mourn—an earthly blessing removed, the transient nature of these blessings demonstrated.

4. The parents shed bitter tears, but their hearts are softened by affliction. 1. Reminded of their Covenant God, His providence displayed to them and their child. 2. Reminded of evil in the world; that evil the cause of these sorrows, separation and death. 3. Reminded of the uncertainty of life and all earthly possessions. 4. Warned not to make anything an idol, nor any created thing a portion.

5. The parents' attention is directed to the other world. 1. The soul. The body in the grave, but not the soul; it has gone to God, who gave it. 2. The habitation of Christ and the blessed, our Father's house; all His children are gathering there,

6. The parents are reminded that their salvation is not infant salvation. Repentance, faith, and a new life are necessary, if they would be saved and join their child again.

7. The babe in heaven speaks to the parents on earth—tells them to prepare. Sin alone can form an impassable gulf between the parents and the child. Become rid of sin.

PREPARATION FOR ETERNITY.

BY JUSTIN EDWARDS, D.D., BOSTON.

But the end of all things is at hand: be ye therefore sober and watch unto prayer.—1 PETER iv. 7.

This warning naturally leads our minds to the end of the world, which, compared with eternity, may be said to be even now "at hand." But to you and to me the end is much nearer than this. For what is your life? A vapor, which appears and vanishes away. I shall, therefore,

I. ILLUSTRATE THIS TRUTH.

A thing is said to be at hand when it is so near that we may come upon it at any time. In this sense the end of all things is at hand. There is not a moment in which we are not exposed, without warning, to death. The merchant's plans may reach into the distant future, his ships may be in many seas; but in a moment the end comes. The mother may indulge countless hopes for her child, but a fall, a fever, may in an instant shatter them. No age, no condition, can keep off death.

II. I SHALL POINT OUT THE DUTIES TO WHICH THE WARNING CALLS US. "Be ye sober, and watch unto prayer."

1. *Be ye sober.* This applies to the body and to the mind. Let your appetites, passions, affections, be governed by the Bible. Keep your eye on eternity and in its light measure the importance of the sorrows and joys of time. Even Christians are often cast down by frowns of the world or elated by its smiles. Let them remember for how short a time these endure. Be ye sober, and the joy unspeakable will be yours on earth, and eternal bliss in heaven.

Moreover your example will exert an influence for good which cannot be measured. The world is full of instances where the humblest life has been the means of the grandest accomplishments. Not the amount but the kind of influence you exert is what tells.

2. *Watch unto prayer.* Prayer is the lever that moves the world. By it a person's influence may reach around the world and into the everlasting future. The prayers of Paul, of David, of Abraham, may still be the agents of unseen good to the world. One blessing a believer's prayer may certainly secure—his own eternal life.

DEATH IN THE MIDST OF LIFE.

BY JABEZ BURNS, D.D.

Her sun is gone down while it was yet day.—JEREMIAH xv. 9

THE sun is well used to represent the life of a saint. Let us note a few points in the resemblance.

I. THE SUN IN ITS SPLENDOR.

1. *Its natural glory.* The most glorious of the heavenly bodies, it well typifies moral excellence and spiritual glory. (See 2 Cor. iii. 18.)

2. *Its constancy.* The centre of the solar system, a million times larger than the earth, it stands forth as the most sublime of God's material works. How constantly, without interruption or decrease, it is fulfilling the purpose of its Creator! What destruction would result from irregularity in the exertion of its power! So with the Christian. (See. 1 Cor. iv. 9.)

3. *Its influence.* Of how much beauty and comfort are its rays the source! Without them life were impossible, and the earth a sterile, uninhabitable mass. Such is every spot where the Christian life is unknown. All the blessings of civilization flow from the Sun of Righteousness. "Ye are the lights of the world," etc.

II. THE SETTING SUN.

1. *The certainty of its setting.* As certain is death.

2. *The diversity in the time of its setting.* We have the short day of winter, the long day of summer. But still more diverse is the period of life. How often does its sun go down while it is yet day!

3. *The frequent beauty of its setting.* "Let me die the death of the righteous, and let my last end be like his."

4. *The sun sets to shine upon another horizon.*

DEATH-BED REPENTANCE.

BY THE MOST REV. JOHN MACHALE, D.D., ARCHBISHOP OF TUAM, IRELAND.

Because you have despised all my counsel, and neglected my reprehensions, I also will laugh in your destruction, and shall mock you when that shall come to you which you feared.—PROVERBS i. 25, 26.

ST. AUGUSTINE remarks that of all the wiles of the adversary for vanquishing our innocence, there is none so frequent or so successful as that by which he persuades us to delay our conversion. The folly and presumption of one who puts off salvation in the hope of a death-bed conversion, are shown in the following considerations :

1. *He devotes his life to the service of sin.*
2. *He hopes to deceive the omniscient God.* The conversion he relies upon is a hollow, hypocritical one, since such must be any conversion which is the result, not of aversion for sin, but of the impossibility of enjoying it longer.
3. *His passions gather strength with each gratification.*
4. *He may have no knowledge of approaching death.* His death may be sudden. Or friends may deceive him to the very last with hopes of life.
5. *He may become the victim of despair.* This is the common fate of the wicked. As his mind is at last turned to his real condition, his sins rise like a mountain between him and God.

THE CHANGING AND THE CHANGELESS.

BY JABEZ BURNS, D.D.

The voice said, Cry, and he said, What shall I cry? All flesh is grass and all the goodliness thereof is as the flower of the field, etc.—ISAIAH xl. 6–8.

I. HUMAN FRAILTY.

What is more fragile than the grass or the flower of the field? Even if no blight from without destroy it, its existence is soon ended. And even this brief existence is often hastened by the withering wind and the scorching sun. Let us observe a few points of resemblance in the corruptible body to the fragile flower.

1. *Its source and sustenance.* The earth is the basis of the body's existence, from which its supplies are drawn, and to which it must at last return. "Dust thou art," etc.

2. *Its loveliness.*

a. The bud of infancy.

b. The opening flower of youth.

c. The blossom of purity and virtue.

3. *On what its existence depends.* Our lives are in God's hands. He gave the lily its beauty, and according to His will it perishes. He gives us strength, and it is His hand that deprives us of it. "The Lord hath given, and the Lord hath taken away."

4. *Living in remembrance of this frailty.*

II. THE UNCHANGING WORD OF GOD.

1. *The grand doctrines of God's word are immutable.* Man's perceptions may vary, but truth is unchangeable. It does not vary with different climes, or different ages, or different worlds.

2. *God's promises are immutable.*

3. *God's warnings are immutable.* They rest upon His justice and purity, and are as unchanging as these qualities. The warnings given to Lot's wife are adapted to every sinner fleeing from destruction.

NOT HERE, BUT RISEN.

BY REV. JOHN LOBB, LONDON.

Why seek ye the living among the dead? He is not here, but is risen.—
LUKE xxiv. 5, 6.

THERE is suggested here

1. *The power of the illusions of sense to cloud the mind and darken hope.* The disciples sought the living among the dead, because universal experience gave them no clew whatever to any other course of action. The past proclaimed that death was king. But here was a new fact which contradicted all experience. And in that fact we have the divine answer to the materialism of all ages.

2. *The marvellous change of which Christ had been the subject, and which His people share.* After long years even, we go to the grave

to weep there. We look downward rather than upward, seeking the living among the dead. But it is indeed the fact that it is death which is transitory, and life which is abiding. They are the living whom we have lost. The gain of dying is unspeakable; the blessedness is immediate.

3. *The redemption and reinstatement of the body.* There was an empty tomb. A dead body saw no corruption. It was reanimated. And the doctrine of Holy Scripture is, as we shall be planted in the likeness of Christ's death, so we shall start up in humanity's new springtime, in the likeness of His resurrection. "He shall change our humiliated bodies that they may be fashioned like unto His glorious body." Why then seek ye the living among the dead? Why go to the grave to weep there? We might weep if destruction were lord, and corruption the only end. But we know that death is but birth into a higher life.

SUDDEN DEATH: IS IT TO BE DEPRECATED?*

BY REV. EDWARD CAPEL CURE, LONDON.

So teach us to number our days, that we may apply our hearts unto wisdom.—PSALM xc. 12.

I. THE UNCERTAIN DURATION OF LIFE.

1. *The high pressure of modern life increases this uncertainty.* Overtaxed hearts and brains yield suddenly, and the frail thread of life snaps as tow when touched by the flame.

2. *The illustrations abound on all sides.* To no community are sudden deaths unknown. On all sides we see strong men suddenly stricken.

3. *It should alter our standard of value of men.* The uncertainty in the time of death involves the instability of the most brilliant talents and richest possessions. What a man has is too often the standard of worth, while a man is living; what he has done, is the ultimate standard of the world; what he has been, is God's standard.

II. WHY SUDDEN DEATH SHOULD BE DEPRECATED.

1. *It inflicts anguish upon the living.*

---

* On the occasion of the death of His Grace, the Duke of Marlborough, K.G.

2. *We need the lessons taught us from sick-beds.* The prayers, the counsel, the exhortations of the dying have brought many to the cross. Christ is brought nearer in suffering.

3. *It deprives those unprepared for death, of a last chance of repentance.*

THE WEB OF LIFE.

BY REV. EDWARD BLENCOWE, IRELAND.

My days are swifter than a weaver's shuttle.—JOB vii. 6.

1. *The swiftness of our days.* We are apt not to prize them till they are gone. Each was full of mercies; did we appreciate them? Each was full of opportunities; did we use or abuse them? "The wheel will never grind to the water that is past."

2. *Each day adds a thread to the web of life.* Each day has its influence for good or evil, for sin or holiness, for God or Satan. Of how great importance then to "number my days"!

3. *What we now weave we shall wear in eternity.* Our life shall be brought into evidence to show whether we have been believers or not. "Whatsoever a man soweth that shall he also reap." If we live after the flesh, death! If we live after the spirit, life eternal! What is the web your life is weaving?

a. On what are you resting your hope for salvation?

b. Is it your sincere desire to be conformed to the likeness of Jesus?

c. Do you live in the spirit of prayer?

d. Consider at the close of each day how it has been spent.

THE SECRET OF A SUCCESSFUL MINISTRY.[*]

BY THOMAS ARMITAGE, D.D., NEW YORK.

Before whose eyes Jesus Christ hath been evidently set forth.—GALATIANS iii. 1.

1. *He had seen the Lord Jesus crucified.*

No man can show the Lord unto others until he has seen Him for himself. Doubt will weaken any man, but it will paralyze the preacher's right arm.

[*] In memory of Rev. Bartholomew Trow Welch, D.D.

2. *He felt it the great end of his life to show Christ crucified to others.*

He looked upon the style, the pen, the type, in publishing the Gospel as subordinate to the voice of the living preacher. He felt he must speak, for the fire was shut up in his bones.

3. *He unsparingly devoted all the time his lofty theme demanded.*

If his study walls could cry out to its timbers, they would tell you that he could not in conscience attempt to preach the Gospel till he had thoroughly studied it.

4. *He consecrated all his ability to setting forth Christ crucified.*

He held up the cross,

   a. In his own originality.
   b. With boldness.
   c. With childlike simplicity.

THE DEATH OF THE RIGHTEOUS.

BY DR. DAVID THOMAS, LONDON.

Let me die the death of the righteous, and let my last end be like his.—
NUMBERS xxiii. 10.

1. *Righteous men die.* Death is no "respecter of persons." While it pays no regard to adventitious distinctions, it is equally regardless of moral ; it strikes down the good as well as the bad, and sometimes the blow is equally sudden and severe. "There is no discharge in that warfare." "Dust thou art, and unto dust thou shalt return." This is the law, rigorous and inexorable.

2. *Bad men would die like them.* "Let my last end be like his." These are the words of Balaam, a bad man. The death of the righteous is a *desirable* death. He dies with no moral remorse, no terrible forebodings, but with a peaceful conscience and a glorious hope. "O death, where is thy sting? O grave, where is thy victory?" While the wicked are driven away in their wickedness, the righteous have hope in their death. This desirable death is only gained by a righteous life. It is useless to say with Balaam, "Let me die the death of the righteous." You must live the life of the righteous, and then you will die the "death of the righteous." A noble life is the guarantee of a lovely death.

SERMONS IN OUTLINE.

The Life Eternal.—Job xxiv. 22 : "No man is sure of life." Then let every one make sure of life eternal.

The sure Support.—Jer. xlviii. 17 : "How is the strong staff broken, and the beautiful rod !" Human props removed to remind us of the only sure support we have in God.

Death in the Prime of Life.—Amos viii. 9 : "I will cause the sun to go down at noon, and I will darken the earth in the clear day." Sudden death, sudden glory to the believer. Taken away in one's prime, yet not "untimely." God's chronometer never mistakes.

A Christian's Contemplation of Death.—"The putting off of my tabernacle cometh swiftly," etc. (2 Pet. i. 14). 1. The body but a tabernacle. 2. The putting off this tabernacle. 3. When our death shall occur, "swiftly." 4. Whence our knowledge of this : "Our Lord hath showed me."

The Golden Bowl.—Eccl. xii. 6. The body of a consecrated disciple of Christ is emphatically a "golden" vessel, and worthy special honor even when emptied. The breaking of such a "bowl" is a special loss to the Church, though the change of habitation to the disciple himself is great gain.

The New Sepulchre.—John xix. 41. Life's pleasures and possessions shadowed by death—sometimes by dead friendships or gnawing grief and cankering care. All of these may be, like the tomb of Joseph, changed into a joy, a treasure, and uplifting inspiration.

Light in Darkness.—Job xxxvii. 21 : "Men see not the bright light which is in the clouds," because of human limitations, but mainly through lack of congenial, sympathetic union with God. "Unto the upright arises light in darkness." "The secret of the Lord," etc. Pillar and cloud led one people, and baffled and perplexed another.

Sorrow too great for Words.—Eccl. xii. 2 : "The clouds return after the rain." Coming home from the burial of his little Agnes, Dr. Nehemiah Adams drew out of his pocket the ribbon-tied key of her casket, "' then the clouds returned after the rain.' I thought for a few minutes that I should lose my reason." Speech then is powerless to comfort.

God in the Valley.—The Syrians (1 Kings xx. 28) thought that Israel gained their victories because their God was a God of the hills. God determined to prove to them that He was a God of the valleys as well, and could succor His people there also. What victories has He given His people in the valleys ! Job, Joseph, Daniel, Paul, saints in all ages can testify God is God of the valleys as well as of the hills, of adversity as well as of prosperity.

Certainty of the Resurrection.—"Thy brother shall rise again" (John xi. 23). Jesus said so, and it came to pass. He has power over the grave. The forces of death are obedient to Him. He surrendered Himself to death in its most terrible form, and freed Himself unharmed. Hence the resurrection is possible, for there is One who has power over death. It is certain ; for that One has promised it, and His word is truth.

Nearness of the Unseen World.—The eyes of the prophet's companion were opened, and he saw the hills covered with an army of angels (2 Kings vi. 17). We are surrounded by clouds of witnesses, are in the midst of the more real and stupendous of the two universes, and yet we see nothing, hear nothing, feel nothing of it. We look with an owl's eye into broad daylight, and declare that it is Egyptian darkness. Two things are essential to vision, an organ and light. A noonday of glory is around us and yet we ask, Where is heaven?

Death the Development of Life.—"To die is gain" (Phil. i. 21). 1. Death is the falling of the flower and the expanding of the fruit. At death we lay aside the body, with its fleshly lusts and appetites, its pains and passions. 2. It is the soul's deliverance from bondage, and its entrance upon the joyful freedom of heaven. 3. It introduces us to holy society, and into scenes of glory and everlasting rest. To a good man it is all gain.

The Glorified Dead.—"And I heard a voice from heaven saying, Write," etc. (Rev. xiv. 13). 1. The interest of heaven in the glorified dead. Proclaimed—"voice;" and is permanent in its continuance—"write." 2. The character of their death—"in the Lord." Complete union between the dead and Christ. 3. Their condition after death—"rest;" not inaction or indolence, but perfection in service and honor. 4. Their posthumous influence—"their works follow them"—going on, ever widening and deepening.

Grandeur of the Christian's Death.—"Death is swallowed up in victory" (1 Cor. xv. 54). 1. The only thing that gives death any power over us is *sin*. In the case of a Christian, sin is pardoned, and so the sting of death is withdrawn. 2. Death hath been abolished, and it is, to the good man, the gate that opens into a higher life and state of being. Through Christ he has wrested the dart from death's hands, and it has now no power over him. In his so-called death he is a conqueror. It is the time of greatest triumph, because the time of nearest home.

Waste of Life.—"To what purpose is this waste?" (Matt. xxvi. 8.) The most precious things seem ruthlessly destroyed, and life, culture, influence, wealth, commanding power for good, seem extinguished, while the worthless and positively bad are allowed to cumber the world. "Shall not the Judge of all the earth do right?" His thoughts and His ways are above ours and past finding out. Moreover, nothing is lost. Social affection cannot die; the fruits of culture are perpetuated in character forever. Memory lives. Nothing is wasted of the soul-treasures of the departed, and nothing of the good which has been done by them while in the flesh.

Christ Comforting Mourners.—"Let not your heart be troubled: ye believe in God," etc. (John xiv. 1, 2). The disciples, it is true, were not mourning over one who was already dead; their sorrow arose from being told by their Master that He was about to be separated from them. They could not bear the thought of parting from Him, although it was for their benefit that He was leaving them. He comforted them in this " trouble" by, 1. Exhorting them to believe in Him. 2. Assuring them that in His Father's house were many mansions, which He was going to prepare for them. 3. Telling them that He would come again and receive them to Himself in the mansions of eternal fellowship.

The Forgotten Dead.—" The righteous perisheth, and no man layeth it to heart," etc. (Isa. lvii. 1). 1. The body only of the righteous can perish. This returns to dust. Why, then, pamper the body, why give to its wants and enjoyments the chief care? 2. Their death is a deliverance from future evils. These are many and grievous. 3. Their death is a step into a better, nobler life. Their bodies sleep. Their souls live on, progressing upward eternally. 4. But how slightly is the death of even the righteous regarded! The thought of death is repugnant to many, and the cares of life are so pressing. We should lay to heart the death of the righteous, and our prayer should be that our latter end may be as his.

Death will not End Us.—" I am the resurrection and the life" (John xi. 25). Christ proved His power over death by going through the grave and back again. Death is the breaking of the shell that gives the bird a world instead of a narrow cell, powers of flight and vision of which no revelation could have given it an adequate conception. The grave, more than the cradle, will mark the commencement of true living. As we stand by the graves of dear ones, we have a right to say :

> " Believing, in the midst of our afflictions,
> That death is a beginning, not an end,
> We cry to them, and send
> Farewells, that better might be called predictions,
> Being foreshadowings of the future, thrown
> Into the vast Unknown."

Human Life.—" What is your life?" (Jas. iv. 14). 1. Life is the gift of God. We cannot breathe a breath apart from His permission. The babe sleeping in its cot breathes involuntarily, because its breath is in God's hands. 2. Being God's gift, it should be devoted to great purposes. The mere lapse of time is not life. Eating, drinking, sleeping, are not life. The end of life is to be like God. In this way do we glorify Him. 3. It is the period of our preparation for a higher and a better life. There is no perfection in this life. The oldest and wisest man is a mere child, and is full of imperfections. It is a probation. 4. Life is transitory and uncertain ; vapor ; voyage ; pilgrimage ; a drama ; a rainbow.

Death a Sleep.—" Asleep in Christ" (1 Cor. xv. 18). Nowhere in the New Testament is death represented by any figure of speech which implies ghastliness and dread. Frequently do the sacred writers compare it to *sleep*. The little child has played all day long, and is tired, and the shadows of evening send it in weariness to its little cot, where its mother lays it to sleep. The strong man has battled all day with the cares and duties of life, and longs to lay his head on the pillow and sleep. So we fall asleep in Jesus. The games of life are over ; the work of the day of life is finished. We are tired out, and we lay our heads on the bosom of Jesus and fall asleep in Him ! 1. Sleep implies rest from labor. 2. Renewed strength. 3. Awaking in the morning.

Death a New Birth.—" It is sown a natural body ; it is raised a spiritual body" (1 Cor. xv. 44). This life is but the womb of the life to come. Here we are perfected for the birth into a higher life. Through the grave we enter upon a new existence. 1. The gates of death, as of birth, are hinged to open only one way. Man can progress from one condition to another, but cannot return. 2. He who prepared for us the natural body, when we entered this sphere of existence, will prepare for us the spiritual body for the next. 3. Adaptation of both to our condition. As the caterpillar in due time throws off its repulsive body, and comes out in beauteous colors ; as from the uncomely egg is produced a bird of gayest plumage, so at our birth into a higher state of being God will give a body resplendent and glorious.

The Dead Child.—" All were weeping and bewailing her, but He said," etc. (Luke viii. 52). The history in which these words are found records one of the most distinguished miracles of Christ. 1. The sorrow at the death of the child. This grief is natural, not forbidden ; yet it often springs from small faith. The certainty of the resurrection, and of the presence of an infinitely powerful and kind God, wipes away tears. Christ did not rebuke the tears at the grave of Lazarus, but the lack of faith. 2. Christ's consoling view of death. "Not dead, but sleepeth." Sleep implies an awaking. Death, then, does not end us. 3. Christ the awakener. No one but Christ could have awakened that maid. Christ makes the grave but a door through which we pass. Henceforth the sting and victory of death and the grave have passed away.

Fellowship and Recognition in Heaven.—" To-day shalt thou be with Me in paradise" (Luke xxiii. 43). There is but a step between the cross and heaven. From the cross Jesus soars to paradise, taking with Him a ransomed soul. The reply of Jesus to the prayer of the penitent thief clearly teaches, among other important truths : 1. Heavenly recognition. We may not know each other here. We live in different countries, cities, homes, and so are strangers. Heaven is represented as the home of the good, and is called " our Father's house," and surely the *children* will all be acquainted. 2. Mutual fellowship. Members of the same family—subjects of the same government—children of the same Father—pursuits, thoughts, desires, one.

From Shadows into Daylight.—" Seek him . . . that turneth the shadow of death into the morning" (Amos v. 8). It is but natural to feel that death is an enemy. It is called by many figures which indicate horror and darkness. Yet in order to get to heaven one must die. Between us and Europe rolls the dreadful ocean. Some make little of crossing it, others cannot pluck up heart enough to encounter it. It is so with death. Even some Christians become timorous and fearful when they contemplate the "narrow sea that divides this heavenly land from ours." It is an ordinance of nature, and like every ordinance of nature it is directed to beneficent ends. Night precedes the morning. To die is to find the morning, beauty and perfect rest. 1. God turns death to *immortality*. 2. The act of dying He turneth into our entrance into heaven. 3. We come out of darkness and shadows, at death, into morning and light.

The Empty Seat.—" Thou shalt be missed, because thy seat will be empty" (1 Sam. xx. 18). 1. Death causes an absence more complete than that Jonathan feared. The silence is unbroken, profound. The separation wrought by death is absolute as far as eye or ear or any physical sense can measure. After death has passed, the seat of our friend is empty indeed. 2. This empty seat recalls and impresses the virtues of him that is gone. His kindly words, his noble resolutions and deeds, how they crowd into memory! 3. That empty seat, however, is proof of the absence only of the material portion of him whose death we lament. The seats of Moses and Elias were vacant on earth, yet they made it manifest on the Mount of Transfiguration that they had not departed wholly from the earth, nor lost interest in earthly affairs. Though his seat is vacant, our friend is still with us. 4. This empty seat reminds us that at death's bidding we must also, sooner or later, leave our places on earth.

Recognition beyond the Grave.—On the Mount of Transfiguration how instantly the disciples recognized Moses and Elias (Matt. xvii. 3, 4), whom they knew only through their minds and their hearts —whom they had never seen with the natural eye. Soul recognizing soul! There is a power of vision apart from the natural eye— immediate soul-sight. Dr. Beard, the late eminent physician in New York, declared that he had demonstrated by exhaustive experiments, that there are conditions of mind in which a man may see everything about him and yet be blindfolded. There are powers within us of which philosophers have scarcely, as yet, dreamed. It is nothing strange that we should know at a glance in the other world, the Wesleys, Calvin, Luther, Paul—the men whose hearts, whose souls, we have studied. We will need no pointing out, no introduction. How quickly the rich man, in torment, recognized Lazarus and Abraham! Distance did not dim his vision. Far easier the mother will recognize her child, the wife her husband. Sad thought were it otherwise.

> "It were a double grief if the true-hearted,
>   Who loved us here, should, on the other shore,
>   Remember us no more."

Acquiescence in Bereavement.—"Is it well with the child? And she answered, It is well" (2 Kings iv. 26). Life abounds with illustrations of the fact that the greater the blessings we enjoy the greater the agony felt at their loss. What greater blessing to a mother than her child? In the case before us a mother is bereaved of a child, and yet when asked, "Is it well with the child?" she answered, "It is well." 1. A great trial acquiescingly endured. What wonderful resignation! In reply to a difficulty suggested by her husband in setting out on her journey she replied: "It shall be well." When she answered the question as to her child, she said, "It is well." Though I left my dear boy a corpse at home, and my heart bleeds, I feel it is all well. 2. The grounds of her resignation. *a.* She knew it was the dispensation of a Father all-wise and all-loving, and she bowed to His will. *b.* She believed that her child was better off and that God would overrule the trial for her own good. A state of mind so magnanimous as this, under great sorrow, is the duty and privilege of all the holy and good.

Crossing the River.—" Prepare you victuals; for within three days ye shall pass over this Jordan" (Josh. i. 11). 1. There is a determinate boundary to every life. This is illustrated by the relation of the Jordan to the pilgrimage of the Israelites. That was a visible limit; the limit of life is invisible. The precise time was known when the Jordan was to be passed—" three days;" of the day and hour when death's border is to be crossed knoweth no man. 2. There is a necessity for crossing the boundary. Palestine could not be entered save through Jordan; the spirit world cannot be entered save through death. Sin has made death a necessity, giving existence to its "cold flood." Yet under God's guidance death may be made a gateway for the soul to a Canaan that will yield a far richer result than " milk and honey." 3. Preparation for crossing required. " Prepare you victuals." Humble confession of sin; a hearty repentance; a turning away from evil; thankful acknowledgment of mercies received; a quickening faith in the Great High Priest who crosses with the pilgrim; a hope of an inheritance on the other side—these constitute the "victuals" which are to stay the Christian as he passes over the Jordan that separates this wilderness of life from the Canaan beyond.

The Withered Gourd.—" God prepared a worm when the morning rose the next day, and it smote the gourd that it withered" (Jonah iv. 7). A child is like Jonah's gourd—God's gift and man's comfort. 1. God has a right to recall His gifts. They are still His property. They are only loaned. 2. God may recall at any time. He has given no lease and specified no length of time that the gift shall be left with us. He has placed Himself under no obligation. 3. God may recall the gift when it is apparently most needed. "When the morning rose" the gourd was smitten. Jonah needed the gourd most then as a shelter from the sun's heat. 4. God may recall the gift when we are beginning to appreciate it most. When "Jonah was exceeding glad because of the gourd" it withered. When parents are saying of their child, "This same shall comfort us," it is smitten. 5. God may recall the gift by any instrumentality He may choose. "A worm" smote the gourd. Some apparently insignificant thing may be God's agent for our deprivation. 6. God, after recalling the gift, can comfort the sorrowing, and can compensate for the loss. Jonah had this experience, and so will all who look to God through Christ.

The Christian's Mastership over Death.—"For all things are yours: whether . . . life or death" (1 Cor. iii. 22). Development in our life on earth is limited, as is the development of the bird in the egg. The bursting of the egg-shell is no disaster, but a relief and a profit. That breaking of the shell brings the bird into a world that is unspeakably more glorious. Death is our servant, not our master—through Christ an immeasurable blessing. Because—

1. It restores us more nearly to our friends who have gone beyond. Yet it does not, if we interpret death rightly, remove us from our friends on earth; for the dead are ministering spirits permitted by God to help more potently the world than when in the flesh. The spirits of Moses and Elias communed with Christ on the mount, doubtless concerning His mission to men. Whose heart does not yearn to meet the dear ones gone?

2. It brings us nearer to Christ. Paul was eager to be absent from the body that he might be present with the Lord. Beyond the grave, in a special sense, is the Christian present with Christ. 3. It places us in a position more favorable for soul-growth. 4. It increases our capacity for usefulness. Those who are faithful in this life in a few things, will be made in the life to come rulers over many things. 5. As a consequence our happiness will be greatly augmented.

Resurrection of the Dead.—" Why is it judged incredible with you, if God doth raise the dead?" (Acts xxvi. 8). It would be difficult to explain how the identity of the body can be preserved while the matter composing it is changed; but our difficulty in explaining can present no reason for denying the fact. 1. It is neither against the Power, the Wisdom, nor the Will of God. God wills nothing that is not wise and good, and whatever He wills He has the power to accomplish. He has performed greater things than raising the dead. 2. We see vital exemplifications of it daily. The matter of our bodies undergoes a change every seven years, yet our body's identity is preserved. Look at trees and plants in winter time, and see them when the breath of spring has touched them into life. Study the insect, at first a crawling worm. The hour arrives when it bursts its cerements and becomes a pure-winged, beautiful creature, sailing in sunny skies. Paul saw our grave in the furrow of the plough; our burial in the corn dropped in the soil; and our resurrection in the grain bursting its sheath to wave its head in summer sunshine. 3. The resurrection of the body is less inexplicable than its creation. It is not the same thing to rekindle an extinguished lamp and to show fire that has never yet appeared. 4. The Lord Jesus Christ purposely rose again in His human body, as a pattern and firstfruit of our resurrection.

Alone in Death.—Moses was alone with God on Nebo in his dying hour (Deut. xxxii. 49, 50; Deut. xxxiv. 5, 6). No relative, no earthly friend, was allowed to witness that strange death scene. Our friends and relatives may approach us more nearly in the last hour; yet, in a sense, we shall be alone in the death struggle, as was Moses. Death is an individual matter. There is a point beyond which the parent cannot accompany the child, nor the husband the wife. In this seemingly the most momentous of all conflicts—the battle of the death-bed—no earthly friend can give us aid. It is only seemingly the most momentous—the vital conflict is fought before that hour—that conflict in choice which determines whether God and good angels will also be absent from our dying bed, or present, as they were with Moses. What is it that can give comfort in that hour of loneliness? 1. The memories of a life spent in striving to obey God. Said the veteran apostle, as he looked grim death full in the face: "I have fought the good fight; I have kept the faith." What illuminating and cheering memories had Moses! 2. A developed Christian character. The consciousness of having been builded in Christ, of having grown to the full stature of Christian manhood—this will cheer the Christian. He knows he enters the other world not a babe, but a man in spirit. 3. The sure hope of a glorious life beyond. It cheered Paul—the hope of the crown that was laid up for him. 4. Above all, the conscious presence of Christ, the beloved, and the assurances of His continued presence forever. The thief on the cross was made glad at the thought that Christ was by his side, and doubly glad at the words: "This day thou shalt be with me in Paradise." How easy to imagine that to the Christian the hour of death is the happiest of all his existence on earth!

EXTRACTS AND ILLUSTRATIONS.

THOUGHTS ON LIFE.

Life is a noise between two silences.

Short is the little that remains to thee of life. Live as on a mountain!—*Marcus Aurelius.*

Pass through life comfortably to nature and end the journey in content, just as an olive falls off when it is ripe; blessing nature who produced it, and thanking the tree on which it grew.—*Marcus Aurelius.*

Life is a turbulent sea. Changing circumstances come rolling after each other like the billows, ever climbing up the climbing wave. In heaven there is no more sea, but perpetual stability of joy—unbroken rest.—*Alexander Maclaren.*

A railroad car once carried a man whose mind had faded into a blank and whose end was to be an asylum; a criminal whose destiny was a dungeon; and a bride on her way to her new home and the welcome of new friends. Time will soon bring all, the good, the bad and the irresponsible to the last stopping place.

I have been always regarded as exceptionally favored by fortune, and I do not wish to complain or find fault with the course of my life. But, after all, it is nothing but labor and toil; and I may truly say that during my seventy-five years I have not had four weeks of real comfort. It is the never-ceasing rolling of a stone which must always be lifted anew.—*Goethe.*

Life a cathedral.—When in its prime, its strength and beauty evoke admiration, and its walls echo to sweetly-solemn strains; but in age, the "well-turned cornices crumble into dust, its arches fall one by one, and its pillars fail to give the needed support. Such a mind seems to be attending the funeral of its own faculties, and mourning their untimely decay."--*Prof. Park.*

Bossuet says that life is like a road that ends in an awful precipice. We know that at the beginning. We would gladly stop, but there is an irresistible force which impels us to walk, and finally to run. The speed increases as the end draws near. Objects that attracted at first, lose their distinctness and beauty. The flowers are less bright, the meadows less blooming, and everything fades. We begin to feel the fatal gulf, but we cannot return, and the shadow of death finally falls. Chrysostom says that life is but a scene in a theatre. We are actors. We play our part for a moment and disappear. The curtain falls, and all is over. The only thing valuable about us is the soul, and that is the very thing about which we occupy ourselves the least.

We are accustomed to think that an eminent and complete character, a character sweet and of majestic purity, insures length of days; that great usefulness makes length of days more probable in the wise administration of God's providence; and yet how striking it is that our divine Master died at the age of thirty-three! I have often thought that if one knowing nothing of the New Testament beforehand, had prepared himself to believe what he learned in the Scriptures of Christ in the earlier chapters of the evangelists, what would be his impression concerning the continued life on earth of our God, Jesus Christ? Would he not say to himself: Here is one coming to the world who has been predicted for centuries, in the splendor of whose foreseen presence every part of the ritual has glowed with a new beauty and glory, whom the prophet and king have alike been predicting in their office as well as in their words, who is coming into the world by the miracle of incarnation, and the world is to be hushed into peace, in order that His coming may be in the fitness and fulness of time? He is coming to regenerate life and bring in at last the fulness of the Gentiles, to bring the glory of the millennial peace and millennial holiness everywhere over the earth. His life then will be protracted for centuries till at last the most eminent, most holy, the most powerful, may have preceded Him, and it will only be after centuries of divine instruction and divine work that He—

this transcendent person, so long prophesied—shall ascend in triumph through the skies which were brightened at His coming—into the heavens which He left to save the world. What significance there was in those words of his: "I have finished the work that Thou gavest me to do." The whole plan of God had been completed concerning the life of Christ in these three years of ministry.—*R. S. Storrs, D.D.*

THOUGHTS ON DEATH.

GIVE me no guess for a dying pillow.—*Joseph Cook on a Second Probation.*

WHAT Belfrage says of John is true of the departure of every believer. It is not like the evening star sinking into the darkness of the night, but like the morning star, lost to our view in the brightness of day.

DEATH a release.—It will be like the breaking of a chain, the close of long confinement, and the opening of a prison door. "Let me pass out!" was the striking utterance of a dying saint as his soul fled, like an imprisoned bird, away from an opened cage.

THE Thracians wept whenever a child was born, and feasted whenever a man went out of the world; and with reason. Death opens the gate of fame and shuts the gate of envy after it; it unlooses the chain of the captive and puts the bondsman's task into another man's hand.—*Sterne.*

GORDON, once a celebrated driver on the Pacific coast, was not less known for his profaneness than for his skill in driving. His end was dreadful. In the delirium of death he thrust out his feet and clutched at the bedclothes. When asked the cause of his trouble, he replied, "Oh, I'm going down a terrible grade and can't find the brake!"

DEATH touches only the body.—In proportion as the body falls into ruin, the spirit becomes disengaged; like a pure and brilliant flame, which ascends and shines forth with additional splendor in proportion as it disengages itself from the remains of matter which held it down, and as the substance to which it was attached is consumed and dissipated.—*Massillon.*

SPIRITUALLY dead.—We see the crape fluttering at the door, here and there, as we walk the streets. Somebody is dead! Had we eyes like God, we should see other dead amid the living—beneath the guise of dress, of rosy health, of ample wealth, of high position, as well as under humbler forms of concealment. Dead in trespasses and sins, as really insensible to the higher verities of life as is the sheeted corpse to its daily actualities.

DEATH seizeth upon an old man, and lies in wait for the youngest. Death is oftentimes as near to the young man's back as it is to the old man's face. It is told of Charles the Fourth, King of France, that, being one time affected with the sense of his many and great sins, he fetched a deep sigh, and said to his wife, "By the help of God, I will now so carry myself all my life long that I will never offend Him more," which word he had no sooner uttered, but he fell down and died.—*Thomas Brooks.*

DOCTOR Gordon, a gentleman of culture, when dying in the prime of life and surrounded with comforts and joys, said, "Death! I see no death at my bedside. I would not have a fear. Christ, not death, is about to take me from earth! There is no death to the Christian. The glorious Gospel takes away death." That which separates the Christian from Christ is not distance, but the veil of the flesh, and therefore the moment that is laid aside the Christian is with his Lord. There is no middle passage of horrors between the two.—*W. M. Taylor.*

EVERY day travels toward death, but only the last one arrives at it. To him that told Socrates, "The thirty tyrants have sentenced thee to death," he said: "And nature has sentenced them." Your death is a part of the order of the universe, a part of the life of the world. Lucretius says:

> "Mortals among themselves by turns do live,
> And life's bright torch to the next runner give,"

alluding to the Athenian games, wherein those that ran a race carried torches in their hands, and, the race being done, delivered them into the hands of those who were to run next.—*Montaigne.*

"'AND He took clay and anointed his eyes.' That is just what Death does with us. Many people are afraid of the doctor, and the more clever the doctor, the more apt to be rough and quick. Old Doctor Death is a wonderful doctor. He wraps us up in clay and heals us. We go in at the back door of the doctor's house, and come out at the front. We go in blind, and come out gazing on golden streets and heavenly mansions; we go in deaf, and we come out with ears unstopped and hearing softest celestial sounds; we go in mute, and we come out with tongues unloosed to join in angelic songs; we go in halt, out of breath, decrepit, and we come out strong, to 'run up with joy the shining way.'"

AN Alpine traveller and his guide, while crossing a glacier, were precipitated into a crevasse, whence no human power could rescue them. At last a rivulet was found that pierced the mountain of ice, which they followed into a dark, cold and ever-narrowing passage, that finally ended in the roaring gulf of a sub-glacial river. To plunge into its gloom and whirl seemed to be a leap into the jaws of death, but there was no other alternative. The guide made the plunge, crying, "Follow me." They were tossed about in the icy waters, and deafened by its roar, but in a few moments were swept out into the summer air and green vale of Chamouni. So Jesus has passed through the sullen stream of death; and with Him we need fear no evil, but shall find ourselves safely conducted to the summer land beyond.

DEATH cannot separate from the love of God. Death does not change the spirit, it only liberates it. We go with a friend up to the last moment on earth. We see the mind still active, the memory clear, the noble impulses of the soul still predominant. Do you suppose that he who wrought the gem into forms of beauty has ceased while the gem still delights the eye? That he who built the cathedral is ended while the work of his hand calls forth the admiration of mankind? We have the assurance in the words of Christ, in the resurrection of Christ, that death does not destroy the soul. Rather it sets the soul free from the lassitude and inactiveness of the body. The body hampers and manacles the soul. Now, can you conceive that death, which so adds to the spirit, can separate from the love of God? Death does not affect our love for our departed friends, save to augment it. How much more will it but augment the love of God! No, says the apostle, and our conscious and sentient being responds, Death cannot separate from the love of God.—*R. S. Storrs.*

OH! what an ado about dying! We become so attached to the malarial marsh in which we live that we are afraid to go up and live on the hill-top. We are alarmed because vacation is coming. Eternal sunlight, and best programme of celestial minstrels, and hallelujah, no inducement! Let us stay here and keep cold and ignorant and weak. Keep our feet on the sharp cobblestones of earth instead of planting them on the bank of the amaranth in heaven. Give us this small island of a leprous world instead of the immensities of splendor and delight. Keep our hands full of nettles, and our shoulder under the burden, and our neck in the yoke, and hopples on our ankles, and handcuffs on our wrists. "Dear Lord," we seem to say, "keep us down here where we have to suffer, instead of letting us up where we might live and reign and rejoice." I am amazed at myself and at yourself for this infatuation under which we all rest. Men, you would suppose, would get frightened at having to stay in this world instead of getting frightened at having to go toward heaven.—*Talmage.*

WHAT have you proved about death?—What then is the case you have made out? You have made out just this: that death allows us to have a perfect body, free of all aches, united forever with a perfect soul free from all sin. Correct your theology. I demand that you correct your theology; and when you see a new gray hair in your head thank God, and when you see another wrinkle on your cheek thank God, and when you feel another physical infirmity thank God, and when another year has passed thank God. What does it all mean? Why, it means that moving-day is coming, and that you are going to quit cramped apartments and be mansioned forever. The horse that stands at the gate will not be the one lathered and bespattered, carrying bad news; but it will be the horse that St. John saw in Apocalyptic vision—the white horse on which the King comes to the banquet. The ground around the palace will quake with the tires and hoofs of celestial equipage, and those Christians who in this world lost their friends, and lost their property, and lost their health, and lost their life, will find out that God was always kind. —*Talmage.*

A DELICATE child, pale and prematurely wise, was complaining on a hot morning that the poor dewdrop had been too hastily snatched away and not allowed to glitter on the flowers like other happier dewdrops, that live the whole night through and sparkle in the moonlight and through the morning onward to noonday. "The sun," said the child, "has chased them away with his heat, or swallowed them in his wrath." Soon after came rain and a rainbow, whereupon his father pointed upward. "See," said he, "there stand thy dewdrops gloriously reset—a glittering jewelry —in the heavens; and the clownish foot tramples on them no more. By this, my child, thou art taught that what withers upon earth blooms again in heaven." Thus the father spoke, and knew not that he spoke prefiguring words; for soon after the delicate child, with the morning brightness of his early wisdom, was exhaled like a dewdrop into heaven. —*Richter.*

MAKE the best of life's finality. Now, you think, I have a very tough subject. You do not see how I am to strike a spark of light out of the flint of the tombstone. There are many people who have an idea that death is the submergence of everything pleasant by everything doleful. If my subject could close in the upsetting of all such preconceived notions, it would close well. Who can judge best of the features of a man—those who are close by him, or those who are far off? "Oh!" you say, "those can judge best of the features of a man who are close by him." Now, my friends, who shall judge of the features of death—whether they are lovely or whether they are repulsive? You? You are too far off. If I want to get a judgment as to what really the features of death are, I will not ask you; I will ask those who have been within a month of death, or a week of death, or an hour of death, or a minute of death. They stand so near the features they can tell. They give unanimous testimony, if they are Christian people, that death, instead of being demoniac, is cherubic. Of all the thousands of Christians who have been carried through the gates of Greenwood, gather up their dying experiences and you will find they nearly all bordered on a jubilate. How often you have seen a dying man join in the psalm being sung around his bedside, the middle of the verse opening to let his ransomed spirit free! Long after the lips could not speak, looking and pointing upward! Some of you talk as though God has exhausted Himself in building this world, and that all the rich curtains He ever made He hung around this planet, and all the flowers He ever grew He has woven into the carpet of our daisied meadows. No. This world is not the best thing God can do. This world is not the best thing that God has done.—*Talmage.*

AT the very instant of our soul's separation from the body, death seems to have a great advantage upon us; but when I consider all, I find it has no cause to boast of the victory. When a valiant captain marches out of a town almost destroyed, to another more secure and better fortified, with his weapons in his hand, we say that he has quitted his station, not that he is overcome. Thus, when the wretched body decays, and our souls depart, well armed with faith and hope, to lodge in a more secure place in the highest heavens, nobody can say, to speak properly, that we have been overcome. As it happens to such as sail on the ocean, when a violent storm threatens them with shipwreck, they think themselves very happy if they can quit the vessel, leave it to the mercy of the winds and waves, and escape to land with their riches and lives safe : thus it is with us who sail upon the tempestuous sea of this world ; when death raises its most cruel storms, we think ourselves happy if we can leave this miserable body, which seems as a ship to our souls, and if we can secure our spiritual life and our heavenly riches. Therefore we may justly say to the faithful, that are frightened when they see death threatening to drown them in its depths, as St. Paul to the ship's company, who trembled for fear at the sight of roaring and swelling waves, "Take good courage, my brethren, for I assure you, in the name of the living God, that your lives are secure, and that you shall lose nothing but this ship." We may furnish them with stronger comforts ; for these good mariners lost their ship without hopes of recovering it again, but we are assured that God will one day gather up every piece of the broken vessels of our bodies, and will join them together in a more perfect estate.—*Drelincourt.*

THOUGHTS ON HEAVEN.

The melody of evening bells has been heard under rare circumstances, it is said, a hundred miles at sea by those who put their ears in the focus of the mainsail, which gathered and condensed the sound. So, in some supreme moment, under specially favorable circumstances, the Christian voyager toward heaven seems to hear the ringing of heavenly bells wafted from his home within the vale.

"I am going to see Jesus," said a dying negro boy; "I am going to see Jesus." And the missionary said, "You are sure you will see Him?" "Oh, yes, that's what I want to go to heaven for." "But," said the missionary, "suppose Jesus should go away from heaven; what then?" "I should follow Him," said the boy. "But if Jesus went down to hell; what then?" He thought for a moment, and then he said: "Massa, where Jesus is there can be no hell!" Oh, to stand in His presence! That will be heaven!—*Talmage.*

In this world, we only meet to part. It is good-by, good-by; farewells floating in the air. We hear it at the rail-car window and at the steamboat wharf—good-by. Children lisp it and old age answers it. Sometimes we say it in a light way—good-by; and sometimes with anguish in which the soul breaks down—*good-by!* Ah, that is the word that ends the thanksgiving banquet; that is the word that comes in to close the Christmas chant—good-by, good-by. But not so in heaven. Welcomes in the air; welcomes at the gates; welcomes at the house of many mansions, but no good-by.—*Talmage.*

What a place that must be which Christ prepares! It must be a place where every purified desire of the heart shall have perpetual satisfaction. The inner soul longs for happiness; it is only the outward and changeable sense that would dictate its form. That it is a pure and holy place and that it has Christ in it, is enough. We know the delicious contents of the vessel, if we do not know the shape and color of the vessel. What a comfort and joy the thought, that Christ is preparing our place! God's consolations are not like men's, mere soothers of a troubled mind; but seeds of positive and independent joy. God's grace comes with a set-off that belittles the earthly care and sorrow. If a soldier in the ranks is wounded, it is one thing to apply soothing cataplasms to stay the pain ; but it is a grander thing and a better thing for his general to come to him and bestow upon him the title, rank, and insignia of a high officer. "To depart" is "to be with Christ ;" this is the "far better" of the Apostle. Again, some may say, Do the departed ones know of and take an interest in what takes place in this world? Angels know of and take an interest in the affairs of men, being ministering spirits, why not then the saints? Agassiz, when alive, could have told you all about fishes, birds, or animals, as to what species they belonged. By seeing the fin of one fish he could declare its tribe. Types determine whole structures in the physical world. Taking this reasoning along with us, in Christ's risen body we find that we know all that we need know of the material, spiritual body, and of heaven, which is a place and no myth. We arrive first at the state, and then the place. I do not, cannot, believe those mythical theories which assert that the saints are to inhabit the space between the stars. No, I believe that heaven is a place, and that we are to have a real, material, spiritual body, like to the risen body of Jesus. No other suggestion, however cleverly framed, meets the wants of the soul. Our Lord is not to-day in the tombs of the prophets.—*J. A. M. Chapman.*

THOUGHTS ON AFFLICTION.

THINK not because you suffer that you are not chosen. As Christ was made perfect in His work, through His suffering, so are we thus to be led. Jesus takes those whom He loves into Gethsemane, and further.—*W. M. Taylor.*

THE mourner may always count on the sympathy of Jesus. Jesus thought not of Mary and Martha alone. There sounded in His ears the dirge of the ocean of human misery. The weeping of Mary and Martha was but the holding of the shell to His ears. That tear of love is a legacy to every Christian.—*W. M. Taylor.*

A SUFFERING believer once remarked to a friend : "When I am very low and dark I go to the window, and if I see a heavy cloud

I think of those precious words, 'A cloud received Him out of their sight,' and I look up and see the cloud sure enough, and then I think—well, that may be the cloud that hides Him. And so you see there is comfort in a cloud."

It is said that gardeners sometimes, when they would bring a rose to richer flowering, deprive it for a season of light and moisture. Silent and dark it stands, dropping one faded leaf after another, and seeming to go down patiently to death. But when every leaf is dropped, and the plant stands stripped to the uttermost, a new life is even then working in the buds, from which shall spring a tender foliage and a brighter wealth of flowers. So, often, in celestial gardening every leaf of earthly joy must drop before a new and divine bloom visits the soul.—*Mrs. H. B. Stowe.*

PRAYERS.

AT THE FUNERAL OF CORNELIUS VANDERBILT.

BY C. F. DEEMS, D.D., NEW YORK.

ALMIGHTY and Most Merciful God, our Heavenly Father, to whom all hearts are open and all thoughts are known, and from whom no secrets are hid, cleanse Thou the thoughts of our hearts with the inspiration of Thy Holy Spirit, that we may perfectly love Thee, and worthily magnify Thy excellent name. We worship and adore Thee, Maker of Heaven and Earth, for all the things Thou hast made in the heavens above and in the earth beneath, and in the waters that are under the earth. And we thank Thee for this human race, of which we are parts, that Thou hast called into existence man, and hast given him reason and remembrance and imagination, and fear and love and hate. We thank Thee that Thou hast given us this earth, that we may till it and improve it, and make it to be the garden of the Lord. And we thank Thee, O Father, for all the generations of men that have come and gone, that have sown and planted, and reaped and replanted, and made for us such harvests of civilization, and garnered for us such results of culture. We thank Thee that we are living men, born into the world, with capacities for indefinite development in this world and in the world to come. We thank Thee that we are not shut up here forever, but having been trained and disciplined on earth, Thou openest unto us the gates of the second birth and the second life—the life that is everlasting.

Above all, we thank Thee for Thine inestimable love in the gift of Thy Son, Jesus Christ, to be the propitiation for our sins and for the sins of the whole world. We thank Thee that He has brought life and immortality to light, and that the blood of Jesus Christ, Thy Son, cleanseth us from all sin.

And now we thank Thee, Holy Father, for those who have assisted us in moral and intellectual development, and this day especially for him, Thy servant, whose remains we are about to bury forever out of our sight. For all his bodily and intellectual and spiritual endowments; for his long continuance among men; for his successful efforts to raise the lowly, to strengthen the weak, to enlarge men's ideas of their own capacities, and to increase the comforts of this present world, we thank Thee, good Lord. We thank Thee, too, that he had such a mother, and that he had such influences about him in the beginning of his life; that during all his career he had perfect trust in Thy Word, as coming from the King Eternal, Immortal, Invisible, the only wise God—and honoring his father and his mother, so that his days were long in the land; and that, at the last, after his weary and troubled life, like a little child, according to the word of his Saviour, he laid his head at the feet of Christ, and being so humbled by himself, was by his Lord lifted up into the embrace of love so that he should die on the bosom of Jesus. And now, Father, that he has been taken from our midst—he who has been the guide and leader of this generation—he who has been so strong to stand and so bold to go forward—he who has been such a fortress and strong tower to so many—now that Thou hast been pleased in Thy providence to take him away, grant us grace to lead such godly and righteous lives that we may be able to carry forward such plans as seemed his purpose. We beseech Thee to send grace and divine consolation to these bereaved ones. Bless his wife. Thou that hast put in the Holy Scriptures so many words for the widow, bless her; and now that the strong staff has been stripped out of her hand, may she rest upon Him who has been her guide from her youth— her divine Saviour. Bless these, his children. Grant unto them grace to feel the immense responsibility of inheriting the fame of their father, and grant unto them grace so to love one another, so to cleave together, so to co-operate, that the blessing of God may be invoked day by day upon their family relations and all the public interests in which they are involved. We pray for them who for years have shared his bounty, and now shall see his face no more, for the lowly, for the broken, for the weak to whom he showed such kindness in secret. God bless them and comfort them, and make them feel that there is a stronger arm than is in man. Bless those who soothed him in his last hours—these faithful nurses, these devoted friends, these skilful physicians, and grant that at the judgment of the last day the divinest lips may say to them, as touching him that hath gone, "Even as ye did it unto the least of these, ye did it unto me."

And while we pray for ourselves, we pray also for those who in distant places are lifting unto God their hearts to-day in solemn worship in memory of this great life and this great death; and especially we pray Thee to bless the solemn services conducted in the university that bears his name, that the Spirit of grace may come and rest upon them, and that the young men who shall bow this day before Thy throne in the church there, may worship God, and may go forth in strength to carry the benefaction of Thy deceased servant, even unto the ends of the earth. And now, God, be merciful to us and bless us, and cause the light of Thy countenance to shine unto us, that Thy name may be known upon earth, Thy saving health among all nations.

BEFORE A SERMON ON "THE REST OF GOD."

BY REV. HENRY WARD BEECHER, BROOKLYN.

WE are in the midst of mortal toils, in uncertainties, in strifes that have no fruit but sorrow; and we are glad to believe that there is a world where all things do move in harmony, where wisdom is perfect, where guidance is without erring, where all do help all, and all love all; where the lowest and the least are great, and the greatest bow down themselves unto the least; where Thou art, O Thou eternal and helpful God; where, without warrings, without shadow of turning, without slumber, or sleep, or weariness, Thou dost bear up the mightiness of creation, and yet hast time, and thought, and desire for love toward every living thing. The circuit of Thy being is further than our thoughts can fly. We wonder at Thy justice, at Thy love, and Thy compassion, which are interpreted to us by no experience in human life. Thy love is deeper than any love we have ever known. Thy sense of kindness, wider than the earth, is more than all its life. Thou art filled with sweetness and gentleness. Thou art the thunderer;

and yet, all Thy creatures do rejoice in the goodness of the unstorming God, unto whose land of rest we are sending pilgrims. They who brought us up, they who taught us to love Thee, they who taught our knees to bow in prayer and our lips to syllable the words—they are chanting before the throne evermore ; not according to the picture that our mind forms, though we struggle as best we may on an undeveloped sketch ; but in a glory without name, and with a power transcending human thought or experience. They rest from earthly care, and from all sin and imperfection, and rejoice with a glory that it hath not entered into the heart of man to conceive. We thank Thee for their rest. We thank Thee for the service that they rendered us. We thank Thee that they have entered into the nobler service of the sanctuary above. There are many of our companions with whom we have taken sweet counsel upon earth. We walked hand in hand, and labored together. They have gone up, while we yet struggle on, doing imperfectly the few things that we are minded to do that are noble and disinterested. Enthralled with care, we drudge on in this material life ; but they have heard the call, and gone before. We do not envy them ; but Lord, grant that we may be ready to follow whenever Thou comest for us.

We rejoice that the little pilgrims are safe. No storm hath pursued their ship, or can, in the land on whose shore breaks no wave, and whose air is distempered by no winds or storms. They rest sweetly. They are in angel charge, nearest to God. Thine own elect angels are their guardians ; and in their bosoms, or led by their hands, they do rejoice, not forgetting their earthly home, yet wandering in the beauty and joy of their heavenly home. . .

We pray that Thou wouldst grant that Thy life may be more and more perfectly shown in our lives. May we walk together in the hope of glory. May we feel that we are not of this world ; that while our feet do press the soil here our heads are above the cloud, and that by faith we walk in the celestial city. So we beseech Thee, O Lord our God, when at last all temptation is over, all suffering, all things intended for our education having been done, we may not be afraid to depart. May we believe that it is better to be with Christ than to live on earth. May that silent voice which draws men away, come to us ; and may love cry " The warfare is accomplished ; come up, come ;" and with exceeding great joy we will throw off the burden of this mortal life, and depart to be with Christ, which is better than life.

And to the Father, Son, and Holy Spirit, forevermore, we will give the praise of our salvation. Amen.

AT THE FUNERAL OF PRESIDENT LINCOLN.

BY REV. DR. GREY, CHAPLAIN UNITED STATES SENATE.

O, LORD God of Hosts, behold a nation prostrate before Thy throne, clothed in sackcloth, who stand around all that now remains of our illustrious and beloved chief. We thank Thee that Thou hast given to us such a patriot, and to the country such a ruler, and to the world such a noble specimen of manhood. We bless Thee that Thou hast raised him to the highest position of trust and power in the nation ; and that Thou hast spared him so long to guide and direct the affairs of the Government in its hour of peril and conflict. We trusted it would be he who should deliver Israel, that he would have been retained to us while the nation was passing through its baptism of blood ; but in an evil hour, in an unexpected moment, when joy and rejoicing filled our souls, and was thrilling the heart of the nation, he fell. O God, give grace to sustain us under this dark and mysterious providence ! Help us to look up unto Thee and say, Not our will but Thine, O God, be done. We commend to Thy merciful regard and tender compassion the afflicted family of the deceased. Thou seest how their hearts are stricken with sorrow and wrung with agony. O, help them, as they are now passing through the dark valley and shadow of death, to fear no evil, but to lean upon Thy rod and staff for support. O, help them to cast their burden upon the great Burden-bearer, and find relief. Help them to look beyond human agencies and human means, and recognize Thy hand, O God, in this providence, and say : It is the Lord ; let Him do what seemeth good in His sight ; and as they proceed slowly and sadly on their way with the remains of a husband and father, to consign them to their last resting-place, may they look beyond the grave to the morning of resurrection, when that which they now sow in weakness shall be raised in strength ; what they now sow a mortal body shall be raised a spiritual body ; what they now sow in corruption shall be raised in incorruption, and shall be fashioned like unto Christ's most glorious body. O God of the bereaved, comfort and sustain this mourning family. Bless the new Chief Magistrate. Let the mantle of his predecessor fall upon him. Bless the Secretary of State and his family. O God, if possible, according to Thy will, spare their lives, that they may render still important service to the country. Bless all the members of the Cabinet. Endow them with wisdom from above. Bless the commanders of our army and navy, and all the brave defenders of the country, and give them continued success. Bless the ambassadors from foreign courts, and give us peace with the nations of the earth. O God, let treason, that has deluged our land with blood, and devastated our country, and bereaved our homes, and filled them with widows and orphans, and has at length culminated in the assassination of the nation's chosen ruler —God of justice, and Avenger of the nation's wrong, let the work of treason cease, and let the guilty author of this horrible crime be arrested and brought to justice. O, hear the cry and the prayer and the tears now arising from a nation's crushed and smitten heart, and deliver us from the power of all our enemies, and send speedy peace unto all of our borders, through Jesus Christ, our **Lord** Amen.

TEXTS FOR FUNERAL DISCOURSES.

1. Death in the prime of life.

Gen. xi. 28.—And Haran died before his father Terah.

Job xxi. 23.—One dieth in his full strength.

Jer. xv. 9.—Her sun is gone down while it was yet day.

Jer. xlviii. 17.—All ye that are about him bemoan him ; and all ye that know his name, say, How is the strong staff broken and the beautiful rod.

Hosea xiii. 15.—Though he be fruitful among his brethren, an east wind shall come, the wind of the Lord shall come up from the wilderness, and his spring shall become dry, and his fountain shall be dried up.

Amos viii. 9.—I will cause the sun to go down at noon.

Luke xiv. 30.—This man began to build, and was not able to finish.

2. Death of an obscure worker.

Ruth ii. 17.—So she gleaned in the field until even.

Eccl. vii. 1.—A good name is better than precious ointment ; and the day of death than the day of one's birth.

Matt. vii. 20.—By their fruits ye shall know them.

Matt. x. 29.—Are not two sparrows sold for a farthing ? and not one of them shall fall on the ground without your Father : but the very hairs of your head are all numbered.

Matt. x. 39.—He that loseth his life for my sake, shall find it.

Matt. xi. 28.—Come unto me, all ye that labor and are heavy-laden, and I will give you rest.

Matt. xxv. 15.—Unto one he gave five talents, to another two to another one.

Matt. xxv. 21.—Well done, good and faithful servant: thou hast been faithful over a few things, I will set thee over many things: enter thou into the joy of thy Lord.

Rev. iii. 1.—I know thy works, that thou hast a name that thou livest, and art dead.

3. Death of a parent.

Gen. xxxv. 18.—And it came to pass, as her soul was in departing (for she died), that she called his name Ben-oni.

Num. xx. 26.—And strip Aaron of his garments, and put them upon Eleazar his son: and Aaron shall be gathered unto his people, and shall die there.

Ps. xxvii. 10.—When my father and my mother forsake me, then the Lord will take me up.

Ps. xxxv. 14.—I bowed down heavily, as one that mourneth for his mother.

Ps. lxviii. 5.—A father of the fatherless . . . is God in his holy habitation.

Prov. xiii. 22.—A good man leaveth an inheritance to his children's children.

Prov. xx. 7.—The just man walketh in his integrity; his children are blessed after him.

Prov. xxxi. 28.—Her children arise up and call her blessed; her husband also, and he praiseth her.

Jer. xlix. 11.—Leave thy fatherless children; I will preserve them alive.

4. Death of the unrepentant.

Deut. xxxii. 31.—For their rock is not as our Rock, even our enemies themselves being judges.

2 Sam. iii. 33.—Died Abner as a fool dieth?

Job iv. 21.—They die, even without wisdom.

Job x. 21, 22.—Before I go whence I shall not return, even to the land of darkness and the shadow of death ; a land of darkness, as darkness itself ; and of the shadow of death, without any order, and where the light is as darkness.

Job xv. 23.—He knoweth that the day of darkness is ready at his hand.

Job xxi. 17.—How oft is the candle of the wicked put out ! and how oft cometh their destruction upon them !

Ps. xviii. 31.—Who is a rock save our God ?

Prov. i. 25-26.—But ye have set at nought all my counsel, and would none of my reproof : I also will laugh at your calamity ; I will mock when your fear cometh.

Matt. xvi. 26.—For what shall a man be profited, if he shall gain the whole world and forfeit his life ?

Matt. xxv. 10.—And while they went away to buy, the bridegroom came.

Luke xii. 20.—Thou foolish one, this night is thy soul required of thee ; and the things which thou hast prepared, whose shall they be ?

John viii. 21.—Ye shall seek me and shall die in your sin.

John xii. 25.—He that loveth his life loseth it.

Rom. vi. 23.—For the wages of sin is death.

Gal. vi. 7.—Whatsoever a man soweth that shall he also reap.

1 John v. 12.—He that hath the Son hath the life ; he that hath not the Son of God, hath not the life.

5. End of an unhappy life.

Josh. xiii. 33.—The Lord God of Israel was their inheritance.

1 Kings xvii. 12.—That we may eat it, and die.

1 Kings xix. 4.—And he requested for himself that he might die ; and said, It is enough ; now, O Lord, take away my life.

Job iii. 22.—Which rejoice exceedingly and are glad, when they can find the grave.

Job vii. 16.—I would not live alway.

Eccl. iv. 2.—Wherefore I praised the dead which are already dead, more than the living which are yet alive.

Isa. xxi. 11, 12.—Watchman, what of the night? The watchman said, The morning cometh.

Dan. xii. 13.—Go thou thy way till the end be; for thou shalt rest.

Jonah iv. 3.—O Lord, take, I beseech thee, my life from me; for it is better for me to die than to live.

Matt. xi. 28.—Come unto Me, all ye that labor and are heavy laden, and I will give you rest.

Rom. viii. 18.—For I reckon that the sufferings of this present time are not worthy to be compared with the glory which shall be revealed to us-ward.

Rev. vi. 11.—And it was said unto them that they should rest yet for a little time.

Rev. vii. 16.—They shall hunger no more, neither thirst any more.

Rev. vii. 17.—And God shall wipe away every tear from their eyes.

Rev. xiv. 13.—That they may rest from their labors.

Rev. xxi. 4.—And He shall wipe away every tear from their eyes; and death shall be no more; neither shall there be mourning, nor crying, nor pain any more.

6. Consolation for the bereaved.

Deut. xxxiii. 27.—The eternal God is our refuge, and underneath are the everlasting arms.

Josh. i. 5.—As I was with Moses, so I will be with thee; I will not fail thee nor forsake thee.

2 Sam. xii. 23.—Can I bring him back again? I shall go to him but he shall not return to me.

Ps. lxviii. 5.—A father of the fatherless, and a judge of the widows, is God in His holy habitation.

Job xxxvii. 21.—And now men see not the bright light which is in the clouds.

Jer. xlix. 11.—Leave thy fatherless children, I will preserve them alive; and let thy widows trust in Me.

Lam. i. 12.—Behold, and see if there be any sorrow like unto my sorrow.

Ezek. xiv. 23.—And ye shall know that I have not done without cause all that I have done in it, saith the Lord God.

Amos v. 8.—Seek Him that . . . turneth the shadow of death into the morning.

Matt. v. 4.—Blessed are they that mourn.

Matt. xi. 28.—Come unto me all ye that labor and are heavy laden, and I will give you rest.

Mark xvi. 3.—Who shall roll us away the stone from the door of the tomb?

Mark xvi. 6.—He is risen; He is not here; behold the place where they laid Him.

Luke vii. 32.—And when the Lord saw her He had compassion on her, and said unto her, Weep not.

Luke viii. 52.—She is not dead, but sleepeth.

Luke xxiii. 28.—Daughters of Jerusalem, weep not for me, but weep for yourselves.

Luke xxiv. 5, 6.—Why seek ye the living among the dead? He is not here, but is risen.

John xi. 13.—Thy brother shall rise again.

John xiii. 7.—What I do thou knowest not now; but thou shalt understand hereafter.

2 Cor. iv. 18.—While we look not at the things which are seen, but at the things which are not seen; for the things which are seen are temporal; but the things which are not seen are eternal.

1. Thess. iv. 13.—But we would not have you ignorant, brethren, concerning them that fall asleep; that ye sorrow not, even as the rest which have no hope.

7. Sudden or accidental death.

Job xv. 21.—In prosperity the destroyer shall come upon him.

Job xxi. 13.—They spend their days in wealth, and in a moment go down to the grave.

Job xxxiv. 20.—In a moment shall they die, and the people shall be troubled at midnight, and pass away : and the mighty shall be taken away without hand.

Ps. xxxix. 11.—Thou makest his beauty to consume away like a moth.

Prov. xxvii. 1.—Thou knowest not what a day may bring forth.

Eccl. ix. 12.—For man also knoweth not his time.

Isa. xvii. 14.—And behold at eveningtide trouble, and before the morning he is not.

Ezek. xxiv. 16.—Son of man, behold, I take away from thee the desire of thine eyes with a stroke.

Matt. xxiv. 42.—Watch therefore : for ye know not on what day your Lord cometh.

Matt. xxiv. 44.—Be ye also ready : for in an hour that ye think not the Son of man cometh.

Matt. xxv. 6.—But at midnight there is a cry, Behold, the bridegroom ! Come ye forth to meet him.

Matt. xxv. 13.—Watch therefore : for ye know not the day nor the hour.

Mark xiii. 29.—Know ye that He is nigh, even at the doors.

Mark xiii. 33.—Take ye heed, watch and pray : for ye know not when the time is.

Mark xiii. 35.—Watch therefore : for ye know not when the lord of the house cometh.

Mark xiii. 37.—And what I say unto you I say unto all, Watch.

1 Thess. v. 2.—The day of the Lord so cometh as a thief in the night.

1 Thess. v. 6.—So then let us not sleep, as do the rest ; but let us watch and be sober.

James iv. 14.—Whereas ye know not what shall be on the morrow.

Rev. iii. 3.—If therefore thou shalt not watch, I shall come as a thief, and thou shalt not know what hour I shall come upon thee.

Rev. xvi. 15.—Behold, I come as a thief. Blessed is he that watcheth, and keepeth his garments, lest he walk naked, and they see his shame.

8. Death of a young man or woman.

Judges xi. 39, 40.—And it was a custom in Israel, that the daughters of Israel went yearly to lament the daughter of Jephthah.

2 Sam. i. 25.—O Jonathan, thou wast slain in thine high places.

2 Sam. xviii. 33.—O my son Absalom, my son, my son Absalom! would God I had died for thee, O Absalom, my son, my son.

1 Kings xvii. 17.—The son of the woman, the mistress of the house, fell sick; and his sickness was so sore that no breath was left in him.

1 Kings xvii. 23.—And Elijah said, See, thy son liveth.

Eccles. xi. 9.—Rejoice, O young man, in thy youth; . . . but know thou that for all these things God will bring thee into judgment.

Eccles. xii. 1.—Remember now thy Creator in the days of thy youth.

Jer. vi. 26.—Make thee mourning as for an only son, most bitter lamentation.

Jer. ix. 21.—For death is come up into our windows, and is entered into our palaces, to cut off the children from without, and the young men from the streets.

Jer. x. 20.—My tabernacle is spoiled and my cords are broken: my children are gone forth of me, and they are not: there is none to stretch forth my tent any more, and to set up my curtains.

Jer. xlviii. 17.—All ye that are about him bemoan him; and

all ye that know his name, say, How is the strong staff broken and the beautiful rod !

Amos viii. 10.—I will make it as the mourning of an only son.

Matt. ix. 24.—The damsel is not dead, but sleepeth.

Luke vii. 12.—Behold, there was carried out one that was dead, the only son of his mother, and she was a widow.

Luke vii. 14.—Young man, I say unto thee, Arise.

Luke viii. 52.—And all were weeping, and bewailing her: but he said, Weep not ; for she is not dead, but sleepeth.

John xi. 24.—Thy brother shall rise again.

9. Death of an aged Christian.

Gen. v. 24.—And Enoch walked with God : and he was not, for God took him.

Gen. xv. 15.—Thou shalt go to thy fathers in peace ; thou shalt be buried in a good old age.

Gen. xxiii. 2.—And Sarah died . . . and Abraham came to mourn for Sarah and to weep for her.

Gen. xxv. 8.—Then Abraham gave up the ghost, and died in a good old age, an old man, and full of years, and was gathered to his people.

Gen. xxvii. 2.—Behold now I am old, I know not the day of my death.

Gen. xxxv. 29.—And Isaac gave up the ghost, and died, and was gathered unto his people, being old and full of days ; and his sons Esau and Jacob buried him.

Gen. xlvii. 9.—Few and evil have the days of the years of my life been.

Gen. xlviii. 21.—And Israel said unto Joseph, Behold, I die : but God shall be with you.

Gen. xlix. 18.—I have waited for thy salvation, O Lord.

Gen. xlix. 29.—And he charged them, and said unto them, I am to be gathered unto my people : bury me with my fathers.

Gen. xlix. 31.—There they buried Abraham and Sarah his wife; there they buried Isaac and Rebekah his wife; and there I buried Leah.

Gen. xlix. 33.—And when Jacob had made an end of commanding his sons, he . . . yielded up the ghost and was gathered unto his people.

Gen. l. 24.—And Joseph said unto his brethren, I die: and God will surely visit you and bring you out of this land.

Deut. xxxiv. 7.—And Moses was an hundred and twenty years old when he died: his eye was not dim nor his natural force abated.

Josh. ix. 13.—And these bottles of wine, which we filled, were new; and, behold, they be rent: and these our garments and our shoes are become old by reason of the very long journey.

Josh. xiii. 1.—Now Joshua was old and stricken in years.

Job v. 26.—Thou shalt come to thy grave in a full age, like as a shock of corn cometh in in his season.

Job xi. 17.—Thine age shall be clearer than the noonday.

Ps. xci. 16.—With long life will I satisfy him and show him my salvation.

Prov. iii. 2.—For length of days, and long life, and peace, shall they add to thee.

Zech. xiv. 7.—At evening time it shall be light.

10. Death of children.

Gen. xxii. 12.—For now I know that thou fearest God, seeing thou hast not withheld thy son, thine only son from me.

Gen. xxxvii. 30.—The child is not.

Gen. xxxvii. 35.—And all his sons and all his daughters rose up to comfort him; but he refused to be comforted, and he said, For I will go down into the grave unto my son mourning.

1 Sam. i. 28.—Therefore also I have lent him to the Lord.

1 Sam. iii. 8.—And Eli perceived that the Lord had called the child.

2 Sam. xii. 19.—David said unto his servants, Is the child dead? And they said, He is dead.

1 Kings xiv. 13.—And all Israel shall mourn for him and bury him . . . because in him there is found some good thing toward the Lord God of Israel.

1 Kings xiv. 17, 18.—When she came to the threshold of the door the child died; and they buried him: and all Israel mourned for him.

2 Kings iv. 20.—And when he had taken him, and brought him to his mother, he sat on her knees till noon, and then died.

2 Kings iv. 26.—Is it well with the child? And she answered, It is well.

2 Kings iv. 31.—And Gehazi passed on before them, and laid the staff upon the face of the child; but there was neither voice nor hearing. Wherefore he went again to meet him, and told him, saying, The child is not awaked.

Job i. 21.—The Lord gave, and the Lord hath taken away; blessed be the name of the Lord.

Ps. xcii. 13.—Those that be planted in the house of the Lord shall flourish in the courts of our God.

Isa. xi. 6.—And a little child shall lead them.

Isa. xl. 7.—The grass withereth, the flower fadeth, because the spirit of the Lord bloweth upon it.

Isa. xl. 11.—He shall gather the lambs with His arm, and carry them in His bosom.

Jer. x. 20.—My tabernacle is spoiled, and all my cords are broken: my children are gone forth of me, and they are not: there is none to stretch forth my tent any more, and to set up my curtains.

Jer. xxxi. 15.—A voice was heard in Ramah, lamentation and bitter weeping; Rachel weeping for her children refused to be comforted for her children, because they were not.

Mal. iii. 17.—And they shall be mine, saith the Lord of hosts, in that day when I make up my jewels.

Matt. xviii. 10.—See that ye despise not one of these little ones; for I say unto you, that in heaven their angels do always behold the face of my Father which is in heaven.

Matt. xviii. 14.—It is not the will of your Father which is in heaven that one of these little ones should perish.

Matt. xix. 14.—Suffer the little children, and forbid them not, to come unto me: for of such is the kingdom of heaven.

11. Death of a prominent person.

Num. xx. 28.—And Aaron died there in the top of the mount.

Num. xx. 29.—And when all the congregation saw that Aaron was dead, they mourned for Aaron thirty days.

Num. xxvii. 12, 13.—Get thee up into this mount Abarim, and see the land which I have given unto the children of Israel. And when thou hast seen it, thou also shalt be gathered unto thy people.

Deut. iii. 27.—Get thee up into the top of Pisgah and lift up thine eyes . . . and behold it with thine eyes: for thou shalt not go over this Jordan.

Deut. iv. 22.—But I must die in this land, I must not go over Jordan: but ye shall go over, and possess that good land.

Deut. xxxii. 49, 50.—Get thee up into this mountain . . . and die.

Deut. xxxiv. 5.—So Moses the servant of the Lord died there in the land of Moab, according to the word of the Lord.

Josh. xxiv. 29.—And it came to pass after these things that Joshua the son of Nun, the servant of the Lord, died, being an hundred and ten years old.

1 Sam. xxv. 1.—And Samuel died and all the Israelites were gathered together and lamented him.

2 Sam. i. 19.—The beauty of Israel is slain upon thy high places: how are the mighty fallen!

2 Sam. i. 25.—O Jonathan, thou wast slain in thine high places.

2 Sam. iii. 32.—And the king lifted up his voice, and wept at the grave of Abner; and all the people wept.

2 Sam. iii. 38.—Know ye not that there is a prince and a great man fallen this day in Israel?

2 Sam. xxiii. 1.—Now these be the last words of David.

1 Kings ii. 10.—So David slept with his fathers.

2 Kings ii. 5.—Knowest thou that the Lord will take away thy master from thy head to-day? And he answered, Yea, I know it; hold ye your peace.

2 Kings xxiii. 30.—And his servants carried him in a chariot dead from Megiddo, and brought him to Jerusalem, and buried him in his own sepulchre.

2 Chronicles xxxi. 21.—And in every work that he began in the service of the house of God, and in the law and in the commandments, to seek his God, he did it with all his heart, and prospered.

2 Chron. xxxii. 27, 33.—And Hezekiah had exceeding much riches and honor. . . . And Hezekiah slept with his fathers.

2 Chron. xxxii. 33.—And Hezekiah slept with his fathers, and they buried him in the chiefest of the sepulchres of the sons of David: and all Judah and the inhabitants of Jerusalem did him honor at his death.

2 Chron. xxxv. 25.—And Jeremiah lamented for Josiah: and all the singing men and the singing women spake of Josiah in their lamentations to this day, and made them an ordinance in Israel: and, behold, they are written in the lamentations.

Job xxxiv. 24.—They are exalted for a little while, but are gone and brought low.

Job xxxiv. 20.—The mighty shall be taken away without hand.

Ps. xlix. 17.—For when he dieth he shall carry nothing away: his glory shall not descend after him.

Isa. iii. 1–3.—For behold the Lord, the Lord of hosts, doth take away from Jerusalem and from Judah . . . the mighty man, and the man of war, the judge, and the prophet, and the prudent, and the ancient, the captain of fifty, and the honorable man, and the counsellor, and the cunning artificer, and the eloquent orator.

Isa. xxiii. 9.—The Lord of hosts hath purposed it, to stain the pride of all glory, and to bring into contempt all the honorable of the earth.

Matt. xxv. 15.—Unto one he gave five talents, to another two, to another one.

John v. 35.—He was the lamp that burneth and shineth : and ye were willing to rejoice for a season in his light.

12. Admonition and exhortation.

Deut. xxxi. 14.—Behold thy days approach that thou must die.

Deut. xxxii. 29.—O that they were wise, that they understood this, that they would consider their latter end !

Josh. i. 11.—Prepare you victuals ; for within three days ye shall pass over this Jordan.

Josh. iii. 4.—That ye may know the way by which ye must go : for ye have not passed this way heretofore.

1 Kings xx. 11.—Let not him that girdeth on his harness boast himself as he that putteth it off.

2 Kings xx. 1.—Set thine house in order ; for thou shalt die, and not live.

Job xxxiii. 14.—For God speaketh once, yea twice, yet man perceiveth it not.

Ps. xc. 12.—So teach us to number our days that we may apply our hearts unto wisdom.

Prov. xi. 4.—Riches profit not in the day of wrath ; but righteousness delivereth from death.

Eccles. vii. 2.—It is better to go to the house of mourning than to go to the house of feasting : for that is the end of all men : and the living will lay it to his heart.

Eccles. ix. 10.—Whatsoever thy hand findeth to do, do it with thy might ; for there is no work, nor device, nor knowledge, nor wisdom, in the grave, whither thou goest.

Eccles. xi. 9.—Rejoice, O young man, in thy youth ; and let thy heart cheer thee in the days of thy youth, and walk in the ways of thine heart, and in the sight of thine eyes : but know thou that for all these things God will bring thee into judgment.

Eccles. xii. 1.—Remember now thy Creator in the days of thy youth.

Jer. v. 31.—What will ye do in the end thereof?

Ezek. vii. 6.—An end is come, the end is come ; it watcheth for thee ; behold it is come.

Dan. xii. 8.—What shall be the end of these things?

Amos iv. 12.—Prepare to meet thy God.

Amos v. 6.—Seek the Lord and ye shall live.

Amos v. 8.—Seek Him that . . . turneth the shadow of death into the morning.

Matt. vi. 19, 20.—Lay not up for yourselves treasures upon the earth, where moth and rust doth consume, and where thieves break through and steal : but lay up for yourselves treasures in heaven, where neither moth nor rust doth consume, and where thieves do not break through nor steal.

Matt. x. 28.—Be not afraid of them which kill the body, but are not able to kill the soul : but rather fear Him which is able to destroy both soul and body in hell.

Matt. xvi. 26.—For what shall a man be profited, if he shall gain the whole world, and forfeit his life? or what shall a man give in exchange for his life?

Luke xii. 33, 34.—Make for yourselves purses which wax not old, a treasure in the heavens that faileth not, where no thief draweth near, neither moth destroyeth. For where your treasure is, there will your heart be also.

Luke xii. 35.—Let your loins be girded about and your lamps burning.

Rom. xiv. 7.—For none of us liveth to himself, and none dieth to himself.

Rom. xiv. 10.—For we shall all stand before the judgment seat of God.

Rom. xiv. 12.—So then each one of us shall give account of himself to God.

2 Cor. v. 10.—We must all be made manifest before the judgment seat of Christ ; that each one may receive the things done in the body, according to what he hath done, whether it be good or bad.

Eph. v. 16.—Redeeming the time, because the days are evil.

Col. iii. 2.—Set your mind on the things which are above, not on the things that are on the earth.

1 Thess. v. 6.—So then let us not sleep, as do the rest, but let us watch and be sober.

Heb. ix. 27.—It is appointed unto men once to die, and after this cometh judgment.

1 Peter iv. 5.—Who shall give account to Him that is ready to judge the quick and the dead ?

2 Peter i. 14.—The putting off of my tabernacle cometh swiftly.

Rev. iii. 11.—I come quickly : hold fast that which thou hast, that no one take thy crown.

Rev. xx. 12.—And I saw the dead, the great and the small, standing before the throne, and books were opened ; and another book was opened, which is the book of life : and the dead were judged out of the things which were written in the books, according to their works.

Rev. xx. 13.—And the sea gave up the dead which were in it ; and death and Hades gave up the dead which were in them : and they were judged every man according to their works.

Rev. xxii. 12.—Behold, I come quickly ; and my reward is with Me, to render to each man according as his work is.

13. Transiency of life.

Josh. xxiii. 14.—Behold, this day I am going the way of all the earth.

Judges ii. 10.—Also all that generation were gathered unto their fathers.

1 Sam. xx. 3.—There is but a step between me and death.

2 Sam. xiv. 14.—For we must needs die, and are as water spilt on the ground, which cannot be gathered up again.

1 Kings ii. 2.—I go the way of all the earth.

2 Kings xix. 26.—They were as the grass of the field, and as the green herb, as the grass on the housetops, and as corn blasted before it be grown up.

Job iv. 19.—Them that dwell in houses of clay, whose foundation is in the dust, which are crushed before the moth.

Job vii. 1.—Is there not an appointed time to man upon earth? are not his days also like the days of an hireling?

Job vii. 6.—My days are swifter than a weaver's shuttle.

Job vii. 8.—The eye of him that hath seen me shall see me no more: thine eyes are upon me, and I am not.

Job vii. 9, 10.—As the cloud is consumed and vanisheth away, so he that goeth down to the grave shall come up no more. He shall return no more to his house, neither shall his place know him any more.

Job vii. 21.—Now shall I sleep in the dust; and thou shalt seek me in the morning, but I shall not be.

Job viii. 9.—For we are but of yesterday, and know nothing, because our days upon earth are a shadow.

Job ix. 12.—Behold, He taketh away, who can hinder Him? who will say unto Him, What doest thou?

Job ix. 25, 26.—Now my days are swifter than a post; they flee away, they see no good. They are passed away as the swift ships; as the eagle that hasteth to the prey.

Job xiv. 1, 2.—Man that is born of a woman is of few days, and full of trouble. He cometh forth like a flower, and is cut down: he fleeth also as a shadow, and continueth not.

Job xiv. 5.—Seeing his days are determined, the number of his months are with thee, thou hast appointed his bounds that he cannot pass.

Job xiv. 10.—But man dieth, and wasteth away : yea, man giveth up the ghost, and where is he?

Job xiv. 11, 12.—As the waters fail from the sea, and the flood decayeth and drieth up ; so man lieth down and riseth not till the heavens be no more, they shall not awake, nor be raised out of their sleep.

Job xiv. 16.—Thou numberest my steps.

Job xiv. 19-21.—Thou destroyest the hope of man. Thou prevailest forever against him, and he passeth : thou changest his countenance and sendest him away. His sons come to honor, and he knoweth it not, and they are brought low, but he perceiveth it not of them.

Job xvi. 22.—When a few years are come, then I shall go the way whence I shall not return.

Job xvii. 1.—The graves are ready for me.

Job xvii. 14, 15.—I have said to corruption, Thou art my father : to the worm, Thou art my mother and sister. And where is now my hope?

Job xx. 8, 9.—He shall fly away as a dream, and shall not be found : yea, he shall be chased away as a vision of the night. The eye also which saw him shall see him no more ; neither shall his place any more behold him.

Job xxi. 26.—They shall lie down alike in the dust, and the worms shall cover them.

Job xxi. 32, 33.—Yet shall he be brought to the grave, and shall remain in the tomb. The clods of the valley shall be sweet unto him, and every man shall draw after him, as there are innumerable before him.

Job xxiv. 24.—They are exalted for a little while, but are gone and brought low ; they are taken out of the way as all other, and cut off as the tops of the ears of corn.

Job xxvii. 18.—He buildeth his house as a moth, and as a

booth that the keeper maketh. (See also St. John xiv. 1.—In my Father's house are many mansions.)

Job xxx. 23.—For I know that thou wilt bring me to death, and to the house appointed for all living.

Job xxxiv. 15.—All flesh shall perish together, and man shall turn again unto dust.

Ps. xxxix. 4.—Lord, make me to know mine end, and the measure of my days, what it is; that I may know how frail I am.

Ps. xxxix. 5.—Behold thou hast made my days as an handbreadth; and mine age is as nothing before thee: verily every man at his best state is altogether vanity.

Ps. xxxix. 6.—Surely every man walketh in a vain show: surely they are disquieted in vain: he heapeth up riches, and knoweth not who shall gather them.

Ps. xxxix. 11.—Thou makest his beauty to consume away like a moth.

Ps. xc. 5, 6.—In the morning they are like grass which groweth up. In the morning it flourisheth, and groweth up; in the evening it is cut down and withereth.

Ps. xc. 9.—We spend our years as a tale that is told.

Ps. xc. 10.—The days of our years are threescore years and ten; and if by reason of strength they be fourscore years, yet is their strength labor and sorrow; for it is soon cut off, and we fly away.

Ps. cii. 11.—My days are like a shadow that declineth; and I am withered like grass.

Ps. cii. 26.—They shall perish, but thou shalt endure: yea, all of them shall wax old as a garment; as a vesture shalt thou change them, and they shall be changed.

Ps. ciii. 15, 16.—As for man, his days are as grass: as a flower of the field, so he flourisheth. For the wind passeth over it, and it is gone; and the place thereof shall know it no more.

Ps. cxliv. 4.—Man is like to vanity: his days are as a shadow that passeth away.

Ps. cxlvi. 4, 5.—His breath goeth forth, he returneth to his earth; in that very day his thoughts perish. Happy is he that hath the God of Jacob for his help, whose hope is in the Lord his God.

Prov. xxvii. 1.—Boast not thyself of to-morrow; for thou knowest not what a day may bring forth.

Eccl. i. 2.—Vanity of vanities, saith the preacher, vanity of vanities; all is vanity.

Eccl. i. 4.—One generation passeth away, and another generation cometh: but the earth abideth for ever.

Eccl. ii. 14.—One event happeneth to them all.

Eccl. iii. 20.—All go unto one place: all are of the dust, and all turn to dust again.

Eccl. v. 15.—As he came forth of his mother's womb, naked shall he return, to go as he came, and shall take nothing of his labor, which he may carry away in his hand.

Eccl. viii. 8.—There is no man that hath power over the spirit to retain the spirit; neither hath he power in the day of death: and there is no discharge in that war.

Eccl. ix. 5.—For the living know that they shall die.

Isa. ii. 22.—Cease ye from man, whose breath is in his nostrils: for wherein is he to be accounted of?

Isa. xl. 6, 7.—All flesh is grass, and all the goodliness thereof is as the flower of the field: the grass withereth, the flower fadeth: because the spirit of the Lord bloweth upon it: surely the people is grass.

Isa. xl. 8.—The grass withereth, the flower fadeth; but the word of our God shall stand forever.

Isa. lxiv. 6.—We all do fade as a leaf.

Dan. iv. 35.—He doeth according to His will in the army of heaven, and among the inhabitants of the earth: and none can stay His hand, or say unto Him, What doest thou?

Dan. xi. 45.—He shall come to his end, and none shall help him.

Dan. xii. 13.—Go thou thy way till the end be : for thou shalt rest, and stand in thy lot at the end of the days.

Hosea xiii. 3.—They shall be as the morning cloud, and as the early dew that passeth away, as the chaff that is driven with the whirlwind out of the floor, and as the smoke out of the chimney.

Micah ii. 10.—Arise ye, and depart ; for this is not your rest.

Zech. i. 5.—Your fathers, where are they ? and the prophets, do they live forever ?

Rom. v. 12.—Therefore, as through one man sin entered into the world, and death through sin ; and so death passed unto all men, for that all sinned.

James i. 10.—As the flower of the grass, he shall pass away.

James iv. 14.—Whereas ye know not what shall be on the morrow. What is your life ? For ye are a vapor, that appeareth for a little time, and then vanisheth away.

1 Peter i. 24, 25.—All flesh is as grass, and all the glory thereof as the flower of the grass. The grass withereth, and the flower falleth : but the word of the Lord abideth forever.

14. Death of the righteous.

Ex. xxxiii. 14.— My presence shall go with thee, and I will give thee rest.

Num. xxiii. 10.—Let me die the death of the righteous, and let my last end be like his.

Num. xxv. 12.—Behold I give unto him my covenant of peace.

Deut. ix. 3.—Understand therefore this day that the Lord thy God is He which goeth over before thee.

Deut. xxviii. 6.—Blessed shalt thou be when thou comest in, and blessed shalt thou be when thou goest out.

Deut. xxxi. 6.—For the Lord thy God, He it is that doth go with thee ; He will not fail thee nor forsake thee.

Deut. xxxii. 39.—I kill, and I make alive ; I wound and I heal ; neither is there any that can deliver out of my hand.

Josh. iii. 17.—And the priests that bare the ark of the covenant stood firm on dry ground in the midst of Jordan, and all the Israelites passed over on dry ground.

2 Kings ii. 9.—Elijah said unto Elisha, Ask what I shall do for thee, before I be taken away from thee. And Elisha said, I pray thee, let a double portion of thy spirit be upon me.

2 Kings ii. 11, 12.—It came to pass, as they still went on, and talked, that behold, there appeared a chariot of fire and horses of fire, and parted them both asunder; and Elijah went up by a whirlwind into heaven. And Elisha saw it, and he cried, My father, my father, the chariot of Israel, and the horsemen thereof. And he saw him no more.

2 Kings iv. 1.—Thy servant my husband is dead; and thou knowest that thy servant did fear the Lord.

2 Kings xviii. 19.—What confidence is this wherein thou trustest?

2 Kings xxii. 20.—I will gather thee unto thy fathers, and thou shalt be gathered into thy grave in peace.

Job xi. 18, 19.—Thou shalt take thy rest in safety. Also thou shalt lie down, and none shall make thee afraid.

Ps. ix. 13.—Thou that liftest me up from the gates of death.

Ps. xii. 1.—Help, Lord; for the godly man ceaseth; for the faithful fail from among the children of men.

Ps. xxiii. 4.—Yea though I walk through the valley of the shadow of death, I will fear no evil: for thou art with me; thy rod and thy staff they comfort me.

Ps. xxxvii. 37.—Mark the perfect man, and behold the upright; for the end of that man is peace.

Ps. cii. 19, 20.—For He hath looked down from the height of His sanctuary . . . to loose those that are appointed to death.

Ps. cxvi. 15.—Precious in the sight of the Lord is the death of His saints.

Ps. cxxvii. 2.—He giveth His beloved sleep.

Ps. cxxxix. 11.—Even the night shall be light about me.

Prov. x. 7.—The memory of the just is blessed.

Prov. xii. 28.—In the way of righteousness is life; and in the pathway thereof there is no death.

Eccles. ii. 16.—How dieth the wise man?

Isa. xl. 2.—Speak ye comfortably to Jerusalem, and cry unto her, that her warfare is accomplished.

Isa. lvii. 1, 2.—The righteous is taken away from the evil to come. He shall enter into peace.

Ezek. xviii. 28.—Because he considereth, and turneth away from all his transgressions which he hath committed, he shall surely live, he shall not die.

Ezek. xx. 29.—What is the high place whereunto ye go?

Dan. xii. 3.—They that be wise shall shine as the brightness of the firmament; and they that turn many to righteousness as the stars forever and ever.

Zech. xiv. 7.—At evening time it shall be light.

Mal. ii. 6.—The law of truth was in his mouth, and iniquity was not found in his lips: he walked with me in peace and equity, and did turn many away from iniquity.

Mal. iii. 17.—And they shall be mine, saith the Lord of hosts, in that day when I make up my jewels.

Matt. v. 8.—Blessed are the pure in heart, for they shall see God.

Matt. vii. 20.—By their fruits ye shall know them.

Matt. x. 39.—He that loseth his life for my sake, shall find it.

Matt. xi. 28.—Come unto Me, all ye that labor and are heavy laden, and I will give you rest.

Matt. xiii. 43.—Then shall the righteous shine forth as the sun in the kingdom of their Father.

Matt. xxiv. 46.—Blessed is that servant, whom his lord when he cometh shall find so doing.

Matt. xxv. 34.—Come, ye blessed of my Father, inherit the kingdom prepared for you from the foundation of the world.

Luke xiv. 17.—Come, for all things are now ready.

Luke xxiii. 43.—To-day shalt thou be with me in Paradise.

John xvii. 4.—I glorified thee on the earth, having accomplished the work which thou hast given me to do.

Rom. viii. 16.—The Spirit himself beareth witness with our spirit that we are children of God.

Rom. viii. 37.—In all these things we are more than conquerors through Him that loved us.

Rom. xiv. 8.—Whether we live therefore **or die, we are the Lord's.**

2 Cor. v. 4.—For indeed we that are in this tabernacle do groan, being burdened ; not for that we would be unclothed, but that we would be clothed upon, that what is mortal may be swallowed up of life.

2 **Cor.** v. 8.—We are of good courage, I say, and are willing **rather to** be absent from the body, and to **be** at home with the Lord.

Phil. i. 21.—For to me to live is Christ, and to die is gain.

Phil. i. 23.—But I am in a strait betwixt the two, having the desire to depart and be with Christ ; for it is very far better.

2 Tim. iv. 6–8.—For I am already being offered, and the time of my departure is come. I have fought the good fight, I have finished the course, I have kept the faith : henceforth there is laid up for me the crown of righteousness.

Heb. ii. 14, 15.—That through death He might bring to nought him that had the power of death, that is the devil ; and might deliver all them who through fear of death were all their lifetime subject to bondage.

Heb. iv. 9.—There remaineth therefore a Sabbath rest for the people of God.

Heb. vi. 18, 19.— . . . the hope set before us ; which we have as an anchor of the soul, a hope both sure and steadfast and entering into that which is within the veil.

Heb. x. 34.—Knowing that ye yourselves have a better possession, and an abiding one.

Heb. x. 37.—For yet a very little while, He that cometh shall come, and shall not tarry. But my righteous one shall live by faith.

Heb. xi. 4.—He being dead, yet speaketh.

Heb. xi. 9.—For he looked for the city which hath the foundations, whose builder and maker is God.

Heb. xi. 13.—Having confessed that they were strangers and pilgrims on the earth.

Heb. xi. 16.—But now they desire a better country, that is, a heavenly: wherefore God is not ashamed of them, to be called their God: for He hath prepared for them a city.

Heb. xiii. 14.—For we have not here an abiding city, but we seek after the city which is to come.

James i. 12.—He shall receive the crown of life, which the Lord promised to them that love Him.

1 Peter v. 4.—Ye shall receive the crown of glory that fadeth not away.

1 John iii. 2.—Beloved, now are we children of God, and it is not yet made manifest what we shall be. We know that, if He shall be manifested, we shall be like Him; for we shall see Him even as He is.

1 John v. 12.—He that hath the Son hath the life.

Rev. ii. 10.—Be thou faithful unto death, and I will give thee the crown of life.

Rev. ii. 17.—To him that overcometh, to him will I give of the hidden manna, and I will give him a white stone, and upon the stone a new name written, which no one knoweth but he that receiveth it.

Rev. iii. 4.—They shall walk with me in white; for they are worthy.

Rev. iii. 5.—He that overcometh shall thus be arrayed in white garments, and I will in no wise blot his name out of the book of life, and I will confess his name before my Father, and before His angels.

Rev. iii. 12.—He that overcometh, I will make him a pillar in the temple of my God, and he shall go out thence no more.

Rev. iii. 21.—He that overcometh, I will give to him to sit down with Me in my throne.

Rev. vi. 11.—And there was given them to each one a white robe ; and it was said unto them, that they should rest yet for a little time.

Rev. vii. 13.—These which are arrayed in the white robes, who are they, and whence came they?

Rev. vii. 14, 15.—They washed their robes and made them white in the blood of the Lamb. Therefore are they before the throne of God ; and they serve Him day and night in His temple.

Rev. vii. 16, 17.—They shall hunger no more, neither thirst any more ; neither shall the sun strike upon them, nor any heat : for the Lamb which is in the midst of the throne shall be their shepherd, and shall guide unto fountains of the waters of life : and God shall wipe away every tear from their eyes.

Rev. xiv. 13.—And I heard a voice from heaven saying, Write, Blessed are the dead which die in the Lord from henceforth : yea, saith the Spirit, that they may rest from their labors ; for their works follow them.

Rev. xv. 3.—They sing the song of Moses, the servant of God, and the song of the Lamb.

Rev. xix. 9.—Write, Blessed are they which are bidden to the marriage supper of the Lamb.

Rev. xxi. 3, 4.—He shall dwell with them, and they shall be His peoples, and God himself shall be with them, and be their God : and He shall wipe away every tear from their eyes ; and death shall be no more ; neither shall there be mourning, nor crying, nor pain any more.

Rev. xxi. 7.—He that overcometh shall inherit these things ; and I will be his God, and he shall be my son.

Rev. xxii. 4.—And they shall see His face; and His name shall be on their foreheads.

Rev. xxii. 14.—Blessed are they that wash their robes, that they may have the right to come to the tree of life, and may enter in by the gates into the city.

15. Heaven and immortality.

Deut. xxxii. 40.—For I lift up my hand to heaven, and say, I live forever.

1 Sam. ii. 6.—The Lord killeth and maketh alive: He bringeth down to the grave and bringeth up.

Job iii. 17.—There the wicked cease from troubling, and there the weary be at rest.

Job xiv. 14.—If a man die, shall he live again?

Job xix. 26.—Though after my skin worms destroy this body, yet in my flesh shall I see God.

Ps. xvi. 10.—For thou wilt not leave my soul in hell; neither wilt thou suffer thine Holy One to see corruption.

Ps. xvi. 11.—Thou wilt show me the path of life: in thy presence is fulness of joy; at thy right hand there are pleasures forevermore.

Ps. xlix. 15.—But God will redeem my soul from the power of the grave, for He will receive me.

Ps. lxviii. 18.—Thou hast ascended on high, thou hast led captivity captive.

Isa. xxv. 8.—He will swallow up death in victory; and the Lord God shall wipe away tears from off all faces.

Isa. xxvi. 19.—Thy dead men shall live, together with my dead body shall they arise. Awake and sing, ye that dwell in dust: for thy dew is as the dew of herbs, and the earth shall cast out the dead.

Isa. xxxiii. 17.—Thine eyes shall see the King in His beauty: they shall behold the land that is very far off.

Isa. xxxiii. 24.—The inhabitant shall not say, I am sick : **the people that dwell therein shall be forgiven their** iniquity.

Isa. xxxv. 9, 10.—The redeemed **shall** walk there ; and the ransomed of the Lord shall return, and come to Zion with songs and everlasting joy **upon** their heads : they shall obtain joy and gladness, **and sorrow and** sighing **shall flee** away.

Isa. xxxviii. 16.—**O Lord,** by these things men live, and **in all these things** is the life of my spirit.

Isa. xl. 31.—They that wait upon the Lord shall renew their **strength** ; they shall mount **up with** wings as eagles ; they shall run and not be weary ; and they shall walk and not faint.

Isa. lx. 20.—**Thy sun shall no more go down,** neither **shall thy moon withdraw itself : for the Lord shall be** thine everlasting light, and the **days of thy mourning shall be ended.**

Isa. lxv. 19.—I will rejoice in Jerusalem, and joy in my people : and the voice of weeping shall be no more heard in her, nor the voice of crying.

Ezek. xxxvii. 3.—**Son of man, can** these bones live ?

Ezek. xxxvii. 9.—**Come from the** four winds, **O** breath, **and breathe upon these slain, that they** may live.

Ezek. xxxvii. 12.—**Behold, O my people, I will** open your **graves and cause you to come up out of your** graves, and **bring you into the land of Israel.**

Hosea xiii. 14.—**I will** ransom them from the power of the grave ; **I will** redeem them from death : O death, I will be thy plagues ; O grave, I will be thy destruction.

Habakkuk i. 12.—**Art** thou not from everlasting, O Lord my God, mine Holy One ? we shall not die.

Zech. iii. 3, 4.—Joshua was clothed **with** filthy garments, and stood before the angel. And he answered and spake unto those that stood before him, saying, Take away the filthy garments from him.

Zech. iii. 7.—**I will give thee places to walk among** these that stand by.

Matt. vi. 20.—Lay up for yourselves **treasures** in heaven, where neither moth nor rust doth **consume,** and where thieves do not **break** through nor steal.

Matt. xiii. 43.—Then shall the righteous shine forth **as the sun in the** kingdom of their Father.

Matt. xxviii. 7.—He is risen from the dead ; **and lo,** He goeth before you into Galilee ; there shall ye see Him.

Luke xx. 36.—Neither can they die any more : for they are **equal unto the** angels ; and are sons of God, being sons of the **resurrection.**

John iii. 16.—For God so loved the world, that He gave His only begotten Son, that whosoever believeth on Him should not perish, but have eternal life.

John iii. 36.—He that believeth on the Son hath eternal life.

John v. 24.—He that heareth **my word** and **believeth on Him** that sent Me, hath eternal life, and cometh not into judgment, but hath passed out of death into life.

John v. 25.—The hour cometh, and now is, when the dead shall hear the voice of the Son of God ; and they that hear shall live.

John v. 28, 29.—For the hour cometh, when all that are in the tombs **shall hear His voice,** and shall come forth ; they that have done good, unto the resurrection of life ; and they that have done ill, unto the resurrection **of judgment.**

John vi. 39.—And this **is the will of** Him that sent Me, that of all that which He hath **given Me I** should lose nothing, but should raise it **up at** the last **day.**

John vi. 40.—For this is the will of my Father, that **every one** that beholdeth **the Son, and believeth** on Him, should have eternal life ; and I will **raise him up** at the last day.

John vi. 48-50.—I am the bread of life. **Your fathers** did eat the manna in the wilderness, and they died. This is the bread that cometh down out of heaven, that a man may eat thereof and not die.

John vi. 51.—I am the living bread which came down out of heaven : if any man eat of this bread, **he shall** live forever.

John vi. 54.—He that eateth my flesh and drinketh my blood hath eternal life ; and I will raise him up at the last day.

John x. 10.—I came that they may have life, and may have it abundantly.

John x. 28.—I give unto them eternal life ; and they shall never perish.

John xi. 25, 26.—I am the resurrection and the life ; he that believeth on Me, though he die, yet shall he live : and whosoever liveth and believeth on Me shall never die.

John xii. 24.—Except a grain of wheat fall into the earth and die, it abideth by itself alone ; but if it die, it beareth much fruit.

John xii. 25.—He that loveth his life loseth it ; and he that hateth his life in this world, shall keep it unto life eternal.

John xiv. 2, 3.—In my Father's house are many mansions ; if it were not so, I would have told you ; for I go to prepare a place for you. And if I go and prepare a place for you, I come again, and will receive you unto myself ; that where I am there ye may be also.

John xiv. 19.—Because I live, ye shall live also.

John xvii. 24.—Father, that which thou hast given Me, I will that, where I am, they also may be with Me, that they may behold my glory, which thou hast given Me.

Rom. v. 17.—For if, by the trespass of the one, death reigned through the one ; much more shall they which receive the abundance of grace and of the gift of righteousness, reign in life through the one, even Jesus Christ.

Rom. vi. 23.—For the wages of sin is death ; but the free gift of God is eternal life in Jesus Christ our Lord.

Rom. viii. 2.—For the law of the Spirit of life in Christ Jesus made me free from the law of sin and of death.

Rom. viii. 13.—For if ye live after the flesh, ye must die ; but if by the spirit ye mortify the deeds of the body, ye shall live.

Rom. viii. 18.—For I reckon that the sufferings of this present time are not worthy to be compared with the glory which shall be revealed to us-ward.

Rom. viii. 38, 39.—For I am persuaded that neither death nor life . . . shall be able to separate us from the love of God.

1 Cor. ii. 9.—Things which eye saw not, and ear heard not, and which entered not into the heart of man, whatsoever things God prepared for them that love Him.

1 Cor. xiii. 12.—For now we see in a mirror, darkly; but then face to face: now I know in part; but then I shall know even as also I have been known.

1 Cor. xv. 20.—But now hath Christ been raised from the dead, the firstfruits of them that are asleep.

1 Cor. xv. 22.—In Christ shall all be made alive.

1 Cor. xv. 26.—The last enemy that shall be abolished is death.

1 Cor. xv. 36.—That which thou thyself sowest is not quickened except it die.

1 Cor. xv. 42-44.—It is sown in corruption; it is raised in incorruption: it is sown in dishonor; it is raised in glory: it is sown in weakness; it is raised in power: it is sown a natural body; it is raised a spiritual body.

1 Cor. xv. 49.—As we have borne the image of the earthy, we shall also bear the image of the heavenly.

1 Cor. xv. 52.—For the trumpet shall sound, and the dead shall be raised incorruptible, and we shall be changed.

1 Cor. xv. 53, 54.—For this corruptible must put on incorruption, and this mortal must put on immortality. But when this corruptible shall have put on incorruption, and this mortal shall have put on immortality, then shall come to pass the saying that is written, Death is swallowed up in victory.

1 Cor. xv. 55-57.—O death, where is thy sting? O grave, where is thy victory? The sting of death is sin; and the strength of sin is the law: but thanks be to God, which giveth us the victory through our Lord Jesus Christ.

2 Cor. iv. 14.—Knowing that He which raised up the Lord

Jesus shall raise up us also with Jesus, and shall present us with you.

2 Cor. v. 1.—For we know that if the earthly house of our tabernacle be dissolved, we have a building from God, a house not made with hands, eternal, in the heavens.

Gal. vi. 8.—He that soweth unto the Spirit, shall of the Spirit reap eternal life.

Eph. iv. 8.—When He ascended on high He led captivity captive, and gave gifts unto men.

Eph. v. 14.—Awake, thou that sleepest, and arise from the dead, and Christ shall shine upon thee.

Phil. iii. 20, 21.—For our citizenship is in heaven; from whence also we wait for a Saviour, the Lord Jesus Christ: who shall fashion anew the body of our humiliation, that it may be conformed to the body of His glory.

2 Tim. ii. 11, 12.—For if we died with Him, we shall also live with Him: if we endure, we shall also reign with Him.

Titus i. 2.—In hope of eternal life, which God, who cannot lie, promised before times eternal.

Heb. xi. 10.—The city which hath the foundations, whose builder and maker is God.

Heb. xi. 19.—Accounting that God is able to raise up, even from the dead.

Heb. xii. 22.—But ye are come unto Mount Zion, and unto the city of the living God, the heavenly Jerusalem, and to innumerable hosts of angels.

1 Peter i. 4.—Unto an inheritance incorruptible, and undefiled, and that fadeth not away.

1 Peter i. 23.—Begotten again not of corruptible seed, but of incorruptible.

1 John ii. 17.—The world passeth away, and the lust thereof: but he that doeth the will of God abideth forever.

1 John ii. 25.—And this is the promise which He hath promised us, even the life eternal.

1 John v. 13.—That ye may know that ye have eternal life.

Rev. i. 18.—I was dead, and behold, I am alive for evermore, and I have the keys of death and of Hades.

Rev. ii. 7.—To him that overcometh, to him will I give to eat of the tree of life, which is in the Paradise of God.

Rev. vii. 16, 17.—They shall hunger no more, neither thirst any more; neither shall the sun strike upon them, nor any heat.

Rev. xxi. 23.—And the city hath no need of the sun, neither of the moon, to shine upon it: for the glory of God did lighten it, and the lamp thereof is the Lamb.

16. Miscellaneous.

Ex. xxxiii. 18.—I beseech thee, show me thy glory.

Ex. xxxiii. 20.—For there shall no man see Me, and live.

Deut. v. 25.—Now, therefore, why should we die?

Deut. xxxii. 43.—For He will avenge the blood of His servants.

Josh. xviii. 3.—How long are ye slack to go to possess the land which the Lord God of your fathers hath given you?

Judges xvi. 30.—So the dead which he slew at his death were more than they which he slew in his life.

1 Sam. iii. 18.—It is the Lord: let Him do what seemeth Him good.

1 Sam. xiv. 17.—Number now, and see who is gone from us.

1 Sam. xx. 18.—Thou shalt be missed, because thy seat will be empty.

2 Sam. iii. 34.—As a man falleth before wicked men, so fellest thou.

1 Kings xiv. 6.—I am sent to thee with heavy tidings.

2 Kings i. 4.—Thou shalt not come down from that bed on which thou art gone up, but shalt surely die.

2 Kings xxiii. 17.—It is the sepulchre of the man of God.

Job xix. 25.—I know that my Redeemer liveth.

Job xxix. 18.—I said, I shall die in my nest.

Job xxxviii. 17.—Have the gates of death been opened unto thee? or hast thou seen the doors of the shadow of death?

Ps. xxxvi. 6.—Thy judgments are a great deep.

Ps. lxviii. 20.—Unto God the Lord belong the issues from death.

Ps. lxxvii. 19.—Thy way is in the sea, and thy path in the great waters, and thy footsteps are not known.

Ps. lxxxii. 7.—Ye shall die like men, and fall like one of the princes.

Ps. cxli. 7.—Our bones are scattered at the grave's mouth as when one cutteth and cleaveth wood upon the earth.

Eccles. iii. 2.—A time to die.

Eccles. xii. 5, 6.—Because man goeth to his long home, and the mourners go about the streets: or ever the silver cord be loosed, or the golden bowl be broken, or the pitcher be broken at the fountain, or the wheel broken at the cistern.

Eccles. xii. 7.—Then shall the dust return to the earth as it was: and the spirit shall return unto God who gave it.

Isa. xvii. 7.—At that day shall a man look to his Maker, and his eyes shall have respect to the Holy one of Israel.

Jonah iv. 7.—God prepared a worm when the morning rose the next day, and it smote the gourd, that it withered.

Haggai ii. 3.—Who is left among you that saw this house in her first glory?

Zech. iii. 2.—Is not this a brand plucked out of the fire?

Luke i. 79.—To shine upon them that sit in darkness and the shadow of death.

Luke xiii. 22.—And He went on His way through cities and villages, teaching, and journeying on unto Jerusalem.

Luke xx. 38.—Now He is not the God of the dead, but of the living: for all live unto Him.

Luke xxii. 33.—Lord, with thee I am ready to go both to prison and to death.

Heb. ii. 9.—That by the grace of God He should taste death for every man.

Rev. iv. 1.—Come up hither, and I will show thee the things which must come to pass hereafter.

MISCELLANY.

ABOUT FUNERAL ADDRESSES.

BY PASTOR RUDOLPH MÜLLER.

[Translated from the German by Rev. G. F. Behringer.]

To preach in Christ's name means to bear witness to Christ; means to offer to the congregation a living testimony from the converted heart. Thus the funeral address must be a testimony of salvation in Christ; it will be, first of all, a witness of the faith, and, in the faith of Jesus, a testimony of our hope through Him. Without Jesus no salvation, either in life, or in death, or in eternity; no salvation for the departed, none for those remaining. And when the newly-made grave testifies of the transitory character of all things; when sorrow and mourning surround the preacher; when the burden of grief rests like a heavy weight upon the hearts; when human comfort is dumb, or does not avail—at that time how elevating is it to hear the preacher of the Gospel speak with joy upon his lips, proclaiming the grace of God in Jesus Christ, illuminating the gloom of the grave, lighting up also the gloom of sorrow through the proclamation of the Lord, who is the resurrection and the life! This is the height up to which every funeral address must lead.

Thus the funeral sermon is essentially a testimony for Christ, and a confession of the hope in Christ that is within us; and this confession at the grave exerts a mighty influence upon the heart not yet completely hardened. Nowhere else so striking as here, where even the careless one cannot resist serious thoughts, does the opportunity present itself to hold the hearts, and direct them to the "one thing needful." Many a one has, perhaps purposely, gone out of the way of the Word of God; but here he must hear it, either for weal or woe. Many a heart has grown hard under the cares and pleasures of life, but pain is a sharper plough which loosens the earth. At this time he is in a receptive condition; instinctively he longs for a word of life that may comfort him. Such an opportunity must be utilized. Let us be mindful of our sacred obligation to scatter divine seed. Let us be painfully conscientious in funeral sermons: we shall be called upon to give an account of every idle word spoken. To this class belongs the useless word that carries with it no power of life.

The difficulty of combining personal matters with the treatment of the text is but an apparent one. For the text should be chosen especially in view of the individuality of the deceased. Philip David Burk correctly says: "The *personal* allusions are not to be saved unto the end of the discourse, but in the very beginning the impression is to be made that these personal matters were in the mind of the speaker during his preparation for and in his meditation upon the address." Emphasizing the personal (which was developed out of the heathen "*laudatio*") is the most original element of the funeral address. We find this, by way of illustration, as thoroughly violating all churchly dignity in the case of the address of Ephraim the Syrian upon Basilius the Great. If a distinguished person is to be buried, possibly here or there may be found some one disposed to lavish his praises extravagantly in an uncalled-for and offensive manner, with a view of pleasing the surviving relatives. Even a common peasant pride, based upon the money bags, demands at times such praise. Let the servant of the Church not belittle himself to found the fame of the deceased upon externals, or to adorn the life-picture of the departed with virtues that he never possessed. But, of course, *that* is to be praised that is worthy of praise—what we know of him by our own observation and experience, or whatever may be known in the common experience of the friends and acquaintances of the deceased. Yet in doing this we should not praise the dead in and for himself, but for the grace of God which glorified itself in him, for "through grace I am that I am;" we should not declare him as saved because of his works, but we may hope and pray for this salvation in Christ's mercy and as a manifestation of grace, provided that the confession may also be reported of him: "The highest praise at my grave shall be that I have loved Thee, Lord!"

If we did not personally know the deceased, and if, after diligent inquiry, we cannot obtain any reliable information, then the greatest caution is to be exercised in praise as well as in blame. The want of this caution has given many an offence. Even if the clergyman in question is innocent in a certain sense of doing any injustice, the truth is expected of him under *all* circumstances. And it is very distressing when he with pathos proclaims as truth and reality what is the very opposite, and presents the same for our example; or when he reproves the deceased when many grateful mourners honestly and sincerely lament his loss. This estranges the heart and impairs authority. Furthermore, attention is to be paid to this point: only such personal matters are to be taken up and considered as are of any value to Christian consideration, only such as can be regarded from an evangelical point of view. Matters of little consequence, at any rate such as are of little importance in the sight of God, are not to be put into a funeral address. In this respect the preacher must regard his word as too high and holy to refer to trifles at the grave, where the breath of eternity touches us. It would be sad indeed if he had nothing important to say.

In regard to the use of personal matters, the text will afford us the right measure to be applied. Let us keep this steadily in view; it will preserve us against errors and unnecessary latitude, and will teach us to emphasize only those points the mention of which will not flatter the individual, but will be of saving influence to all. It is pleasing if we can bestow praise and in this way impress the image of the departed indelibly upon the memory of the survivors (*e.g.* in the case of a father or mother). Then the grave exerts an influence upon the mourners, and in the case of many an erring one has proven to be in later years an awakening voice.

But how shall we proceed if, on the other hand, the life-picture of the deceased present dark spots? It would be wanting in tact and imprudent did we appear at the grave with the lightning and thunder of Mount Sinai. We are servants of Christ who, with all earnestness, carry not only the rod "WOE," but also the rod "EASY," that is, peace. "This one receives sinners." This is His highest praise. We should not only wound, we should also heal; and remember that we preachers are not infallible. "How seest thou the mote in thy brother's eye, and regardest not the beam that is in thine own eye?" This passage also will apply to the servant of the Word: "Judge not, that ye be not judged." There is no man but has some good sides to his character; let us dwell upon these: the bad sides are known to the people without our telling them. And why mention such things when the deceased is now standing before his judge, perhaps has become reconciled to God through sorrow and repentance? But, if nothing good whatever can be said of the deceased, then it would be best to make the address a general one—that is, to speak of the destroying influences of sin, the necessity of conversion, etc. The people understand right well how to read between the lines. What must be said can be said without offending any one: there is but tact needed.

Let us hold fast to this: the funeral address shall be a testimony of love. The sinner is rather the object of pity than of condemnation. Sin is condemned by the Scripture under any and every circumstance. But the sinner remains the object of our love. If we could know all the secret ways by which one has gone to destruction, how many things should we find have co-operated to bring this about, and which would essentially modify our judgment! To paint as light that which is dark, we dare not do. When one has died unconverted, when he has persevered unto hardness in his vice, this dare not be ignored, even for the sake of those who have come out to hear. It would mark the preacher with the brand of cowardice. The more boldly he can swing the sword of the Spirit, the better will it be. Yet love must guide the hand, that love which bewails, which does not condemn without mercy. And the sword must not be drawn against the deceased brother, but against his vice, especially if this be prevalent in others among the congregation. Thus the object of the address will be gained, and truth will be honored without causing offence or arousing bitterness of feeling. The funeral address should not cast a shadow upon the deceased, but light from a higher world upon the life of the living.

The funeral address becomes a very difficult matter when the deceased was a modern heathen, whose burial is nevertheless demanded of the Church. The Roman Catholic Church simply ignores him—that is, in case he ignores the Church up to the last moment. But the Evangelical Church must be tolerant. Up to the present time, whoever pays church dues can demand a church burial. Such people, since they led a "*civil*" life, should receive a civil burial—thus thinks the hot-head. And yet, if either the departed or his relatives have asked for a religious interment, does not this involve the confession, even if external reasons seem to contradict, that the Church is a power, and that only a churchly burial hallows the ceremony at the grave? And even if the Church have no power or influence over the dead, have not the living been intrusted to her care for her to seek them, and, if possible, to save them, and to give them to know and to experience what of reality there is in the neglected salvation by faith?

The preacher must here honor the truth, and yet confess with regret that the eyes of the deceased were holden to the treasures of the Church. Perhaps God's all-seeing eye may have discerned elements of faith upon the background of the heart; perhaps the deceased in his secret hours may have experienced an ardent desire for that God whom he outwardly denied; perhaps God's mercy had begun its work of repentance within him in a quiet but particular way, and that He will lead him up above to a fuller knowledge of salvation. At any rate, we dare not presume to prescribe bounds to God's mercy, nor to close heaven against any one, small as may be our hope that God will *know* one who despises Him here. "Yet not as man regardeth," etc.

The funeral sermon ought to be, furthermore, a testimony of love to the survivors. If the deceased did not occupy a prominent position in life, his special relation to his relatives affords us sufficient material. And that we are addressing mourners will also determine the tone of our remarks. We ought to be mindful of these things in determining our thoughts.

Yet there are rocks even here. "Yes, it was a beautiful address; not one eye that was not bathed in tears." Such laudation seems to many a one to be the principal thing. He seems fairly to exhaust himself "to drum upon the hearts" of the people, to open the floodgates of tears, to inflict deep wounds that bleed right well. With hard-boned natures and thick-skinned hearts this may pass. But if there be nervously constituted persons present, then fainting fits are unavoidable, with accompanying disorders, and upon the educated such a course produces the opposite effect from that desired. "Weep with the weeping ones." This is the advantage which the older minister has over the younger one, that his long experience indicates to him the right tone and temper of mind which will re-echo in the wounded hearts and lead them to feel involuntarily: the minister knows just how *I* feel. If the minister has himself stood at the grave of father or mother, or of wife or child, how differently will he speak from the youth to whom life smiles through rosy glasses! **Hence** this rule must be observed: put yourself in the place **of the sorrowing ones,** into their real feelings.

"The pastor remains untouched: burying belongs to his business!" These are public remarks. We ought to prevent their being made. Although our natures may be different, yet we must never forget that people look for a warm heart under the minister's gown; that "the heart makes the theologian;" that not only as ministers but as men **we speak** to men; that above all other things love should both develop **and edify** faith.

But the chief thing is: "Comfort ye, comfort ye my people." This cannot be too strongly emphasized. The funeral sermon should be, above **all** things, an address of consolation, to stanch the weeping eyes, to raise **up those that are bowed down,** that they may pursue their journey with **new courage and earnestness.** Mere shedding of tears but increases the pain; a **passing impression lacks power.** But to comfort in the right way is an **art that we can learn only in the school of the Holy** Spirit. How vapid it is, for example, if at the burial of children **continual reference is** made to how much the departed has been delivered **from; that perhaps the** hope of salvation might have been lost if he or she had lived longer. In reference to this, Palmer asks: "Why has not God taken others who really fell into evil ways? Is He not unjust to these? Or would my child really have grown up as bad or worse? And as regards any unfavorable fate or fortune that might have threatened the child—well, we adults also **have survived severe** experiences, and **with God's help we have passed through them all, and** enjoy **our life in spite of all afflictions."** The mere **preaching** of woe and misery awakens no **wholesome view of life, nor** arouses the necessary life-courage, it simply **depresses. This** is not our mission, to diminish, if possible, our pain; sorrow remains sorrow, and **when it** comes it hurts—yes, it is intended to hurt. The right comfort lies in emphasizing our faith in that wonderful Providence, who, little as we **understand** His ways, yet doeth all things well; in that Saviour who, as the eternal High-priest, as *our* Saviour, watches over us and speaks to us: "Only believe."

In the next place, the words of the text are to be applied as comfort to the survivors, and in the light of this word death was to the deceased **not** a loss but a gain, and to the survivors not as the blow **of blind fate, but as** an expression of love of an infallible divine wisdom. Such afflictions, grievous as they sometimes are, belong to our education in righteousness. The cross is a school; as such it must be presented. Through much tribulation runs the path of life below, but the end is the kingdom of God, **and** the end will justify God's mysterious leadings in Providence. And to this comfort and consolation may very naturally be added the *admonition*, which should not be wanting in any address, and which should be well used, according to the special and surrounding circumstances. "Enter into the strait gate;" "Lord, make me to know mine end," etc.

With text in hand, first a glance into the grave, then above and beyond the grave to the heavens, then forward into life with its tasks and duties; this is the aim and object of the funeral sermon.

But there is one essential matter that we dare not overlook: God's blessing in all things, even in the ordinary course of our life, is dependent upon "praying and working." As to all our sermons, so to the funeral address, prayer must be added. The Lord must enlighten His servant that he truly discharge his duties as servant of the Lord. With praying heart seek thy text; with praying thoughts apply thyself to the work of preparation; God will give it unto thee, even in difficult positions, to decide upon the right matter. To His honor ought we to speak, and we can only do this when we first of all accord to Him the honor, when we permit His spirit of peace to flow upon us, when we permit ourselves to be guided by His spirit of truth and love. To God alone be the glory: let that be the motto of our funeral addresses.

POINTS OF ETIQUETTE IN FUNERALS.

THE following questions were addressed to a number of leading clergymen in New York and Brooklyn. The answers returned are given below.

QUESTIONS.

I. What circumstances will justify a minister's refusal to officiate at a funeral? (*a*) Will the fact that the deceased was an unbeliever? or (*b*) belonged to another church? or (*c*) was personally unknown to the minister?

II. Where should the minister's direction of affairs cease and the undertaker's begin?

III. Is it advisable for the preacher to visit the house of mourning immediately after the funeral? If so, how long should his stay be? If not, how soon should he make such visit?

IV. What do you consider the best order of exercises — singing, prayer, reading, sermon, etc.?

V. What rule do you observe with respect to calling on other ministers for remarks?

VI. What do you consider the most proper relative positions for preacher, corpse, and mourners—(1) during the service; (2) on the way out of the church or house?

VII. What do you consider the most objectionable features in modern funerals, and what remedy would you suggest?

VIII. Is it proper for a minister to receive compensation for officiating at a funeral?

REPLIES:

Rev. G. F. BEHRINGER, Grace English Evangelical Lutheran Church, Brooklyn, N. Y.:

I. Insincerity on the part of **those inviting, or inability on** the part of the minister **to perform** the duties requested. (*a*) No, providing he were not hindered from speaking the whole truth. (*b*) If the deceased had been a member of another **church** it would be necessary to investigate all the facts involved, especially so as not to give offence to a brother minister; this is a very important matter in a small town or village. (*c*) If the deceased were personally unknown to the minister, he must, for obvious reasons, avoid personal **allusions**.

II. **If services are concluded at the house,** then **the minister's** duties end with the amen of the benediction. If he accompany the remains to the cemetery, he resumes *there*, and concludes with the final sentence of the committal service. Then and there his work ceases.

III. Where it is customary to fee him for his services, it **makes it a** delicate matter **to visit** the family **again.** Otherwise he should do so within the first week (not make a long stay), **with a few words of comfort,** Scripture, and prayer.

IV. As to the order of exercises, I would not favor a stereotyped form, but, as a general rule: singing, Scripture, prayer, singing, address, prayer, **benediction. As to singing,** it depends *where* and *when* the services are held. **Unless appropriate and** well rendered, omit.

V. As to calling upon other ministers, I do not do it, except at the request of the family, for the simple reason that I would be held responsible for his remarks.

VI. **If possible, (1) the minister at** the head of the coffin, **the relatives on the right, friends, etc. on the left**; (2) in leaving house **or church, minister, coffin, relatives, friends, general** crowd.

VII. Display: mourning **garments,** expensive coffins, **flowers, carriages, and general fuss** and **feathers.** Also **the** abomination of refreshments, **etc.** after funerals, **near the** cemetery. No reform possible unless *all* adopt the Roman Catholic idea of refusing to serve if these abuses are indulged in.

THEODORE L. CUYLER, D.D., Lafayette Avenue Presbyterian Church, Brooklyn, N. Y.:

I. *No* "**circumstances**" except such **as** arise from previous engagements or physical impossibilities.

II. The minister has charge of *all* that properly belongs to the *religious* service—no more.

III. Common-sense will **dictate the** times of visits and their duration. **The** unpardonable **sin is** *neglect*.

IV. My usual order is: Scriptures, singing, address, prayer, and some**times** second singing.

V. I call on **other ministers to take just such parts in** the service as the *family* may desire or request.

VI. Nothing to say about such **trivialities.**

VII. *All* funerals do not have "objectionable features." Some are made too much a floral exhibition, and some are too formal and ostentatious. The services should be brief, simple, natural, tender, and devout, and *spiritual* in the best sense.

VIII. Yes, if a fee is *offered,* let it be received (except from **the very poor**) and used for a good object. To decline it in most cases would give offence. A service for those *outside* of a pastor's congregation often involves much extra labor, and a "fee" is proper.

CHARLES F. DEEMS, D.D., Church of the Strangers, New York :

I. A previous engagement, or the fact that the hour of the funeral was published before the minister was consulted, will justify him in declining to officiate. The previous state and condition of the deceased should have nothing to do with a Protestant minister's decision in this case. **A funeral** is to him an opportunity of setting forth **the blessed Gospel of the Son of God, and he should rejoice therein.** A funeral service is held for the living, not for the dead. The fact that the deceased was an unbeliever, a suicide, a murderer, or even a grogseller, should have nothing to do with it. If the deceased belonged to **another church, the minister should be sure that the pastor of the** deceased could not attend **the** service, in which case he should cheerfully officiate in the place of the absent pastor.

II. **The undertaker** has general charge of the funeral. The minister performs the religious service. **The undertaker resumes** charge when the officiating minister requests **him to do so.** Families should be instructed **to** employ the sexton of the church **the pastor** of which is to officiate. They know each other's methods.

III. **It is the** pastor's *duty* to visit the bereaved family of a deceased **person** who had belonged **to** his church. In general it is advisable for him to visit any house of mourning, especially if he has lately been called thereto for service at a funeral. But he must use his discretion. In a great city the pastor of a large congregation can scarcely find time to visit every unknown **family from which there** has been a funeral, especially if he be "popular" in this department of work. **A minister who has** been wise and tender and profitable at **one funeral will probably make for himself** five calls **to other funerals. Non-church-going families are proud of having the services of a noted pastor.**

IV. I have seen no "order of exercises" equal to that for the burial of the dead of the Protestant Episcopal Church, a shortened form of which I always use. Funeral sermons should be delivered only in cases in which the character of the deceased affords an opportunity for the minister to make the Gospel more impressive. He should never be *asked* to preach such **a sermon.**

V. I have no rule. If the family desire it, a visiting minister may be requested to take a part of the exercises. One man in ordinary health is sufficient for one funeral, and two ministers should never be invited to take charge. It complicates and embarrasses matters.

VI. I have never thought of this matter before. In our church the pastor precedes and the mourners follow the remains.

VII. Several: (1) Taking the sexton from one church and the officiating minister from another. (2) Advertising the hour of the funeral before consulting the minister. (3) Failing to put in the hands of the undertaker in advance at least half enough to cover the expenses. (4) Extravagant expenditure for flowers, carriages, etc., when the family have not money in hand to pay the bills. (5) Exposure of the living to pay honor to the dead. Very often one funeral brings on another. The service should be simple, and the rooms well ventilated. Sometimes in broad daylight every crevice is closed and curtained, and the gas lighted. (6) The fussiness of some sextons in seating late comers after the service has begun.

VIII. A minister should never make charges for funerals, nor should any fee be tendered him by members of his church. But when people who have no claim upon him, who contribute nothing to the support of the church and charities in which he is engaged, occupy his time, employ his talents, and expose his health, why should not some remuneration be made? Why should there not be funeral fees, if there be marriage fees? To a sympathetic man the former is much more wearing. Nevertheless, when nothing is proffered, the minister should avoid saying or doing anything to show that he expected remuneration.

Emory J. Haynes, D.D., Washington Avenue Baptist Church, Brooklyn, N. Y.:

I. None whatever, if he be requested, and has no previous engagement.

II. The minister has nothing to do save performing the strictly religious part of the service.

III. Within a few days—not delaying more than a week at the longest—he should by all means call.

IV. Begin with "the Infallible Word." Then sing, if it be desired. Next go direct to God in prayer—better without singing: it is no place for song, which is always heart-rending. Then kindly, briefly speak your human words last. Sing again, if they will have it. Benediction.

V. Never do, except the afflicted ask it.

VI. Stand where the living can hear. Enter a church or depart from it leading the way before the body.

VII. The trick of "gloves," and similar impositions on the part of undertakers; want of promptness; prolonged stay about a chilly grave; unseemly display of any kind.

VIII. Never. He might properly receive travelling expenses; not a cent more, unless to refuse would wound the sore hearts that offer it.

J. O. PECK, D.D., Hanson Place M. E. Church, Brooklyn, N. Y.:

I. (a) Of course, when he has a positive engagement. (b) When any secret order, like Masons or Odd Fellows, attempt to control the services and make the clergyman and religious services a mere tail to their kite. These orders should only hold their services at the grave. (c) Peculiar circumstances, where self-respect or the honor of religion is involved. (d) I answer, No, to the instances named, in the abstract. Discrete circumstances *may* modify this general answer.

II. The undertaker should be limited to the movement of the casket, and possibly the direction of the congregation in viewing the face of the dead.

III. The visit of the pastor to the house of mourning *ordinarily* should be after the lapse of a few days only, and the time should be governed by his common-sense. Above all, this is the occasion for his greatest spiritual benefit to the afflicted. Their hearts will never be so receptive again, and his opportunity never so hopeful.

IV. Singing, Scripture lessons, address or sermon, prayer, singing, benediction—for services in the private house.

V. The pastor of the deceased should make the only address, except in cases of an old pastor, or where some *particular* relation of some other minister suggests his special fitness.

VI. (1) That must be determined by the shape and size of the rooms and other conditions. It is not important. (2) Preacher, casket, mourners.

VII. (1) Sunday's being selected for the funeral, because greater parade and numbers can be gained. Remedy: pastors to unite and give notice that they will not attend funerals on Sunday, unless under very exceptional circumstances. (2) Too much fashion, worldly pomp, and floral display. Remedy: more religion. (3) Too much crape, heathen gloom, and hopeless sepulchral paraphernalia. Remedy: more study of the New Testament. (4) Relatives taking leave of the dead before a gaping crowd. Remedy: private farewells. (5) Too much gush, sentiment, eulogy, and indiscriminate admission of all deceased persons into heaven, by ministers. Remedy: more significant silence at times; more exemption from being the echo of what the friends *like* to have said; more fear of God. (6) Reading the same funeral service from a Liturgy over saint and sinner, in which both are equally perfumed with piety.

VIII. (1) Never, in his own parish or among the poor. (2) Never to demand it as the condition of his services. (3) But when families of other churches, or who support no minister, and thus have no claim upon him, demand his services, often for hours, they ought to have the decent honesty to make some compensation for his time and service. In short, ministers ought not to **demand compensation, but** *outsiders* ought to tender it.

O. H. TIFFANY, D.D., Madison Avenue M. E. Church, New York

I. Nothing but absolute inability to attend. The facts suggested concerning the deceased are reasons *for*, not against, officiating.

II. At the close of the religious service.

III. Not unless personally intimate with the family. The next day a **brief visit, or** a longer call **in a** day or two; but certainly a call within a week.

IV. Prayer, Scripture reading, and a brief address (but **it would be** better to omit this); singing when specially desired and **provided for by family**, or suggested by the circumstances of the deceased.

V. **Only invite those who have been pastorally connected with the deceased.**

VI. In a church this first matter regulates itself; in a private house the mourners should be near **the corpse, the minister located where he** can best be heard. On the way out of the church or **house, the minister** always should go first, the bearers following, and the mourners in the order of their nearness in relationship.

VII. Fussy undertakers. Remedy: make them understand that you have charge during the religious service; **after that** they **cannot** be restrained.

VIII. Any minister may **receive a gift, but no one should exact payment, as of a debt.**

J. M. SHERWOOD, D.D., Presbyterian, Brooklyn:

I. No, nothing but sickness, distance, engagement, or something extraordinary in the circumstances, making the case exceptional, would justify a refusal.

II. This is a delicate point, and no rule can be safely laid down. It must depend greatly on the custom prevailing in the community. What might be proper and best in the city, might not be in the country. One thing, however, the officiating clergyman should assert any and every where, **quietly, but** firmly—viz., that he alone is the sole and absolute judge as to the character and time allowed for the *religious part* of **the funeral service.** The regulation of the ceremonial and business part pertains to the undertakers, or whoever has been chosen by the **friends to have** the "charge" of the funeral. With that the minister has nothing to do, and equally **the man of** "ceremony" has no right in any **way** or degree to interfere with the servant of God **in** the exercise of **the** proper functions of **his** holy **office.** He owes a duty to his Master, to himself, and to the friends who have invited or who have a right to claim his sympathy and instruction on so sad and solemn an occasion, which it would be the height of impudence or impertinence in any undertaker whose convenience or business views might conflict, to interfere with in any way. My course always has been, where practicable, to confer in advance with "the master of ceremonies," and come to a definite understanding, so that there should not be any conflict, or any jar in the order of service.

III. Yes ; call the moment he hears of the death, if the deceased person or the family belonged to his congregation. Endeavor to have a word with the family just before the funeral service begins. And call as soon after the funeral and as frequently as the time of the pastor and the circumstances of the family may seem to demand, of which of course every man must be his own judge.

IV. Depend on circumstances ; how much time is allowed for the service, and the surroundings, and the wishes of the family, which should be consulted. My order would be to read first select portions of Scripture ; remarks, or brief sermon, governed by circumstances ; prayer and singing, if desired or thought best.

V. The friends should be consulted on this point. Often they wish a particular ministerial friend or friends to take part. If left to the discretion of the officiating clergyman, courtesy and propriety would prompt me to invite any brother minister present, whom I had reason to believe was not objectionable to the relatives, to assist me in some minor part of the service.

VI. This must depend largely on the *place* of the funeral. If in a church, that fact settles the question. If in a private house, the position of the minister must be governed by the size and arrangement of the house and the attendance. I have officiated at many funerals where the dead, the friends, and the audience were all crowded into a single room. In such cases I took my stand by the head of the coffin. If the friends and audience are all on the same floor, the right position of the speaker is where he has the best command of his hearers, irrespective of other considerations. The prevalent custom to-day (a most infelicitous one) is for the family and friends to gather on the second floor, out of sight both of speaker and of the main audience below ; in which case the only position of the preacher is on the *stairs* in the hall, subject to drafts and constant interruption of people coming in, and forced to speak chiefly to two high walls closing him in.

As to the order of procession on leaving the church or house, my own habit is to precede the coffin uncovered, and stand by the carriage till the chief mourners enter, and then take the lead of the procession to the place of burial, the hearse and pall-bearers following, then the friends, and lastly the public. Some ministers excuse themselves from attendance at the burial ; but it seems to me heartless. The friends feel it keenly. Is it not eminently fitting that the minister of religion should stand with the mourners by the open grave and officially commit "ashes to ashes, dust to dust," and then and there, in that supreme moment of grief, ring out the words of Him who is the Resurrection and the Life ?

VII. The show and extravagance are the most objectionable features,

They have reached a point absolutely intolerable, at which public sentiment begins to revolt. Fashion has run to riot over the dead, and the funeral ceremony been turned into a heartless and showy and costly pageant. It has been a very carnival for florists, undertakers, and liveries! The cost is a terrible tax on multitudes. And the elements of pageantry which enter into the scene are in sorry keeping with aching hearts and solemn thoughts. The only remedy for the evil is, mainly, in the hands of the rich—the higher classes. If they will set the example of **reform in the** way of floral display, costly caskets, a long array of carriages, and extravagant mourning outfit, it will be speedily followed by **the public;** and millions of dollars will be saved annually to those who can ill afford the present outlay. A movement is just begun that promises good results—viz., to have the funeral *services* at the house in the evening, and the *burial* a private one, at **the convenience of** the family. This course will lessen the motive for display, and cut off a large item of expense, in the city at least.

VIII. Clearly, if the funeral is outside of his congregation, and those tendering it are abundantly able; otherwise not, in either case. If it were a "wedding" service, no one would hesitate to accept a fee; **why should** he decline a reasonable offering? Funerals are a very heavy tax upon a minister's time, sympathy, and bodily health, and where they occur among those who have no claim upon him other than that of our common humanity and religion, he is clearly **entitled to** pay. Seldom, however, does he get it. In a long ministry, the writer has in only *three* instances been tendered anything; and yet in several cases he has spent an *entire day* in journeying to and from the house of death and the grave, and that in storm and cold of intense severity, and at the request of entire strangers, and those in good circumstances. Still, I would not decline to go for such a reason; nor would I ask for a dollar.

A. C. WEDEKIND, D.D., St. John's Lutheran Church, Brooklyn, N.Y.:

I. Viewing the amplified points of this question as objective truths, there can be but one answer given to them, and that is, that there are no circumstances at all that will justify such a refusal. But the **answers will largely** be given from a subjective standpoint, and will therefore depend, to some extent, upon the ministers themselves. **If, for example, a minister is called** in the supposed case (unbeliever), and he must rely exclusively upon a stereotyped form, originally designed for *Christian* burial only, and cannot adapt himself or his form to circumstances, then he is fully justified to refuse officiating at such a funeral. For his "form," however "beautiful," would be a shocking travesty on funeral rites. So is any other minister, with or without a form, whose conceptions of funeral services **reach** no higher and embrace no **more** than a mere eulogy of the departed one. He is certainly justified in refusing to officiate at such a funeral, because he has no ground at all on which to stand.

But the minister who regards a call to a funeral in the light of a providence, summoning him to serve his Master by instructing the living, and thus "sowing beside all waters," will rarely regard these specifications as a sufficient cause for the refusal of his service. And for the simple reason that he has to do with the living, and *not with the dead.*

II. Where each *understands* and *minds* his own business, there can be no difficulty in "the direction of affairs" at funerals; and where neither has this requisite knowledge, it would be next to impossible to prescribe rules. One principle, however, is always applicable to ministers at funerals, and that is, "Possess ye your souls in patience."

III. About the advisability of a minister's visiting the house of mourning after the funeral, there can be no question. Where God has entered with His special providence, God's ministers should enter with a view of improving that providence. Such afflictions are eminently calculated to soften the heart. God meant that they should. On no occasion does He approach us so closely or speak to us so personally. God has applied to the family in question his highest effort of compassion, His reserved agency of means with which to gain its members to His service. That family is in a most critical condition. It will come out of this furnace either hardened or softened. And it may largely depend on these *pastoral visits* which it shall be.

The mere accidents of this question, as to "how soon" or "how long" should such visits be, are of small account, and may be safely left to the discretion of each minister. My own practice ordinarily is to pay my first visit within a week after the funeral. I think it best to suffer the family to settle into a calmer mood after the harrowing scenes through which they have passed.

IV. If at church, I commence with a short invocation, followed by singing, Scripture lesson, prayer, sermon, prayer, interment service, benediction. If at the house, I usually commence with a prayer, repeat the text from memory, and then make my remarks as strictly *textual* as possible. This gives variety and freshness to each service, prevents the repetition of stale platitudes, and forestalls giving unnecessary offence, since it is not the minister but God's word that reproves, rebukes, exhorts, and comforts. I then close with prayer, the interment service, and benediction.

V. In this matter I am mainly governed by the wishes of the family.

VI. Wherever it is at all possible, I consider that the most natural and therefore the most proper relative position at funerals is where the corpse, preacher, and mourners can be in one room. At church, that is the position as a matter of course, and it should be so at the private house. Fashion has sadly altered this. The corpse stands in the midst of strangers; the preacher is stationed somewhere on the stairs, to talk against blank walls, and the mourners are hid away up-stairs! This is style —modern style. God pity the style! The blessed Master stood face to face with the weeping, widowed mother, whilst speaking words of comfort to her sorrowing heart. He stood near the bier, touched it—yea, took the hand of the dead young man while He spoke His mighty words of help. He held familiar intercourse with Martha and Mary; He was not hustled away from the corpse, but taken to it.

Going out of the house or church, the preacher should precede the corpse, and the mourners immediately follow it.

VII. One word will answer that question: *an indecent struggle for display.* Funerals have been taken out of the sacred precincts of private grief, and become the occasions of public shows. This insane struggle pervades all ranks, from the top to the bottom of society. It is a crying evil and a crushing weight on those not ranked with the rich. "What remedy would you suggest?" That's a conundrum I give up. I know of but one remedy—viz., a revival of humility and of *Christian propriety* among the leaders of society, and then an earnest following of all ranks.

VIII. If any be offered, no one should hesitate to receive it, since in most cases it is not regarded as a compensation—a *quid pro quo*—but rather as a grateful recognition of the services rendered. In hardly any case can the reception of such a *present* be improper, but in very many instances it would be right to demand compensation. Where the party served, for example, has no claim upon the minister's time, is in no way connected with his church, perhaps with no church, is "well to do in the world," why should a minister be debarred from receiving a proper compensation for his labor? Why should he be at all expected to give his labor for nothing under such circumstances? Neither the physician that attended the departed one, nor the lawyer that wrote his will, is expected to give his time and labor for nothing; why should the minister? Here is an illustration: I visited a sick man twice a week for five years. He was not a member of my church, but boarded with one of my families. Each visit took at least two hours, and in bad weather necessitated a change of cars. The time devoted to him per week was *four hours*, or a legal half day's work, equal to twenty-five days a year, making in all one hundred and twenty-five days; deducting for vacations, etc., one-fifth, would leave one hundred days devoted to this man. Each visit cost me ten cents for car fare, or eighty cents per month, making nine dollars and sixty cents a year, or forty-eight dollars in all; but deducting as above one-fifth, would leave a cash outlay in car fare of thirty-eight dollars and forty cents. The man died, and I had to bury him. He had a respectable library, and left an estate valued at thirty thousand dollars. His brother, a warden in a church, and president of a fire-insurance company in this city, was considerate enough to send me, from the deceased man's library, an English copy of *Luther's Commentary on the Galatians*, with the following note accompanying it: "Please, sir, accept this book as a slight token of our appreciation of your kind, long-continued, and invaluable services rendered to our departed brother, and believe us to be, yours, etc., in behalf of the family." As I had already a Latin, two German, and an English copy of this excellent work, I returned the book and note to this appreciative and pious warden, which closed this interesting affair. The man that would controvert the propriety of receiving, or even demanding compensation—a thing which I have never done—under such circumstances, is just the man that has no experience in such work, and is, therefore, practically disqualified to give a proper opinion in the case.

WORDS FROM THE DYING.

Jeremiah Evarts.—" Glory ! Jesus reigns."
John Wesley.—" The best of all is, God is with us."
Rev. A. C. Hall, missionary to Ceylon.—" I triumph."
John Adams.—" Thomas Jefferson still survives."
Mrs. Anna Cordeux.—" Lord, thou art mine, and I am thine."
Jonathan Edwards.—" Trust in God, and you have nothing to fear."
John Quincy Adams.—" This is the last of earth. I am content."
James D. Burns.—" I have been dying for years : now I shall begin to live."
Thomas Jefferson.—" I resign myself to my God, and my child to my country."
Mrs. Mary Wilcock.—" I have a long journey before me ; but I dare follow my guide."
Alexander Hamilton.—" I have a tender reliance on the mercy of God in Christ."
Rev. Alfred Cookman.—" I'm sweeping through the gates, washed in the blood of the Lamb."
Rev. A. C. Waugh, D.D.—" REWARD ! Do not speak of *reward*. I am going to receive *mercy, mercy !*"
Melanchthon, in reply to the question if he would have anything.— " Nothing but heaven."
Dr. Edward Payson.—" The battle is fought ! the battle is fought ! and the victory is won forever !"
Keats, the poet, in response to the question, " How do you feel ?"— " Better, my friend ; I feel the daisies growing over me."
Voltaire, to his physician.—" I will give you half of what I am worth, if you will give me six months of life."
Hobbes, the infidel philosopher.—" If I had the whole world to dispose of, I would give it to live one day."
Lady Huntingdon.—"I am encircled in the arms of love and mercy. I long to be at home ! Oh, I long to be at home !"
Theodore Parker.—" Oh that I had known the art of life, or found some book, or some one had taught me how to live."
Rev. Augustus M. Toplady, writer of " Rock of Ages."—" The sky is clear ; there is no cloud. Come, Lord Jesus, come quickly !"
Zachary Taylor.—" I am ready for the summons. I have endeavored to do my duty. I am sorry to leave my friends."

George Washington.—"I find I am dying; *my breath cannot last long.*' Again, "Doctor, I die hard, but I am not afraid to go."

Gibbon, the historian, a sceptic.—"The present is a fleeting moment, the past is no more, and my prospect of futurity is dark and doubtful."

John Mason, a royal favorite.—"Were I to live again, I would change the whole life I have lived in the palace for an hour's enjoyment of God in the chapel."

Philip III., King of Spain.—"Ah! how happy it would have been for me had I spent these twenty-three years I have held my kingdom, in retirement."

Ziegenbalger, the missionary.—"Washed from my sins in the blood of Christ, and clothed with His righteousness, I shall enter into His eternal kingdom."

Rev. John Mishke.—"Oh, wretched philosophy, how much would thy comforts fail in the circumstances I now am in! But, Jesus, thou art still my Jesus!"

Altamont.—"Oh time, time, how art thou fled forever! A month! oh, for a single week. I ask not for years, though an age were too little for the much I have to do."

Daniel Webster, a few days before his death, dictated the following as an inscription for his tombstone: "Lord, I believe; help thou my unbelief."

Andrew Jackson.—"My sufferings, though great, are nothing in comparison with those of my dying Saviour, through whose death I look for everlasting happiness."

Dr. Janeway, the eminent clergyman.—"Oh, my friends, we little think what Christ is worth on a death-bed. I would not now for a world, nay, for millions of worlds, be without Christ and pardon."

Grotius, the historian.—"Ah I have consumed my life in a laborious doing of nothing. I would give all my learning and honor for the plain integrity of John Urick"—a poor man of eminent piety.

Richard Baxter, author of "Saint's Rest."—"God might justly condemn me for the best deeds I ever did, and all my hopes are from the free mercy of God in Christ." Again, "I am almost well."

Rev. John Adams.—"No clouds now darken my prospect, no doubts disquiet my mind; a perfect peace and tranquillity fill the heart, and a hope of glorious immortality gladdens the soul."

Salmasius, one of the greatest scholars of his times.—"Oh, I have lost a world of time—time, the most precious thing on the earth, whereof if I had but one year more, it should be spent in David's Psalms and Paul's Epistles. Oh! mind the world less, and God more."

Dr. Rivet, speaking of his suffering.—"This little cloud hides not from me the light of heaven; it shines in my soul. . . . Grace upon grace! Oh what a lovely chain! It is a golden chain. There is no more than the last link of it to be finished in me."

Lord Chesterfield, a sceptic.—"When I reflect upon what I have seen, what I have heard, and what I have done myself, I can hardly persuade myself that all the frivolous hurry and bustle and pleasure of the world are a reality; but they seem to have been the dreams of restless nights."

Duke of Buckingham, after a life of folly and sin.—"Oh! what a prodigal have I been of the most valuable of all possessions—time! I have squandered it away with the persuasion that it was lasting; and now, when a few days would be worth a hecatomb of worlds, I cannot flatter myself with the prospect of half a dozen hours."

A Dying Nobleman.—"Good God! how have I employed myself! In what delirium has my life been passed! What have I been doing while the sun in its race and the stars in their courses have lent their beams, perhaps only to light me to perdition! I have pursued shadows, and entertained myself with dreams. I have been treasuring up dust, and sporting myself with the wind. I might have grazed with the beasts of the field, or sung with the winged inhabitants of the woods, to much better purpose than any for which I have lived."

CURIOUS FACTS CONCERNING FUNERAL RITES.

THE Mohammedans bury without a coffin of any kind.

The rudest method of burial was to lay the corpse on the ground and pile stones upon it.

The custom of burying the dead with the head and feet pointing east and west used to be nearly universal.

The Greenlanders bury with a child a dog, to guide it in the other world, saying, "A dog can find his way anywhere."

The Norseman had horse and armor interred in his grave, that he might ride to Valhalla in full panoply.

The music continuously kept up at the Irish wakes used to be for the purpose of warding off evil spirits.

The Chippewas lighted fires on the grave for four nights to guide the soul in its journey

The early Christians avoided the use of the word death, using instead such expressions as "Sleep in Christ," "Rest in God," etc.

The Mexicans gave slips of paper to the dead, as passports to take them safely by cliffs, serpents, and crocodiles.

The Russians place in the hand of the corpse a paper certificate of the character of the deceased, to be shown to Peter at the gate of heaven.

The natives of Dahomey kill a slave from time to time, that he may carry to the departed news from the living.

The Fijians strangled wives, slaves, and even friends of the dead, that his spirit might not be unattended.

In India the devoted wife ascended her husband's funeral pyre and perished in the flames.

Certain tribes in Guinea throw their dead into the sea, thinking thus to rid themselves of both body and ghost.

The Parsees carry their dead to round towers, where they are left to the vultures that make their nests therein.

At Dahomey the body of a person killed by lightning is hacked into pieces, which the priests pretend to eat.

Some tribes of Mexicans bury their children by the wayside, that their souls may enter into the persons passing by.

The Colchians suspended the corpses of the men from trees, in order to dry them preparatory to burial.

The Todas of India burn all their dead except the victims of infanticide, whom they bury.

The Australians tie the hands of the corpse and extract the finger nails, that the dead may not scratch his way out of the grave.

The Badages of the Nilgherry Hills, in India, release at the grave a scapegoat, which is supposed to bear away the sins of the dead.

The negroes of Guinea preserved the bones of their deceased friends in chests, which from time to time they opened to hold converse with the dead.

The Siberians fling a hot stone after the corpse as it is taken to the grave, and the Brandenburg peasants empty after it a pail of hot water, to prevent the spirit's return.

The Dyaks of Borneo made head-hunting the principal business of life, believing that they would be served in the life to come by all whose heads they secured.

The North American Indians buried with the corpse a kettle of provisions, bow and arrows, and moccasins, with pieces of deerskin and sinews of deer for the purpose of patching the moccasins.

The Hawaians, upon the death of a king, feign universal madness, and commit all manner of crimes, even murder, to indicate that their grief has driven them frantic.

In Wales, at one time, "sin-eaters" were employed to eat a loaf of bread above the grave, thereby, as was supposed, taking upon themselves the sins of the deceased.

The Chinese scatter paper counterfeits of money on the way to the grave, that the evil spirits following the corpse may, by delaying to gather them, remain in ignorance of the locality of the grave. They also scatter in the wind, above the grave, paper images of sedan-bearers and other servants, that they may overtake the soul and act in its service.

The Egyptians turn the corpse around several times before coming to the grave, to make it giddy, in order that the ghost may be unable to find its way back to torment the living. For the same reason the Greenlanders take the corpse out of the house by a window, instead of by a door; and the Siamese make a new opening in the wall, through which the corpse is carried, and then borne three times around the garden.

The Greeks sometimes buried and sometimes burned their dead. They anointed the body, dressed it in white, crowned it with flowers, and placed an obolus in the mouth to pay Charon for passage over the Styx, and a honey-cake with which to appease the watchdog Cerberus. The kinsfolk gathered around it, as it lay in state, and lamented, tearing their hair and clothes. Before sunrise on the third day it was carried out in an earthen coffin, men walking before it, women behind. It was buried outside the town, and a monument with inscription was raised over the grave. All present at the funeral services had to be purified before allowed in a temple. On the third, ninth, and thirteenth days after burial, sacrifices were offered.

In the Roman empire the body was invariably burned, being prepared by the hired *pollinctores*. On the eighth day the body was carried, dressed in the best apparel that could be afforded, to the crematory. In the procession the sons of the deceased went veiled, and the women beat their breasts. Sometimes professional players gave a representation of the merits and deeds of the deceased. As the corpse burned, oil, perfumes, spices, and ornaments were thrown into the fire. The attendants afterward purified themselves by sprinkling with water or stepping over a fire. Mourning ended on the ninth day with a sacrificial feast and gladiatorial combats.

Among the Mohammedans the body is usually buried on the day of death. Male relatives precede the funeral procession, and are themselves preceded by four or six old men, generally blind, chanting the profession of faith, and are followed by the same number of schoolboys chanting poetical passages descriptive of the last judgment. Behind the corpse come the female relatives, wailing and eulogizing the dead, assisted by hired tambourine women. If the deceased were rich, camels follow the procession, with provisions to be distributed at the grave among the poor, a buffalo following last, to be slaughtered at the grave for the same purpose. The priest, or imam, officiating at the grave, calls for testimony concerning the character of the dead, when those present respond, "He was of the virtuous." After the body is laid in the tomb it is instructed in the answers to such questions as "Who is God?" "Who is His Apostle?" which the angels, it is supposed, will ask.

In ancient Egypt the funeral rites were most elaborate. The body was embalmed, and often kept in the house for a year, feasts from time to time being held in its honor. In the funeral it was taken to the sacred lake of the nome, and on the shore forty-two judges were summoned to pass judgment on the life of the deceased, any one being allowed to make accusations. If the verdict were unfavorable, burial was refused for a length of time proportioned to the magnitude of the crimes. If the verdict were favorable, a gold or silver plate was placed in the mouth of the corpse, as a certificate of good character ; the body was taken in a boat, and carried to the other side of the lake by a boatman called Charon, and there buried.

Some of the more marked changes in funeral rites made under the influence of the Christian religion were: Hired mourners were forbidden; cremation disappeared from Europe; the preparation of the body was done by friends as a labor of love; the funeral took place by day, as significant of victory; the branches of cypress carried by the Romans in funeral processions gave place to palm and olive branches, the symbols of victory and peace; at the grave the last kiss of peace was given by the priest and friends.

APPROPRIATE HYMNS FOR FUNERAL SERVICE.

Abide with me, fast falls the eventide.—Lyte.
Asleep in Jesus! blessed sleep!—Mrs. Mackay.
Beautiful valley of Eden.—Cushing.
Beyond the smiling and the weeping, I shall be soon.—Bonar.
Blessed hope that in Jesus is given.—W. W. D.
By thy birth and by thy tears.—Grant.
Calm on the bosom of thy God.—Mrs. Hemans.
Come, ye disconsolate, where'er ye linger.—Moore.
Deem not that they are blest alone.—Bryant.
Down life's dark vale we wander.—Bliss.
Fade, fade, each earthly joy.—Mrs. Bonar.
Forever with the Lord.—Montgomery.
Gliding o'er life's fitful waters.—Fannie Crosby.
Gone to the grave is our loved one.—Anon.
He leadeth me, O blessed thought!—Gilmore.
Home at last on heavenly mountains.—Sankey.
How blest the righteous when he dies!—Mrs. Barbauld.
I am waiting for the morning.—Irvin.
I have heard of a land far away.—Cushing.
I have read of a beautiful city.—Atchison.
I know that my Redeemer lives.—C. Wesley.
I know not the hour when my Lord will come.—P. P. Bliss.
I need thee every hour.—Mrs. Hawes.
In my Father's home there is many a room.—Pierson.
In the Christian's home in glory.—Harmer.
In the silent midnight watches.—Coxe.
It is not death to die.—Bethune.
I've found a joy in sorrow.—Jane Crewdson.
I've reached the land of corn and wine.—Page.
I would not live alway.—Muhlenberg.
Jerusalem the golden.—Neals.
Jesus, lover of my soul.—C. Wesley.
Jesus wept; those tears are over.—Denny.
Light after darkness, gain after loss.—Frances Havergal.
Lead, kindly Light, amid the encircling gloom.—Newman.

Look away to Jesus. —Burton.
My faith looks up to thee.—Palmer.
My heavenly home is bright and fair.—Hunter.
My Jesus, as thou wilt.—Miss Borthwick.
Nearer, my God, to thee.—Sarah Adams.
Oh for the peace that floweth as a river.—Anon.
Oh! safe to the rock that is higher than I.—Cushing
Oh, think of the home over there.—Huntington.
Oh! to be over yonder!—Florence Armstrong.
Oh, where shall rest be found?—Montgomery.
One sweetly solemn thought.—Phœbe Cary.
On Jordan's stormy banks I stand.—Stennett.
Only a little while.—Mrs. Crozier.
Only waiting till the shadows are a little longer grown.—Frances Mace.
Rise, my soul, and stretch thy wings.—Seagrave.
Rock of Ages, cleft for me.—Toplady.
Safe in the arms of Jesus.—Fanny Crosby.
Saviour, more than life to me.—Fanny Crosby.
Shall we gather at the river?—Lowry.
Shall we meet beyond the river?—Hastings.
Silently the shades of evening.—C. C. Cox.
Sun of my soul, thou Saviour dear.—Keble.
There is a land of pure delight.—Watts.
There's a beautiful land on high.—Nicholson.
There's a land that is fairer than day.—Bennett.
There's a light in the valley once shrouded by darkness.—Anon.
The sands of time are sinking.—Mrs. Cousin.
The way is dark, my Father.—Cobb.
Thou art gone to the grave, but we will not deplore thee.—Heber.
Through the valley of the shadow I must go.—P. P. Bliss.
'Twill not be long, our journey here.—Fanny Crosby.
Unveil thy bosom, faithful tomb.—Watts.
Vital spark of heavenly flame.—Pope.
We are waiting by the river.—Mary Griffin.
We are waiting, Jesus, waiting.—Palmer.
We're going home, no more to roam.—Paulina.
We shall meet beyond the river.—Atkinson.
We shall sleep, but not forever.—Mrs. Kidder.
We speak of the land of the blest.—Mrs. Mills.
What a Friend we have in Jesus!—Anon.
What tho' clouds are hovering o'er me!—Hattie Conrey.
When my final farewell to the world I have said.—P. P. Bliss.
When shall we meet again?—A. A. Watts.
When the mists have rolled in splendor.—Anon.
When we get home from our sorrow and care.—Gabriel.
While with ceaseless course the sun.—Newton.

Who are these arrayed in white?—C. Wesley.
With tearful eyes I look around.—Charlotte Elliott.

SCRIPTURE READINGS.

READINGS of any length and of almost endless variety **may be made** by each pastor to suit himself, out of the texts on pages 298–331.

Admonition.

    Job xiv. 1–22.
    Job xxxiv. 12–21.
    Psalm xxxix. 4–13.
    Psalm xc. 1–12.
    Ecclesiastes i. 2–11.
    Ecclesiastes iii. 1–22.
    Ecclesiastes viii. 6–13.
    1 Thessalonians v. 1–10.

Consolation.

    Psalm xviii. 1–6.
    Psalm xxiii. 1–6.
    Psalm xlii. 1–11.
    Psalm xci. 1–15.
    Psalm cvii. 8–21.
    Psalm cxxi. 1–8.
    John xiv. 1–31.
    2 Corinthians iv. 6–18.
    2 Corinthians v. 1–10.

Death of Children.

    2 Samuel xii. 15–23.
    Ecclesiastes xii. 1–8, 13, 14.
    Isaiah xl. 6–8.
    Matt. xviii. 1–6, 10–14; xix. 13–15.

Heaven.

    Rev. v. 1–14.
    Rev. vii. 9–17.
    Rev. xiv. 1–3; xv. 2–4.
    Rev. xxi. 1–27.
    Rev. xxii. 1–7.

Resurrection.

    John v. 24–29.
    John xx. 1–18.
    Romans viii. 9–24.
    1 Cor. xv. 20–28; 35–58.
    1 Thess. iv: 13–18.

Trust.

    Job xxiii. 1–10.
    Psalm xx. 1–9.
    Psalm xxvii. 1, 4–14.

Miscellaneous.

    Job iii. 17–26.
    Job xii. 9–22.
    Psalm xxv. 14–22.
    Psalm cxliii. 4–11.
    John vi. 27–58.
    John xvii. 1–5.

PRACTICAL HINTS.

1. BE on hand punctually. Overwrought nerves can ill bear any anxiety over your delay.

2. There is no other occasion where the sensibilities are so awakened. Delicacy and tact in the highest degree are demanded.

3. Consolations drawn from Scripture are of much more value than those drawn from *any* other source.

4. "Search the Scriptures" *before* the service, and mark the passages you wish to use, so that you can find them at once. Awkward pauses greatly detract from the impressiveness of the service.

5. At such a time the hardest heart is more or less susceptible. It may be the one chance of a lifetime to turn it to Christ.

6. Very often little or no time is given the preacher for preparation. He should prepare, particularly if he be a young preacher, for such an emergency; a sermon or two made ready beforehand may save him many embarrassments.

7. Remarks particularly adapted to each occasion are always expected, are most effective, and should never be lacking. The life of the deceased, the circumstances of the death, the friends bereaved, are always topics of interest.

8. Be brief. Funeral occasions, especially when held in a private house, are always trying: nerves are on a severe tension; the house is usually crowded; many are in uncomfortable positions.

9. Be subdued. Avoid anything startling in word or voice or gesture. Any attempt at a mere display of oratory is almost insufferable.

10. Do not try to awaken too deep an emotion. Some preachers seem to think the success of an address is in direct proportion to the number of tears started. Your business is to *calm* emotion.

11. A preacher who does not feel sympathy on such an occasion will probably have little success in affecting it.

12. Do not be too persistent or officious in offering consolation to the bereaved, or expect to allay grief by merely arguing about it.

13. The truth has as strong claims upon you by the side of the dead as anywhere else. Avoid extravagant eulogy while not withholding merited praise.

14. Your chief aim should be to strengthen and comfort the living, not to bewail or eulogize the dead.

15. Control, not repress, your own emotions. You who are to support others should support yourself.

16. "Judge not, that ye be not judged." It is too true that "the evil that men do lives after them; the good is oft interred with their bones." The preacher ought not to strengthen such a tendency. It must be a most desperate case if there is nothing good he may truthfully say of the deceased.

APPROPRIATE POEMS FOR QUOTATION AND READING.

A Dirge.—Mrs. Hemans.
Adonais.—Shelley.
At a Funeral.—Heber.
Babe Christabel.—Gerald Massey.
Ballad of Babie Bell.—Aldrich.

Beyond the Veil.—Vaughan.
Burial of the Dead.—Keble.
Cowper's Grave.—Mrs. Browning.
Death in Arabia (" He who died at Azan").—Edwin Arnold.
Elegy in a Country Churchyard.—Gray.
Hamlet's Soliloquy.—Shakespeare (Hamlet—Act iii. Scene 1).
Hymn to Death.—Bryant.
In Memoriam.—Tennyson.
Lalla Rookh (line 278 seq.).—Moore.
Lycidas.—Milton.
Ode : Intimations of Immortality.—Wordsworth.
Oh may I join the choir invisible.—George Eliot.
Over the river they beckon to me.—Nancy Priest.
Resignation.—Longfellow.
Thanatopsis.—Bryant.
The Conqueror's Grave.—Bryant.
The Deathbed.—Hood.
The First Snowfall (on the death of a child).—Lowell.
The Grave.—Blair.
The Hour of Death.—Mrs. Hemans.
The Reaper and the Flowers.—Longfellow.
The Sleep.—Mrs. Browning.
The Two Angels.—Longfellow.
The Two Voices.—Tennyson.
Threnodia (on the death of an infant boy).—Lowell.
To Bear, to Nurse, to Rear.—Mrs. Hemans.

THE CARNAGE OF WAR.

IN his "Vindication of Natural Society," published in 1756, Edmund Burke, the English statesman, makes the following rough estimate of the number of lives sacrificed in war, as far as history gives us any knowledge on the subject :

	Lives Lost.
In the expedition of Sesostris out of Egypt,	1,000,000
In wars of Semiramis against India,	3,000,000
In wars of Persians against Greeks and Scythians,	4,000,000
In wars of Alexander the Great,	1,200,000
In wars between Alexander's successors,	2,000,000
In the wars of Greece,	3,000,000
In the wars of Sicily,	2,000,000
In wars of Græcia Magna, prior to Roman dominion,	1,000,000
In wars at the beginning of the Roman Empire,	2,000,000
In Punic wars,	3,000,000

	Lives Lost.
In wars between Rome and Mithridates,	1,000,000
In wars waged by Julius Cæsar,	1,200,000
In conquest of Judea and destruction of Jerusalem,	2,000,000
In conquest of Spanish America,	10,000,000
In all the wars of the world (rough estimate),	36,000,000,000

Since the above estimate was made, the following wars, among others, have been prosecuted: The Seven Years' War (1756-63); French and Indian War, in part (1754-59); American Revolution (1775-81); French Revolution (1789-95); Napoleonic wars (1796-1814); War of 1812 (1812-15); war between United States and Mexico (1846-47); Crimean War (1854-56); Mutiny in India (1857); war between France and Italy (1859); American Rebellion (1861-65); Franco-German War (1870-71); Russo-Turkish War (1877-78).

TEXTUAL INDEX.

	PAGE
Numbers xxlii : 10. Let me die the death of the righteous, etc.	269
Deuteronomy xxxii : 49, 50. Get thee up into this mountain, etc.	279
Deuteronomy xxxiv : 1-5. And Moses went up from the plains of Moab unto the mountain of Nebo. . . . So Moses, the servant of God, died there in the land of Moab, according to the word of the Lord	94
Joshua i : 11. Prepare you victuals, for within three days ye shall pass over this Jordan	277
1 Samuel xx : 18. Thou shalt be missed because thy seat will be empty	275
2 Samuel i : 19. How are the mighty fallen!	13
2 Samuel iii : 38. Know ye not that there is a prince and a great man fallen this day in Israel?	123
1 Kings vii : 22. Upon the top of the pillars was lily work	250
1 Kings xx : 28. The Lord is God of the hills, but he is not God of the valleys	271
2 Kings iv : 26. Is it well with the child? and she answered, It is well	276
2 Kings vi : 17. Behold, the mountain was full of horses and chariots of fire	271
Job v : 26. Thou shalt come to thy grave in a full age, like as a shock of corn cometh in in his season	232
Job vii : 6. My days are swifter than a weaver's shuttle.	268
Job xiv : 14. If a man die, shall he live again?	202
Job xxiv : 22. No man is sure of life	270
Job xxxvii : 21. Men see not the bright light which is in the clouds	270
Psalm xvi : 11. In thy presence is fulness of joy	251
Psalm xxxv : 14. I bowed down heavily as one that mourneth for his mother	66, 245
Psalm xc : 12. So teach us to number our days, that we may apply our hearts unto wisdom	207, 218, 267
Proverbs i : 25, 26. Because ye have set at naught all my counsel. . . . I also will laugh at your calamity, etc.	265
Ecclesiastes iii : 2. A time to die	164
Ecclesiastes xii : 2. The clouds return after the rain	271
Ecclesiastes xii : 6. Or ever . . . the golden bowl be broken	270
Isaiah iii : 1-3. Behold the Lord . . . doth take away from Jerusalem and from Judah the stay and the staff, etc.	100
Isaiah xxxviii : 16. O Lord, by these things men live, and in all these things is the life of my spirit	194
Isaiah xl : 6-8. The voice said, Cry ; and he said, What shall I cry? All flesh is grass, etc.	265
Isaiah li : 11. The redeemed of the Lord shall return . . . and sorrow and mourning shall flee away	244
Isaiah lvii : 1. The righteous perisheth and no man layeth it to heart	273
Jeremiah xv : 9. Her son is gone down while it was yet day	264
Jeremiah xlviii : 17. How is the strong staff broken and the beautiful rod!	270

TEXTUAL INDEX.

PAGE

Lamentations iii : 33. Though He cause grief, yet will He have compassion, etc...... 223
Daniel iv : 17. This matter is by the decree of the watchers ... that the living may know that the Most High ruleth in the kingdom of men.......... 123
Amos iv : 12. Prepare to meet thy God.................. 247
Amos v : 8. Seek Him that ... turneth the shadow of death into the morning...... 275
Amos viii : 9. I will cause the sun to go down at noon.............................. 270
Jonah iv : 7. God prepared a worm when the morning rose the next day, and it smote the gourd that it withered 277
Matthew xvii : 3, 4. There appeared unto them Moses and Elias talking with Him, and Peter answered, etc............. 276
Matthew xxv : 46. And these shall go away into everlasting punishment............ 133
Matthew xxvi : 8. To what purpose is this waste?................................. 272
Luke viii : 52. All were weeping and bewailing her, but He said, etc.............. 274
Luke xxiii : 43. To-day shalt thou be with me in Paradise............ 275
Luke xxiv : 5, 6. Why seek ye the living among the dead? He is not here, but is risen 266
John xi : 23. Thy brother shall rise again................................... 271
John xi : 25. I am the resurrection and the life, etc........ .... 259, 273
John xi : 28. The Master is come and calleth for thee... 230
John xiii : 7. Jesus answered and said unto him, What I do thou knowest not now, but thou shalt know hereafter... .... 198, 254
John xiv : 1, 2. Let not your heart be troubled: ye believe in God, etc.............. 272
John xix : 41. And in the garden a new sepulchre................................. 270
Acts xx : 24. But none of these things move me, neither count I my life dear unto myself, etc........................ 79
Acts xxvi : 8. Why is it judged incredible with you if God doth raise the dead?...... 279
Romans viii : 10, 11. If Christ be in you, the body is dead because of sin, but the Spirit is life, etc.. 226
Romans xiii : 11. Now is our salvation nearer than when we believed................ 260
1 Corinthians iii : 21, 22. All things are yours: whether ... life or death.......... 278
1 Corinthians xiii : 12. Now we see through a glass darkly 235
1 Corinthians xv : 18. They also which are fallen asleep in Christ...... 274
1 Corinthians xv : 20. Now is Christ risen from the dead, and become the firstfruits of them that slept. ..;... 256
1 Corinthians xv : 26. The last enemy that shall be destroyed is death.............. 37
1 Corinthians xv : 44. It is sown a natural body ; it is raised a spiritual body.......... 274
1 Corinthians xv : 54. When this corruptible shall have put on incorruption ... death is swallowed up in victory................................ 272
1 Corinthians xv : 55-57. O death, where is thy sting? O grave, where is thy victory? The sting of death is sin, etc... .... 186, 228
1 Corinthians xv : 56, 57. The sting of death is sin, and the strength of sin is the law; but thanks be to God, etc... 181
2 Corinthians ii : 14. Thanks be to God which always causeth us to triumph in Christ. 167
2 Corinthians v : 6. Knowing that whilst we are at home in the body we are absent from the Lord.............................. 237
Galatians iii : 1. Before whose eyes Jesus Christ hath been evidently set forth....... 268
Philippians i : 21. For to me to live is Christ, and to die is gain................. 215, 271
Philippians i : 23, 24. But I am in a strait betwixt the two, having a desire to depart, etc.. 221
1 Thessalonians iv : 13. I would not have you to be ignorant, brethren, concerning them which are asleep, etc..102, 197
Hebrews ii : 15. And deliver them who through fear of death were all their lifetime subject to bondage... 255
Hebrews vi : 20. Whither the forerunner is for us entered, even Jesus, made an high priest, etc.................... 257
Hebrews ix : 27. It is appointed unto men once to die.......................52, 211

	PAGE
Hebrews ix : 27, 28. And as it is appointed unto men once to die, but after this the judgment: So Christ was once offered, etc.	31
Hebrews xii : 10. For they verily for a few days chastened us after their own pleasure, but He for our profit, etc.	113
James iv : 14. For what is your life?	248, 273
1 Peter iv : 7. The end of all things is at hand: be ye therefore sober and watch unto prayer.	263
2 Peter 1 : 14. The putting off of my tabernacle cometh swiftly, etc	270
Revelation iii : 11. Behold, I come quickly	234
Revelation iii : 12. Him that overcometh will I make a pillar in the temple of my God.	250
Revelation xiv : 13. I heard a voice from heaven saying unto me, Write, etc.	252, 272
Revelation xxi : 25. For there shall be no night there	239

INDEX OF SUBJECTS.

A.

AARON, 149 seq.
Abel, 162.
Accident, Death by, 303.
Acquiescence in bereavement, 276.
Adams, John, 347.
Adams, Rev. John, 348.
Adams, J. Q., 347.
Admonition, 310, 336.
Affliction, 223 seq., 230, 290.
Altamont, 54, 61, 348.
Anger of God, 117.
Aspirations, 205.
Australians, 350.

B.

BADAGES, of India, 350.
Baxter, Richard, 60, 348.
Bereavement, The national, 94 seq.
Blandina, 93.
Bolingbroke, Lord, 202.
Bowl, The golden, 270.
Boyle, Robert, 29.
Blessed dead, The, 252 seq.
Brevity of life, 207 seq., 219.
Buckingham, Duke of, 55, 61, 349.
Burns, J. D., 347.
Byron, 206.

C.

CAIN, 162.
Call, The Master's, in affliction, 230 seq.
Change, 82; in funeral rites, 351.
Changing, The, and the changeless, 265.
Character, Strength and beauty in, 250.
Chastisements, Divine, 113 seq.
Chesterfield, Lord, 54, 61, 348.
Childhood, 147.
Children, 160, 235 seq., 262, 274; death of, 306, 336.
Chinese, 350.
Chippewas, 349.
Christ, and immortal life, 257; comforting mourners, 272; consolation in, 31 seq.; destroyer of death, 43 seq., 255; resurrection of, 256, 266; length of the life of, 282.
Christians, Death of, 89 seq., 215 seq., 226, 228 seq., 269, 272, 275, 278, 283 seq., 317.
Colchians, 350.
Comfort in death, 144.
Condé, Prince of, 172 seq.
Confessions of dying men, 52 seq.
Consolation for the bereaved, 301.
Constancy, 86.
Cookman, Rev. Alfred, 347.
Cordeux, Mrs. Anna, 347.
Corn, Shock of, 232.
Cross, The, 132.

D.

DAHOMEY, natives of, 349 seq.
Daughter, Death of an only, 153 seq.
Davies, President, Mother of, 107.
Dead, The forgotten, 273; the glorified, 272; Voice of the, 179 seq.
Death, 31 seq., 37 seq., 89 seq., 121, 125, 131, 164 seq., 181 seq., 186 seq., 193, 216, 222, 234 seq., 264, 270, 271, 273, 274, 283 seq.; in the prime of life, 270.
Despondency, 177.
Display at funerals, 338 seq.
Distrust, 176.
Dog, The Master's shepherd, 167 seq.
Doubt, 183.
Duelling, 13 seq.
Dyaks of Borneo, 350.
Dying, 142.
Dying men, Confessions of, 52 seq.
Dying, Words from the, 347.

E.

EARTH, 221.
Edwards, Jonathan, 60, 347.
Egyptians, 202, 350 seq.

INDEX OF SUBJECTS.

Eleazar, 149.
Emotions of a saint in heaven, 251
Eternal life, 270.
Eternity, Preparation for, 263.
Etiquette at funerals, 337.
Evarts, Jeremiah, 347.
Evarts, Jonathan, 60.
Exhortation, 310.

F.

Facts, Curious, concerning funeral rites, 349.
Faith, 79 seq., 146, 183, 200, 220, 236.
Fatherhood of God, 114 seq.
Fear of death, 184, 255.
Fees for officiating at funerals, 338 seq.
Fidelity, 150.
Fijians, 349.
Friends, Death of, 102 seq.
Funeral addresses, 141 seq., 332.

G.

Genius and Christianity, 29.
Gibbon, 348.
God, Meeting, 247 seq.
Goths, 203.
Gourd, The withered, 277.
Grave, 74 seq., 186.
Greatness, Human, 126 seq., 172.
Greeks, 350.
Greenlanders, 349.
Grotius, 55 seq., 348.
Growth in grace, 232 seq.
Guiltiness, 182.
Guinea, 350.

H.

Hall, Rev. A. C., 347.
Hamilton, Alexander, 13 seq., 347.
Harrison, President, 124 seq.
Hawaiians, 350.
Heaven, 151, 158, 222, 260, 289, 323.
Heavenly world, The, 239.
Hindoos, 202.
Hints, Practical, 354.
Hobbes, 347.
Home, 70 seq.
Home, Going, to heaven, 244.
Honors, 149.
Hooker, Richard, 58.
Huntington, Lady, 347.
Hymns for funeral service, 352.

I.

Idolatry, 176.
Immortality, 201 seq., 257 seq., 323.
India, 349.

Indians, North American, 350.
Infidelity, 170.
Influence, 161.
Irish wakes, 349.
Irving, Washington, 191 seq.

J.

Jackson, Andrew, 348.
Janeway, 57, 348.
Jefferson, Thomas 347.
Johnson, Dr. Samuel, 58.
Jordan, Crossing the, 277.
Judgment Day, 136, 189 seq., 214.

K.

Keats, 347.
Killing, 16 seq.

L.

Lazarus, The death of, 259.
Life, 54, 82, 147 seq., 155, 195, 207 seq., 215, 219 seq., 221 seq., 248 seq., 264, 273, 281 seq.
Light in darkness, 270.
Lincoln, Abraham, 95 seq.
Living after death, 161 seq., 296.
Locke, John, 29.
Loneliness in death, 182, 279.
Louis the Great, 174 seq.
Love, Funeral sermon a testimony of, 334.
Luther, 120.

M.

Martyn, Henry, 60.
Mason, John, 56, 348.
Melancthon, 347.
Mexicans, 349 seq.
Ministry, Secret of a successful, 268.
Mishke, Rev. John, 348.
Mohammedans, 349, 351.
Morality, 56.
Moses, The prophet, 94.
Mother, Death of a, 66 seq., 158 seq., 243 seq.
Mystery of Providence, 198.

N.

Nation, God's voice to the, 123 seq.
Nature, 178, 204, 229, 232.
Newport, 61.
Newton, Sir Isaac, 29.
Night, No, in heaven, 239.
Nobleman, A dying, 56, 57, 51, 348
Norseman, 349.

O.

Old age, Death n, 305.
Order of exercises at funerals, 338 seq.
Owen, John, 60.

INDEX OF SUBJECTS.

P.

PARENTS, 116 seq., 235 seq. ; death of, 299.
Parker, Theodore, 347.
Parsees, 350.
Party strife, 128.
Paulinus, 87.
Payson, Edward, 60, 347.
Personal matters in funeral addresses, 333.
Peter, the Apostle, 89.
Philip III., King of Spain, 56, 348.
Poems for quotation and reading, 355.
Prayer at funerals, 292 seq. ; before funerals, 337.
Preparation for death, 219 seq., 247 seq., 263, 277.
Prime of life, Death in the, 298.
Probation, 194 seq.
Prominent persons, death of, 308.
Providence, 198 seq., 254.
Punishment by parents, 116 seq.
Punishment, Future, 48, 229.

R.

RECOGNITION in heaven, 275, 276.
Readings, Scripture, 354.
Regret, 73 seq.
Repentance, 178 ; death-bed, 265.
Responsibilities of the living, 141, seq.
Rest of God, 294 seq.
Resurrection, 47, 139, 185, 188 seq., 212, 227, 256, 271, 278.
Revelation, 211, 225.
Review of life, 155 seq., 168.
Richter, 206.
Righteous, Death of the, 317.
Rivet, Dr., 348.
Romans, 350.
Russians, 349.

S.

SALADIN the Great, 126.
Salmasius, 55, 348.
Science, 201.
Seat, The empty, 275.
Separation, Eternal, 110.
Sepulchre, The new, 270.
Siberians, 350.
Sins, National, 129.
Slavery, 99 seq.
Sorrow, 102 seq., 176 seq., 223 seq., 271.

Soul, Funeral of the, 133 seq.
Sovereignty of God, 125 seq., 198.
Steadfastness, 143.
Submission, 104, 199.
Success, 210.
Sudden death, 267, 303.
Support, The sure, 270.
Sympathy, 178.

T.

TAYLOR, Zachary, 347.
Time, A, to die, 164 seq.
Todas of India, 350.
Toplady, Augustus M., 347.
Transiency of life, 312.
Turner, 204.

U.

UNDERTAKERS, Duties of, 338 seq.
Unhappy life, End of a, 300.
Unrepentant, Death of the, 177, 299.
Unseen world, Nearness of the, 271.

V.

VALLEY, God in the, 271.
Vanderbilt, Cornelius, 141 seq., 292 seq.
Vanity, 209.
Vassar, John, 168 seq.
Victory over death, 186 seq., 228 seq.
Visiting the house of mourning, 338 seq.
Voltaire, 54, 347.

W.

WALES, 350.
War, The carnage of, 356.
Washington, George, 348.
Waste of life, 272.
Waugh, A. C., D.D., 347.
Web of life, 263.
Webster, Daniel, 207, 348.
Wesley, John, 347.
Wilcock, Mrs. Mary, 347.
Worker, Death of an obscure, 298.
Wrath, Divine, 229.

Y.

YEARS fleeting, The, 260.
Young, Death of the, 304.
Youth, 147.

Z.

ZIEGENBALGER, 59, 348.